Putting
Body & Soul
Together

Robin Scroggs

Essays in Honor of
ROBIN SCROGGS _____

Putting
Body & Soul
Together

Edited by

Virginia Wiles
Alexandra Brown
and
Graydon F. Snyder

TRINITY PRESS INTERNATIONAL   VALLEY FORGE

Trinity Press International, P.O. Box 851, Valley Forge, PA 19482-0851
Trinity Press International is a division of the Morehouse Publishing Group.

Cover art: *Jerome* by Jonathan Paul Scroggs

Library of Congress Cataloging-in-Publication Data

Putting body and soul together : essays in honor of Robin Scroggs / edited by
    Virginia Wiles, Alexandra Brown, Graydon F. Snyder.
        p. cm.
    Includes bibliographical references and index.
    ISBN 1-56338-206-7 (pbk. : alk. paper)—
    ISBN 1-56338-209-1 (cloth : alk. paper)
    1. Bible. N.T.—Criticism, interpretation, etc. 2. Bible. N.T.—
Theology.   I. Scroggs, Robin.   II. Wiles, Virginia, 1954–
III. Brown, Alexandra R., 1955–   IV. Snyder, Graydon F., 1930
BS2395.P87 1997
225.8—dc21   97–227
                                                    CIP

Printed in the United States of America

97   98   99   00   01   9   8   7   6   5   4   3   2   1

Contents

PART II
READING THE JEWISH CONTEXT
OF EARLY CHRISTIANITY

PART III
UNDERSTANDING PAUL

PART IV
INTERPRETING THE NEW TESTAMENT
FOR A NEW DAY

Acknowledgments

The editors acknowledge with gratitude the many people who have helped to make this tribute to Robin possible. Vincent Wimbush and S. C. Winter initiated the project, and Holland Hendrix provided support by securing its publication with Trinity Press. We were helped immeasurably by the secretarial assistance of Elsie Schmoyer at Muhlenberg College and Karen Lyle at Washington and Lee University. The reference staff at Trexler Library, Muhlenberg College, assisted us in bibliographical matters. George Landes graciously gave his time and expertise to check Hebrew and Aramaic passages in the essays. Emily Peters assisted in preparing the indexes.

For checking our summary of Robin's biographical data and for assistance with other matters important to the production and presentation of the volume we are indebted to Marilee Munger Scroggs. As the volume began to take shape and the day of its presentation came into view, Frederick Weidmann took on the task of organizing the celebration in Robin's honor. Together with the Biblical Field and President's office at Union Theological Seminary, Fred assured that the celebration be suited to Robin, both in dignity and in joy. Finally, it has been our great privilege to have the excellent guidance and support of the editorial staff at Trinity Press International. We are especially indebted to Harold Rast, whose vision of what a Festschrift for Robin should look like inspired us to carry on, and to Laura Barrett whose steady competence, good judgment, and day to day commitment to the project saw it to its completion in record time.

Contributors

Cameron Afzal. Professor of Religion, Sarah Lawrence College, Bronxville, New York

Alexandra Brown. Associate Professor of Religion, Washington and Lee University, Lexington, Virginia

Celia Deutsch. Adjunct Associate Professor of Religion, Barnard College and Columbia University, New York, New York

Pamela M. Eisenbaum. Assistant Professor of Biblical Studies and Christian Origins, Iliff School of Theology, Denver, Colorado

Agneta Enermalm. Associate Professor of New Testament, Lutheran Theological Southern Seminary, Columbia, South Carolina

Gary Gilbert. Assistant Dean for Academic Affairs and Lecturer, Religion, Chatham College, Pittsburgh, Pennsylvania

Deirdre Good. Professor of New Testament, The General Theological Seminary, New York, New York

Judith Gray. Head of Reference for the American Folklife Center, The Library of Congress, Washington, DC

Robert Jewett. The Henry R. Kendell Senior Professor of New Testament Interpretation, Garrett-Evangelical Theological Seminary, Evanston, Illinois

Peter Iver Kaufman. Professor, History of Christian Traditions, University of North Carolina, Chapel Hill, North Carolina

André LaCocque. Professor Emeritus, Hebrew Scriptures, Chicago Theological Seminary, Chicago, Illinois

Perry LeFevre. Professor Emeritus, Constructive Theology, Chicago Theological Seminary, Chicago, Illinois

J. Louis Martyn. Edward Robinson Professor Emeritus of Biblical Theology, Union Theological Seminary, New York, New York

Carol Munro Mosley. Associate Pastor of St. Pauls United Church of Christ, Chicago, Illinois

Daniel Patte. Professor of New Testament and Chair of the Department of Religious Studies, Vanderbilt University, Nashville, Tennessee

Calvin J. Roetzel. Arnold Lowe Professor of Religious Studies, Macalester College, Saint Paul, Minnesota

Claudia Setzer. Assistant Professor of Religious Studies, Manhattan College, Riverdale, New York

Kevin L. Smith. Reference Librarian for Harry C. Trexler Library, Muhlenberg College, Allentown, Pennsylvania

Graydon F. Snyder. Professor of New Testament, retired, Chicago Theological Seminary, Chicago, Illinois

Burton L. Visotzky. Appleman Chair of Midrash and Interreligious Studies, Jewish Theological Seminary, New York, New York

Frederick W. Weidmann. Assistant Professor of New Testament, Union Theological Seminary, New York, New York

Virginia Wiles. Assistant Professor of Religion, Muhlenberg College, Allentown, Pennsylvania

Vincent L. Wimbush. Professor of New Testament and Christian Origins, Union Theological Seminary and Adjunct Professor of Religion for Columbia University, Graduate School of Arts and Sciences, New York, New York

Michael Winger. Practicing attorney, Fennell & Chiappone LLP, New York, New York

S. C. Winter. Director of Religious Studies Program, Eugene Lang College, New School of Social Research, New York, New York

Abbreviations

AAR	American Academy of Religion
AB	Anchor Bible
ABD	*Anchor Bible Dictionary*, ed. D. N. Freedman
AJA	*American Journal of Archeology*
AnBib	Analecta Biblica
ANRW	*Aufstieg und Niedergang der römischen Welt*
AV	Authorized Version
BAGD	W. Bauer, W. F. Arndt, F. W. Gingrich, and F. W. Danker, *Greek-English Lexicon of the New Testament*
BAR	*Biblical Archaeologist Reader*
BDF	F. Blass, A. Debrunner, and R. W. Funk, *A Greek Grammar of the New Testament*
BEvT	Beiträge zur evangelischen Theologie
BETL	Bibliotheca ephemeridum theologicarum lovaniensium
BJS	Brown Judaic Studies
BTB	*Biblical Theology Bulletin*
BZNW	Beihefte zur *Zeitschrift für die neutestamentliche Wissenschaft*
CBQ	*Catholic Biblical Quarterly*
CBQMS	Catholic Biblical Quarterly—Monograph Series
CCSL	Corpus Christianorum. Series Latina.
CIL	*Corpus inscriptionum latinarum*
CNT	Commentaire de Nouveau Testament
ConBNT	Coniectanea biblica, New Testament
CPS supp.	Cambridge Philosophical Society, supplement

CSEL	Corpus scriptorum ecclesiasticorum latinorum
CTM	*Concordia Theological Monthly*
EDNT	*Exegetical Dictionary of the New Testament,* ed. H. Balz and G. Schneider
EKKNT	Evangelisch-katholischer Kommentar zum Neuen Testament
EncJud	*Encyclopaedia Judaica* (1971)
EphTheolLov	*Ephemerides theologicae lovanienses*
ExpTimes	*Expository Times*
HNT	Handbuch zum Neuen Testament
HNTC	*Harper's NT Commentaries*
HTS	Harvard Theological Studies
HWP	*Historisches Wörterbuch der Philosophie,* ed. R. Eisler
IBS	*Irish Biblical Studies*
ICC	International Critical Commentary
IDB	*Interpreter's Dictionary of the Bible,* ed. G. A. Buttrick
Int	*Interpretation*
JAAR	*Journal of the American Academy of Religion*
JBL	*Journal of Biblical Literature*
JEarlyChrSt	*Journal of Early Christian Studies*
JJS	*Journal of Jewish Studies*
JQR	*Jewish Quarterly Review*
JR	*Journal of Religion*
JRA	*Journal of Religion in Africa*
JSJ	*Journal for the Study of Judaism in the Persian, Hellenistic and Roman Period*
JSNT	*Journal for the Study of the New Testament*
JSNTSS	Journal for the Study of the New Testament— Supplement Series
JSOT	*Journal for the Study of the Old Testament*
JSPSup	Journal for the Study of the Pseudepigrapha— Supplement Series
JTS	*Journal of Theological Studies*
LCL	Loeb Classical Library
LSJ	Liddell-Scott-Jones, *Greek-English Lexicon*
MM	J. H. Moulton and G. Milligan, *The Vocabulary of the Greek Testament*
NAB	New American Bible
NCB	New Century Bible
Neot	*Neotestamentica*
NICNT	New International Commentary on the New Testament
NIV	New International Version
NJB	New Jerusalem Bible

NovT	*Novum Testamentum*
NovTSup	Novum Testamentum, Supplements
NRSV	New Revised Standard Version
NRT	*La nouvelle revue théologique*
NTAbh	Neutestamentliche Abhandlungen
NTS	*New Testament Studies*
PG	*Patrologia graeca*, ed. J. Migne
PL	*Patrologia latina*, ed. J. Migne
RB	*Revue biblique*
REB	Revised English Bible
REJ	*Revue des études juives*
RSV	Revised Standard Version
RV	Revised Version
SBL	Society of Biblical Literature
SBLASP	SBL Abstracts and Seminar Papers
SBLDS	SBL Dissertation Series
SBLMS	SBL Monograph Series
SBT	Studies in Biblical Theology
SJT	*Scottish Journal of Theology*
SNTS	Studiorum Novi Testamenti Societas
SNTSMS	Society for New Testament Studies Monograph Series
SR	*Studies in Religion/Sciences religieuses*
TDNT	*Theological Dictionary of the New Testament*, ed. G. Kittel and G. Friedrich
ThQ	*Theologische Quartalschrift*
USQR	*Union Seminary Quarterly Review*
WBC	Word Biblical Commentary
WMANT	Wissenschaftliche Monographien zum Alten und Neuen Testament
WUNT	Wissenschaftliche Untersuchungen zum Neuen Testament
WW	*Word and World*
ZKT	*Zeitschrift für katholische Theologie*
ZNW	*Zeitschrift für die neutestamentliche Wissenschaft*
ZThK	*Zeitschrift für Theologie und Kirche*

Introduction

Alexandra Brown

The theme of this volume came to us as an obvious choice, a fact which is itself a tribute to Robin Scroggs and to the clarity and coherence of his work throughout his career. For Robin's scholarly work, like his life, communicates unmistakably and persistently a sense of connection and integration, body and soul. Anyone who knows Robin knows that he is not one for disembodied ideas. New Testament interpretation, his stock-in-trade, is legitimate for him only insofar as it takes place on the ground, that is to say, in reference to the "everyday lives and social needs and contexts of real human beings." In an essay on the use of sociological method in New Testament studies, Robin urged interpreters to "put body and soul together again" by moving beyond an interpretive method that operated "as if believers had minds and spirits unconnected with their individual and corporate lives" and attending instead to the "[dynamic] interaction between social reality and theological assertions." The essays collected here reflect in various ways the kinds of connections—social condition to theological assertion, context to text, text to reader—to which Robin has dedicated his efforts as scholar, teacher, and theologian.

Many of the essays in this volume reflect appreciation particularly of Robin's work on social context and of the way in which, as one writer puts it, "he points us to the human dimensions, individual and social, of the ancient dramas we study." Whether by echoing Robin's concern to situate Christianity in the context of formative Judaism or Hellenism more broadly conceived, or by exploring new methods to get at questions of social location, all reflect the discipline, so central to Robin's work, of connecting ideas to the lives of real people.

Other essays in this volume reflect the more explicitly theological or ethical concerns that pervade Robin's work from the beginning. Here the existential connection of body to soul is clear. In several different ways, these essays remind us that Robin is not content simply to *describe* the faith claims of New Testament authors by setting them in social context; he seeks also "to *inform* the faith affirmations of succeeding generations of believers." The clarity with which Robin identifies central and enduring existential questions that link ancient texts to contemporary life is one of his greatest gifts. He continually "in-forms" us by casting theology in the forms of our common life. In Robin's writings on Paul, for example, we are drawn to share in what one writer calls his "appreciation of Paul as a human being." Indeed, as several essays here reveal, we are "in-formed" by Robin's extraordinary ability to bring Paul, the real human being of the first century, into focus "for a new day," and by his determination to connect Paul's defining moments and convictions with our own.

Robin is primarily and unapologetically a biblical theologian, but his profound connection to his own times also keeps him vigilantly honest about presuppositions and methods in theological interpretation. He continually and rigorously rethinks what it means to be a biblical theologian in the late-twentieth century. Thus, he has recently wondered aloud (and not without irony), "Can New Testament Theology Be Saved?"—a question which is taken up directly or indirectly by the writers of the final set of essays in this volume as they address, in conversation with Robin, the future of biblical and theological studies in the academy.

When he introduced his own collected essays, *The Text and the Times,* Robin stated what he takes to be the raison d'être of the scholar, namely, the responsibility to share that branch of wisdom with which one has been entrusted so as "to illuminate perplexities, to make suffering as comprehensible as possible, to help make the terrors of the times endurable." As we open this volume, we honor Robin's ever-embodied faithfulness to his vocation and acknowledge his lasting contribution to our own and future generations' efforts to "put body and soul together again."

Robin Scroggs
A Tribute

"Putting body and soul together"—no phrase could better describe the life and scholarship of Robin Scroggs. To pay tribute to Robin's scholarship without simultaneously paying tribute to other aspects of his presence among us would represent a failure on our part to recognize the many important ways in which Robin has sought for integration in his own life and work. We honor him as scholar, as teacher, as colleague, as musician, and as friend, for in all these ways and more Robin Scroggs has put body and soul together. Robin, with this volume we your colleagues, students, and friends salute you for your thoughtful and stimulating contributions to our life, our scholarship, and our faith.

A Scholar_____ *Graydon F. Snyder*

Like many other New Testament scholars Scroggs presents a complex combination of skills and interests. At the undergraduate level he majored in music and continued that interest as an organist at Chicago Theological Seminary. Robin's major contribution to the academic world has been in Pauline studies and sociological method. Yet his work with W. D. Davies and at Hebrew Union College instilled in him a deep interest in Judaism as it related to the New Testament writings. Scroggs's first major work resulted from that initial Princeton interest in Judaism: *The Last Adam* (1966). At the same time, *The Last Adam* indicated a hermeneutical approach to Paul that was to mark nearly all of Robin's contributions. The last Adam was the eschatological human: humanity in the new age.

Continuing with his studies in Paul, Scroggs sought to make more accessible and functional the theology of Paul by penning a work entitled *Paul for a New Day* (1977). The chapters in *Paul for a New Day*, originally given as lectures to ministers in the Colorado Conference of the United Church of Christ, evidence his continuing interest in Paul's description of a new humanity. In this study, he creatively engages the work of Norman O. Brown and Herbert Marcuse as resources for helping us to understand Paul's vision of an eschatological reality that "is better, truer, more authentic for human existence than that reality lived by the culture of sin and death." Justification, community, ethics, and faith itself were elements of Paul's eschatological expectation. Because in our day we still live in the end time, Paul's eschatological materials are valid for us, too.

Even prior to the publication of *Paul for a New Day,* Scroggs had published two significant articles that tried to show that Paul's attitude toward women was revolutionary, not reactionary ("Paul and the Eschatological Woman," and "Paul and the Eschatological Woman: Revisited," see bibliography). Scroggs argued that in 1 Corinthians Paul was not addressing women in general, but women at Corinth who were living an overly realized eschatological existence while still in the old age. Paul's eschatological expectation of equality for women (e.g., Galatians 3:28) abides as the present-day expectation. Despite wide appreciation for Scroggs's attempts to interpret Paul in a manner useful for our time, for some there were questions about Paul's directives for women in his own time. Robin is not at all a controversial person, but he has a penchant for writing on what will become controversial subjects.

A somewhat similar fate awaited Scroggs's next major work: *The New Testament and Homosexuality* (1983). In a careful study of all ancient (extant) texts relating to homosexuality, Scroggs concluded that it was not adult homosexuality that was condemned in the New Testament, but rather pederasty, a style of life embraced by Greek men as a natural way of life. Scroggs's work has been widely accepted as the classic study on the subject (see Gordon Fee, *The First Epistle to the Corinthians* [Grand Rapids: Eerdmans, 1987] 243; and John Boswell's review in *JR* 67 [1987] 365). Once again, Scroggs's research has contributed significantly to what, in recent years, has become a hotly politicized debate about the place of homosexuality in the church. A major note of Scroggs's work, both in his published pieces and in his many addresses to lay audiences, is his confidence that the New Testament can offer wisdom for the present. But he insists that his own writings are not "cause" pieces. Rather, "they take as their primary task the exposition of the 'then' and do not belabor contemporary application or argue passionately for a particular view that is 'true' for our day." (See his introduction to *The Text and the Times,* 1993.) His work is characterized by a careful attention to the text and a conviction that such attention, while it may leave us in what he has called "the abyss of a continual uncertainty," can and does yield wisdom for "a new day" in which we can take creative stances regarding the issues of our time. (See "Tradition, Freedom, and the Abyss," 1970.)

While Scroggs was always interested in "putting body and soul together," it was at Chicago Theological Seminary that he picked up strands of the research of earlier sociologists of religion like Shirley Jackson Case and turned more seriously to the social context of the New Testament. At the 1977 meeting of the Studiorum Novi Testamenti Societas in Tübingen he read a seminar paper defending, for theological reasons, the use of a sociological methodology. The next year in Paris he read a similar main paper entitled "The Sociological Interpretation of the New Testament: The Present State of Research." The response was electrifying. Few will forget Ernst Käsemann's distraught reaction when he perceived that the mass of American scholarship might shift from a theological analysis to a sociological interpretation. That oft-quoted paper was published in *New Testament Studies* 26 (1980). Scroggs's continuing interest in a sociological methodology can be seen, for example, in his analysis of the early Christian community as a sect, an article that has been widely used to understand the social nature of the early church in its first-century environment ("The Earliest Christian Communities as Sectarian Movement," 1975), and in his study of the social roots and functions of the early Christian confessions ("Christ the Cosmocrator and the Experience of Believers," 1993).

Despite the complexity and variety of Scroggs's contributions to the study of the New Testament, finally theology has always been his major concern. In 1988, in his inauguration lecture at Union Theological Seminary, he came back to his concern for New Testament theology ("Can New Testament Theology Be Saved? The Threats of Contextualisms," 1988). In the same year Robin attempted to answer his question by comparing Paul with John (*Christology in Paul and John,* 1988). True to his initial perceptions Robin sees in both Paul and John a realized eschatology that is, through Christ, made available for humans in the present—for Paul the end time brings "freedom, joy, peace, and love," while for John it offers "divine reality."

Many of these articles can be found in a volume of important essays entitled *The Text and the Times* (1993). The purpose of those essays selected is "to show, on the one hand, how the New Testament, a collection of ancient texts from a culture so different from our own, might have something to contribute to reflection on the issues of our times; and, on the other hand, how intellectual models and ethical concerns of our day may give new illumination of an ancient culture."

Robin Scroggs has made many and varied contributions to us all, as the following tributes evidence. He is an attentive scholar who not only takes his role as interpreter of the text seriously but is also a conscientious, gracious, and attentive colleague. His numerous careful reviews of books in the area of New Testament studies evidence the seriousness with which he takes his collegial responsibilities. He is musician; he is caring friend. But perhaps none of his contributions surpasses his gift as a teacher.

A Teacher _____ *Carol Munro Mosley*

In the course of receiving an elementary and secondary education and undergraduate and graduate degrees, I have had a lot of teachers. A few were quite awful, most were fairly adequate, some were pretty good, and a couple were truly outstanding. Robin Scroggs was the latter. That I should feel this way is somewhat remarkable, because I encountered Robin Scroggs, the teacher, with every intention of disliking and dismissing both him and his message.

I came to Chicago Theological Seminary in 1979 with a bad attitude. I had taught high school for five years while simultaneously working on a graduate degree in education administration, and had experienced graduate school largely as people who didn't know how to teach trying to teach teachers to teach. I expected that seminary would be no different, populated with scholars, philosophers, and authors, but not with teachers. To make matters worse, I had read just enough before entering seminary to have decided that the Scriptures were clearly the cause of centuries of oppression of women, and that if they couldn't be destroyed, they should, at the very least, be ignored. At our orientation session another woman asked the New Testament professor whether or not he felt, in light of feminist theology, that the Scriptures held integrity. I had no idea what feminist theology was (I hadn't read *that* much), but I liked the sound of it and waited with bated breath to see if this guy would squirm under the pressure of female outrage. Without the least hint of discomfort, without any embarrassment over having spent his professional career immersed in this chauvinistic literature, not only studying it, but spreading it around, Robin Scroggs replied that "Scripture holds integrity as Scripture. The sole fact that it is Scripture is its value to us"—or something to that effect. Clearly, there wasn't much this guy was going to say that I was going to like. I began to thumb through the catalogue to see what was the minimum amount of New Testament we had to take.

I entered Robin's Synoptic Gospels class with my bad attitude perched squarely on my shoulder. I decided after the first class session or two that I could probably tolerate it. Even if he never got around to saying anything that I would think was worthwhile, Robin Scroggs had the most incredible voice and—the greatest shock yet—he seemed actually to be a good teacher! There was an energy to what he was doing, an intensity that made me want to pay attention to what he was saying. So I did. And my world has not been the same since. Robin Scroggs taught me that Scripture does have integrity, and most important, that it makes sense. As I listened, as I allowed myself to be drawn in by his own fascination in what the Scriptures held, my cynicism melted. I began to admit to myself, somewhat sheepishly, that this was pretty interesting stuff, and this was a mighty good teacher, for being in a graduate school.

The true test came, however, when I took the Paul course. I was convinced that Paul had been the original and quintessential male chauvinist and therefore should be expunged from the canon—and nobody was going to convince me otherwise. But Robin did. He managed it. Robin was not offended that I disliked Paul; he merely challenged me to be sure I knew *why* I disliked Paul. And what I learned was that I had no idea who Paul was, or what he had really written. I found that once I did know, I liked what Paul had written very much. Score another one for Professor Scroggs!

As I've reflected, in preparing this piece for this Festschrift, on what it is that makes Robin Scroggs such an excellent teacher, I've narrowed it down to two things: his love for his subject matter and his love for his students. Robin loves the Scriptures. Not in the "God wrote it, I believe it, that settles it" sort of way, but in the way of someone who is in relationship with these texts, has fought with them from time to time, and has grown to trust them. Robin shares in his teaching his own struggles with understanding, interpreting, and applying the Scriptures. He shares that excitement and fascination with others—the many layers of meaning in the wordplay in a certain passage, the way the telling of a story is changed from one Gospel writer to another, the way the societal pressures are reflected in what the earliest Christians wrote about. Robin feels passionately the injustice of bad interpretation of the Scriptures and exudes that passion in the classroom. Everything about the way he teaches proclaims his belief that this is very important stuff—too important to be taught poorly.

Everything about the way Robin Scroggs teaches proclaims his belief that his students are very important as well, whether they are seminary students, or clergy at a denominational seminary, or laypeople attending an adult education class. Among Robin's many gifts is a remarkable capacity for bringing the power of the Scriptures to the people of the church. It is so often the case that people, particularly those already feeling intimidated by the confusing nature of the Scriptures, feel even more intimidated by scholars who seem to understand them and seek to explain them. Many people whose faiths are based in certain understandings of the Scriptures don't want some professor telling them that the person they thought wrote the passage didn't in fact write it, and that it doesn't in fact mean what they have always thought it meant. Robin Scroggs is not one of those intimidating academicians. He is able to impart the difficult lesson that things are not as people have always thought they were, and to do so with confidence, integrity, humor, and compassion. Perhaps the single most important way to describe Robin Scroggs as a teacher is to turn again to the theme of this Festschrift, the theme embodied by Robin himself. Robin is an incredible teacher because he teaches with his soul. To sit in Robin's class is to see a man who has learned through his own embodied experience to pay attention to what feeds his soul, and to take those things and share them with others in what has been a remarkable contribution to us all. And I feel truly blessed to have had a chance to share in even a small part of that contribution.

A Colleague _____ *Perry LeFevre*

On the occasion of another retirement some years ago, Robin Scroggs noted that there were often persons who helped hold an institution together either through sharing a creative vision or by keeping it from fracturing and falling apart. One hopes that there are such persons in every institution, and it is clear to those of us who were his colleagues in Robin's seventeen years at the Chicago Theological Seminary that Robin played such a role in our company.

The very possibility of collegiality out of which creativity and the sharing of a vision can emerge and be maintained depends on the capacity to transcend divisions and tensions of disagreement and to contribute to the building up of persons and institutions alike. Robin Scroggs was one amongst us who shared in that process.

A Musician _____ *Judith Gray*

In 1971 I moved into a residence hall owned by Chicago Theological Seminary. Almost immediately, I began hearing about an organization known as the Radical Renaissance Revivalists (which, I was told, was short for "Robin's Radical Renaissance Revivalist Polymorphous Perverse All-Baritone Cantata"!). Loving to sing, I investigated, and thus met the conductor, one Robin Scroggs. From those first encounters with him as director, singer, and passionate partisan of motet repertory, I soon learned to know Robin as pianist (and owner of a beloved baby grand Steinway), as the host for memorable musical evenings, and as someone who enjoys singing a different vocal part on every verse of a hymn.

Robin started his musical life both with keyboard and with brass instruments. After a rather short career with cornet and baritone, ending around the tenth grade, he focused on the piano and eventually considered life as a soloist. Though he chose another path, Robin is still the musician, the lover of music. The radio or stereo goes on in the morning even before the coffee is made. Concertgoing is a frequent part of visits to his and Marilee's home, as is the "name the composer" game when driving someplace and tuning in the radio to a piece in progress. Conversation with Robin is often peppered with allusions to favorite works (e.g., "Was ist das? Das ist der Mond" from Orff's "Der Mond"). Robin enjoys a broad spectrum of music and has introduced many of us to an array of contemporary composers. For a long time he resisted mightily the notion that he might actually like late-nineteenth-century Romantic music, but more than once we've shared a look during a Mahler symphony, a Mussorgsky opera, or even (gasp!) during a composition by Wagner, that conveyed how much the performance of the music itself has touched us.

Looking forward to fewer meetings and other obligations, Robin plans to study cello, which leads him to wonderfully elaborate fantasies of the day when he will give the definitive performance of works for open-string cello and piano left-hand! (Perhaps we should encourage him to add that first baritone horn to the mix?) In any case, Robin will always be surrounded by music and will always have roles in creating it and in nurturing the love and experience of music in others. I thank him.

A Friend_____*Peter Iver Kaufman*

I remember Robin turning forty. Odd that the memory should be so clear and distinct when nothing was particularly distinct at the time; the rooms of that small apartment just north of 55th Street were filled with billowing smoke. Who brought the cigars? Was it Paul or Wayne? Jean? Max? We were all Robin's students at the seminary and, though he'd only recently come to Chicago from New Hampshire, nearly all the seminary students were there. With all the smoke—even without it—we could never locate boundaries between student and friend. We could only cross them with ease, unself-consciously.

Teacher—tyrant—siren—partner, Robin ritually wrestled with cellophane at the start of each class. A fresh cigar soon emerged (no rival to those puffed above), but I can't recall him lighting up. Lighting into easy answers, received opinion—that was sport. Robin transformed presentations into conversations, effortlessly obliterating caste-lines dividing fellow travelers, a pedagogue from pupils, a pastor from laypersons. Yet there was something predatory about his sifting through students' submissions, his hunt for unintelligent and unintelligible remarks. Nonetheless, Robin could molest one's prose at an afternoon conference, only to cover one's backcourt at dusk, host the evening gathering of friends from the piano in his parlor, and find ways to put each bruised soul back on course. He proves that it's possible for a teacher to do as a friend and for a friend to do as a teacher. I'd follow him down a rabbit hole. In fact, I did just that.

With all the chatter about "information management" and "distance learning," I'm more and more frightened to look far west of the future. Our profession was no tea party when Robin turned forty, of course, but should we ever manage to distance ourselves in education from educators, or to replace them with managers, we'll be a sorry lot indeed. With Robin at eighty and out ahead, I expect that I'll get by. For there is something to the reassurance one derives from an encounter with a monumental dignity that long ago passed beyond defensiveness, as well as from the experience of a friend's inexhaustible goodwill.

PART I

EXPLORING

THE SOCIAL WORLDS OF THE

NEW TESTAMENT

1

The Social Context of the
Ironic Dialogues in the
Gospel of John

Graydon F. Snyder

Putting body and soul together in the Gospel of John has been an enterprise nearly impossible to achieve.[1] Failing to discover an appropriate social context for the Fourth Gospel has led us to make many assumptions which cannot be substantiated and to leave many incongruities. One of the most significant advances in the search for a context has been the use of literary criticism to determine context. One major proposal assumes that the redactional use of the man born blind (chapter 9) indicates the Johannine concern for a conflict between church and synagogue.[2] In a similar vein, the Nicodemus story calls secret Christian sympathizers to become public supporters.[3] I have argued elsewhere that the use of the beloved disciple as a foil to Peter indicates a location where the church has a competitive relationship with

---

In the early 1980s, when the concern for the social context of New Testament material was first being raised, I had the privilege of team-teaching several seminars on the sociology of the New Testament with Robin Scroggs. This article is written in appreciation for Robin's work during those seminal days.

1. Mark W. G. Stibbe believes the future of Johannine research is to move away from hypothetical reconstructions to more sociological approaches. Stibbe, *John as Storyteller: Narrative Criticism and the Fourth Gospel* (Cambridge: Cambridge University Press, 1992) 61.

2. J. L. Martyn, *The Gospel of John in Christian History* (New York: Paulist, 1978); David Rensberger, *Johannine Faith and Liberating Community* (Philadelphia: Westminster, 1988) 25–26; Rodney A. Whitacre, *Johannine Polemic: The Role of Tradition and Theology* (Chico, CA: Scholars Press, 1982) 7–10; Dwight Moody Smith, "Johannine Christianity: Some Reflections on Its Character and Delineation," *NTS* 21 (1975) 238–40.

3. The crypto-Christian is a particular concern of Rensberger's analysis of the Nicodemus narrative. *Johannine Faith*, 40 and passim.

3

Rome.[4] The purpose of this study will be to extend the use of literary analysis as a means of describing the social context of the Fourth Gospel.

First, two preliminary observations about the Gospel of John.

1. Inculturation

One of the more critical issues in New Testament scholarship is the question of how the various cultures in the first century interacted with one another. This issue is, of course, important in our understanding of present-day Christianity as well, and the terminology used in these current discussions about Christianity and culture may well be of use to us in our analysis of the emergent Christian traditions of the first century.[5] I propose, in this essay, the use of one of these terms— "inculturation"—for the purposes of describing the interaction between the "Jesus tradition" and the various cultures of Greco-Roman and Jewish societies in the first century. The term describes a style of mission that allows for an aggressive promotion of the Jesus tradition without seeking to dominate or destroy another culture. According to Pedro Arrupe, of the Society of Jesus, inculturation is

> the incarnation of the Christian life and of the Christian message in a particular cultural context, in such a way that this experience not only finds expression through elements proper to the culture in question, but becomes a principle that animates, directs and unifies the culture, transforming and remaking it so as to bring about a "new creation."[6]

In terms of the early church, then, we may say that the Jesus tradition enters a social matrix, makes use of the cultural elements of that social

---

4. Graydon F. Snyder, "John 13:16 and the Anti-Petrinism of the Johannine Tradition," *Biblical Research* 16 (1971) 5–15. This position has been examined and expanded by Kevin Quast, *Peter and the Beloved Disciple* (Sheffield: Sheffield Academic Press, 1989).

5. For works on inculturation and interaction, see David J. Bosch, *Transforming Mission* (Maryknoll: Orbis, 1991); Ray O. Costa, ed., *One Faith, Many Cultures: Inculturation, Indigenization, and Contextualization* (Maryknoll: Orbis, 1988); Bolaji Idowu, *Towards an Indigenous Church* (London: Oxford, 1965); Robert Redfield, *The Little Community* (Chicago: University of Chicago Press, 1955); Lamin Sanneh, *Translating the Message: The Missionary Impact on Culture* (Maryknoll: Orbis, 1989); Peter Schineller, *A Handbook on Inculturation* (New York: Paulist Press, 1990); Robert Schreiter, *Constructing Local Theologies* (Maryknoll: Orbis, 1985); Aylward Shorter, *Toward a Theology of Inculturation* (Maryknoll: Orbis, 1988).

6. Pedro Arrupe, "Letter to the Whole Society on Inculturation," *Aixala* 3 (1978) 172–81. There is an important distinction in the literature on inculturation between the processes and results of acculturation and inculturation. Acculturation occurs when one (usually subordinate) culture is assimilated into another (usually dominant) culture. Thus, acculturation is more passive than inculturation. Acculturation occurs when a subculture is *overtaken* by and assimilated into the dominant culture. Inculturation, by contrast, describes those occasions when a subculture impacts and transforms a dominant culture.

matrix, and may in an undetermined way create a new culture which expresses the Christian faith for that matrix.

In recent years those who espouse a Jesus tradition have reduced, by means of redaction and form criticism, the canonical Jesus tradition to a more universal, deculturized Jesus. The premise that the real Jesus tradition should be devoid of prior Jewish materials and later Christian materials has essentially made the historical Jesus acultural. Of course, that cannot be true; Jesus was a Jew of the first century. Nevertheless, the process of inculturation can be seen. We do not know what Jesus said. We have only the tradition of the first witnesses.[7]

According to some, especially Burton Mack,[8] the sayings of Jesus were adapted by specific Jewish communities (around Q, around the *Gospel of Thomas,* around miracle stories, around pronouncement stories, and around leading Jerusalem tradents). For Mack, at least, the Gospels and the genuine letters of Paul are indeed already incultura-tions of these early tradition communities. He means by this that as the Jesus tradition spread into various cultures it was transformed according to the nature of that particular culture. In the first letters of Paul we find the Jesus material joining with a Jewish apocalyptic framework. That apocalyptic motif eventually resulted in the identification of the death and resurrection of Jesus as the defining symbol of Christianity.[9] Each of the three synoptic Gospels resulted from the impact of the Jesus tradition on a particular Jewish mind-set. In the Gospel of Mark the Jesus tradition was impacting a well-known Jewish framework—the narrative myth of the suffering righteous.[10] In Matthew the Jesus tradi-tion moved into and transformed a Jewish narrative myth about the per-secuted righteous. Luke's Gospel results from the impact of the Jesus tradition upon a Jewish teleological framework found in the Priestly document (promise and fulfillment). In both Paul and the Gospels there were also Hellenistic motifs, such as the dying and rising god and the cult meal, which made possible the implantation of the early Christian message into the culture of the Roman world.

At least one Gospel redactor recognized the danger of accultura-tion: a Jewish tradition caught in Jewish cultural patterns (or any

7. Willi Marxsen, *Jesus and the Church: The Beginnings of Christianity* (Philadelphia: Trinity Press International, 1992) 4.

8. Burton L. Mack, *The Lost Gospel: The Book of Christian Origins* (San Francisco: HarperSanFrancisco, 1993); and Q in book form, *The Lost Gospel Q: The Original Sayings of Jesus*, ed. Marcus Borg, Mark Powelson, and Ray Riegert (Berkeley, CA: Ulysses Press, 1996).

9. Burton L. Mack, *Who Wrote the New Testament? The Making of the Christian Myth* (San Francisco: HarperCollins, 1996) 75. I consider the death and resurrection motif of Paul to be apocalyptic by definition.

10. Douglas A. Hare, *The Theme of Jewish Persecution of Christians in the Gospel According to Matthew* (Cambridge: Cambridge University Press, 1967).

cultural patterns) could not be universal. So the Gospel of John was written primarily to deculturize Jesus. Hence, in the Fourth Gospel there is no ethic, but there is love; there is no dogma, but there is faith; there is no community organization, but there is the Spirit. The death and resurrection myth has been shifted to a sign of God's love (3:14–16), and the so-called cultic meal has been rejected and re-attached to the presence of Jesus (6:35).

2. Irony in Johannine Dialogue

A second observation concerns the dialogic style of the Gospel. The final redactor of John's Gospel intended to use the dialogues as a means of convincing the reader that the words of Jesus give life, while the words of his dialogue partner do not. Conversations in the Gospel of John are constructed in such a way that the words of Jesus refer to faith concerns while, by means of double entendre, puns, or synonymns, the dialogue partner speaks from a nonfaith level. The proposal of this paper is that the dialogues or dialogical pro-nouncements serve not only to convince the reader of the redactor's point of view, but also to state a case against the point of view represented by the dialogue partner. If in fact the dialogues present a critique of a rival position then the redactor has given us some clue to the socio-historical context of the Gospel. The conversants may not be actual rivals, but they surely represent in a symbolic way alternatives to "Jesus" that the author would want to depreciate.

More specifically, there are two ways to read Johannine irony—as an outside reader or as an inside reader. The implied outside reader (who may or may not be inside the Johannine community) does not know the language and does not yet know the faith stance of the Fourth Gospel. This reader only knows through irony that the conversant has badly misunderstood the intent of Jesus. The implied inside reader, however, does know the language and to some degree recognizes the theology of the author. This reader sees more than misunderstanding, for the dialogue takes on the form of a debate with known rival posi-tions.[11] My goal is to discern how both implied readers (outside and inside) read key ironic passages and from that investigation to charac-terize the nature of the rivals so as to suggest the social context of the Gospel.

---

11. Duke sees three basic elements of irony: (1) It is a double-layered conversation or statement. The double layer depends on a word or phrase which can be understood two ways. (2) The two layers stand in opposition to each other. (3) There is an element of unawareness on the part of the reader or listener—that is, some do not see the irony. See Paul D. Duke, *Irony in the Fourth Gospel* (Atlanta: John Knox, 1985) 13–18.

EXAMINING THE IRONIC DIALOGUES:
OUTSIDE READERS AND INSIDE READERS

The following passages could be classified as ironic dialogues or dialogical pronouncements:

A.	1:35–42	Call of the Disciples
B.	1:43–51	Nathanael
C.	2:1–11	The Wedding at Cana
D.	2:13–22	Cleansing of the Temple
E.	3:1–15	Nicodemus
F.	4:1–30	The Samaritan Woman
G.	7:32–36	Seeking Jesus
H.	9:1–41	The Man Born Blind
I.	11:1–44	Raising of Lazarus
J.	13:1–20	Last Supper
K.	12:1–8; 13:21–30; 18:1–5	Judas
L.	13:36–38	Peter
M.	14:1–7	The Way

While there are other Jesus dialogues in John's Gospel, after he says he will speak plainly, none depend on irony.[12] In what follows, I will examine each of these passages first by identifying what I will term its "hinge phrase" (the phrase which marks the ironic turn of the dialogue), and then by showing how each type of reader would have understood it.

A. 1:35–42 CALL OF THE DISCIPLES

Hinge phrase: ποῦ μένεις;

The Outside Reader

John the Baptist has indicated to his disciples that there will be a significant person who comes after him (vv. 24–27). In this passage the promised person appears and two disciples of John follow him. They ask where he lives.[13] From a purely literary perspective they are simply asking where his living quarters are. In the context of the Baptist's pronouncement, the two men are asking where the cult of Jesus occurs. Jesus invites the two to his home, where after some time they decide to leave John the Baptist and follow Jesus.

---

12. 16:25, Ταῦτα ἐν παροιμίαις λελάληκα ὑμῖν· ἔρχεται ὥρα ὅτε οὐκέτι ἐν παροιμίαις λαλήσω ὑμῖν, ἀλλὰ παρρησίᾳ περὶ τοῦ πατρὸς ἀπαγγελῶ ὑμῖν. An exception is the dialogue with Pilate (18:33–38) which reflects an ontological context.

13. 1:38, οἱ δὲ εἶπαν αὐτῷ· ῥαββί, ὃ λέγεται μεθερμηνευόμενον διδάσκαλε, ποῦ μένεις;

The Inside Reader

The inside reader who knows the language of John realizes the irony. From the theological perspective of the author, the two disciples are asking about Jesus' relationship to God. John consistently coins new meanings from simple words. The term μένω is one of his major redefinitions. John claims that the Jews have the written scriptures, but they do not have the Word of God "abiding" in them (5:38). In another passage John's Jesus implies that those who participate in the Eucharist are not really appropriating (abiding in) the reality of Jesus unless they eat his flesh (i.e., participate in his presence, 6:56). The vine analogy of chapter 15 makes the meaning of μένω quite clear. The believer attaches to the divine reality of Jesus as Jesus attaches to the Father.[14]

Jesus responds to the question ποῦ μένεις; with the crucial Johannine slogan ἔρχεσθε καὶ ὄψεσθε.[15] It is the Johannine phrase used to invite the reader to recognize Jesus, the Word become flesh. The same phrase is used by Philip to call Nathanael (1:46) and by the Samaritan woman to the citizens of Samaria (4:29). The intent of the ironic dialogues is to enable the reader to recognize Jesus as the divine presence. Since the plot of the Fourth Gospel is set in such a way that recognition will occur, the ironic dialogues are simply key elements which have the same purpose as the larger narrative.[16]

The inside reader recognizes the nature of the ironic dialogue. The question ποῦ μένεις; assumes there is a correct place where God is to be approached and understood. The answer ἔρχεσθε καὶ ὄψεσθε signals the Johannine theme: divine reality can only be found in the presence of the incarnate Jesus.

B. 1:43–51 NATHANAEL

Hinge phrase: πόθεν με γινώσκεις;

---

14. Generally μένω is understood and translated as "lodge." Raymond Brown recognizes the double meaning. See Brown, *The Gospel According to John* (Garden City, NJ: Doubleday, 1979) 1:75, 79.

15. C. K. Barrett says the phrase has "no special significance here." See Barrett, *The Gospel According to St John* (London: SPCK, 1958) 151. Others consider it a common Aramaic phrase, but Brown, *John*, considers it a Johannine description of faith (79).

16. R. Alan Culpepper, *Anatomy of the Fourth Gospel: A Study in Literary Design* (Philadelphia: Fortress Press, 1983) 88–89. Culpepper has compared the recognition scenes in John with stories of recognition or *anagorisis* in literature contemporary with the New Testament. The intent of the recognition is to describe when and how the characters recognize the divine or angelic being that has appeared in human form. Culpepper, "Recognition Scenes in the Gospel of John," paper presented in the Gospel of John Seminar, SNTS, 1996.

The Outside Reader

Because Jesus recognizes Nathanael from afar, the outside reader understands that Jesus has the power of clairvoyance. He has seen Nathanael in miraculous detail, sitting under a fig tree. Though the outside reader may be impressed by the magical powers of Jesus, she or he is bewildered by Nathanael's remarkably high confession: ῥαββί, σὺ εἶ ὁ υἱὸς τοῦ θεοῦ, σὺ βασιλεὺς εἶ τοῦ 'Ισραήλ. Indeed, Nathanael himself is surprised by the performance of Jesus and asks, πόθεν με γινώσκεις;

The Inside Reader

The inside reader sees something entirely different. S/he knows that Nathanael is a complete Jew (ἐν ᾧ δόλος οὐκ ἔστιν) who has reached the Jewish end state: sitting under his own vine and fig tree, for in the Hebrew Bible, the fig tree serves as a symbol of ultimate satisfaction.[17] Nathanael does not reflect on the clairvoyant powers of Jesus, but asks how (or when) Jesus recognized him as a Jew who had reached the end state. Although γινώσκω most often refers to the Johannine process of recognizing Jesus (e.g., 1:10; 6:69; 7:26; 8:28; 14:7, 9; 16:3), here and elsewhere the author can speak of Jesus knowing others (e.g., 2:24, 25). Jesus responds that Nathanael should be impressed: at this very moment Jesus could see him already in the end state. However, it will be more important for Nathanael when he recognizes in Jesus, the Son of Man, the divine presence ascending and descending (v. 51).[18]

A telling parallel to this scene is the story of the rich man whom Jesus loved (Mark 10:17–22). He, too, was a Jew who knew no sin. Jesus loved him as an end-state Jew, but said he lacked one thing: to deny the material blessing of his end state and become a disciple of Jesus. The man could not. As for Nathanael, we know no more except that he, as an end-state Jew, lacked one thing: recognition of the divine presence in Jesus.

C. 2:1–11 WEDDING AT CANA

Hinge phrase: τὸ ὕδωρ οἶνον γεγενημένον

---

17. Deut 8:8; 2 Kgs 18:31; Ps 105:33; Hos 2:12; 9:10; Joel 1:7, 12; 2:22; Isa 36:16; and especially Zech 3:10—ἐν τῇ ἡμέρᾳ ἐκείνῃ λέγει κύριος παντοκράτωρ συγκαλέσετε ἕκαστος τὸν πλησίον αὐτοῦ ὑποκάτω ἀμπέλου καὶ ὑποκάτω συκῆς.

18. Wayne Meeks, "The Man from Heaven in Johannine Sectarianism," *JBL* 91 (1972) 44–72.

The Outside Reader

Jesus and the disciples travel from Jerusalem to Cana in Galilee in order to attend a family wedding. No sooner does Jesus arrive than his mother presents him with a critical problem: they have run out of wine. Perhaps the arrival of the new band that follows Jesus has helped precipitate the crisis. Jesus responds with an enigmatic, even insulting statement: τί ἐμοὶ καὶ σοί, γύναι; The phrase τί ἐμοὶ καὶ σοι was used by the unclean spirit in Mark 1:24 to upbraid Jesus. If the idiom is used similarly here, Jesus was attacking his mother! Furthermore he addressed her as γύναι, not insulting necessarily, but at least reflecting a formal distance.[19] No matter who the reader, the phrase οὔπω ἥκει ἡ ὥρα μου remains something of a mystery. For the outside reader it was yet another insult: "I don't have time for your concerns."

It is a commonplace that ironic dialogues in John are often composed in such a way that Jesus and the dialogical partner do not actually converse in the same frame of reference. This is the first such dialogue in the Gospel. If Jesus did insult his mother she does not notice. Following her first concern about the lack of wine, she tells the servants to do whatever Jesus says. Jesus responds by changing jars of water into wine. For the outside reader this is an incomprehensible dialogue between mother and son followed by a miracle story (just as it was in the Gospel's precursor, the Sign Source).

The Inside Reader

The inside reader knows Jesus himself is the bridegroom (3:29) and presumably has already associated the wedding at Cana with the eschatological marriage feast. So the mother of Jesus is asking for the end-time gift of the Spirit or, at least by analogy, the life of the new age (6:53; 15:1–7). Jesus' insulting response reminds the reader that the end time is not something that can be sought, even in a time of crisis. The enigmatic οὔπω ἥκει ἡ ὥρα μου continues the theme, for the inside reader knows that the Spirit will be released from the cross (19:30) and given to the disciples on resurrection Sunday (20:22). At Cana it was not yet time. Nevertheless, Jesus stood beside six stone jars of water, collected for Jewish purification rites, and changed that water into the wine of the Spirit. Whether or not it was Jesus' hour, at Cana he made the Johannine case very clear. The end time could not be reached by reform measures (purification), but by the gift (miracle) of new Spirit/wine.

---

19. Matt 15:28; Luke 22:57; John 4:21; 8:10; 19:26; 20:13, 15. See Rudolf Bultmann, *The Gospel of John: A Commentary* (Philadelphia: Westminster Press, 1971) 116.

D. 2:13-22 CLEANSING OF THE TEMPLE

Hinge phrase: ἐν τρισὶν ἡμέραις ἐγερῶ αὐτόν

The Outside Reader

Since this pericope carries its own explanation little needs to be said. From the Sign Source we have the well-known narrative of Jesus entering the temple precinct and disturbing both the selling of animals and the temple bank. When accosted by the Jews he responded: λύσατε τὸν ναὸν τοῦτον καὶ ἐν τρισὶν ἡμέραις ἐγερῶ αὐτόν. Like the Jews in the narrative, outside readers assume Jesus is speaking of his recent attack on the temple and the possible destruction of it. They, too, gasp at his audacity, or foolishness, in saying he could rebuild in three days what it took forty-six years to construct.

The Inside Reader

After Jesus was raised from the dead in three days, the disciples became insiders. They realized then that Jesus was speaking of the new faith community, his body, over against the temple in Jerusalem. There can hardly be any other meaning, but one must admit that John never identifies temple with body in the Pauline sense.[20] Nor do Johannine authors identify the faith community with the body of Christ. In any case the conflict is clear. The rivals think of a physical, stationary place of worship instead of the spiritual, moveable worship of the Johannine community.

E. 3:1-15 NICODEMUS

Hinge phrase: τις γεννηθῇ ἄνωθεν

The Outside Reader

A leader of the Jews came to Jesus at night and made an approbative remark to Jesus. In typical Johannine style, Jesus ignored the pleasant opening and answered: ἀμὴν ἀμὴν λέγω σοι, ἐὰν μή τις γεννηθῇ ἄνωθεν, οὐ δύναται ἰδεῖν τὴν βασιλείαν τοῦ θεοῦ. Taking the ἄνωθεν as "again" rather than "above," Nicodemus asks how he can go back into his mother's womb and experience birth once more. The outsider, following the words of Nicodemus, assumes that the physical idea of rebirth is ridiculous.

---

20. See 1 Cor 3:16–17; 6:19.

The Inside Reader

The inside reader knows Nicodemus comes in ignorance (i.e., darkness, 12:35); his affirmation about Jesus lacks significant substance. Jesus responds to Nicodemus with the statement that participation in the kingdom depends upon παλινγγενεσσία—a well-known term for spiritual rebirth from above (ἄνωθεν). For the inside reader the response by Nicodemus does not sound ridiculous. His question is: Can we actually go back and start all over? Jesus insists that σάρξ is σάρξ and πνεῦμα is πνεῦμα. Flesh may be reformed but spirit blows where it will and creates new life. The rivals here, represented by Nicodemus, are those who would reform their religious institution rather than anticipate a new beginning.[21]

F. 4:1-30 THE SAMARITAN WOMAN

Hinge phrase: ὕδωρ

The Outside Reader

Jesus walks through Samaria and stops at Sychar, near the well of Jacob. A woman of Samaria approaches the well in order to draw water. The scene is set for a masterpiece of noncommunication. Jesus asks for a drink; the woman is shocked that a Jewish man would speak to her at all. Jesus says that if the woman had recognized him she would have asked for running or spring water (ὕδωρ ζῶν) rather than well water. The woman assumes Jesus is speaking of the spring water of an artisan well. She objects that Jesus has no way to reach the bottom of the well; after all, even Jacob could not have done that. Jesus replies that the well water does not quench thirst, but that the ὕδωρ ζῶν Jesus gives will satisfy forever. Now the woman becomes excited and asks for the gift of running water in her own self so that she would never have to come back to the well. The outside reader sees a very foolish discussion between Jesus and the Samaritan woman. Jesus pretends he can reach the level of running water, while the Samaritan woman stupidly thinks Jesus can give her a source for running water right in her own throat.

The Inside Reader

While the outside reader supposes ὕδωρ ζῶν means running water, the inside reader knows that ὕδωρ ζῶν refers to the gift of the Spirit.[22] It is

---

21. See David Rensberger, *Johannine Faith and Liberating Community*, 115.

22. 7:37. See Isa 44:3; 55:1; 58:11. For an extended discussion of water as a faith symbol, see Craig R. Koester, *Symbolism in the Fourth Gospel* (Minneapolis: Augsburg Fortress, 1995) 167-72.

the life of the Spirit that Jesus offers the Samaritan woman. She does foolishly misunderstand the term, but eventually throws a challenge at Jesus: our father Jacob could not reach the running water at the bottom of the well. Are you better? That, of course, sets up the point of the narrative. Jesus responds that those who drink of the water of tradition will need to have it constantly replenished, while those who drink of the water of the Spirit will never thirst again. For the inside reader, the Samaritan woman is no longer a foolish person, but a rival who maintains the authority of tradition over against the Johannine life of the Spirit.

G. 7:32-36 SEEKING JESUS

Hinge word: ζητήσετε

The Outside Reader

The Jews send officers to arrest Jesus. Jesus tells them they have only a little time to arrest him because he is going back to the one who sent him. There is no use seeking him because they cannot go where he is and they would not find him anyway. The Jews are confused by this nearly incomprehensible statement. They wonder where Jesus is going that will be so inscrutable. They suspect he is going to the Dispersion, not to teach Jews, but Greeks. In any case they ask among themselves what Jesus means with the phrases ζητήσετέ με καὶ οὐχ εὑρήσετέ [με] and ὅπου εἰμὶ ἐγὼ ὑμεῖς οὐ δύνασθε ἐλθεῖν.

The Inside Reader

To seek Jesus is to recognize him.[23] The first narrative about Jesus (1:35-42) begins with Jesus asking John's two disciples τί ζητεῖτε; The disciples want to know who he is. In this pericope the inside reader knows that John is first (v. 33) speaking of Jesus' crucifixion and return to the Father (9:3-5; 14:1-7, 18-19). But the two key phrases ζητήσετέ με καὶ οὐχ εὑρήσετέ [με] and εἰμὶ ἐγὼ ὑμεῖς οὐ δύνασθε ἐλθεῖν refer to the inability of the adversaries to recognize him. They, the Jews of the text, will seek to know him and cannot. In fact, they cannot even approach the real existence he makes manifest. Why not? While they might know him, the divine presence, in terms of Jewish culture, even that of the Dispersion, they could not possibly recognize

---

23. Alan Culpepper has shown that ζητέω translates דרשׁ which means in a technical sense the study of the Scriptures. John has shifted the meaning to "appropriating the Word." Culpepper, *The Johannine School* (Missoula: Scholars Press, 1975) 291-99.

him among the Greeks! They (the Jews of the text) are exclusionists! They have no mission and have no sense of universalization. As is sometimes the case in Johannine irony, the outside reading takes on yet another meaning. The Jesus of the Fourth Gospel is going to the Greeks!

H. 9:1–41 THE MAN BORN BLIND

Hinge phrase: ἕν οἶδα ὅτι τυφλὸς ὢν ἄρτι βλέπω

The Outside Reader

Jesus passes a man born blind. He makes a ball of clay and spit, places it on the man's eyes, and asks him to wash in the pool of Siloam. The man is questioned by neighbors and eventually by the Pharisees. The man born blind cannot respond well to questions, for he does not know Jesus. But he does suppose the man who healed him must have been a prophet. The Pharisees are incensed and attack Jesus. The man responds: ἕν οἶδα ὅτι τυφλὸς ὢν ἄρτι βλέπω. The man refuses to alter his story, and maintains furthermore that such a miracle must be of God. At that the Pharisees cast him out of the synagogue. The Pharisees excommunicate the man born blind because he neither renounces the miracle nor submits to their interpretation.

The Inside Reader

While the story of the blind man may indeed be based on a miracle story, the inside reader knows that "seeing" in John is an analogical term for recognition. We have already discussed ἔρχεσθε καὶ ὄψεσθε as the Johannine invitation to recognize Jesus (v. 40). Indeed, according to the final key pronouncement of the narrative (v. 39), that is exactly the function of Jesus—to bring recognition to those who cannot see, and offer blindness to those who falsely suppose they can see (i.e., recognize ultimate reality). Chapter 9 is John's formulation for faith development. The man born blind was unable to perceive reality. While still blind, Jesus offered him sight, even though the man did not know the agent of his change. The story traces the process of recognition until finally the man says πιστεύω, κύριε. Throughout the narrative the blind man insists that he can now recognize reality and that fact cannot be taken from him. His experience eventually leads him to recognize and affirm Jesus.[24]

---

24. Duke, *Irony in the Fourth Gospel*, considers chapter 9 a sustained narrative irony, where the entire story in itself is an irony (117–26).

The key to the story is not the excommunication of the man born blind, but a statement about the process of recognition.[25] Recognition of Jesus depends on the experience of seeing, rather than any prior *credentia*. The rivals in this narrative are those who believe that in their *credentia,* or faith system, they can see divine reality. They cannot. Recognition comes only through experiencing that reality. Only then are concrete affirmations about the nature of Jesus possible.

I. 11:1–44 RAISING OF LAZARUS

Hinge phrase: ἀναστήσεται ὁ ἀδελφός σου

The Outside Reader

The best friend of Jesus, Lazarus of Bethany, has died. For inexplicable reasons, Jesus does not go immediately, but using linguistic double-talk explains that Lazarus is only sleeping. Nevertheless, after three days Jesus and his disciples travel to Bethany. There, Jesus is met by the sister of Lazarus, Martha, who complains that had Jesus come sooner he could have healed her brother. Jesus responds ἀναστήσεται ὁ ἀδελφός. Martha answers with an acceptable eschatological statement: οἶδα ὅτι ἀναστήσεται ἐν τῇ ἀναστάσει ἐν τῇ ἐσχάτῃ ἡμέρᾳ. The response shows the great faith of Martha in the final resurrection of the dead. She can take solace in the death of her beloved brother because she knows he will someday live again. Jesus, however, surprises her and everyone else by miraculously raising Lazarus from the dead. The outsider understands that the miraculous resurrection of Lazarus led to the execution of Jesus.

The Inside Reader

But the inside reader knows that Jesus refers to an atemporal existence in divine reality. In fact if one participates in that reality, s/he will never die (vv. 25–26). Jesus hears that Lazarus died, and he waits three days in order to make sure, by Jewish custom, that Lazarus is officially dead.[26] Jesus then walks to Bethany where Lazarus had been buried. The sister of Lazarus, Martha, comes out to meet Jesus. She expresses regret that Jesus has been delayed. She knows Jesus as a healer and believes he could have intervened. Somewhat hesitantly she notes that Jesus could still perform a miracle (v. 22). Jesus responds with his key statement: ἀναστήσεται ὁ ἀδελφός σου. Martha hears the

---

25. Koester, *Symbolism in the Fourth Gospel,* 102.
26. Another possibility is that the author ironically plays with the delay of the *parousia* (21:20–23).

words but does not understand. She supposes Jesus refers to the end-time resurrection. When Jesus asked Martha if she believed him, she answered with another acceptable, eschatological affirmation: ἐγὼ πεπίστευκα ὅτι σὺ εἶ ὁ χριστὸς ὁ υἱὸς τοῦ θεοῦ ὁ εἰς τὸν κόσμον ἐρχόμενος. To demonstrate the immediacy of the resurrection Jesus calls Lazarus from death back to life.

The rival in the narrative has a traditional eschatology vis-à-vis the present life offered by the incarnational Jesus. The christological nature of Martha's second response would suggest that the rival is a Christian with a well-formulated set of faith statements.

J. 13:1–20 LAST SUPPER

Hinge word: νίπτω

The Outside Reader

Jesus joined his disciples at a final supper. Although normally a servant might have washed their feet, in this case, somewhat tardily, Jesus washes the feet of his disciples. An encounter occurs between Jesus and a major disciple, Peter, when Peter refuses to let Jesus do this act of humble service. Jesus responds with the warning that unless Peter lets him wash his feet, Peter cannot be a member of the disciples (ἐὰν μὴ νίψω σε, οὐκ ἔχεις μέρος μετ᾽ ἐμοῦ). Peter acquiesces to the warning and requests that Jesus also wash his hands and his head. Jesus brushes off the ludicrous request and continues washing feet.

The Inside Reader

The reader who understands the Gospel of John recognizes the contrived nature of the Supper. No one would wash the feet of the others after the meal had begun. Furthermore the term νίπτω must have special significance. It is a term nearly unique to John's Gospel where it occurs here and in the story of the man born blind.[27] For the man born blind, "washing" is a prerequisite for seeing and marks the paradigm shift from misperception to the beginning of recognition. At the final supper, as the disciples share in a community-forming meal, Jesus takes this last opportunity to offer the possibility of recognition.[28] Peter misses the point and refuses, in no uncertain terms, to have his feet washed: οὐ μὴ νίψῃς μου τοὺς πόδας εἰς τὸν αἰῶνα.[29] Jesus makes

---

27. Elsewhere only Matt 6:17; 15:2; Mark 7:3; 1 Tim 5:10.

28. The argument that νίπτω refers to baptism has attractive possibilities. The Outside Reader might well read the reference to νίπτω as a reference to baptism. The Inside Reader, however, would recognize Peter's misguided zeal.

29. We assume the washing of other disciples' feet has only narrative value.

it clear that Peter can have no part in divine reality unless he first is washed: ἐὰν μὴ νίψω σε, οὐκ ἔχεις μέρος μετ' ἐμοῦ. While Peter understands the severity of Jesus' admonition, he still misses the point. He supposes that Jesus is talking about water when he asks that Jesus wash his head and his hands also.

Strange as it may seem, a redactor of the Gospel understood this event somewhat as Peter did. In verses 12–16 the redactor has the Gospel take the position that to express humility we should continue to wash one another's feet.[30] Then, in a very clever way, the author uses that misunderstanding to state that the apostle (Peter) is not greater than the sender (Jesus, v. 16).[31]

The inside reader recognizes the rival as one who uses water for renewal or even for conversion. The rival believes the water itself is an agent of change.

K. 12:1-8; 13:21-30; 18:1-5 JUDAS

Hinge phrase: τοὺς πτωχοὺς γὰρ πάντοτε ἔχετε μεθ' ἑαυτῶν, ἐμὲ δὲ οὐ πάντοτε ἔχετε

The Outside Reader

The reading of the Judas passages is complex because, just as the author used the outside reading of the feetwashing narrative to attack Peter, so he uses the outside reading of these passages to attack Judas. In the enigmatic narrative about Mary anointing the feet of Jesus with expensive perfume, Judas comes across as one concerned for the poor. He would have sold the ointment rather than waste it on Jesus' feet. The outside reader shares the sentiments of Judas. When Jesus admonishes Judas—τοὺς πτωχοὺς γὰρ πάντοτε ἔχετε μεθ' ἑαυτῶν, ἐμὲ δὲ οὐ πάντοτε ἔχετε—clearly Jesus has advocated the diversion of resources away from his primary mission—liberation of the poor and outcast—to a rather reprehensive self-adoration.

The author does not stop with this mission conflict. He adds two even more negative stories. At the last supper Jesus acts as if Judas is a beloved member of the disciple band. He even shares a morsel with

---

30. John Christopher Thomas concludes that in the Fourth Gospel footwashing is an act of preparation. John 13:1-20 is a unit since the "example section" is a sacramental preparation. See Thomas, *Footwashing in John 13 and the Johannine Community* (Sheffield: Sheffield Academic Press, 1991) 186–89. It is difficult to understand why Jesus was preparing Peter!

31. See G. F. Snyder, "Anti-Petrinism," 9–10. Lutz Simon sees the conflict as one between *Amt* (Peter) and *Authorität* (the Beloved Disciple). However, he argues that through the presence of both "wird die Integration von joh Christen in die petr Gemeinde, Tradition und Theologie vollzogen." *Petrus und der Lieblingsjünger im Johannesevangelium: Amt und Autorität* (Frankfurt am Main: Peter Lang, 1993) 290.

him. At the same time he indicates that the one with whom he shares the morsel will betray him. The disciples, so worried about their own potential betrayal, miss the action and actually suppose their treasurer is doing quickly what he had wanted to do—buy food for the poor. The final scene becomes more difficult. Judas did not buy food for the poor, but instead changed sides. So at this denouement Judas no longer appears with the disciples, but with the officers of the chief priests.

It is hard to read these stories about Judas from an outsider's perspective because the author uses his own outsider narrative to create yet another Judas—the one who betrayed Jesus. The author presents him first as one concerned for the poor, but then as a person seeking financial gain. In that sense, because of his conflict with Jesus over money and the purpose of their mission, Judas can be portrayed as a self-centered thief who eventually became a betrayer.[32]

The Inside Reader

Few of John's characters actually recognize Jesus, but the inside reader would see that at least two persons "caught on": the beloved disciple and Mary of Bethany. In 12:1–8, the author describes in a most audacious way how a person who had recognized Jesus would relate to him. Mary used an expensive bottle of ointment on the feet of Jesus and then dried them with her hair. The daring intimacy and adoration expressed by Mary in this scene almost defies imagination. Judas cannot see the act of intimate worship because he has not recognized Jesus. He betrays his own blindness with his outcry: τί τοῦτο τὸ μύρον οὐκ ἐπράθη τριακοσίων δηναρίων καὶ ἐδόθη πτωχοῖς; The reader easily supposes Judas was genuinely concerned. He had joined the Jesus movement because he supposed alleviation of poverty was a major part of the Jesus mission. Jesus knows Judas's concern and agrees with it, but calls for Judas to know the divine reality while it is available: τοὺς πτωχοὺς γὰρ πάντοτε ἔχετε μεθ' ἑαυτῶν, ἐμὲ δὲ οὐ πάντοτε ἔχετε.

The original rival expressed considerable social concern. S/he could not tolerate or even fathom the use of expensive resources to express love for Jesus. The resources of the Jesus movement belonged to the people who were poor and outcast. Personal wealth is considered by this person to be an impediment to knowing the kingdom. This rival may be any socially concerned person and could well be an early

---

32. The notion that Judas was himself betrayed is receiving wide acceptance. See particularly William Klassen, *Judas: Betrayer or Friend of Jesus?* (Minneapolis: Fortress, 1996). Danillo Nunes argues that Judas identified Jesus to the chief priests as a punishment for misleading the people. *Judas, Betrayer or Betrayed?* (New York: Vantage Press, 1992) 303–4.

Christian who follows the teachings of Jesus as found in one of the synoptics. The Judas stories reveal, almost certainly, a conflict between the Johannine theology of present divine appropriation and the early Christian concern for end-time liberation.

L. 13:36–38 PETER

Hinge phrase: τὴν ψυχήν μου τίθημι

The Outside Reader

After the encounter with Peter over feetwashing, Peter's loyalty has come into question. Following a discourse on love by Jesus, Peter picks up on the enigmatic theme of Jesus that he is going away. Peter wants to know where he is going. Jesus answers, as in 7:32–36, that Peter cannot follow. Peter is indignant. He will follow Jesus, and if that means death, he will die for Jesus: τὴν ψυχήν μου ὑπὲρ σοῦ θήσω.

The Inside Reader

The discussion with Peter follows the all-important command to love one another. It is by love that the world will know them to be his disciples (13:35). And how does this love occur? Jesus explains it in the pericope 13:36–38. The disciples cannot follow Jesus in his oneness with the Father, though someday they will. Indeed that is Jesus' prayer in 17:23—ἐγὼ ἐν αὐτοῖς καὶ σὺ ἐν ἐμοί, ἵνα ὦσιν τετελειωμένοι εἰς ἕν. Unity with divine reality is the goal of Jesus' presence among us. Peter insists that he can follow Jesus now, for he is prepared to lay down his life for Jesus. But Peter has missed the point of his own exclamation. In Johannine language τίθημι has a double meaning. The author uses it primarily to mean "pass on" (10:11, 15, 17, 18 *bis*; 15:13, 16).[33]

For the inside reader there is no place in the Gospel where ψυχή means life (10:11, 15, 17, 24; 12:25, 27; 13:37, 38; 15:13). In 12:27 it cannot mean physical life—νῦν ἡ ψυχή μου τετάρακται. Ψυχή means rather "person" or "personhood" and most of its uses are connected with τίθημι. Here we have the definition of love in the Johannine worldview: love means to share, or make available for others, your own personhood as Jesus made available his ψυχή. In chapter 15 John states it clearly: μείζονα ταύτης ἀγάπην οὐδεὶς ἔχει, ἵνα τις τὴν ψυχὴν αὐτοῦ θῇ ὑπὲρ τῶν φίλων αὐτοῦ. Authentic human life in the Fourth Gospel requires a sharing of received ontology rather than specific actions; actions will proceed from the giving and receiving of divine reality.

---

33. Τίθημι has the meaning "lay down" in 2:10; 13:4; 19:19, 41–42; 20:2, 13, 15.

M. 14:1–7 THE WAY

Hinge word: ἡ ὁδός

The Outside Reader

In a reassuring way Jesus reports that there are many places in the Temple[34] and that he is going there soon to make ready for the disciples. To be sure, he may be absent for a time, but he will return to them. Anyway they know the way, so they can make the trip themselves. One of the disciples, Thomas, says he doesn't really know what Jesus is talking about, so how can he know the way? Jesus doesn't answer the question, but again reassures Thomas by saying that he (Thomas) has the correct directions.

The Inside Reader

Jesus starts by recognizing that there are different ways of expressing divine reality. He uses his own *terminus technicus—μοναί—*to designate the multiple possibilities. The ascension of Jesus to the Father will make it possible for all people to know the ὁδός. Thomas exclaims that he does not even know where Jesus is going, that is, the goal of the journey. How could he possibly know the ὁδός? The protest is very reasonable. If Thomas, or the implied reader, does not know the theological direction, how can he know the ethics (for some readers the הלכה or the Way)? While this protest may seem reasonable, it misunderstands the nature of Johannine theology. There is no ethic as such, so Jesus responds: ἐγώ εἰμι ἡ ὁδὸς καὶ ἡ ἀλήθεια καὶ ἡ ζωή· οὐδεὶς ἔρχεται πρὸς τὸν πατέρα εἰ μὴ δι' ἐμοῦ. The divine reality expressed in Jesus is in itself the way. In Johannine theology there is not a lifestyle that results from faith. The divine reality is in itself the lifestyle, albeit expresssed in a variety of culture patterns. Put another way, the decultured Jesus of the Gospel of John has no specific ethical demands. Because Jesus is not culturally determined the author can say there is no ὁδός to the Father except that ultimate reality which is found in Jesus. The μοναί are the various cultural expressions of the divine reality.

---

34. James McCaffrey recognizes the outside and inside readers, except that he refers to the outside as pre-Paschal and the inside as post-Paschal (26). The outside reader assumes Jesus speaks of the Jerusalem Temple, while the inside reader assumes it is the heavenly or eternal Temple created by the passion of Jesus and his resurrection (254). McCaffrey, *The House with Many Rooms: The Temple Theme of Jn. 14.2–3* (Rome: Editrice Pontificio Instituto Biblio, 1988). In a significant article, Tod D. Swanson argues that the Gospel of John is universalizing the Christian faith by developing spacelessness. See "To Prepare a Place: Johannine Christianity and the Collapse of Ethnic Territory," *JAAR* 62 (1994) 241–63.

Rivals in this dialogue are persons who have identified their own ὁδός or הלכה with the truth. By so doing they have equated their own cultural expression of faith with divine reality. John's Jesus responds that he is the way and the truth. Anything else is a secondary cultural expression.

THE QUALITIES OF FAITH (INSIDE VIEW) AS KEY TO JOHN'S RIVALS (OUTSIDE VIEW)

When, as we examine these dialogues, we assemble the qualities of faith exhibited by the inside readers, we see yet another set of qualities exhibited by the outside readers. These qualities are those of John's rival(s). The qualities of faith (and their implied opposites) that have emerged from our investigation are the following:

1. True faith (recognition) begins with experience rather than dogma, tradition, or pronouncements. We see this in Jesus' invitation to the prospective disciples: ἔρχεσθε καὶ ὄψεσθε (1:35–42). It is also the theme of the narrative of the man born blind: ἕν οἶδα ὅτι τυφλὸς ὤν ἄρτι βλέπω (9:1–41).

2. The end time is present in Jesus. Jesus can see Nathanael already in an end-time state (1:43–51). Jesus corrects the eschatological faith of Martha with a present-time sense of resurrection (11:1–44).

3. Traditional faith cannot be reformed. At the wedding in Cana the water of purification (reform) was changed into wine (Spirit, 2:1–11). Nicodemus cannot enter again his social and personal formation with the intent to change it (3:1–15). Likewise water from the well of Jacob would not suffice—only the living water of the Spirit satisfies (4:1–30).

4. Real faith cannot be found in any location. The temple will be destroyed and the new location will be the mobile body of Christ (2:13–22).

5. Attachment to Jesus (recognition) cannot be achieved by espousal of causes. Judas was rejected because he wanted to feed the poor (12:1–8). Ethics in the Gospel of John derive from love, and specific actions depend upon what is required to pass on that divine reality (τὴν ψυχὴν μου τίθημι).

6. Attachment to Jesus (recognition) cannot be achieved by religious acts. At the final supper Peter learns that the use of water for cleansing cannot bring recognition of divine reality (13:1–20).

7. Attachment to Jesus (recognition) is not a religion, but a universal truth. The contenders seek divine reality among themselves rather than among those who are outside their religious context (7:32–36). Jesus has been universalized so radically that he has become the only ὁδός (14:1–7).

THE SOCIAL CONTEXT OF THE
FOURTH GOSPEL

Assuming we have correctly identified the dialogue partners (or contenders), we can reverse the process and try to identify the social context in which the Fourth Gospel was written:

1. The Johannine community does not have a permanent place of worship. The Jewish contenders were developing synagogues, while the Christian contenders must have developed permanent places—that is, regularly used house churches. The Johannine community must have been sufficiently new that it floated from house to house. Furthermore there are no officers of the Johannine community—a fact that would support the conclusion that no house(s) had yet gained sufficient ascendancy to furnish a "head of the house."

2. The Johannine community places the experience of faith prior to expressions of faith. The author believes that the other Christian communities have become ossified in their faith. He does not believe reform of the traditions would be sufficient to revitalize the church. So in this Gospel he makes concrete expressions of faith dependent upon a prior moment of faith (*fides*), a moment arising from an encounter with divine reality in Jesus.

3. The Johannine community insists on an attitude of love rather than commitment to ideological causes. While one cannot know whether the common meals of the church—the Agape meal—actually began in Jerusalem (Acts 2:43–47), or whether the first Christians actually had all things in common (Acts 4:32–37), there can be little doubt that the life of the church, especially the Agape, served as a "welfare" system.[35] The Johannine community believes that such social concern does not constitute love, and does not lend itself to appropriation of the divine reality. John does record the feeding of the five thousand, the apparent narrative basis for the Agape, but severely scolds the participants for simply wanting the food—ἀμὴν ἀμὴν λέγω ὑμῖν, ζητεῖτέ με οὐχ ὅτι εἴδετε σημεῖα, ἀλλ' ὅτι ἐφάγετε ἐκ τῶν ἄρτων καὶ ἐχορτάσθητε. Just as it rejects doctrinal statements, so the Johannine

---

35. See 1 Cor 11:22; Jude 12.

community rejects the notion that social action is equivalent to the divine reality of love. It would appear that the community had no common meal. The author not only rejected the prototype meal, the feeding of the five thousand, but committed possible historical mayhem in order to avoid the institution of a Last Supper (by using a different date for the Passover). If there is a social concern nevertheless, it cannot be substantiated in the Gospel as we have it.

4. The universal Jesus of the Gospel of John has been deculturized.[36] John does not depend on an independent Jesus tradition which was, *mirabile dictu,* without cultural expressions. Instead, as can be seen in the ironic dialogues, the author opposes those groups which depend upon location, tradition, doctrine, ethics, and sacraments. The intent of the opposition is to present a Jesus not dependent on any of these cultural expressions. The author is poised for a new mission, one different from those traditions known to us as Jamesian, Pauline, or Petrine.

The Johannine community is relatively new at 100 C.E. It first depended on the Sign Source, but then took a different tack. In order to make the Jesus tradition more acceptable to other cultures it stripped away cultural accretions. There is no particular reason to suppose that the rival in these dialogues was actually Jewish. The author's aim was to renew the Christian faith, not to attack the synagogue. If there was no specific attack on Judaism, then, the provenance of this Gospel need not be Palestine. At the same time, while this Gospel was hardly written in the Petrine/Pauline stronghold of Rome, it must have been written in a place where the Petrine/Pauline influence was strong enough to create a rival church.[37]

---

36. Donald Senior, "The Struggle to Be Universal: Mission as Vantage Point for New Testament Investigation," *CBQ* 46 (1984) 63–81.

37. Ernst Käsemann, "Ketzer und zeuge: Zum johanneischen Verfasserproblem," *Exegetische Versuche und Besinnungen* (Göttingen: Vandenhoeck & Ruprecht) 1:68–87.

2

A Speech Act of Faith

The Early Proclamation of the Resurrection of Jesus

Pamela M. Eisenbaum

Biblical scholarship has witnessed an explosion of new methods in recent years. While once scholars were trapped by a single dominant paradigm, members of the scholarly guild now have their choice of many competing approaches to the study of the biblical text. This diversity of methodological perspectives is, it seems to me, a welcome state of affairs, and one which Robin Scroggs helped to inspire through his pioneering exploration of sociological models and their usefulness for the study of early Christianity.

One method recently introduced into the domain of biblical scholarship is speech act theory. For reasons not entirely clear to me, speech act theory has not caught the imagination of biblical scholars the way other recent methods have.[1] Yet it has tremendous potential for exploring questions relevant to the study of biblical texts. In this essay I will first provide an overview of the insights of speech act theory. I will then utilize these insights to analyze the earliest Christian resurrection proclamations. The well-known Christian proclamation

---

1. There was one concerted effort to bring speech act theory to the study of biblical texts: H. White, ed., *Speech Act Theory and Biblical Criticism, Semeia* 41 (1988). While this volume includes an extremely helpful introduction by White, has some creative essays and a good annotated bibliography, its focus is primarily on theory, rather than specific texts (although two essays attend to Genesis 2–3). Furthermore, most handling of speech act theory in this volume is mediated through literary criticism. Indeed, speech act theory has demonstrated its enormous potential for literary critics, and it surely has such potential for biblical texts. Still, it seems to me that biblical scholars have missed the most obvious place to use speech act theory: on actual biblical speech acts, such as ritual language, hymns and hymnic fragments, and pronouncements and proclamations.

"Jesus is risen"—or, as translated by the NRSV, "Jesus was raised"[2]— can be traced back to the earliest stratum of recoverable Christian tradition. Before there were written narratives describing the appearance of the risen Jesus to the disciples, Christians proclaimed his resurrection—hence the common scholarly designation for early Christian preaching: the *kerygma*. In my estimation, speech act theory provides new insights into these early traditions, insights that not only clarify the meaning of these claims, but that also offer a glimpse of an early Christian theology that turns out to be rather surprising.

SPEECH ACT THEORY

In the study of linguistics and the philosophy of language scholars recognize three dimensions of communication: semantics, syntactics, and pragmatics. While semantics is the study of how language relates to the world to make meaning (viz., how words, phrases, or sentences refer to objects, concepts, and the like) and syntactics is the study of the relationship between the component parts of language which enable coherent discourse, pragmatics is the study of the relationship between language and the users of language. Loosely put, pragmatics is the study of the social function of language.[3] Speech act theory falls under the domain of pragmatics.

J. L. Austin, the founder of speech act theory,[4] observed that the meaning of certain kinds of expressions is not dependent on their truth correspondence to the world. For example, if I say "I am writing a paper," the meaning of this statement is derived from the fact that it corresponds to the true fact that I am writing a paper. In this case meaning is fundamentally semantic. Austin and subsequent writers on this issue call such a statement—i.e., a statement that describes a state of affairs in the world—a *constative*.[5] If, however, I make a statement such as "I promise to write a paper," the meaning of the statement is

---

2. There are many subtle variations in the extant Greek forms of these words, but the expression usually takes the aorist passive, e.g., ἠγέρθη Ἰησοῦς, or the perfect passive, e.g., ἐγήγερται Χριστός. The titles vary and participial forms are common. According to R. E. Brown, the older translation, "Jesus is risen," derives from Jerome's Latin translation. Brown, *The Virginal Conception and Bodily Resurrection of Jesus* (New York: Paulist, 1973) 79.

3. For a more thorough definition of pragmatics and its relationship to semantics and syntactics, see S. C. Levinson, *Pragmatics* (Cambridge: Cambridge University Press, 1983) 1–35.

4. Austin, *How to Do Things with Words* (Cambridge: Harvard, 1975) is the fullest expression of Austin's work on speech act theory, but for a simplified statement see also "Performative Utterances," in *Philosophical Papers*, ed. J. O. Urmson and G. J. Warnock (Oxford: Clarendon, 1970) 233–52.

5. Austin, *Words*, 3. See also Levinson, *Pragmatics*, 226–36.

not derived from its truth correspondence; it is not describing some-thing in the world which can be either true or false; it is not pointing to something outside itself at all, it is *performing* something. Austin therefore called it a performative utterance, or simply a *performative*, thus designating a class of statements distinct from constatives. By the very utterance "I promise," I perform the action of promising. If one begins a statement with "I promise," one not only commits oneself to whatever follows in the statement but also engages in the formal act of doing so.[6]

Austin isolated three components within a speech act: *locution, illocution,* and *perlocution.* The locution is what was said, i.e., "I promise to write a paper." The illocution is what was done. In the case of promising, the illocution is easy to identify: it is the ritual act of promising. I have enacted something in the world by an utterance; I have made a commitment to someone to do something in the future. Finally, the perlocution is the result or uptake on the part of the hearer. The hearer of the promise expects the fulfillment of the promise.[7]

Scholars of various fields, including philosophy, linguistics, literary theory, and religion, have taken up the study of speech acts and elaborated upon the theory.[8] In most cases those who work with speech

---

6. Meaning in this case is derived from the speaker's use; the speaker must be sincere, must use the correct expression, and if need be the speaker must be a person of authority (as in the case of pronouncing someone husband and wife), etc. These requirements are what Austin called "felicity conditions" (*Words,* 12–24). Felicity conditions ensure the successful delivery of the speech act. While performative utterances cannot be right or wrong, they can misfire (viz., the speech act does not have the intended effect) or be abused (wherein the speech act is deliberately flouted).

7. It is important to realize that all three components are *acts.* The locution, for example, is the act of making the statement. For more technical definitions of these terms, see Levinson, *Pragmatics,* 236. For a critical reappraisal, see D. Holdcroft, *Words and Deeds: Problems in the Theory of Speech Acts* (Oxford: Clarendon, 1978) 14–24.

8. In philosophy the two most influential scholars who took up Austin's work were J. R. Searle, *Speech Acts: An Essay in the Philosophy of Language* (Cambridge: Cambridge University Press, 1969), and H. P. Grice, "Logic and Conversation" in *Syntax and Semantics,* vol. 3, ed. P. Cole and J. L. Morgan (New York: Academic Press, 1975) 41–58. Among linguists, the most influential was E. Benveniste, who had a fairly rigid conception of what constitutes a speech act. See Benveniste, *Problems in General Linguistics,* Miami Linguistic Series 8 (Coral Gables, FL: University of Miami, 1971). Others who have tried to systematize the study of speech acts include O. Ducrot, *Les mots du discours* (Paris: Les Éditions de Minuit, 1980), and J. Saddock, *Toward a Linguistic Theory of Speech Acts* (New York: Academic Press, 1974). A variety of recent perspectives can be found in S. L. Tsohatzidis, *Foundations of Speech Act Theory: Philosophical and Linguistic Perspectives* (London and New York: Routledge, 1994). Outside of linguistics, literary theory has given speech act theory its warmest reception. Among the earliest and most influential literary critics to make use of the theory for the study of literature were S. Fish, "How to Do Things with Austin and Searle: Speech Act Theory and Literary Discourse," *Modern Language Notes* 91 (1976) 983–1025; M. L. Pratt, *Toward a Speech Act Theory of Dis-course* (Bloomington: Indiana University Press, 1977); and R. Ohman, "Literature as Act," in *Approaches to Poetics,* ed. S. Chatman (New York: Columbia University Press, 1973). The work of both Derrida and Fish has had influence in both philosophical and literary circles. J. Derrida "Signature Event Context," in *Glyph 1* (Baltimore: Johns Hopkins University Press, 1997) 172–92; S. Fish, "With the Compliments of the Author: Reflections of Austin and Derrida," *Critical Inquiry* 8 (1982) 693–721. Among religionists, the first one to make use of the theory was S.

acts come to realize that the illocution—or what is now commonly called the *illocutionary force*—is the essential component in analyzing the speech act.[9] Although the locution is always the starting point in the analysis, the illocution determines what kind of speech act is manifest in any given instance. The perlocution is a more evasive and unpredictable aspect and one which in any case is sometimes conflated with the illocution.[10] Furthermore, while the illocution is understood to be the conventional force implicit in the speaker's utterance,[11] an infinite number of perlocutions can accompany any verbal exchange because unique circumstances are always possible.[12]

Initially Austin seems to argue that the category of speech acts includes only formalized utterances such as promising, taking vows, and saying blessings.[13] As one progresses through his discussion, however, Austin says that many, if not all, utterances are speech acts because all coherent utterances have illocutionary force.[14] As a result, linguists and philosophers have primarily applied speech acts to ordinary language.[15] Searle has composed a comprehensive taxonomy of speech acts comprised of five types, including direct and indirect speech acts.[16]

A direct speech act is one where the illocution coincides with the propositional content represented in the locution—as in the command,

---

Tambiah, "The Magical Power of Words," *Man* n.s. 3 no. 2 (1968) 175–208. Surprisingly few historians of religion have taken up the task, although one particularly insightful article which applies speech act theory to liturgical language is by W. T. Wheelock, "The Problem of Ritual Language: From Information to Situation," *JAAR* 50 (1982) 49–71.

9. This is evident in that speech acts are normally categorized according to their illocution; see Searle, *Speech Acts*, 23–24, 66–67.

10. See Levinson, *Pragmatics*, 236–37, 241–42. Since the perlocution is especially difficult to determine in written texts, I will not evaluate that component of the resurrection proclamation.

11. The one person who takes exception to this is Benveniste (*Problems in General Linguistics*) because he argues that every individual speech act is unique.

12. See Searle, "A Taxonomy of Illocutionary Acts," in *Expression and Meaning: Studies in the Theory of Speech Acts* (Cambridge: Cambridge University Press, 1979) 3.

13. Because Austin distinguishes between constatives and performatives in order to illustrate what a speech act is, it at first appears that only performatives count as speech acts.

14. As White says, "The concept of the illocutionary act ultimately displaces the distinction between performative and constative for Austin." White, "Introduction: Speech Act Theory and Literary Criticism" *Semeia* 41 (1988) 19. See also Searle, *Speech Acts*, 17–18; and Levinson, *Pragmatics*, 231.

15. The ultimate example of this kind of work is Grice, "Logic and Conversation," who applied the insights of speech act theory to conversation.

16. They are as follows: (1) Assertives: where the speaker's purpose is to assert the truth of a proposition; (2) Directives: where the purpose is to get the hearer to do something; (3) Commissives: where the speaker commits to some future course of action; (4) Expressives: where the purpose is to express a psychological state or attitude about a state of affairs (examples include apologizing or congratulating); and (5) Declarations: where the purpose is to initiate a state of affairs in the world (examples include christening a ship or pronouncing a couple married). Searle's taxonomy, which is really a revision of Austin's, can be found in "Taxonomy," 1–29.

"Shut the door!"—or where the utterance contains an *illocutionary force indicating device*,[17] as in formalized utterances like promising (I promise . . . , I bet . . . , I bless . . . , etc.). Conversely, an indirect speech act is an utterance in which the illocution does not directly correspond to the propositional content. In the words of John Searle, such a situation occurs when "a speaker utters a sentence, means what he says, but also means something more."[18] Thus, in an indirect speech act, illocutionary force is not discernible from the locution; it may even correspond to another locution which is implied but not verbally communicated. Searle offers the question "Can you reach the salt?" as an example. What the speaker of this question really wants is for the hearer to pass the salt—*pass the salt* being the implied locution. The linguist Stephen Levinson uses the following example:

> Setting: Primary school classroom
> *Teacher:* What are you laughing at?
> *Child:* Nothing.[19]

In a classroom setting, where laughing is a restricted activity, one can be fairly sure that although the teacher asked a question—which on the surface is an inquiry about the object of the child's laughter—the illocutionary force is really that of a command to stop laughing. Furthermore, the child's reply is most likely not true—in the sense that she or he most likely laughed at *something*. The point, however, is not that the child lied or is insincere, but rather that the child has been humbled—she or he demonstrates knowledge that students are not supposed to laugh in class.

Of course in this example, because the setting is a classroom, there are indicators which can be derived from the conventions of the setting.[20] A classroom may not be as formalized and predictable as a ritual setting, but it does provide a certain degree of structure, and thus the setting itself can help to convey much of the illocutionary force. However, studies of indirect speech acts demonstrate that indirect

---

17. Levinson, *Pragmatics*, 238.
18. Searle, "Indirect Speech Acts," in *Expression and Meaning: Studies in the Theory of Speech Acts* (Cambridge: Cambridge University Press, 1979) 30.
19. Levinson, *Pragmatics*, 279.
20. As Searle points out ("Taxonomy," 5–7) some speech acts are dependent upon extra linguistic factors to work. Two such factors relevant to this example would be the institutional setting of a classroom or educational environment, and the fact that the teacher has a status the student does not have. Comparable examples where these factors play a role would be pronouncing two people husband and wife, where the speaker must have a certain ecclesiastical or civil status, and pronouncing an assembly of students graduated, where the existence of a school provides the context.

speech acts can and do happen apart from structured context indicators.[21] Consider the following example:

> Setting: A husband and wife are dining at a restaurant and the wife is eating her dessert. She puts down her fork.
> *Husband:* Are you finished with your cake?

The locutionary content of this question is an inquiry about whether or not the woman has finished her dessert. But the illocutionary force is something quite different. It may be that the husband wants to know if *he* can finish his wife's cake. The question may even have the force of persuading the woman to hand over her cake, in which case perlocutionary uptake has been successful. In this case there are no verbal clues, nor does the context dictate the illocutionary force. The couple is dining in a restaurant, but they might just as well be dining anywhere. The two are engaged in ordinary conversation. To be sure, the context plays an important role in the delivery of a successful speech act, and we need information about the context to interpret the illocution. But the context in this case does not constitute a structured setting that guarantees the illocution. One can imagine other functions to the question: Perhaps the couple is trying to catch a movie and the husband feels pressured for time, so when he asks his wife, "Are you finished with your cake?" he is trying to tell her to hurry up. If, however, a waiter asks the question "Are you finished with your cake?" he most likely wants to know if he can clear the woman's plate.

In all three cases, what is most important about the utterance is the illocutionary force; it constitutes the essential component that enabled effective communication. In none of these examples was the asker *ultimately* interested in whether the woman had finished eating her cake. To assume that he was is to privilege the semantic dimension at the expense of the pragmatic one. To be sure, the husband/waiter most likely meant what he said. There is no reason to believe that either asker was insincere, but the force of the question was to get something to happen that was not literally reflected in the propositional content. Indeed, whenever an indirect speech act occurs, the meaning of the locution itself is likely to be secondary to the illocutionary force.

---

21. How then do people recognize indirect speech acts? As Searle says, "In indirect speech acts the speaker communicates to the hearer more than he actually says by way of relying on their mutually shared background information, both linguistic and non-linguistic, together with their general powers of rationality and inference on the part of the hearer" ("Indirect Speech Acts," 31–32). For more on this issue, see the work of Grice, "Logic and Conversation"; and J. J. Gumperz, "Sociocultural Knowledge in Conversational Inference," in *Linguistics and Anthropology*, Georgetown University Round Table on Languages and Linguistics 1977 (Washington, DC: Georgetown University, 1977) 191–211.

THE RESURRECTION PROCLAMATION

The early resurrection proclamation[22] is an excellent candidate for speech act analysis. Although no doubt Paul (or any other NT author who makes use of the proclamation) meant what he said when he said "Jesus was raised," he may well have meant something more.[23] In other words, while the proposition makes a truth claim—namely, that Jesus has been raised from the dead—that truth claim is not necessarily the impetus or the force behind the proclamation. As demonstrated in the examples above, the force of an utterance is frequently not found in its propositional content. Indeed, as Wade Wheelock has shown, the conveyance of information is frequently not a priority in the stating of religious utterances.[24]

Scholars have already demonstrated they have an implicit awareness that the statement "Jesus was raised" is much more than a simple proposition. By means of a form-critical approach, many have argued (and even more have assumed) that the statement "Jesus was raised" is a proclamation or confession of faith, which, to be sure, sounds very much like a conclusion a speech act theorist might draw. A confession of faith can easily be classified as an assertive, a direct speech act that asserts the speaker's belief in the truth of something. The trouble is that such a judgment about the early resurrection proclamation is based largely on semantics; the pragmatic dimension remains unexplored. That is, the very words "Jesus was raised"—together with general notions about the development of early Christian theology and Christology—determine for the form critic the possible function(s) of the statement.[25] "Jesus was raised" by itself is an assertion that in a

---

22. By using the term proclamation, I am not naming the illocution. This designation is common in scholarly discourse and I therefore use it as a matter of convenience.

23. Searle (*Speech Acts*, 29–30) distinguishes between a proposition or a propositional act and an illocutionary act. In other words, speech acts often contain propositions, but only the way the proposition is expressed can reveal the illocutionary force. If the proposition forms an assertion, then the speaker is indeed asserting the truth of the proposition. The proposition can, however, take a different form or be embedded in another statement, as the resurrection proclamations usually are.

24. Wheelock, "The Problem of Ritual Language," esp. 58–59.

25. Since form criticism has been the dominant method in the study of these early Christian traditions, I feel compelled to articulate where my approach stands in relation to it. Ever since the critique of form criticism by E. Güttgemanns and the rise of narrative criticism, scholars have become appropriately leery about analyzing small form-critical units in order to ascertain socio-historical information about the earliest Christian communities. Among the many problems that Güttgemanns correctly identifies are, first, that scholars had not adequately accounted for the transformation that a speech event undergoes when it moves from the oral to the written, and second, that *Formgeschichte* as traditionally conceived was really aimed at settling theological questions about the historical development of early Christianity. That is, form criticism was more interested in the *Geschichte* and its theological implications and not so much in the *Form*. Indeed Güttgemanns argues that although the kerygma should be a form-critical *terminus technicus* (*Candid Questions*, 322) or stereotypical word field, it is more often used to refer to the original worldview of the first Christians which blossomed into the gospel, the seed from which the

religious context constitutes a faith statement. With this fundamental assumption in mind, studies of the resurrection proclamations of early Christianity usually have one of two intentions: to discover early christological beliefs[26] or to discover the earliest Gospel traditions about what actually happened at the resurrection or immediately following the resurrection.[27] In contrast to these endeavors, this essay does not strive to answer these questions because they are semantic—they are concerned exclusively with what the proclamation *refers to*. Furthermore, these questions may even be misguided because they are based on a faulty understanding of the proclamation as a direct speech act, when, as I argue in the following analysis, the early resurrection proclamation is really an indirect speech act.

Locution

While the ultimate purpose of this essay is to discover the illocution of the early Christian resurrection proclamation, determining the locution is an essential first step—especially because there is some dispute regarding what constitutes the earliest form of the proclamation. I will therefore attempt to sort out the debate as well as lay out the form of the locution.

Christian religion grew. Although the initial impetus for my work here did not come from Güttgemanns, I now see my study of the early resurrection proclamation as a potential response to the crisis that currently exists in form criticism. While my initial remarks about the proclamation may resemble form-critical judgments, I have tried to be more precise by separating the semantic/syntactic dimension, which I address under "Locution," from the pragmatic dimension discussed under "Illocution." Indeed, Güttgemanns thinks the corrective to the vagueness and unreliability of form criticism can be found in linguistics. See Güttgemanns, *Candid Questions Concerning Gospel Form Criticism: A Methodological Sketch of the Fundamental Problematics of Form and Redaction Criticism* (Pittsburgh: Pickwick, 1979).

26. As was the case with W. Kramer, *Christ, Lord, Son of God*, SBT 50 (London: ACM, 1966) 15; K. Wengst, *Christologische Formeln und Leider des Urchristentums* (Gütersloh: Mohn, 1972) 92–95; R. Brown, *Virginal Conception and Bodily Resurrection*; A. B. du Toit, "Primitive Christian Belief in the Resurrection of Jesus in Light of Pauline Resurrection and Appearance Terminology," *Neot* 23 (1989) 320; and most recently, G. Leudemann, *The Resurrection of Jesus: History, Experience, Theology* (Minneapolis: Fortress, 1994).

27. The classic study written with this intention is by W. Marxsen, *The Resurrection of Jesus of Nazareth* (Philadelphia: Fortress, 1970). Among more recent works I would include M. J. Harris, *Raised Immortal: Resurrection and Immortality in the New Testament* (Grand Rapids: Eerdmans, 1983); W. Lunny, *The Sociology of the Resurrection* (London: SCM, 1989); and Leudemann (*Resurrection*) who also tries to reconstruct events. Several German scholars show interest in both early Christology and reconstructing history because of their understanding of the importance of the ἀποκάλυψις of the risen Jesus to the disciples. For these scholars, the origin of belief in the resurrection of Jesus lies in the fact that the disciples experienced visions of Jesus after he died. See the essays collected in P. Hoffmann, *Zur neutestamentlich Überlieferung von der Auferstehung Jesu* (Darmstadt: Wissenschaftliche Buchgesellschaft, 1988), especially those of U. Wilckens, "Der Ursprung der Überlieferung der Erscheinungen des Auferstandenen. Zur traditionsgeschichtlichen Analyse von 1 Kor. 15, 1–11," 139–93; and R. Pesch, "Zur Enstehung des Glaubens an die Auferstehung Jesu. Ein neuer Versuch," 228–58.

There are three different verbs used to describe the resurrection of Jesus in the New Testament: ἐγείρω, ἀνίστημι, and ζάω, but those forms using ἐγείρω dominate at the earliest stages. Ἐγείρω is overwhelmingly the most frequent verb in our earliest texts: the Pauline corpus. Only once does Paul use ἀνίστημι when he makes his proclamation (1 Thess 4:14). Ζάω appears three times (Rom 6:10, 14:9; 2 Cor 13:4), but since only Paul uses it, one cannot know whether it is pre-Pauline.[28] The strongest reasons for concentrating on the ἐγείρω formulation of the kerygma are twofold. First, there are more examples of the ἐγείρω formulation; and second, this formulation represents the most standardized construction. The other two verbs are not repeated in the earliest texts with enough frequency and fixity to constitute a formulaic expression. To be sure, the early Christians must have described the resurrection of Jesus in a variety of ways in casual conversation. The object of this study, however, must be the standardized form. Focusing on the standardized form eliminates uncontrolled variables, since alteration of the locution could well mean a different illocutionary force. Furthermore, the most standardized formula has the greatest chance of being a genuinely common Christian expression and not an idiosyncratic one. My goal is not to identify the idiosyncrasies accompanying particular instances of the proclamation of the resurrection of Jesus, but rather the most essential illocutionary force common to most, if not all, occurrences of this speech act.

It is not clear why ἐγείρω became the verb of choice to proclaim the resurrection of Jesus.[29] A few scholars speculate that since the verb is commonly used to awake from sleep, and since resurrection in Jewish terms is metaphorically understood as awakening from sleep, the verb was a natural choice over ἀνίστημι.[30] Another point of distinction between the two verbs is that ἐγείρω appears exclusively in the passive when Jesus is the subject of the proclamation, while ἀνίστημι most often appears in the active with an intransitive meaning. The use of the passive form of ἐγείρω implies that God is the agent who caused Jesus' raising, and this is what we would expect from the earliest layer of tradition.[31] In post–New Testament texts, the active form of the verb

---

28. In all cases the theme of "life" or "living" is the topic of the moment. Paul thus seems to be modifying the formula to fit the context of his discussion. See du Toit, "Primitive Christian Belief," 318.

29. Ἐγείρω is an unusual choice with regard to the raising of the dead; ἀνίστημι is the typical verb used by other Greek authors; see A. Oepke, *"ἀνίστημι" TDNT* 1:369; and idem, *"ἐγείρω" TDNT* 2:333–35.

30. C. F. Evans, *Resurrection and the New Testament* (London: SCM, 1970) 22–23.

31. The idea of Jesus raising himself implies a more developed Christology. See Evans, *Resurrection*, 21.

becomes more common.[32] Thus the tradition evolves from a statement about God raising Jesus to one where Jesus is understood to have raised himself or at least participated in the event with God. The problem of determining the construction of the early formula is more complex than that of determining which verb was used. The early resurrection proclamation varies in two ways. First, there is an active form in which God is the subject, "God raised Jesus (from the dead)," and a passive form in which Jesus is the subject, "Jesus was raised (from the dead)." Second, when the formula occurs with only a reference to the raising, it is commonly known as a one-member formula. When it is prefaced by a reference to the death—"Jesus died and was raised"—it is known as a two-member formula, and in this case Jesus is always the subject.[33] Scholars debate whether the one-member or the two-member formula came first. I will first address the arguments for the priority of the two-member proclamation.

In the speeches in Acts, a variation of the two-member formula appears that some think is the earliest version of the resurrection proclamation.[34] Two examples will suffice to illustrate this version of the formula:[35]

> But you rejected the Holy and Righteous One, and asked to have a murderer given to you, and killed the author of life, whom God raised from the dead. (Acts 3:14–15)

> Let it be known to all of you, and to all the people of Israel . . . , that by the name of Jesus Christ of Nazareth, whom you crucified, whom God raised from the dead. (Acts 4:10)

Scholars argue that because the description of the death here reflects a scandalous embarrassment, this formula must be more original than that which appears in the Pauline epistles. Jesus' dying is not seen as part of God's plan, or in any way salvific. The resurrection is seen as

---

32. Evans (*Resurrection*, 22) cites Ignatius, *Smyrn* 2:1 ("He truly raised himself . . . ") and *Epistle to Rheginos* 45:17–18 ("He transformed himself into an imperishable *eon* and raised himself up."). The idea that Jesus raised himself is already found in John (2:19; 10:17–18), but John also uses the passive formula (2:22).

33. My survey of Paul's letters yields the following examples of the proclamation: The one-member ἐγείρω formula can be found in Rom 4:24; 6:4; 6:9; 7:4; 8:11; 10:9; 1 Cor 6:14; many times throughout Paul's famous discussion on resurrection of the body in 1 Cor 15; 2 Cor 4:14; Gal 1:1; and 1 Thess 1:10. Among the deutero-Pauline literature, examples appear in Col 2:12; Eph 1:20; and 2 Tim 2:8. Other examples of the one-member formula include Acts 13:37 and 1 Pet 1:21. The two-member formula appears many times in Acts (see n. 35) and four times in the genuine letters of Paul: Rom 4:25; 8:34; 1 Cor 15:3–4; 2 Cor 5:15. 1 Thess 4:14 contains an example of the two-member formula but uses the verb ἀνίστημι.

34. Evans, *Resurrection*, 133; Brown, *Virginal Conception and Bodily Resurrection*, 80–81, n. 137.

35. The other examples from Acts include 5:30; 10:39–40; 13:28–30.

God's vindication for the martyred Jesus. This proclamation constitutes a contrasting formula—that is, the death and resurrection are not seen as one salvific event, but as contrasting events. Human beings did something which God overturned. The proclamation in Acts, then, represents a primitive Christology whose foundation is the story of the passion. While the logic of this thesis is sensible, it fails to convince because its reasoning is based on theological assumptions not inherent in the standardized form of the early proclamation.[36]

First, the two-member proclamations in Acts are not good candidates for an early dating.[37] The literary context indicates that they are here for a Lucan apologetic purpose. The first member of the formula, which refers to Jesus' death, is addressed in the second person to the Jews in the audience (i.e., "Jesus Christ of Nazareth, whom *you* crucified"). The goal of these proclamations is to convince the Jews or Jewish authorities of their misdeeds and misperceptions regarding Jesus.[38] This squares well with Luke's desire to exonerate the Romans in hopes of ameliorating relations between Christianity and the State, while blaming the Jews for any hostile crimes.[39] Second, that Peter, a

---

36. The argument that the earliest kerygma was a contrasting formula in which the death and resurrection are set over against each other is at least partly dependent upon the work of G. Nickelsburg, *Resurrection, Immortality, and Eternal Life in Intertestamental Judaism*, HTS 26 (Cambridge: Harvard University Press, 1972). Nickelsburg has ably demonstrated that one of the earliest forms through which the Jewish concept of resurrection developed was that of the "Persecution and Exaltation of the Righteous Man." The notion of resurrection, which developed during the intertestamental period, was a religious response to the unjust suffering of individuals. New Testament scholars who have looked for antecedents to the early belief in the resurrection of Jesus have found these antecedents in the model of the persecuted and exalted righteous man. There is no doubt that what we know about the death of Jesus resonates with the intertestamental model (see also Nickelsburg, "Resurrection" in *ABD* 5:688). However, my task here is the evaluation of the earliest *linguistic forms* of the early Christian kerygma, and what I find is that these forms do not reflect this model. Perhaps the model was operative but did not manifest itself in the early proclamation, but only in christological hymns. Perhaps this model was not the most powerful one for understanding the resurrection of Jesus at this time. Nickelsburg himself says that in the later intertestamental period, "resurrection theology loses its connections with persecution and suffering" and instead takes on the function of fulfilling more general notions of reward and punishment (*Resurrection, Immortality*, 173).

37. Ever since Dibelius argued that the speeches in Acts were composed by the author, the argument for the preservation of early material in the speeches has been highly suspect. Dibelius, "The Speeches in Acts and Ancient Historiography," *Studies in the Acts of the Apostles* (New York: Charles Scribner's Sons, 1956) 26–77, 138–85. See also H. Conzelmann, *Acts of the Apostles*, Hermeneia (Philadelphia: Fortress, 1987) xliv.

38. Brown (*Virginal Conception and Bodily Resurrection*, 80) acknowledges that there is an anti-Jewish element in these formulae, but argues that while the anti-Jewish tone reflects a later setting, the two-member formula that portrays the death negatively is still the earliest formula and is best represented by these constructions in Acts. However, I see no evidence for an *urformula* underlying these polemical statements in Acts, as my discussion here should demonstrate.

39. E. Haenchen, *The Acts of the Apostles* (Philadelphia: Westminster, 1971) 102, 106. Attempts to deny the anti-Jewish polemic in Acts in general or the speeches in particular such as that of J. R. Wilch and F. Matera, fail to be convincing against the more comprehensive contributions of other scholars such as J. Sanders. See Wilch, "Jewish Guilt for the Death of Jesus—Anti-Judaism in the Acts of the Apostles?" *Lutheran Theological Journal* 18 (1984) 236–49; Matera, "Responsibility for the Death of Jesus according to the Acts of the Apostles," *JSNT* 39 (1990) 77–93; and Sanders, *The Jews in Luke–Acts* (Philadelphia: Fortress, 1987). Exactly how thorough-

Jewish preacher, would speak in the second person—"you did such and such . . ."—rather than using the first person "we," might well reflect an "us and them" consciousness, pointing to a separation between Judaism and Christianity,[40] which in turn implies a later stage of development. The third and final reason why this two-member formula in Acts is not a likely candidate for an early dating is that the first half is not truly formulaic. The mention of the death is really a mention of crucifixion, which does not display the stereotypical speech form found in other versions of this formula attested elsewhere in the New Testament.[41] Each instance in Acts constitutes an accusation that reflects a typical Lucan theme concerning Jesus' death, which is then attached to the one-member formula.

The description of the death of Jesus in the Acts formulae further demonstrates that the proclamations in Acts function as synopses of the story of the passion and are dependent on Gospel traditions. Indeed, the context of many of the proclamations in Acts include details of the passion narrative:

> The God of our ancestors has glorified his servant Jesus, whom you handed over and rejected in the presence of Pilate, though he had decided to release him. But you rejected the Holy and Righteous One and asked to have a murderer given to you, and you killed the Author of life, whom God raised from the dead. (3:13–15)[42]

> Even though they found no cause for a sentence of death, they asked Pilate to have him killed. When they had carried out everything that was written about him, they took him down from the tree and laid him in a tomb. But God raised him from the dead. (13:28–30)

Thus, I consider it unlikely that the two-member formula in Acts—where the death and resurrection are set over against each other—represents the earliest, common proclamation of the resurrection of Jesus. The presence of Lucan redaction is overpowering.

---

going the anti-Jewish polemic really is continues to be debated, but to argue that statements like those quoted above are not polemical seems to me to deny the obvious. I suspect that Wilch and Matera are motivated by current theological considerations: they do not want those texts used in contemporary discourse to be used to justify modern anti-Semitism. I sympathize with these motivations, but cannot condone such exegetical conclusions. See also the thoughtful essay by D. Tiede, "'Fighting Against God': Luke's Interpretation of the Jewish Rejection of the Messiah Jesus," in *Anti-Semitism and Early Christianity: Issues of Faith and Polemic*, ed. C. A. Evans and D. A. Hagner (Minneapolis: Fortress, 1993) 102–12.

    40. See J. D. G. Dunn, *The Parting of the Ways: Between Christianity and Judaism and Their Significance for the Character of Christianity* (London: SCM, 1991) esp. 241.

    41. The verb used nearly everywhere else outside of Acts to describe Jesus' death is ἀποθνῄσκω. See BAGD, 91, for examples.

    42. The choice of words in this citation also indicates a connection to the passion predictions in the synoptic Gospels. The verbs παραδίδωμι and ἀποκτείνω, which appear here, appear consistently in the passion predictions. See Mark 8:31; 9:31; 10:33–34 and par.

In distinction to Jesus being *killed*, as is proclaimed in Acts, in the Pauline literature Jesus is said to have *died*.[43] The fullest form of course appears in 1 Corinthians 15:3–4: "that Christ died for our sins in accordance with the scriptures, and that he was buried, and that he was raised on the third day in accordance with the scriptures." The mention of scriptures and being buried do not appear in any other occurrence of the two-member proclamation.[44] Although the statement that "Christ died for our sins" does not literally occur anywhere else, Paul does say in Romans 4:25 that Jesus was "handed over for our justification," which conveys the same theological idea.[45] In any case, everyone agrees that 1 Corinthians 15:3–5 reflects a later, expanded proclamation.[46]

Even if one were to grant, as most scholars do, that "for our sins" or "for justification" is a later addition,[47] it is nevertheless the case that proclaiming "Jesus died" assumes that the death of Jesus is worth proclaiming. Unless Jesus' death had theological meaning, there would have been no reason to proclaim that he died. No one had to be convinced of the fact of his death; it was the resurrection that needed proclaiming. Thus, if the salvific notion of Jesus' death evolved later, then so did the two-member proclamation.[48]

---

43. There is one exception to this: Rom 4:25 says that Jesus was "handed over," ὅς παρεδόθη διὰ τὰ παραπτώματα ἡμῶν, similar to the proclamations in Acts.

44. The third day, however, appears in the passion predictions.

45. It is important to note that no particular title for Jesus dominates in the early resurrection proclamation, as Kloppenborg has pointed out. See Kloppenborg, "Analysis of the Pre-Pauline Formula: 1 Cor 15:3b-5 in Light of Some Recent Literature," *CBQ* 40 (1978) 356 n. 38. Although some (e.g., Kramer, *Christ*, 20-44) have tried to construct a developmental chronology according to christological title, I have found no adequate way to stratify the proclamations by title.

46. While the substance of 1 Cor 15:3b–5 is assumed to be a pre-Pauline formula, the particulars are debated; see U. Wilckens, *Die Missionreden der Apostelgeschichte: Form- und traditionsgeschichtliche Untersuchungen* (Neukirchen-Vluyn: Neukirchener, 1963) 73–81; J. Jeremias, *The Eucharistic Words of Jesus* (New York: Charles Scribner's Sons, 1966) 101–5; H. Conzelmann, "On the Analysis of the Confessional Formula in I Corinthians 15:3–5," *Int* 20 (1966) 15–25; idem, *1 Corinthians*, Hermeneia (Philadelphia: Fortress, 1975) 248–58; J. Kloppenborg, "An Analysis of the Pre-Pauline Formula 1 Cor 15:3b–5 in Light of Some Recent Literature," *CBQ* 40 (1978) 351–67; and J. Murphy-O'Conner, "Tradition and Redaction in 1 Cor 15:3–7," *CBQ* 43 (1981) 582–89. It is also well established that the formula in 1 Cor 15:3b–5 is older than the formulaic list of appearances which follows it in vv. 6–7; see R. Deichgraber, *Gotteshymnus und Christushymnus in der frühen Christenheit* (Göttingen: Vandenhoeck, 1967) 108; Kramer, *Christ, Lord, Son of God*, 15; and Wengst, *Christologische Formeln und Leider des Urchristentums*, 92–95.

47. So Jeremias (*Eucharistic Words*, 101–2) and Kloppenborg ("Analysis of the Pre-Pauline Formula," 362–63).

48. On the other hand, if one wishes to argue that the two-member proclamation is as old or older than the one-member, it is also necessary to believe that Christians developed a salvific understanding of the death concurrently. The majority of scholars do not believe this is the case. However, some believe that the soteriological understanding of Jesus' death developed remarkably early. See E. Käsemann, "The Saving Significance of the Death of Jesus in Paul," in *Perspectives on Paul* (Philadelphia: Fortress, 1971) 39; and M. Hengel, *The Atonement: The Origins of the Doctrine in the New Testament* (Philadelphia: Fortress, 1981).

Furthermore, the one-member formula more often than not includes the phrase *from the dead*. By contrast, since the two-member formula refers both to the death and to the resurrection, the phrase *from the dead* is redundant and so never appears. Obviously, if Jesus died, then he had been raised *from the dead!* It is highly unlikely that the phrase *from the dead*, which is so often attached to the one-member formula, would have evolved after a two-member formula already existed, precisely because of this redundancy. In other words, the one-member formula does not constitute a truncated version of the two-member formula. On the other hand, *from the dead* makes good sense if one assumes the priority of the one-member formula, *Jesus was raised*. In the earlier one-member formula, one would not know what kind of raising is implied without the qualifying phrase *from the dead*.[49] Thus, if the two early proclamations are genetically related,[50] the two-member formula is more likely an expansion of the one-member, reflecting the growing interest in the story of the passion and in the theological meaning of Jesus' death.

The final reason to entertain the possibility that the one-member formula represents the earliest stage of tradition depends upon factoring in the other major variable: whether the statement is active or passive. The two-member proclamation employs the passive verb because Jesus is the subject of the sentence.[51] A survey of the one-member proclamations reveals that the majority of them are active—*God raised Jesus from the dead*—though there are a few examples of the passive, *Jesus was raised from the dead*.[52] Although the grammatical subject of the sentence varies, the implied subject of the action is always God. Whether the one-member formula is constructed actively or passively, God is consistently recognized as the agent of the salvific event.

I have found no way to determine which came first, the active or the passive, or whether they emerged simultaneously. However, because God's agency is consistently implied, I think it is fair to say

---

49. This makes all the more sense if we recall that the verb ἐγείρω has many meanings, including raising a person to an elevated status; see BAGD, 214–15. Furthermore, there were those like the members of the Qumran community who believed in eternal life but not necessarily in resurrection from the dead; see Nickelsburg, *Resurrection, Immortality*, 152–69. Death does not seem to have been a prerequisite for a post-earthly life at Qumran. Thus, "from the dead" may have had an important specifying function in the Christian proclamation.

50. Of course, one can entertain the possibility that they are not genetically related, that they sprang up as separate expressions, or that some people used one and some used the other.

51. This is not true of the Acts proclamations but, as I argued above, that is because the Acts proclamations are really active, one-member proclamations attached to a mention of the crucifixion.

52. The only examples of the one-member formula that are passive are Rom 6:4, 9; and 2 Tim 2:8. For a complete list of NT examples of the proclamations, see n. 33.

that the active form is linguistically—perhaps one could even say existentially—prior to the passive form. Both variations possess the same semantic meaning; they refer to the same event. But the active proclamation—*God raised Jesus from the dead*—constitutes a complete, independent assertion in which all the pertinent information is supplied by the sentence. The passive proclamation does not mention *who* raised Jesus—that information is presumed known. In other words, the statement that "Jesus was raised" is dependent upon knowing the other statement, that "God raised Jesus." In this way the active one-member formula has linguistic priority over the passive.

Although the raising is stated passively in the two-member formula, thus also implying God's agency, the first half of that formula, *Jesus died*, makes no reference to God. Semantically speaking, the two-member formula refers primarily to events in Jesus' life, while the one-member refers primarily to God's actions regarding Jesus. If one assumes with most scholars that christological reflection becomes greater as time progresses,[53] then one can argue that a later proclamation would have focused more on Jesus and less on God. This too, then, supports the hypothesis that the one-member formula existed earlier than the two-member. Thus, the simple one-member formula, *God raised Jesus (from the dead)* or *Jesus was raised (from the dead)* with God's agency implied, stands as the earliest determinable form of the tradition.[54]

Even if one doubted my argument that the one-member formula represents the most likely candidate for the earliest resurrection proclamation, one must admit that it is the most common locutionary component within any form of the proclamation. In fact, it is the essential component—without it, *there is no kerygma!* "Jesus died" or "from the dead" are locutionary accoutrements. The reference to raising is the nucleus of the speech act.

---

53. By this remark I do not mean that Christology becomes higher (the christological hymns demonstrate otherwise) but that more sophisticated and more esoteric Christologies develop more fully with the passing of time. See Dunn, "Christology," *ABD* 1:979–90. See, however, Hengel, who argues that the early church's christological reflection was nearly complete in the first twenty years. Hengel, "Christological Titles in Early Christianity," in *The Messiah: Developments in Earliest Judaism and Christianity*, ed. J. H. Charlesworth (Minneapolis: Fortress, 1992) 425–48.

54. X. Leon-Dufour reaches similar conclusions, although his reasoning differs from mine. Leon-Dufour, *Resurrection and the Message of Easter* (New York: Holt, Rinehart, and Winston, 1974) 12–14.

Illocution

The next step is to determine whether this early Christian statement about the resurrection of Jesus is a direct or indirect speech act. It is important to realize that there are no free-floating examples of the kerygma. All the actualized examples of this early Christian claim lie embedded in statements whose function differs from the function of the proclamation.[55] Such embedding provides the context within which one can make inferences about the illocution. Here are some representative examples:

Now the words, "it was reckoned to him," were written not for his sake alone, but for ours also. It will be reckoned to us who believe in him *who raised Jesus our Lord from the dead. . . .*[56] (Rom 4:23-24)

If the Spirit of him who raised Jesus from the dead dwells in you, he *who raised Christ from the dead* will give life to your mortal bodies also through his Spirit that dwells in you. (Rom 8:11)

If you confess with your lips that Jesus is Lord and believe in your heart that *God raised him from the dead*, you will be saved. (Rom 10:9)

Because we know that the one *who raised the Lord Jesus* will raise us also with Jesus, and will bring us with you into his presence. (2 Cor 4:14)

Paul an apostle—sent neither by human commission nor from human authorities, but through Jesus Christ and God the Father, *who raised him from the dead—* (Gal 1:1)

When you were buried with him in baptism, you were also raised with him through faith in the power of God, *who raised him from the dead.* (Col 2:12)

God put this power to work in Christ *when he raised him from the dead* and seated him at his right hand in the heavenly places. (Eph 1:20)

Through him you have come to trust in God, *who raised him from the dead* and gave him glory, so that your faith and hope are set on God. (1 Pet 1:21)

Remember Jesus Christ, *raised from the dead*, a descendant of David—that is my gospel. (2 Tim 2:8)

---

55. This in no way means that the force of the embedded performative is absent; see Saddock, *Linguistic Theory of Speech Acts*, 51–71.

56. Interestingly, this one-member formula is followed by the two-member construction in the following verse.

A direct speech act occurs in only one of these cases: Romans 10:9— "If you . . . believe in your heart that God raised him from the dead, . . ." The statement is preceded by the verb "to believe" followed by "that." Romans 10:9 is an assertive, in which the speaker asserts the truth of whatever the proposition refers to. None of the other examples, however, constitutes a direct speech act. In the two other cases where the verb πιστεύω precedes the proposition (Rom 4:24; 1 Pet 1:21), the object of belief is God, Godself, not Jesus or his resurrection. The mention of the resurrection is appended as a description of God: "[We] believe in him who raised Jesus." Although the locution semantically makes an implicit assertion, asserting the truth of the resurrection is not the point of the utterance. The point is to identify God by this salvific act. Furthermore, when an assertive speech act transpires, it means that the assertion is not *assumed* to be true. Either it is not the reigning opinion or it is disputed; otherwise there is no reason to make an assertion. Yet a glance at these examples, with the possible exception of Romans 10:9, points to the proposition's use as an assumption, something viewed as commonly true, and the basis upon which to assert something else.

Thus I find two primary illocutions that typically accompany this early resurrection proclamation. First, and most important, *the formula is a name*. It distinguishes the God who raised Jesus from other gods, and it redefines God by a new salvific act as opposed to previous acts, like the exodus. Second, *the formula is a condition used in asserting God's power to resurrect the believer.*[57]

A name means that something can always be identified by it; it is a permanent label.[58] One can compare the early proclamation of the

---

57. I will largely refrain from categorizing these functions according to Searle's taxonomy (see n. 16 above), because, as Wheelock points out, it is inadequate for religious language ("Problem of Ritual Language," 59–65). Furthermore, my goal is not to identify a generic function (i.e., whether the formula has an expressive or declarative function) but rather to isolate the actual function!

58. An interesting observation that Searle makes about declarative speech acts, of which naming is one, is that the words fit the world and the world fits the words ("Taxonomy," 3–4, 19). What he is referring to here is the *directional fit* of a speech act. Assessing the directional fit of a speech act means judging whether the words are spoken to match the world, or whether they are designed to get the world to match the words. To illustrate this characteristic, Searle uses the following example: A man is sent to the grocery store by his wife with a shopping list which includes the words, "beans, butter, bacon, bread." This locution has the function of getting the husband to act in accordance with the list, i.e., purchase those items listed. We could say that the goal of this speech act is to get the world (the man's actions) to match the words. Now let us suppose that a detective is following the shopper, writing down everything he purchases. If successful, the detective's list will be the same as the shopper's, but the detective's goal is to get the list to match the man's purchases, i.e., to get the words to match the world. Now, what is unique about declarative speech acts, according to Searle, is that the directional fit works both ways. The function of naming is to get *both* the words to fit the world *and* the world to fit the words. By naming or labeling things, I confer a status on something (world to words) and at the same time my labeling of it is a way of expressing my relationship or experience of the same something (words to world).

resurrection of Jesus to that well-known extended appellation for God in the Hebrew Bible, "I am the Lord your God, who brought you out of the land of Egypt."[59] This phrase occurs throughout the Hebrew Bible, not just in the exodus story.[60] Throughout the scriptural memory of the Jewish people, the God of Israel was defined by this quintessential salvific act.[61]

Similarly, the early resurrection formula defined for the early Christians who their God was. The God whom the Christians believe in is the God who raised Jesus from the dead. Indeed, most of the resurrection proclamations where God is the subject occur in relative clauses and attributive participial phrases—they serve as identification markers of who God is and what makes God, God. In 2 Corinthians 4:14 Paul says, εἰδότες ὅτι ὁ ἐγείρας τὸν κύριον Ἰησοῦν καὶ ἡμᾶς σὺν Ἰησοῦ ἐγερεῖ ("[we] know that the one who raised Lord Jesus will raise us also with Jesus"). Instead of simply calling God θεός, Paul uses the formula, "the one who raised Lord Jesus," which constitutes a paraphrastic expression for God. Similarly Romans 4:24 reads: τοῖς πιστεύουσιν ἐπὶ τὸν ἐγείραντα Ἰησοῦν τὸν κύριον ἡμῶν ἐκ νεκρῶν ("[We] who believe in him who raised Jesus our Lord from the dead"). Here again, Paul substitutes the participial expression, "the one who raised . . ." for the simple θεός. The confession asserts that the believer acknowledges this God, the God who raised Jesus, not that the resurrection is true.[62] In a Greco-Roman context this serves to distinguish the Christian God from pagan gods, while in a Jewish context it

---

59. Although I made this observation by studying the examples of the early proclamation, I subsequently found two scholars who had already made this observation: O. Michel, *Der Brief an die Römer* (Göttingen: Vandenhoeck & Ruprecht, 1966) 127 n. 3; and Nickelsburg, "Resurrection," 688. Both of them make their observations only briefly in the context of a more general discussion. I offer my study here as further support for and corroboration of their conclusions.

60. For a list of references, see M. Noth, *A History of Pentateuchal Traditions* (Englewood Cliffs, NJ: Prentice-Hall, 1972) 49. Interestingly, many observations made about the "out of Egypt" formula parallel those of the early Christian resurrection formula: that it became a fixed formula at an early stage, that it occurs in a participial formulation reflective of hymnic style, and that it functioned as an affirmation of faith.

61. The ultimate expression of this use of "I am the Lord your God who brought you out of the land of Egypt" can be found in the Passover Haggadah. As B. Bokser notes, in the Haggadic narration of the exodus, as well as in the Mishnaic, Moses plays virtually no role in the story. The intended effect of Moses' absence is that God is *the* savior—from Egypt or from whatever else might afflict the Jewish people. Bokser, *The Origins of the Seder: The Passover Rite and Early Rabbinic Judaism* (Berkeley: University of California Press, 1984) 78–79.

62. Thus, statements like the following one by Conzelmann should be called into question: "It is to be noticed that the confession to the one God is mostly absent but virtually presupposed (in early Christianity)" ("Analysis of the Confessional Formula," 17). See also Leon-Dufour, *Resurrection*, 5.

provides God with a new non-ethnic label,[63] which may be why Paul liked it so much.[64]

The second illocutionary force of the formula consists in the Christian's affirmation of faith in the potential resurrection—or at least salvation—of the believer.[65] As Paul says in Romans 10:9, "if you confess with your lips that Jesus is Lord and believe in your heart that God raised him from the dead, you will be saved." Romans 10:9 may be an obvious example of this function of the formula, but the formula more often than not occurs within the protasis of a conditional sentence, followed by an apodosis which ascribes some beneficial result to the believer. Paul says in Romans 10:9 that the believer will be "saved"; in other contexts he says one will walk in the newness of life (Rom 6:4), life will be given to mortal bodies (Rom 8:11) and, most concretely, the believer will be raised (2 Cor 4:14).

In other words, the proclamation had the power to effect salvation. I think one can safely assume that for Paul these expressions are various ways of asserting one kind of salvation, i.e., resurrection from the dead. To believe that God raised Jesus from the dead was not itself an expression of belief in Christ—"Jesus is Lord" constitutes such a statement, not the resurrection proclamation. Indeed, the lack of consistency in the locutionary designations for Jesus—God is said to have raised Jesus, the Lord, Christ, Christ Jesus, and more—indicates that the illocutionary force does not lie with the christological meaning of the resurrection.[66] Neither does the proclamation function to assert that the resurrection happened—that would be to mistake the locution for the illocution. Rather, to believe God raised Jesus meant that one believed in the God who performed the resurrection and that this God had the power to effect one's own resurrection. Believing that Jesus had been raised was a presupposition for believing in one's own resurrection. Resurrection from the dead was a common enough concept in first-century Judaism, but it was not necessarily a commonly held

---

63. In addition to the exodus appellation, the other traditional designation for the Jewish God would have been "the God of Abraham, Isaac, and Jacob."

64. See Noth who points out that the appellation "who brought you out of the land of Egypt" shapes Israel's identity as much as the divinity's identity. For example, some laws are "based upon the recollection that the Israelites were strangers and unfree men ('slaves') in Egypt before Yahweh led them out; so especially in the Deuteronomic law (Deut 15:15; 16:12; 23:8; 24:18, 23) . . . the Holiness Code (Lev 19:34) and in secondary passages of the Book of the Covenant (Exod 22:29; 23:9)" (*Pentateuchal Traditions*, 47–49).

65. Wilckens, too, recognizes this function of the proclamation in 1 Cor 15:3b–5 ("Der Ursprung der Überlieferung," 146–48).

66. Conversely, the christological hymns, which contain the earliest known reflections on the nature of Jesus, do not make use of the proclamation. See Phil 2:6–11; Col 1:15–20; 1 Tim 3:16. 1 Pet 3:18–22 comes close with "he was put to death in the flesh, but made alive in the spirit."

belief. In fact we know it was a debated topic.[67] For Paul and at least some of his followers, the resurrection of Jesus was proof positive that resurrection in general was possible.[68]

This illocutionary force is not exclusive to the authentic writings of Paul but is also found once in Colossians (2:12) and once in Ephesians (2:6). However, there is one place where it appears that the formula did not have this function for some Christians. In 1 Corinthians 15, the famous chapter on the resurrection of the dead, Paul cites the formula repeatedly as evidence for the general resurrection. Although Paul's argument here is a bit circular, his perspective confirms what I have observed elsewhere, that Paul considered the resurrection of Jesus indisputable evidence that resurrection awaits the believer. But the discussion in 1 Corinthians 15 also implies that while the Corinthians know and accept the resurrection of Jesus, they do not think it necessarily implies the resurrection of the believer. At the beginning of the chapter, Paul acknowledges that the Corinthians have accepted the proclamation: "the good news that I proclaimed to you, which you in turn received, in which also you stand, through which also you are being saved. . . ." And as Paul says in verse 12, "Now if Christ is proclaimed as raised from the dead, how can some of you say there is no resurrection of the dead?" The common point of agreement between Paul and the Corinthians is that Christ has been raised from the dead.[69] Nevertheless, the Corinthians do not therefore accept the resurrection of the believer. Perhaps they thought Christ's resurrection was unique, due to his semi-divine status, and thus human beings were not eligible. Of course the nature of the Corinthians' doubt is not so obvious. They may for example have believed that it did effect some kind of salvation, like immortality of the soul, but not bodily resurrec-

---

67. See Mark 12:18; Matt 22:23; Luke 20:27; Acts 23:8; Josephus, *B. J.* 2.8.14 §162ff. For discussions of the differing views on the resurrection of the dead among Jews at this time, see E. Schürer, *History of the Jewish People in the Age of Jesus Christ* (Edinburgh: T. & T. Clark, 1979) 2:391–92, 411; W. S. Vorster, "The Religio-Historical Context of the Resurrection of Jesus and the Resurrection Faith in the New Testament," *Neot* 23 (1989) 163–69; and G. J. Riley, *Resurrection Reconsidered: Thomas and John in Controversy* (Minneapolis: Fortress, 1995) 7–68. Greco-Roman writers represent various perspectives, from those who think it is impossible (Homer *Il.* 24.551) to those who assume it is a reality (Philostratus, *Vit. Ap.* 4.45); see Oepke, "ἀνίστημι," 369.

68. This function also possesses an eschatological dimension (which space does not allow me to explore here), since the general resurrection is often associated with the end times; see G. Nickelsburg, "Resurrection" and Wilckens, "Der Ursprung der Überlieferung," 142–45.

69. J. Lambrecht, "Paul's Christological Use of Scripture in 1 Cor 15:20–28," *NTS* 28 (1982) 515. For a sophisticated but concise analysis of Paul's argument and what it implies about the audience, see A. C. Wire, *The Corinthian Women Prophets* (Minneapolis: Fortress, 1990) 163–76.

tion.[70] The point I wish to make is that even if there was no uptake on the part of the Corinthians, Paul's argument in chapter 15 demonstrates that he thinks the statement about Jesus' resurrection clearly carries with it the implication that the believer is also raised.

CONCLUSION

A speech act analysis of the earliest resurrection proclamation—or at least the one-member version of that proclamation—calls into question two common assumptions: one, that the proclamation was a christological confession of faith; and two, that it was a summary statement of the passion and resurrection of Jesus. First, if the formula functions as a name for God, this means it is primarily a theological statement, not a christological one. It did not define for early Christians who Jesus was or is.

Second, if I am right that the one-member formula dominates the earliest stratum of tradition, the first resurrection proclamation can hardly be said to have relied upon the story of the passion and subsequent resurrection of Jesus. R. H. Fuller has already argued that the resurrection was first proclaimed, not narrated.[71] There is no early narrative of the resurrection. The Gospels contain empty tomb narratives and appearance narratives, not resurrection narratives. Even if these Gospel traditions could be shown to be as old as the formulaic proclamations, they do not tell the story of the resurrection.[72] The only direct information about the resurrection the synoptic Gospels provide is exactly the same simple proclamation we have seen at the pre-Pauline level.[73]

---

70. Several scholars have argued that the Corinthians believed they were already in a "raised," i.e., spiritual, state. The difference then between Paul and his audience is that of a future versus a present condition. See J. M. Robinson, "Kerygma and History," in *Trajectories through Early Christianity*, ed. J. M. Robinson and H. Koester (Philadelphia: Fortress, 1971) 32–36; and D. R. MacDonald, *There Is No Male and Female: The Fate of a Dominical Saying in Paul and Gnosticism* (Philadelphia: Fortress, 1987) 67–69. Cf. Lambrecht, "Paul's Christological Use of Scripture," 515–16, 525–26.

71. *The Formation of the Resurrection Narratives* (Philadelphia: Fortress, 1980).

72. The one place where we do have a narration of the resurrection is the *Gospel of Peter*. Although J. D. Crossan has argued that the *Gospel of Peter* is early, this argument has not received a broad following. See Crossan, *The Cross That Spoke: The Origins of the Passion Narrative* (San Francisco: Harper & Row, 1988). See reviews by R. H. Fuller, *Int* 45 (1991) 71–72; J. Green, *JBL* 109 (1990) 356–58; and J. P. Meier, *Horizons* 16 (1989) 378–79. For a partial acceptance of Crossan's argument, see G. Nickelsburg, *JAAR* 59 (1991) 159–62.

73. The statement "he was raised" is put into the mouth of the angel at the tomb (Matt 28:6 and Mark 16:6), or is miraculously declared to the eleven by the disciples returned from Emmaus (Luke 24:34), or is put into the mouth of Jesus in the Son of Man prediction (Mark 8:31; 9:31; 10:33–34). *The narrator never speaks descriptively of Jesus' being raised.* The characters in the story simply proclaim Jesus' resurrection.

In addition to the lack of evidence for some sort of narrative underlying the first resurrection proclamations, their use does not presuppose a narrative. Of all the various ways the formula appears, it is never used apologetically.[74] At least for the people associated with New Testament texts, the resurrection of Jesus appears to be common knowledge. Apparently no one to whom Paul wrote denied this early Christian claim.[75] This lack of apologetic motive distances the early proclamation of the resurrection from the Gospel traditions of the empty tomb and appearance stories. Those Gospel stories emerged out of a need to defend the truth of the resurrection of Jesus. This radical contrast in motive once again indicates a lack of connection between the kerygma and the Gospel traditions about the passion and resurrection.

Scholars have misunderstood these early statements of belief in the resurrection of Jesus because they have confused them with modern statements of belief, which are very different. When Christians today say, "I believe that God raised Jesus from the dead," they are in fact saying they believe in the truth of this statement (this is a direct speech act). This is not the function of the ancient proclamation, which was not a truth claim. Modern people start from a position of skepticism. A faith claim is then a challenge to skepticism that asserts the truth of the belief. But skepticism was not the starting point for the first Christians. The lack of apologetic force in these early proclamations indicates they met with receptivity. Because the first proclamation was not a truth claim, studying it as such has put its emphasis in the wrong place. The first proclamation of the resurrection provided the Jewish God with a new name, and by this new name it inspired confidence in those who aspired to eternal life.

---

74. Conzelmann (*1 Corinthians*, 250) makes this point for 1 Corinthians 15.

75. Of course in other Christian communities, the resurrection of Jesus may have been a debatable issue. See Riley, *Resurrection Reconsidered*.

3

Why Is Christianity Anti-Body?
Or Is It?

S. C. Winter

"Why is Christianity anti-body?" The question was posed by graduate students from political science, anthropology, and sociology in a course I teach entitled "Issues in Gender and Religion." They meant by this, "Why does Christianity negate the human body?" I tried to explain that Christianity isn't anti-body, it's just that some denominations interpret it to be. I explained that rejecting sexuality does not mean rejecting the body; to the contrary, an ascetic may recognize that the body is the most important domain of the struggle to attain righteousness. But I only succeeded in convincing them, after weeks and after they read the fifteenth-century writer Julian of Norwich (the description of her vision of the physical suffering of Christ and her explanation that Christ is our mother, who gave birth to our salvation[1]) that perhaps at one time Christianity wasn't "anti-body." My students, on the other hand, succeeded in convincing me that perhaps they had a case. The most intriguing instance that came up in class was Christian Science. Mary Baker Eddy, who found extraordinary public acclaim and financial success, based her theory that matter is error and only what is eternal is real on New Testament accounts of healing.

I reformulated the students' question: "Is there something integral to Christianity at its formation, but submerged in the ancient context, that encourages post-Enlightenment negation of the body?" The Neo-

I am pleased to contribute to this volume in honor of Robin Scroggs. I value highly his deep love for the New Testament, and his appreciation of Paul as a human being. Robin has been a good friend and a most helpful critic.

1. Julian of Norwich, *Showings*, ed. and trans. Edmund Colledge and James Walsh (New York: Paulist, 1978), esp. chap. 10 (short text), and chaps. 55–63 (long text).

platonism of some early Christians does not suffice to explain it. The apostle Paul, a Jew and a stoic who wrote some of the most influential texts, was not anti-body, as even Daniel Boyarin, who reads Paul as a Neoplatonist, recognizes.[2]

A factor, I suggest, integral to Christianity but submerged in the ancient context and central to how Christianity developed is the negation of (Jewish) ritual in canonical texts. Ritual engages the body because it asks the body to carve out a domain for the sacred in space and time. In the terminology of Emile Durkheim, ritual brings the profane into sensory communication with the sacred. Some rituals bring human beings (bodies) into time and space that has been set apart, some rituals bring sacred elements physically into the profane, and some, such as prayers over food, sacralize the profane in profane space.[3] Even religions that privilege spirit over matter, when they consider ritual central, will value matter in fact even if not in theory. I suggest that regardless how much the cultural context may affirm spirit over body and thought over matter, a religion in which specified rituals are central will not fully devalue the body. From this perspective we should expect to find Catholicism more affirming of the body than Protestantism, and indeed the case can be made.

Here, because space permits me to address only certain aspects of this very large issue, I shall examine how certain canonical texts treat Jewish ritual. To be sure canonical texts by no means represent the full picture of early Christianity. Some groups whose texts were not accepted as canonical (e.g., the *Didache*) were more committed to the ritual dimension of early Christianity. Often the rituals were derived from Judaism but not always (e.g., possibly a ritual of the bridal chamber alluded to in the *Gospel of Philip*). Other groups presumably were even less committed to ritual. For this present inquiry canonical texts are significant because of the way in which they influenced the Reformation thinkers, who in turn influenced Enlightenment thought.[4]

Two significant factors are apparent in the treatment of rituals in the canon. First, two Christian rituals, Eucharist and baptism, are found only embedded in narrative and apparently were transmitted

---

2. Daniel Boyarin, *A Radical Jew: Paul and the Politics of Identity* (Berkeley: University of California Press, 1994) 7. See the review of Boyarin's book by Robin Scroggs, in *Princeton Seminary Bulletin* 13 (1996) 101–2.

3. My formulation. See Emile Durkheim, *Les Formes élémentaires de la vie religieuse: Le système totémique en Australie* (Paris: F. Alcan, 1912), especially book 3.

4. A millennium and a half after the New Testament received final form, Martin Luther classified (priestly) ritual with the carnal as "external things" that cannot "touch either the freedom or the servitude of the soul." See Luther, "The Freedom of a Christian," in *Martin Luther*, ed. John Dillenberger (New York: Bantam Doubleday Dell, 1962) 54.

thus; they became fixed only in reference to their place in Jesus' life. Paul, for example, refers to the Eucharist in its "historical setting" in 1 Corinthians 11:23–26. No text that simply spells out how to perform these rituals (as does, for example, the *Didache*) found its way into the canon. As a result the practice and importance of these two rituals continues to vary widely in the course of Christian history.

Second, canonical Christian texts reject Jewish ritual sharply, in many and various ways, sometimes without suggesting rejection of the sensory world. Their collective impact derives from differing rejections of ritual read in combination. Here I shall consider four texts whose positions are clearest—Hebrews, Acts, Galatians, and Philippians. Ironically Matthew, which treats Jewish ritual favorably, has contributed to the effect because Christians have generalized Matthew's anti-Pharisee polemic and interpreted it as an anti-Jewish (anti-works) polemic. Without the ritual, however, Christianity became something different from what a religion customarily was in the ancient world.

RELIGION AND PHILOSOPHY
IN THE ANCIENT WORLD

Although ancient Judaism differed from the religions of neighboring regions in its monotheism and its requirement that adherents not participate in rituals acknowledging other gods, in many ways it resembled other religions of the Mediterranean. Religions in the ancient world were defined by ritual practices.[5] Most of these rituals touched on public life or if carried out in "private" were publicly regulated. Most religious officials had some connection with governance either directly or indirectly through social class affiliations. If not exerting political power themselves, for example, they were selected from the politically dominant class(es). Rituals included calendrically determined ceremonies and prayers and public sacrifices of animals or vegetable products. Even private petitions would be accompanied by an offering. Worship was strongly connected with location, and deities varied by region, although gods were always being borrowed, assimilated, and forced on subject populaces.[6] There were cults, those of Isis and

---

5. Here I sketch in broad strokes salient features of religion in the ancient world. For a full picture, see, e.g., Ramsay MacMullen, *Paganism in the Roman Empire* (New Haven: Yale University Press, 1981).

6. The detachment from location in early Christianity has been explored recently in connection with the Fourth Gospel. See Tod D. Swanson, "To Prepare a Place: Johannine Christianity and the Collapse of Ethnic Territory," *JAAR* 62, no. 2 (1994) 241–63.

Mithras, for example, that flourished far from their region of origin. These exotic cults had places in the social structure different from the place of the public religions, and they offered avenues for social interaction other than the public rituals. The exotic cults were, however, like the public religions, based on ritual observances.

Ancient Judaism, like other religions of the ancient world, was defined by ritual practices associated with a specific location (the temple in Jerusalem). Most rituals pertained to public life or were publically regulated, although the various sects sometimes differed among each other regarding points of regulation. Furthermore, even under Roman rule, religious officials had a part in regional governance through the office of high priest and through the Sanhedrin.

Many of the issues now associated with theology—ethics, the existence and nature of God, how to live a worthwhile and fulfilling life—were the concerns of philosophy in the Hellenistic world.[7] Already by the second century, however, the main concerns of Christianity—ethics, exegesis of authoritative texts of the founder, and instructing others in them—made it look more like a philosophy than a religion. Indeed, apologists such as Justin and Athenagoras explicitly advocated Christianity as a philosophy.[8] But not only did Christianity have characteristics of a philosophy, it retained few if any of the characteristics of an ancient religion. It was not centered around ritual, nor centered at specific locations; it was not public; its officials were as far as can be imagined from governance. Christian practices had moved away from the Judaism in which it originated, and had moved toward those of a philosophy.[9]

---

7. Some exotic cults resembled philosophies in some aspects of their social organization as did associations of rabbis with disciples.

8. A. D. Nock, *Conversion: The Old and the New in Religion from Alexander the Great to Augustine of Hippo* (London: Oxford University Press, 1933), chap. 11. See the corrective observations of Ramsay MacMullen, *Christianizing the Roman Empire A.D. 100–400* (New Haven: Yale University Press, 1984), chap. 1. An observation quoted by Loveday Alexander clarifies how the analogy between Christianity and a philosophy might be drawn. She writes, "in them [three texts by Galen (late second century)] Galen treats both Judaism and Christianity as defective philosophies, characterized by faith as opposed to reason." "Paul and the Hellenistic Schools: The Evidence of Galen," in *Paul in His Hellenistic Context*, ed. Troels Engberg-Pedersen (Minneapolis: Fortress, 1995) 64.

9. Wilcken sees this as a response to negative perceptions of the early Christians. He writes, "One way in which the Christian movement began to achieve self-identity in the formative years of the second century was to respond to the charge that Christianity was a superstition. By presenting Christianity as a philosophical school, i.e., a way of life marked by piety (not superstition) towards the gods and moral earnestness, Christian apologists forged a self-understanding which diverged sharply from the self-understanding of the rank and file. . . . The course of development . . . led Christians to present themselves as a philosophical way of life founded by Christ." E. P. Sanders, ed., *Jewish and Christian Self-Definition*, 3 vols. (Philadelphia: Fortress, 1980–82) 1:109–10.

NULLIFYING JEWISH RITUAL:
HEBREWS

The New Testament text most thoroughly concerned with Jewish ritual is the "letter" to the Hebrews, the only canonical text to deal in depth with the priesthood and the temple. In a rhetorical *tour de force* the author contrasts the priesthood of the temple in Jerusalem with the priesthood of Christ. Extraordinarily elegant language disguises a devastating critique of Jewish sacrificial ritual, as subtle as it is devastating because the foundation of the argument is an affirmation of Jewish history and tradition.

The author contrasts Moses as founder with Christ as founder (3:1–6), the Levitical priesthood with the Melchizedek priesthood of Christ (4:14–5:10; 6:13–7:28), sacrifices of goats, calves, and bulls with the sacrifice of Christ (9:12–14; 10:1–14), the earthly sanctuary entered by the high priest with the heavenly sanctuary entered by Christ (9:1–10; 9:24), and the former covenant with the new covenant (9:15–22). Christ as founder supersedes Moses, and the new order of high priest according to Melchizedek brings with it the nullification (ἀθέτησις; 7:12, 18) of the old. The two covenants, the two priesthoods, etc., do not differ in degree or simply follow a sequence; they differ essentially, qualitatively. Moses is *builder* of the household of God (Heb 3:2–6 citing Num 12:7), but Jesus is the *son* over the household (3:6). Christ entered not a sanctuary built by human hands (9:24) but *heaven itself*. Christ is a high priest of the order of Melchizedek, who ministers in the *true tent* (ἡ σκηνὴ ἡ ἀληθινή; 8:2), the mediator of a *better* covenant (κρείττονός ἐστιν διαθήκης μεσίτης; 8:6). Christ's sacrifice is able to perfect the worshipper (10:1; 10:14). So the worshipper, through faith, can enter heaven itself (10:19–20).

The qualitative distinction between the elements of the pairs reflects the author's platonism.[10] The earthly sanctuary is a shadow of the heavenly sanctuary (8:5). Similarly, the law provides a shadow, not the true form (10:1).[11] For Plato the distinction between shadow and

---

10. William Lane is a recent and significant representative of those arguing that the theology of Hebrews does not derive from platonism or platonism via Philo (but see n. 12 below). William L. Lane, *Hebrews*, Word Biblical Commentary, 47A, B (Dallas: Word, 1991). Lane notes that the writing of Hebrews indicates a thinker with an educational level equal to Philo's (ibid., xlix–l), and concedes that 8:1–2 is influenced by Greek philosophy (ibid., 1.205).

11. I.e., "that the phenomenal is but an imperfect, shadowy transcript of what is eternal and real. He [the author of Hebrews] applies this principle to the past. . . . The idea that the seen and material is but a poor, provisional replica of the unseen and real order of things . . . pervades [Hebrews]." James Moffatt, *Epistle to the Hebrews*, ICC (Edinburgh: T. & T. Clark, 1979) xxxi. Attridge writes, "Not only the phrase but also the contrast between image and shadow recall Plato's well-known allegory of the cave, where what human beings perceive in the phenomenal world is likened to shadows cast by imitations of truly real entities, that is, ideas or forms. . . . The emphatic αὐτήν with εἰκόνα suggests that the 'image' is not sharply distinguished from the

reality is ontological. Sensory phenomena are inferior (with respect to their being) to the forms because sensory phenomena are changeable (mutable), whereas forms are immutable. Plato distinguishes the copies, which are plural, from forms, which are unique. The author of Hebrews picks up on the theme of multiplicity and asserts that whereas the former priests were many (7:23), Christ the priest is unique (7:24). Hebrews extends this to a distinction in time: whereas the sacrifices in the temple must be repeated each year, the model sacrifice of Christ was required only once (9:25).[12] Hebrews also offers an analog for Plato's concept of attaining knowledge. For Plato the soul may attain knowledge through contemplation; for the author of Hebrews, the worshipper attains the heavenly sanctuary through faith.[13] The worshipper may follow the path through the curtain made by Christ (10:20; 12:2),[14] and attain the sabbath rest made possible by Jesus going ahead (6:19-20).

Philo, like the author of Hebrews, calls on platonism to explain religious concepts. The difference between Hebrews and Philo, however, points up the significance of Hebrews in the development of Christian theology. Attridge writes regarding "a shadowy copy of the heavenly things" (8:5):

> The use of 'shadow' (σκιά) as an image for components of the phenomenal world is Platonic. This imagery recurs in Philo, where it indicates both the inferiority of the sensible to the ideal and also the positive function of the 'shadow' in leading one to the 'reality'.[15]

In Hebrews, however, the shadow has no positive function, except to point up the superiority of the priesthood and sacrifice of Christ. The

---

reality and that the εἰκων is in fact used for the reality itself. While εἰκων does not usually have this sense, and certainly does not have it in Plato, it does come to be used among middle Platonists as a designation, virtually synonymous with ἰδεα, for the forms or ideas." Harold W. Attridge, *Hebrews* (Philadelphia: Fortress, 1989) 270.

12. Lane (with Williamson) correctly observes that the author of Hebrews is doing something quite different from Philo and from Plato by making the ontological distinction temporal. For this reason Lane argues that the primary influence on Hebrews is eschatological not platonic. The terminology is, however, platonic and I think that the author, who appears to have been not only highly educated but also quite brilliant, applied platonism to history. Lane writes concerning 8:5, "For the writer of Hebrews, the temporal contrast was decisive. . . . The categories of time and history are inextricably bound up with the thought of v 5 in a way that is inconsistent with Platonism. . . . The distinction between 'earthly' and 'heavenly' in 8:1-5 is eschatological" (*Hebrews*, 207-8).

13. I.e., faith in contrast to reason; see above, note 8.

14. The verse is difficult to understand (Attridge, *Hebrews*, 285-87). For Plato the soul may recover its state of heavenly bliss but only when (among other things) it is released from the body. For Hebrews, however, Christ's sacrifice obviates the necessity of death to attain the heavenly state.

15. Attridge's translation (*Hebrews*, 219).

critique of Jewish sacrificial ritual is devastating for just that reason. The traditions of Moses, the high priesthood, and the sanctuary in Jerusalem are the foundation for understanding the work of Christ, but the work of Christ nullifies them completely.

EARLY CHRISTIANITY
DEPICTED AS PHILOSOPHY

The author of Hebrews argues directly that faith in Christ makes Jewish sacrificial ritual obsolete. Acts sets out a similar position through narrative.[16] Stephen's speech is a locus of anti-temple material, perhaps traditional, which appears to have links with Samaritan beliefs.[17] The stoning of Stephen precipitates dispersal of the Jerusalem church (Act 8:1), introduces the major figures who will carry the church traditions to Rome (7:58), and leads to the formation of the church at Antioch where for the first time the disciples have the name *Christianoi* (Acts 11:19-21, 26).[18]

The progression of the church toward Rome begins, however, not in 8:1 but earlier when Luke has the believers move away from the temple. The literary structure of Acts 2-4 highlights the account of the arrest of Peter and James by temple authorities as the incident that motivates the believers to abandon the temple. In Acts 2-4 there are two accounts of the giving of the spirit (Acts 2:1-13 and 4:31), and each of them is followed by a summary describing the life of the believers (2:42-47 and 4:32-35). These summaries depict the believers as an ideal philosophical community sharing all things in common.[19] Set in the middle of the two accounts of the giving of the spirit and the two summaries is the account of the arrest of Peter and John by temple authorities (4:1-12) and their release.[20] The second (mini) Pentecost

---

16. William Manson argues that the theology of Hebrews derives from the anti-temple "teachings" of Stephen. See William Manson, *The Epistle to the Hebrews: An Historical and Theological Reconsideration*, 2d ed. (London: Hodder & Stoughton, 1953).

17. Robert Maddox, *The Purpose of Luke-Acts* (Edinburgh: T. & T. Clark, 1982) 52-54.

18. Rau argues that this sequence suggests that the anti-temple position was foundational for the church at Antioch. See Eckhard Rau, *Von Jesus zu Paulus. Entwicklung und Rezeption der antiochenischen Theologie im Urchristentum* (Stuttgart: Kohlhammer, 1994) passim.

19. Gregory E. Sterling, "'Athletes of Virtue': An Analysis of the Summaries in Acts (2:41-47; 4:32-35; 5:12-16)," *JBL* 113 (1994) 679-96. Abraham Malherbe writes, "so he [Luke], too, sketches a picture of the Jerusalem church in which it realizes the philosophical ideal of a communal sharing of resources, and does so in language that would have made his intention clear to a cultivated reader (Acts 2:44-45; 4:32)." Malherbe, "'Not in a Corner': Early Christian Apologetic in Acts 26:26," in *Paul and the Popular Philosophers* (Minneapolis: Fortress, 1989) 150. See also Alan C. Mitchell, "The Social Function of Friendship in Acts 2:44-47 and 4:32-37, *JBL* 111 (1992) 255-72.

20. Not surprisingly the temple authorities are depicted negatively. In 4:11 Peter paraphrases Ps 118:22 saying, Christ is the stone that *you* rejected.

(4:31) occurs after the release of Peter and John.[21] The believers express fear of the temple authorities (4:29). The second summary (4:32-35) resembles the first (2:42-47) except that the believers no longer pray at the temple as they did before the arrest of Peter and John (2:46). The believers have already abandoned the temple and constituted themselves primarily as a philosophical community.

That Luke's earliest Christians opposed the temple need not imply, of course, that they opposed ritual as the formative element for community. The sectarians of the Dead Sea community opposed service in the temple but only as it was being carried out in their time, because they disapproved of the priests and the calendar. But they constructed their own community around ritual.

In addition to depicting the believers moving away from the temple and villainizing temple authorities, Acts has the early Christians abandon Jewish ritual in three ways: (1) Acts 15 shows the early Christians abandoning Jewish ritual observance unproblematically, even with the approval of James. Acts 15:1 refers to conflict but does not name the troublemakers (although they may well have been "men from James"). This stage of the departure from ritual is, like everything, set narratively into the progression toward Rome. (2) Scripture in Acts is a witness (*the* witness) to Jesus and nothing else; the reader has barely a hint that Scripture might be the foundation of a ritual practice. (3) The narrative, as noted above, paints early Christians as an ideal philosophical community. The philosophical character of the community intensifies as the narrative proceeds, culminating in the last major figure, Paul, who is shown increasingly becoming more of a philosopher.[22] The cumulative effect is to show the formation of the church as a group of philosophers who move progressively further from the religion of Judaism, taking with them what Acts considers its central feature, the texts that witness to the "founder of the philosophy" and leaving behind everything Luke considers useless, including religious ritual. Acts resembles Hebrews in that it shows Christianity founded on, yet superseding, ancient Judaism, but it shows this supersession as an historical as well as conceptual progression.

---

21. At this time the gift of frank speech, which is a defining feature in the *ekklesia* and its progression to Rome, extends to the entire group of believers (4:31), not just Peter as previously (2:29). So S. C. Winter, "*Parrhesia* in Acts," in *Friendship, Flattery and Frankness of Speech*, ed. John T. Fitzgerald, 187-92 (Leiden: Brill, 1996).

22. Malherbe, "'Not in a Corner,'" 147-63; see also Winter, "*Parrhesia* in Acts," 196-99.

PAUL: PHILOSOPHICAL COMMUNITY
REPLACES RITUAL COMMUNITY

Luke's Paul is clearly a philosopher with scarcely an attachment to ritual law. His "Judaism" is that of a philosopher in that it consists mostly of public debate. The Paul of the Epistles, however, agonized over ritual law (e.g., in Rom 7:14–25), the significance of which he felt keenly (Phil 3:4–5). Although for Paul the validity of ritual law had passed with the old aeon, he expresses a painful awareness that he had separated himself from his community of origin, a community which defined itself by observance of ritual law (Rom 9:1–5).

Galatians, which contains Paul's bitterest attack on those who would require law observance of Gentile Christians, concludes with admonitions about building up the community that include a list of vices (5:19–21) and virtues (5:22–26). These lists, Abraham Malherbe observes, "were effectively used in protreptic, the vices frequently listed first to depict the diseased soul . . . in moral slavery . . . from which philosophy would rescue it."[23] Protreptic speeches of the philosophers "called people to turn to the philosophical life and, having taken that initial step by their own free will . . . to continue living the rational disciplined life."[24] That Paul concludes his attack with philosophical material raises two questions with regard to Paul and ritual law. First, could Paul have found in Greco-Roman moral philosophy a basis for constructing community to replace ritual law? And second, does Paul's concept of community tell us anything about why he rejected ritual law?

The answer to the first question is apparently "yes." A concept of the ideal community may have played a part in Paul's rejection of ritual law, and here it is significant which philosophical traditions Paul drew on for his concept of community. Various philosophical traditions had an impact on early Christianity.[25] For insight into philosophical backgrounds for Paul's concept of community we look into what, if anything, the various schools had to say concerning moral development (and the role of the philosopher and philosophical community in promoting it) and concerning the structure of the philosophical community.[26] Troels Engberg-Pedersen has studied Philippians and the

---

23. Abraham J. Malherbe, *Moral Exhortation, A Greco-Roman Sourcebook* (Philadelphia: Westminster, 1986) 138.

24. Ibid., 55.

25. Abraham J. Malherbe, "Hellenistic Moralists and the New Testament," *ANRW* 2.26/1 (267–333). Note also Boyarin's reading of Paul as a Neoplatonist in *A Radical Jew*.

26. Interesting in this connection is Robin Scroggs's "Paul and the Eschatological Body," in *Theology and Ethics in Paul and His Interpreters*, ed. E. Lovering, Jr. and J. Sumney, 14–29 (Nashville: Abingdon Press, 1996). See also Abraham J. Malherbe, "Paul: Hellenistic

possible role of Stoic concepts pertaining to community formation, among them the concept of the Stoic ideal community.[27] Engberg-Pedersen finds the concept of the ideal community from Chrysippus "most directly relevant to Paul"[28] and writes of it, "In Chrysippus . . . the ideal community . . . appears as a community of all those people who are morally good wherever they live on earth. They all belong to that very same community (so there is only one such community) just by being morally good."[29]

This Stoic *politeuma* in which the Stoic claims citizenship has characteristics inhospitable to ritual; it has no designated place (it is everywhere the morally good individuals are), and it prescribes no ritual actions that might occasionally affirm the community in time and space.[30]

On the other hand, The Stoic community ideal was nonhierarchical.[31] In principle a mixed community of Jews and Gentiles could have taken shape in three ways: the community may have had a two-tiered system of membership (Jews forming the inner circle with gentile adherents the outer circle); or the community may have required the Gentiles to convert to Judaism; or the community may have determined that ritual law would be suspended. Hyam Maccoby argues that evidence from Acts shows that the two-tiered community was practiced among some.[32] The Stoic *politeuma* however, was grounded in equality

---

Philosopher or Christian Pastor?" in *Paul and the Popular Philosophers*, 67–77. Paul's approach to community formation becomes especially clear in Philippians. See John T. Fitzgerald, "Philippians in the Light of Some Ancient Discussions of Friendship," in *Friendship, Flattery, and Frankness of Speech*, 141–60.

27. Troels Engberg-Pedersen, "Stoicism in Philippians," in *Paul in His Hellenistic Context*, ed. T. Engberg-Pedersen, 256–90 (Minneapolis: Fortress, 1995).

28. Ibid., 269.

29. Ibid., 267.

30. Stoicism, however, was not opposed to the sensory world. Quite to the contrary, the philosopher was to engage the world of human society on all levels.

31. ". . . Zeno appears to have envisaged an ideal community where all social institutions, all socially based distinctions between people, possibly also all distinctions based on gender and finally all political distinctions have been abolished. There were to be no hierarchies whatever, no subordination, since the only thing that counted was moral goodness or the lack of it" (Engberg-Pedersen, "Stoicism in Philippians," 266). "[T]his probably means that Chrysippus too maintained the radically antihierarchical content of Zeno's original conception . . . the Cynic links served the purpose of doing away with conventional social and political distinctions and so making room for the idea of what remains, an anarchic, radically nonhierarchical community that ran directly counter to all ordinary societies" (ibid., 268).

32. Concerning the report in Acts of the decision of the Jerusalem council, Maccoby writes, "James's remark thus implies his own unquestioning adherence to Judaism, and his confidence that Judaism would continue. There is therefore a tension in our passage between two opposing interpretations of the debate in Jerusalem. One interpretation (evidently that of the author of Acts) is that this debate marked the breakdown of all distinctions between Jews and Gentiles in the Christian movement. The other interpretation (which can be discerned as the substratum of the discussion, and is thus the authentic and original meaning of the incident) is that it was decided that the Jesus movement should consist of two categories of people: Jews, practising the whole Torah; and Gentiles, practising the Noahide laws only. . . . It was quite in accordance with Judaism to make a distinction between the two kinds of believers in monotheism, Torah-

in the here and now.[33] Paul, the Stoic, would have found a two-tiered community to be contrary to his principles.[34] And that may have contributed to the bitterness of his argument in Galatians.[35]

CONCLUSION

In this paper I have considered Jewish ritual in connection with Hebrews, Acts, and two Pauline epistles. I have observed that the author of Hebrews constructed a Neoplatonic rationale for abandoning Jewish ritual, that Acts depicts early Christianity as a philosophical endeavor from the outset, and that Paul argued to replace Jewish ritual with moral philosophy as the foundation for community in Christ. This paper only begins my exploration of this topic. What I have sketched in the preceding remains to be filled out in a number of directions. A more detailed historical inquiry is in order; in history I include both the formation of Christianity in antiquity and the appropriation of that formation over time and across cultures.

In conclusion, returning to whether Christianity is anti-body, I have argued that central canonical texts severed the connection between faith and embodied expressions of faith in ritual. Canonical texts prescribe ethical action as the "fruit" of faith and endorse rituals based on Jesus' life (baptism and Eucharist) with little specification on how they are to be carried out. Christianity has depended on material from its cultural contexts and theological reflection to make explicit how faith is to bear fruit. (In the Middle Ages, for example, it was assumed that spiritual truth expresses itself in the sensory world.) Furthermore, early Western Christianity developed a corpus of texts alongside Scripture, maintained by Catholicism, one concern of which is embodied faith—embodied, that is, in ritual and in ethical action. For Protestants, however, who rely on *sola scriptura* in a post-Enlightenment world that posits mind distinct from body, the need to connect faith with action and make action accountable to faith poses a challenge to theo-

---

practisers and Noahides." Maccoby, *The Mythmaker* (New York: Harper and Row, 1986) 144.

33. Engberg-Pedersen, "Stoicism in Philippians," 264–69.

34. Of the various models for the Christian *ekklesia* proposed by Meeks—household, voluntary associations, synagogue, and philosophical school—all except the last could introduce social inequalities between participants. In Wayne A. Meeks, *The First Urban Christians* (New Haven: Yale University Press, 1983) 75–84. I have argued elsewhere that Paul opposed social inequalities not in principle, but when they affected the *ekklesia*. In Philemon Paul wanted to correct inequalities introduced from the household. S. C. Winter, "Philemon," in *Searching the Scriptures: A Feminist Ecumenical Commentary and Translation*, ed. Elisabeth Schüssler Fiorenza, 306–8 (New York: Crossroads, 1995).

35. Less admirable motives have been suggested, e.g., by Maccoby, *The Mythmaker*, chap. 13.

logy and ethics. Yet these are not impossible challenges. Regarding the title question, therefore, "Why is Christianity anti-body?" I recommend a reply: "There are historical reasons why certain forms of Christianity at certain times may be anti-body, but even these need not necessarily remain so."[36]

---

36. I am indebted to the students who refused to let go of this problem (especially Beth Rollins, Jennifer Hammer, Daniel Jasper, Greg Snyder, Bonnie Thurston, Nancy Wadsworth, and Suzanne Kelley) and to the editors of this volume.

4

The Communal Icon

Complex Cultural Schemas, Elements of the Social Imagination (Matthew 10:32//Luke 12:8 and Revelation 3:5, A Case Study)

Cameron Afzal

How do human beings inherit complexes of ideas from previous generations or exchange them among different groups over time? The question is more acute when applied to the emergence of a new worldview, or to a new constellation of symbols entering the stage of cultural history. How did the complex and pluriform world of first-century Judaism give birth to what would become a distinct religion, Christianity? This question informs much of modern New Testament study and lies at the foundation of this paper.

This study presents a new conceptual tool, *the communal icon,* for tracing the transmission, transformation, and preservation of tradition among early Christians. By communal icon, I mean to describe a cognitive-social *appropriation of an image by a community,* that is, an element of the collective imagination. I use the term to refer to patterns of the imagination that participants in communal conversation can assume they have in common, and that can be taught, edited, satirized, and referred to as a quick means of communicating a complex of ideas. These configurations of symbols can in turn be manipulated by individuals and groups in order to change how a community perceives

This study began as graduate work under Robin Scroggs at Union Theological Seminary. It is fitting that it should see the light of day in a volume of essays expressing appreciation for his scholarship and for his work as a teacher.

aspects of reality embodied in the constituent symbols. Communal icons are patterns of canonized thought that are shared among groups of people.

My proposal of this new conceptual tool arises in response to a vexing problem regarding the tradition history of the Apocalypse of John. I draw on some established ideas that have emerged from the fields of sociology of knowledge and anthropology, as well as on some recent proposals made in the field of cognitive anthropology.[1] Moreover, I will have recourse to some aspects of Paul Ricoeur's theory of the social dynamics of narrative.[2]

THE TRADITION HISTORY OF THE APOCALYPSE

My case study involves a striking resemblance between a reference in Revelation 3:5 and a Jesus saying preserved in Matthew 10:32//Luke 12:8:

> He who conquers shall be thus clad in white garments, and I will not blot his name out of the book of life; I will confess his name before my Father and before his angels. (Rev 3:5 NRSV)

> So everyone who confesses me in public, I also will confess before my Father who is in Heaven. (Matt 10:32, au. trans.)

> And I say to you, every one who confesses me in public, the Son of Man will confess before the angels of God. (Luke 12:8, au. trans.)

How do we account for the similarities between this Jesus saying in the Apocalypse and the Jesus saying preserved in the Q tradition? And, what then would be the implications for establishing the tradition history of the Apocalypse?

The tradition history of the Apocalypse has long been an intriguing yet elusive question in the history of New Testament scholarship. The Apocalypse is dissimilar in many ways to the Fourth Gospel,

---

1. I.e., the work of Clifford Geertz with regard to his work on defining human culture as "socially established structure of meaning," as well as Peter Berger and Thomas Luckmann's position that we function in a "symbolic universe"; that is, a culture's perception of the real world is the result of a socially constructed interaction. Geertz, *The Interpretation of Cultures* (New York: Basic Books, 1973) 207; Berger and Luckmann, *The Social Construction of Reality: A Treatise in the Sociology of Knowledge* (Garden City, NY: Doubleday, 1967). I will also have some recourse to recent proposals made in the field of cognitive anthropology known as "schema theory" (see p. 66 below).

2. Ricoeur's highly complex understanding of both the social function of narrative and the dynamics of how communication can take place between an author and a recipient of a text may be found in *Time and Narrative*, 3 vols., trans. K. McLaughlin and D. Pellauer (Chicago: University of Chicago Press, 1984–88).

both in its eschatology and in its use of Jewish apocalyptic imagery. So too with regard to the deutero-Pauline literature and the Letters of Ignatius, all of which are associated with communities inhabiting the areas associated with the Apocalypse.[3] Yet, despite the difficulties involved in interpreting the text, a portrait of the prophet himself is beginning to emerge in the academic community. John is currently being sketched in the scholarly literature as a Christian prophet at work in Asia Minor with roots in Palestinian Jewish Christianity.[4] These primitive roots are held to account for the dissimilarity with other forms of Christianity in Asia Minor.[5] An important factor shaping this conception of the prophet is the association of aspects of his work with the circles responsible for traditions preserved in the synoptic Gospels.[6]

The association of the Apocalypse with the synoptic tradition relies in no small measure on perceived similarities between passages found in it and the synoptic Gospels. Let us ask, then, what traditions has the prophet of Patmos inherited? On what kinds of sources does he depend?[7]

---

3. This observation was apparently first made by W. Bauer in 1934. Bauer, *Orthodoxy and Heresy in Earliest Christianity*, trans. Philadelphia Seminar on Christian Origins, ed. R. A. Kraft and G. Krodel (Philadelphia: Fortress, 1971) 84. For a review and critique of scholars who have held this position, see E. Schüssler Fiorenza, "Apocalypsis and Prophetia: Revelation in the Context of Early Christian Prophecy," in *L'Apocalypse johannique et l'Apocalyptique dans le Nouveau Testament*, ed. J. Lambrecht, BETL 53 (Leuven: Leuven University Press, 1980) 114–21, reprinted in *The Book of Revelation: Justice and Judgment* (Philadelphia: Fortress Press, 1985) 133–56.

4. See A. Yarbro Collins, *Crisis and Catharsis: The Power of the Apocalypse* (Philadelphia: Westminster, 1984) 25–53, for a review of the most influential theories as well as her own position; also Akira Satake, *Die Gemeindeordnung in der Johannesapokalypse*, WMANT 21 (Neukirchen-Vluyn: Neukirchen Verlag, 1966); Schüssler Fiorenza, "Apocalypsis," 105–28; F. D. Mazzaferri, *The Genre of the Book of Revelation from a Source Critical Perspective*, BZNW 54 (Berlin: De Gruyter, 1989) 197–218, 318–74.

5. Since the Apocalypse itself serves as one of our most significant pieces of literary evidence of Christianity from Asia Minor at the end of the first century, I think the burden of proof rests upon those who would assert that the Christianity represented therein was not a common feature of the Christian landscape.

6. There are numerous passages in the Apocalypse which contain phrases, Jesus sayings, and images which are similar to passages in the synoptic Gospels. These similarities have been noted in the classic commentaries of H. B. Swete, *The Apocalypse of John*, 3d ed. (London: Macmillan, 1909) clvi–iii; R. H. Charles, *A Critical and Exegetical Commentary on the Revelation of St. John*, 2 vols, ICC (Edinburgh: T. & T. Clark, 1920) 1:lxxiv–vi; and E. B. Allo, *L'Apocalypse de St. Jean*, 3d ed. (Paris: Gabalda, 1933) passim; as well as in the more recent studies by E. Lohmeyer, *Die Offenbarung des Johannis*, 2d ed., HNT 16 (Tübingen: Mohr, 1953) passim; M.-E. Boismard, "Rapprochment littéraires entre l'évangile de Luc et l'Apocalypse," in *Synoptiche Studien: Alfred Wikenhauser zum siebzigsten Geburtstag*, ed. J. Schmid and A. Vögtle (Munich: Karl Zinc, 1953) 53–63; L. A. Vos, *The Synoptic Traditions in the Apocalypse*, Virje Universiteit te Amsterdam (Kampen: Kok, 1965); H. Kraft, *Die Offenbarung des Johannis*, HNT 16a (Tübingen: Mohr, 1974) passim; P. Prigent, *L'Apocalypse de Saint Jean*, CNT 14 (Paris: Delachaux & Niestlé, 1981) 368–69; and E. Schüssler Fiorenza, "Quest for the Johannine School," 419–24 (reprinted in *The Book of Revelation: Justice and Judgment*, 85–113).

7. Classic assertions of a relationship involved theories of literary dependence. For example, some commentators, beginning perhaps with Charles (Charles, 1:lxv), suggest that John had

The published dissertation of L. A. Vos, *The Synoptic Traditions in the Apocalypse*, is the only study to date that has attempted a comprehensive examination of relations between the Apocalypse and the synoptic Gospels.[8] As such, Vos's work has become influential in establishing a perception of ties between Revelation and traditions preserved in synoptic Gospels.[9] Vos enters the scholarly discussion at the end of an era when grand theories involving the tradition history of the synoptic Gospels were being founded on the source criticism of the previous generation. The nature of the project dates Vos's work. Vos ascribes most of the instances where there is similarity in the reading of the Apocalypse and a synoptic passage to a common underlying tradition. He concludes that the source of the Jesus sayings of Revelation lies in an oral tradition independent of the synoptic tradition and is referred to in the Apocalypse as "the testimony of Jesus" (Rev 1:9).[10] This independent tradition has been "kept" or "held" in a manner similar to "Jewish tradition," and so preserved by leaders in the communities of Asia Minor.[11]

The major shortcoming in Vos's proposal lies in his use of source-critical methods which, though applicable to the synoptic Gospels, have not been proven useful to the study of the Apocalypse. When, for example, in classic form-critical studies the interpreter observes slightly different wording to a Jesus saying as preserved in Matthew and Luke, for the most part it is appropriate to attribute this to a common source, because (1) we can be fairly sure these evangelists used sources (at least Mark), and (2) where we have the source we can

---

one or another of the synoptic Gospels before him as he wrote. Charles sees in Revelation a literary dependence on the Gospels. Others, beginning perhaps with Swete (Swete, clviii), see rather a dependence of both the synoptic Gospels and Revelation on a common tradition, specifically with regard to the sayings of Jesus.

8. I'm overlooking here the cursory reviews or work on specific passages found in others' works, e.g. Satake, 171–88; Schüssler Fiorenza, *Priester für Gott: Studium zum Herrschafts und Priestermotiv in der Apokalypse*, NTAbh 7 (Münster: Aschendorff, 1972) 185–98; R. Bauckham, "Synoptic Parousia Parables and the Apocalypse," *NTS* 23 (1977) 162–76, and idem, "Synoptic Parousia Parables Again," *NTS* 29 (1983) 129–34. Both articles by Bauckham are reprinted in *The Climax of Prophecy Studies in the Book of Revelation* (Edinburgh: T. & T. Clark, 1993) 92–117.

9. See for example Schüssler Fiorenza, "Quest for the Johannine School," 420–24, especially n. 1 on p. 421 and n. 2 on 423; idem, "Apocalypsis," 123, n. 45; R. Bauckham, "Parousia Parables," 163 n. 4; D. Aune, *Prophecy in Early Christianity and the Ancient Mediterranean World* (Grand Rapids: Eerdmans, 1983) 243, especially n. 80.

10. He therefore reads this highly debated and problematic phrase with a subjective genitive (222). On the meaning of this phrase see most recently B. Dehandschutter, "The Meaning of Witness in the Apocalypse," in *L'Apocalypse johannique et l'Apocalyptique dans le Nouveau Testament*, ed. J. Lambrecht, BETL 53 (Leuven: Leuven University Press, 1980) 283–88.

11. Vos (222), basing his view on those of Gerhardsson, means that Jesus' sayings were kept as oral tradition with the same rigor as is generally associated with the rabbinic schools. See Gerhardsson, *Memory and Manuscript: Oral Tradition and Written Transmission in Rabbinic Judaism and Early Christianity* (Uppsala: Alquist & Wiksells, 1961) 197, 199–202.

observe numerous situations where one or the other writer has altered the source for particular reasons. That is, through the repetition of such examples patterns emerge in the use of sources, and further inferences can be drawn based on these patterns.

The most damaging argument against using this kind of source-critical approach in the study of the Apocalypse may be seen in how John uses his one known source: the Hebrew Bible. Few early Christian documents are so steeped in the ideas and images of the Hebrew Scriptures or are so riddled with allusions to its characters and stories.[12] Interpreters of the Book of Revelation have perceived literally hundreds of references to the HB,[13] yet we do not find in it one single direct quotation.[14] John, according to Schüssler Fiorenza, felt a prerogative in his role as prophet to use "its words, images, phrases and patterns as a language arsenal in order to make his own theological statement."[15] Arriving at a conclusion similar to Vos's on Revelation's use of the HB,[16] she calls John's use of Scripture "anthological."[17]

---

12. On John's use of the OT see: Swete, cxxxi–cliv; A. Schlatter, *Das Alte Testament in der johanneischen Apokalypse* (Gütersloh: Bertelsmann, 1912); Charles, *Revelation* 1:lxv–lxxxii; J. Cambier, "Les images de l'Ancien Testament dans l'Apocalyspe de Saint Jean," *NRT* 77 (1955) 113-22; A. Vanhoye, "L'Utilisation du livre d'Ézékiel dans l'Apocalypse," *Biblica* 43 (1962) 436-76; E. Lohse, "Die Alttestamentliche Sprache des Seheres Johannes," *ZNW* 52 (1961) 122-26; Vos, 1-20; G. K. Beale, *The Use of Daniel in Jewish Apocalyptic Literature and in the Revelation of St. John* (Lanham, MD: University Press of America, 1984); F. D. Mazzaferri, 36-46, 85-156, 185-96; J. Paulien, *Decoding Revelation's Trumpets: Literary Allusions and Interpretation of Revelation 8:7-12*, Andrews University Seminary Doctoral Dissertation Series 11 (Berrien Springs, MI: Andrews University Press, 1988); J-P. Ruiz, *Ezekiel in the Apocalypse: The Transformation of Prophetic Language in Revelation 16, 17-19, 10*, European University Studies, Theology Series 23 (Frankfurt: Lang, 1989).

13. Swete (cxl) counts 278 references; Charles (*Revelation*, 1:lxvi–lxxxii) lists 229; see also Vanhoye, who notes the reference lists of various scholars; A. Vanhoye, 439. Vanhoye cites A. Gelin (*L'Apocalypse in Bible Pirot* [Paris: 1938] 589–90) as being the one who finds the most HB references: "En 404 versets, on trouve 518 citations."

14. Swete, liii; Charles, *Revelation*, 1:lxvi; Lohmeyer, 191; Vanhoye, 439; Vos, 18. This is the current consensus, but it has been challenged by Mazzaferri (39–42), whose position has not met with general acceptance. Vanhoye (437) notes that there is in fact only one explicit mention of a HB passage—a reference to the Song of Moses in Rev 15:3. Yet, what follows is not a quotation from the Song, as might be expected, but "un amalgame de thèmes scripturaires" representing it.

15. Schüssler Fiorenza, "Apocalypsis," 108; see also Ruiz, *Ezekiel in the Apocalypse*, 531–36.

16. Vos, 51–53.

17. Schüssler Fiorenza, "Apocalypsis," 108. Schüssler Fiorenza maintains that John's use of the HB involves a presentation of traditional elements informed by a creative reworking of the HB, a process guided by John's reading of, say, Daniel or Ezekiel; yet as prophecy it is an original work nonetheless. See the studies of Beale and Ruiz for examples of the use of Daniel in reading the Apocalypse. Though Beale's argument (*Ezekiel in the Apocalypse*) for the influence of Daniel has found favor, many of his conclusions regarding this influence have not been accepted. See for example the review of Beale's dissertation by A. Y. Collins in *JBL* and also by Ruiz, 97–122. Both scholars fault the impression left by Beale that the interpretation of Daniel was the object of the prophet's activity, rather than the means to his own ends. Moreover, W. Meeks argues this reworking of older traditions is characteristic of apocalyptic writing. See Meeks, "Social Functions of Apocalyptic Language in Pauline Christianity," *Apocalypticism in the Medi-*

The way John uses the Hebrew Bible highlights a significant problem in trying to determine any pattern in his use of sources. May we not expect his use of Christian tradition to follow this example?[18] If so, we can conclude that John would use Christian sources or traditions with the same prophetic freedom he exhibits in his use of Scripture; that is, he can combine, change, or reconfigure elements in any tradition he has inherited in accordance to his apprehension of the spirit guiding his work. John shows a freedom, then, in his use of his sources that far exceeds the liberties taken by the redactors of the synoptics. That is, he does not use sources as do the synoptic Evangelists.[19] Should we therefore even use the term "sources" when referring to John's dependence on inherited tradition?

Nevertheless, in the texts cited above, the uniquely common way the verb ὁμολογέω is used (with Jesus as the subject of the verb) militates against the possibility that Revelation is completely independent of the synoptic tradition. Surely it is not coincidental that only in these texts do we find Jesus confessing his followers before God.[20] Moreover, John's use of fleeting images depends on the prior knowledge of these images by his audience, and these underlying images require explanation on the part of the interpreter. Since there is as yet no consensus on a tradition history for the Apocalypse, there is no context for setting such similarities in perspective.[21] Terms such as

---

terranean World and the Near East, ed. D. Hellholm (Tübingen: Mohr, 1983) 688. For a much broader and poetic, though very informative approach to John's reworking of HB traditions, see A. Farrer, *A Rebirth of Images: The Making of St. John's Apocalypse* (London: A. & C. Black, 1949).

18. This is Vos's (51–53) own conclusion to his study of John's use of the HB.

19. One recalls the wise words of M. Eugene Boring: "Any sort of source analysis is out of the question [with regard to the Apocalypse], but that John made use of previous apocalyptic tradition is clear." Boring, "The Apocalypse as Christian Prophecy: A Discussion of the Issues Raised by the Book of Revelation for the Study of Christian Prophecy," SBLASP (1974) 51.

20. The verb ὁμολογέω has acquired a technical sense in the NT; it has to do with public acclamation, especially of Jesus and/or his relationship to the father. More significant for our purposes is the use of this verb in connection with a preposition translated "before," and specifically that Jesus confesses before God. Not only is ὁμολογέω common to all three texts under consideration, but it is used in a uniquely common way. With the exception of Acts 7:17, every other use of the verb in the NT involves believers confessing before human beings (The verse in Acts concerns God's confessing his promise to Abraham). Only in these three texts is it said that Jesus confesses his follower before God. Can it really be only coincidence that this verb is used only this way in these three texts?

21. Prigent's comments on this issue typifies the current state of affairs:

En ce qui concerne les relations de l'Apocalypse avec les autre écrits du NT (exeptée la littérature johanninque qu'il faudra étudier à part), on ne parvient pas non plus à des conclusions extrêmement précises: Des ressemblances indiquent des relations littéraires, mais jamais on ne peut aller jusqu'à conclure à la dépendance de l'Apocalypse par rapport à un évangile ou l'inverse. Ou bien il s'agit de dépendance médiate, ou bien on peut supposer que l'Apocalypse et le passage parallèle remontent tous deux à une tradition commune: cf. 1,3.7; 3,21; 19,9; 21,7 sans parler du chapitre 6 qui semble utiliser une tradition apocalyptique juive assez proche de celle qui est mise en œuvre dans l'apocalypse synoptique (368–69).

"allusion" or "reminiscence" are meaningless beyond the trite observation of a similarity between the texts in question.[22] Yet the pervasive use of these and other terms implies that scholars concur that there was some reliance on a common reference point by the prophet and the Evangelists, a reference point that is as yet undefined.[23]

Does this mean nothing can be said about the similarity of images preserved in Revelation and the synoptics? Μὴ γένοιτο! I hope to show that we need not establish a literary dependence of the Apocalypse on one or another Christian text in order to draw meaningful conclusions regarding an author's use of traditional elements found in other early Christian literary artifacts. I believe the relationship between these texts can be best addressed by reference to a communal icon that stands behind both the Evangelists' and John's use of an image of Jesus confessing his followers before his father.

THE COMMUNAL ICON: A PROPOSAL

Let me turn now to some preliminary proposals regarding the notion of communal icon. First, use of the term *communal icon* assumes that human beings do in fact communicate ideas one to another through narrative, both individually and in groups.[24] Ricoeur argues that the world of the author can be described as interacting with the world of the reader over time through the production and reception of texts.[25] He understands this interaction in terms of a threefold process of

---

22. In recent scholarship, when interpreters of the Apocalypse encounter similarities between the Apocalypse and one or another of the synoptic Gospels, these similarities are generally referred to as "echoes," "reminiscences," or "allusions." On Rev 3:3 see, for example, Lohmeyer ("ein Anklang," 32); Prigent ("L'exhortation à veiller rappelle," 63); on Rev. 3:5c, see Lohmeyer ("Anspielung," 34) and Prigent ("allusion," 67). In his recent commentary J. Roloff goes so far as to assert that in Rev 3:5 "the image of the Book of Life is translated . . . through appropriation of a saying of Jesus (Luke 12:8/Matt 10:32–33 [Q])." Roloff, *Revelation*, trans. John E. Alsop (Minneapolis: Fortress Press, 1993) 59.

23. Such an allegedly common reference point is then easily ascribed to a major actor in the New Testament drama. Vos, for example, implies that the common source was Jesus. Vos himself admits that his intent is essentially to contribute to the study of the sayings of Jesus as preserved in the synoptic tradition. He feels that the Apocalypse represents a neglected source providing further parallels to sayings of Jesus preserved there. In short, he studies the Apocalypse as another witness to the Jesus tradition assumed to lie behind the synoptic tradition (Vos, 6–9).

24. I decided on the word "icon" for several reasons. The common use of the word, as in a Byzantine icon, commonly refers to highly stylized, highly symbolic works of art which are canonized by religious communities representing in visual form some of their most profound and deeply held doctrinal beliefs, beliefs (like the Trinity) which are not usually conceived in a visual way. Specifically in this study, I also intend the term to be used as Hayden White uses it, to refer to historical icons, that is, to refer to the image-making capabilities inherent in the verbal structures of historiographic literature. White, *Metahistory: The Historical Imagination in Nineteenth-Century Europe* (Baltimore: Johns Hopkins University Press, 1973) 30.

25. Albeit for Ricoeur's purposes texts are very broadly defined. See Ricoeur, "The Model of the Text: Meaningful Action Considered as Text," *Social Research* 38 (1971) 529–62.

mimesis.[26] A configuration of symbols appropriated from the symbolic universe of the author is inscribed in the mind of the author. This "prefiguration" is called $mimesis_1$.[27] Based on the prefiguration of symbols embodied as $mimesis_1$, the author is able to transcribe a *text*—i.e., a physical work—through the process Ricoeur calls "emplotment."[28] This literal text Ricoeur calls $mimesis_2$. The process of emplotment gives the text its own integrity; it is therefore given its own voice, a point of view that can address itself to a reader.[29] When a text is read, the symbols transcribed therein interact with the symbolic world of the reader. This interaction results in a prefiguration of symbols in the mind of the reader, or "$mimesis_3$."[30] For $mimesis_3$ to take place, the integrity of the world of the text must be maintained in the reading.[31] The reader must in the words of Gadamer join in the "play" or "game," or else the written words will never become "text" (Ricoeur) or "art" (Gadamer). This mimetic activity may or may not have been exactly the one planned for in the rhetorical strategy of the author, that is, the implied or "potential reader"[32] may not be the actual reader. Yet if the actual reader can enter into the narrative world with a degree of trust, a second naivete, communication at some level (inscribed as $mimesis_3$) will take place.[33]

The communal icon represents a pattern of thought that an author inherits by virtue of participation in society. Communal icons are

---

26. *Time*, 1:54–76.

27. Ibid., 54–64.

28. Ibid., 64–70.

29. Ibid., 2:98–99.

30. Ibid., 1:70–71.

31. The written text has an integrity of its own, as Hans-Georg Gadamer's work on the hermeneutics of art has shown. A play (drama) is not a play until it is performed, and a text is not a text until it is read. See Gadamer, *Truth and Method*, trans. G. B. Garrett and J. Cumming (New York: Continuum, 1975) 91–150.

32. In the words of Gérard Genette, *Narrative Discourse Revisited*, trans. J. E. Lewin (Ithaca: Cornell University Press, 1988) 149.

33. The idea expressed by Ricoeur in terms of the relationship of this threefold mimesis is perhaps no more clearly or humorously expressed than by contemporary composer and musician Frank Zappa in his use of the analogy of a recipe to describe the process of composing and making music.

When someone writes a piece of music, what he or she puts on the paper is *roughly the equivalent of a recipe*—in the sense that *the recipe is not food, only instructions for the preparation of the food.* Unless you are very weird, you don't eat the recipe.

If I write something on a piece of paper, I can't *actually* 'hear' it. I can conjure up visions of what the symbols on the page *mean*, and imagine a piece of music as it might sound in performance, but *that sensation is non-transferable; it can't be shared or transmitted.*

It doesn't become a 'musical experience' in normal terms until 'the recipe' has been converted into *wiggling air molecules.* (*The Real Frank Zappa Book*, with P. Occhiogrosso [New York: Poseidon Press, 1989] 161, emphasis is Zappa's.)

All texts, I would argue, can be thought of as recipes which when read recreate the food for thought encoded by the author. The recipe is not the food, but to the degree that it is a good recipe, it provides its reader, to the degree that he or she is a good reader, access to the food encoded therein.

integrated with the thought of the author at the level of mimesis$_1$. The author can in turn assume these patterns of thought are also available to the intended recipients of his or her text (=mimesis$_2$). Having received the text, the narrative thus invoked (mimesis$_3$) in turn invokes these icons by using certain key images which function as tips to a conceptual iceberg. The text of the author (mimesis$_2$), having invoked these images not by wholly reproducing them but simply through these conceptual tags, can then manipulate (at the level of *mimesis$_3$*) the recipient's perception of the realities represented by these complex patterns of thought through the manipulation of the images in the narrative.

Some ideas from what has come to be known in the field of cognitive anthropology as *schema theory* may clarify my use of Ricoeur.[34] To be sure, this study does not intend a full-scale adoption of schema theory through its application to the interpretation of historical texts. Nevertheless, certain elements of schema theory are helpful, perhaps only by way of analogy, in clarifying what I mean by the invocation of a communal icon in a text.

In a paper influential to the emergence of schema theory,[35] Charles Fillmore wrote:

> It seems to me that what is needed in discourse analysis is a way of discussing the development, on the part of the interpreter, of an image or scene or picture of the world that gets built up and filled out between the beginning and the end of text-interpretation experience. . . . The first part of a text creates or "activates" a kind of schematic or outline scene, with many positions left blank, so to speak; later parts of the text fill in the

---

34. For a good introduction, see R. D'Andrade, *The Development of Cognitive Anthropology* (Cambridge: Cambridge University Press, 1995) 122–49. The communal icon involves an idea which relates to but is quite distinct from certain ideas being realized in the study of the preservation and transmission of oral tales, folklore. For example, I am not referring here to a biblical or religious equivalent of folktale "types" or "motifs," nor yet to something analogous to Propp's "form," or Lord and Parry's "themes." These ideas are conveniently introduced to the biblical scholar in the very accessible work by S. Niditch, *Underdogs and Tricksters*, New Voices in Biblical Studies (San Francisco: Harper & Row, 1987), see especially pp. 2–22. These hypotheses refer to ways of telling the tale, structures inherent in the story process involving character formation and plot. Again, I see the communal icon as more closely related to but still distinct from Lévi-Strauss's "deep structures," which constitute cultural building blocks, or genetic structures, perceived in the text of the mythic narrative. See Claude Lévi-Strauss, *Structural Anthropology*, trans. C. Jacobsson and B. G. Schoepf (New York: Basic Books, 1963). My proposal would have the communal icon involve synchronic patterns in the social imagination, that is, as a coherent image produced in the imagination by communal narratives. The work of the folklorist focuses on structure in the narrative at the stage of *mimesis$_2$*, the communal icon involves structures of the human imagination produced at the stages of what Ricoeur calls *mimesis$_1$*, for the author, or *mimesis$_3$*, with regard to the receiver of a narrative. I am thankful to my colleague Robert Desjarlais of Sarah Lawrence College for introducing me to schema theory and the discipline of cognitive anthropology.

35. See Roy D'Andrade, *Development*, 123.

blanks (or some of them anyway), introduce new scenes, combine scenes through links of history or causation or reasoning, and so on. In other words, a person, in interpreting a text, mentally creates a partially specified world; as he continues with the text, the details of the world get filled in; and in the process, expectations get up which later on are filled or thwarted or so on. What is important is that *the ultimate nature of this text-internal world will often depend on aspects of the scene never identified explicitly in the text.* (Emphasis added)[36]

The term "schema" refers to "a simplified interpretive framework used to understand events"[37] and which is invoked by a text. A schema is not "a picture in the mind . . . [but] it is a cognitive structure through which interpretations of the world are made."[38] Such schemas are not simply created by individuals but rather develop in the brain as a result of human social interaction; they are the biological result of cultural interaction. As individuals communicate with one another, the schemas themselves become part of what facilitates communication.[39] More-over, an important characteristic of schemas is that they can be "constructed out of other schemas," or nested.[40] They can therefore be represented in human thought as complex interrelations of many diverse human cultural interactions.

I do not, however, wish simply to identify schemas with com-munal icons because schema theory deals primarily with human cogni-tion. Can communities really be said to have cognitive structures in the biological sense? I use, instead, the term "communal icon" to refer to highly complex patterns of thought representing *communal beliefs*. Per-haps we can say that the communal icon functions at the level of the collective imagination analogous to the way schemas function in the interpretive processes of the individual human mind. These icons, like schemas, integrate differing elements of human experience into an intelligible whole. They are patterns of thought created through social interaction which are integral to the construction and maintenance of community. These patterns of thought would include beliefs concerning

---

36. Charles Fillmore, "An Alternative to Checklist Theories of Meaning," *Proceedings of the 1st Annual Meeting of the Berkeley Linguistics Society* 1 (1975) 125.

37. R. D'Andrade, "Cognitive Anthropology," in *New Directions in Psychological Anthropology*, ed. T. Schwartz, G. White, C. Lutz, Publications for the Society for Psychological Anthropology (Cambridge: Cambridge University Press, 1992) 48.

38. Ibid., 52.

39. See D'Andrade, *Development*, 130–32; and Sherry Ortner, who illustrates how cultural schemas function not simply in the production of literary artifacts but as political and ideological forces in the growth and development of a given society. Ortner, "Patterns of History: Cultural Schemas in the Foundings of Sherpa Religious Institutions," in *Culture through Time: Anthropological Approaches*, ed. E. Ohnuki-Tierney (Stanford: Stanford University Press, 1990) 57–93.

40. D'Andrade, "Cognitive Anthropology," 52.

human origins, eschatology, the nature of human existence, and so on. Communal icons, therefore, represent the coherence of extremely diverse, complex, and sometimes contradictory aspects of human experience. The reference to communal icons in literary artifacts is intended to produce certain results in the community, that is, in the thinking and behavior of the communities for which they are intended.

The communal icon provides a significant component of the cognitive backdrop against which the threefold process of *mimesis* can occur. Such icons constitute a repository of communal patterns of thought that are at the disposal of those who create texts. In turn, while creating a text the author can assume knowledge of these icons on the part of the intended receivers of the text. The text does not therefore simply reproduce these icons, nor would it necessarily legitimate or re-enforce a reader's apprehension of the communal icons. The text may function in such a way as to annihilate an icon, or even more subtly to manipulate the reader's perception of reality through deft use of symbols which already possess meaning for the reader as a result of his or her apprehension of a communal icon. The communal icon therefore plays a role in the *social function* of narrative at the level of *mimesis*$_1$ and *mimesis*$_3$.

Let me flesh out this proposal in relation to the tradition history of the Apocalypse. Lars Hartman, in his important study, *Prophecy Interpreted*, began to examine in detail the complexities of the development of Christian eschatological tradition, especially as it is preserved in the synoptic eschatological discourse.[41] In order better to understand the roots of the traditions preserved therein, he developed the idea of a prophetic midrash of Daniel which predates the Gospels themselves.[42] He uses the term "midrash" to refer to an interpretation of Scripture that can take on a life of its own and be transmitted from one community to another, thereby being adapted from one situation to another.

Hartman describes an apocalyptic substructure in a variety of intertestamental works that he believes derives mainly from a reading of Daniel, but also from other books of the Hebrew Scriptures. This substructure involves "patterns of thought or conceptual frameworks which seem to have played a part in the formation of individual por-

---

41. L. Hartman, *Prophecy Interpreted: The Formation of Some Jewish Apocalyptic Texts and the Eschatological Discourse of Mark 13 and Par.*, ConBNT 1 (Lund: C. W. K. Gleerup, 1966).

42. His use of the term "midrash" has proved problematic, but his ideas regarding the way in which these eschatological traditions developed and were used has, I believe, proven useful. Hartman (174) himself acknowledges the limitations of his use of the term "midrash" by putting it in quotation marks.

tions of the text."[43] For Hartman, the writing of these texts represented a stage whereby "mythical fragments may have begun to be transformed into parts of a symbolic language."[44] Hartman argues that the eschatological discourse reflects the application of this Daniel "midrash" to the life-setting of those who are responsible for the creation and preservation of the traditions preserved in the eschatological discourse. That life-setting, according to many scholars, was determined by pressures stemming from the tumultuous events of the Jewish war with Rome.[45]

Hartman's work is important for this present investigation because his examination of specific texts suggests *how* the process of transmission of particular teachings took place within certain apocalyptic communities, especially those teachings derived from the interpretation of scriptural sources. He has shown convincingly that interpretive traditions from diverse sources could be brought together to form a coherent picture. The picture thus obtained exhibits a structure stable enough to be transmitted to others and adapted to different times and places.[46] A multifaceted picture of the "coming of God" (his example) furnished from diverse symbols developed over time through interpretation of Scripture and became incorporated into the collective imagination of the community. Hartman's mention of "patterns of thought" and "conceptual frameworks" points to structural elements in a community's "symbolic universe."[47] Although Hartman may be referring to a real-life text (*mimesis₂* in Ricoeur's terms) predating the eschatological discourse, this cannot be proven. I would argue, however, that this narrative need not be physical; it can describe a set

---

43. Ibid., 14. Hartman (28–49, recap 238) divides the "raw material" of this aspect of Jewish apocalyptic into five basic categories: (A) the preliminary time of evil; (B) divine intervention; (C) the Judgment; (D) the fate of sinners; (E) joy of the elect. When describing this phenomenon with regard to the visionary material in texts like *1 Enoch, 4 Ezra, 2 Baruch,* he warns his reader that the elements he has isolated as being a part of that substructure ought not to be taken as autonomous elements of different traditions but "parts of a complex of ideas, or as different motifs in a stage picture" (62–63; here specifically with regard to *1 Enoch* 47:1–48:10).

44. Ibid., 141.

45. See A. Feuillet, "Le discours de Jésus sur la ruine du Temple d'après Marc XIII et Luc XXI, 2–36," *RB* 55 (1948) 481–502, 56 (1949) 61–92, though I reject his thesis that it was either Mark's or Jesus' intention to predict the coming of the Son of Man as meaning specifically the destruction of the Temple; D. Nineham, *Saint Mark,* Westminster Pelican Commentaries (Philadelphia: Westminster Press, 1963) 351; W. L. Lane, *The Gospel According to Mark,* NICNT (Grand Rapids: Eerdmans, 1974) 466.

46. I.e., when abstract thought can be expressed in such a way that it is perceived in terms of visual metaphors, the very reification of such thought into an image becomes part of the preservation process. Images imply spatial relations and as such they embody an easily apprehended structure in the relation of various aspects of the image one to another.

47. A community's "texts"—its stories, art, and literature—reflect, indeed reify, particular configurations of symbols derived from the symbolic universe which itself is an evolutionary creation of the community. See Geertz, "Art as a Cultural System," in *Local Knowledge: Further Essays in Interpretive Anthropology* (New York: Basic Books, 1983) 73–120.

of ideas, present in the mind of the author of the eschatological discourse, at the stage of *mimesis*$_1$.

Communities, in the context of debate and conversation, gradually shape various ideas into commonly held pictures, or communal icons. This is to say that a complex of ideas becomes "canonized" by its acceptance. It is my hypothesis that a highly complex structuring of symbols in the collective imagination of a community can take on a life of its own. The icon is communal, because it is not something generated by just one person, even if that person be a prophet. When someone utters a prophecy jarring the generally accepted picture, the icon has then to be revised, or the offending statement dismissed. Thus, the communal icon's constitutive elements evolve, change, or recede in the context of communal discussion on matters of central significance associated with the image.

SANCTIFICATION OF THE NAME

With this understanding of the dynamic social function of the communal icon, let us return to the issue of the similarity between Revelation 3:5 and the Q tradition of Matthew 10:32//Luke 12:8. As we move beyond a purely literary understanding of the sources used by the prophet and delve into the symbolic world in which these early Christian traditions developed, can we better understand the "anthological" way in which John uses his sources?

Our investigation begins with the hypothesis that there were certain common ways of thinking about God, and about the believing community's relationship with God, among Jews of the first century— communal icons which though not necessarily embodied in narrative form, are reflected in narratives, or texts. This is to say that *these icons yield traditions,* traditions that are reflected in sayings and stories present in the Hebrew Scriptures, the Apocrypha, and in tannaitic sources. The sayings at the heart of this study are best understood as having crystallized in a milieu characterized by debate concerning traditionally held Jewish beliefs.[48]

Two factors point strongly in the direction of a Jewish Aramaic-speaking, if not a Palestinian, milieu for the origin of the Q saying preserved in the synoptic Gospels. First there are philological con-

---

48. One may reasonably assume that the Jews responsible for preserving Christian traditions, traditions which themselves share in the broader Jewish worldview regarding God and the believing community's relationship with him, influenced and contributed greatly to emergent Christian traditions later canonized in the New Testament.

siderations: the use of the dative in ὁμολογήσει ἐν ἐμοι reflects Aramaic syntax.[49] Second, the oracular form of the synoptic saying reflects prophetic speech which has been associated with early Palestinian Christian prophets.[50] It is interesting that the Apocalypse, which is thought most to reflect Semitic syntax in its use of Greek,[51] does not here in 3:5c reflect the Aramaic syntax observed above. This fact does not, however, lend itself to any easy conclusions regarding the relationship of Rev 3:5 to the Q saying. What we can conclude at this stage is that if the seer knew an Aramaic original to this saying, his Greek doesn't reflect it.

Where the Q saying has the phrase ὁμολογήσει ἐν αὐτῷ[52] John has the fuller phrase ὁμολογήσω τό ὄνομα αὐτοῦ. John's phrase includes the term τό ὄνομα—a term that is important for John.[53] Although it could be invoked simply as a result of his own peculiar reliance on this theme, I believe the use of the term τό ὄνομα here in the Apocalypse provides a significant clue to a prefiguration of symbols present to the mind of the author, a clue to an element of *mimesis₁*. The saying reflects a communal icon involving the divine name. It is an icon des-

---

49. See BDF §220 (2); J. Fitzmeyer, *The Gospel According to Luke*, AB 28a (New York: Doubleday) 960; A. H. McNiel, *The Gospel According to Matthew* (London: Macmillan, 1961) 146. Boring concludes that "this saying, especially in its Q-form, contains very old material that reflects the linguistic milieu of Palestine." Boring, *Sayings of the Risen Jesus*, SNTSMS 46 (Cambridge: Cambridge University Press, 1982) 165.

50. See Käsemann, "Sentences of Holy Law," in *New Testament Questions for Today* (Philadelphia: Fortress Press, 1969) 79–80; Boring, *Sayings*, 165; Aune, 181–82. This conclusion seems warranted with the qualification that prophetic speech could apply to Jesus as well as to his followers (no conclusion is being drawn here as to whether the saying originated with Jesus or some time after the resurrection). Moreover, this is not to say that later prophets outside the Palestinian milieu could not have inherited this form of speech, but that examples from other writings reflecting a Greek-speaking milieu and which preserve some form of this saying do not reflect the Aramaic grammar; see 2 *Clement* 3:2, and significantly Rev 3:5; also the similar ideas expressed in *Herm. Vis.* II 2:7–8.

51. Charles's work at the beginning of the century established an explanation for the strange Greek of the Apocalypse: it reflected the Semitic language of the author. See Charles, *Studies in the Apocalypse* (Edinburgh: T. & T. Clark, 1913) 79–102, and *Revelation* 1:cxvii–clix. His view for the most part still represents a scholarly consensus. Recently, there is some controversy on whether the language reflects a conscious attempt to reproduce the style of the Hebrew Bible (S. Thompson, *The Apocalypse and Semitic Syntax*, SNTSMS [Cambridge: Cambridge University Press], followed by Mazzaferri, 42–47), or whether it reflects a later mishnaic Hebrew and Aramaic contemporary with the time of the author. See G. Mussies, *The Morphology of Koine Greek as used in the Apocalypse of John*, NovTSup 27 (Leiden: Brill, 1971), and "The Greek of the Book of Revelation," in *L'Apocalypse johannique et l'Apocalyptique dans le Nouveau Testament*, ed. J. Lambrecht, BETL 53 (Leuven: Leuven University Press, 1980) 167–77. Mussies builds on and supports Charles's original contention.

52. Luke 12:8; Matt reads ὁμολογήσω κἀγὼ ἐν αὐτῷ.

53. Note its use in 2:3, 13, 17; 3:1, 8; 6:8; 8:11; 9:11; 11:13, 18; 13:1, 6, 8, 17; 14:1, 11; 15:2, 4; 16:9; 17:3, 5, 8; 19:12, 13, 16; 21:12, 14; 22:4. In addition, the use of τὸ ὄνομα here fits well the context of the letter to the Church in Sardis. There is a play of the word "name" in the letter: 3:2—"you have the name of being awake"; 3:4—"a few names who have not defiled their garments"; and 3:5b—"name I will not blot out of the Book of Life." See A. Farrer, *The Revelation of St. John the Divine* (Oxford: Clarendon Press, 1964) 79.

cribing a relationship between God and Israel (God's people) as having a mutually determined reputation. That is, the icon involves a pattern of ideas expressing the view that public actions on the part of God's people, specifically with regard to God's commandments, bear on God's reputation. Moreover, one's culpability before God in times of judgment is directly related to the impact of one's behavior on God's reputation.

The idea that Israel in some sense bears God's name, and that what happens to Israel in the world has therefore a bearing on God's name, has its roots in the Hebrew Bible. Israel is a people "called by God's name,"[54] and Israel is therefore capable of profaning the divine name by certain forms of misbehavior.[55] In the Maccabean era we read that "the lawless killing" of God's people is perceived as blasphemy against the divine name (2 Macc 8:4); and, by the rabbinic era, it is a commonplace belief that good behavior in public, that is fulfilling God's commandments, in turn sanctifies the divine name.[56]

The idea that God and Israel have a mutually identified reputation attained a certain maturity in rabbinic literature and is traditionally expressed by the phrases "sanctification of the name" (קידוש השם) and "profanation of the name" (חילול השם).[57] Tannaitic and amoraic material give evidence to support the view that the public witness to the God of Israel became one criterion for the rabbis in determining the importance of following certain commandments.[58] An insignificant transgression of the Torah, if performed in public, especially among Gentiles, could be considered much more grave since it has the effect

---

54. E.g., Deut 28:10; Isa 43:7; 63:19; Jer 14:9; 2 Chr 7:14.

55. This can be done either directly by swearing falsely by God's name (Lev 19:12), or more importantly indirectly through one's behaviour (Lev 18:21, 21:6, Amos 2:7). Observing the commandments of the Torah ensures that God's name is not profaned (Lev 22:31-33); see also Ezek 22:16, 26; 36:22-33.

56. The trajectory from the stories of martyrdom during the Maccabean era to the rabbinic use of the term קידוש השם is so clearly a part of Jewish tradition that H. H. Ben-Sasson can write in the *Encyclopaedia Judaica*, "The Fourth Book of The Maccabees is almost entirely a philosophical sermon on the meaning and glory of *kiddush ha-shem* in Hellenistic times" (10:982).

57. See the discussion in E. E. Urbach, *The Sages: Their Concepts and Beliefs* (Jerusalem: Magnes Press, 1979) 356-60. I am well aware of the problems involved in using rabbinic material to elucidate NT issues; however in this case, I am simply using early rabbinic texts that contain ideas clearly parallel to those expressed in the Maccabean era as well as in the NT material itself. I believe these rabbinic materials give voice most clearly to the ideas which lie behind the Maccabean and NT material. I am not arguing dependence of NT material on rabbinic ideas, but am simply pointing to a common fount from which they emanate.

58. We see already in 4 Macc 6-7 in the story of the martyrdom of Eleazer how the confrontation hinges on the keeping of seemingly insignificant commandments dealing with *kashrut*. By the amoraic period the rabbis are identifying the gravity of sin in relation to the degree that the divine name is profaned; see Urbach, 56-57.

of profaning God's name in the world.[59] Similarly, holding to a seemingly trite commandment, if accomplished publicly to the glory of God, has the effect of sanctifying God's name before the world.[60] Early rabbinic Judaism thus maintains a form of retributive justice based on the degree to which God's reputation is damaged or enhanced by one's public behavior.

The idea of קידוש השם becomes particularly relevant in times of persecution. Under these circumstances, seemingly unimportant events could have great consequences with regard to maintaining the distinctive practice of the Jewish community over and against a dominant culture.[61] Adherence to "trivial" or lesser commandments has therefore a great impact on the integrity and cohesive nature of the community— especially during times of persecution. The cohesion that binds Israel together as a body is its relationship to the Torah. The degree to which this relationship is made visible through practice constitutes God's reputation: the public acknowledgment of his name. Therefore proper adherence to the law is not only an individual act but an act that reflects on the community as a whole. The degree to which God's reputation is affected by one's behavior establishes the degree of culpability for one's sins.

The idea of retributive justice is, of course, a notion common in the Hellenistic world. There are well-known non-Jewish Hellenistic examples of *jus talionis*.[62] However, the significant aspect of its Jewish expression, especially as preserved in rabbinic materials, involves the idea that public action bears on one's relationship with the God of Israel and, more important, it bears on *God's* reputation. It is particularly significant that by tannaitic times the term קידוש השם itself carries the implication of martyrdom.[63] This is probably a logical exten-

---

59. See *t. Sanh.* 74a–b for example where in "the house of Nithza in Lydda" the rabbis take up the issue of when one is bound to adhere to even minor precepts of the Torah at the risk of one's life rather than profane the name. And see the famous Baraita אמר רבי אביהו משום רבי חנינא נוח לו לאדם שיעבור עבירה בסתר יאל יחלל שם שמים בפרהסיא (*t. Qidd* 40a). This Baraita is followed by another tradition with a similar warning against profanation of the name; see *t. ʿAbod. Zar.* 27b–28a; *t. Sanh.* 74a; *Cant. Rab.* vii, 8.; *Midr. Pss* on 68:13 (159a §8).

60. See Urbach, 52–60; D. Daube "Limitations on Self-Sacrifice in Jewish Law and Tradition," *Theology* 73 (1969) 291–304.

61. See Daube, 294–95.

62. See the discussion in Käsemann, 67.

63. See discussion in *EncJud* 10:978–79. See *mek. Ba-Hodesh* 6:135–40 (Lauterbach, 247) on God's attitude toward those who keep Torah in times of persecution. There is a parallel here in the Christian use of the term "martyr" which originally meant "to bear witness," but since this so often meant losing one's life it came to have the meaning which directly invoked this one kind of bearing witness; see A. A. Trites, "'Μαρτυς' and Martyrdom in the Apocalypse: A Semantic Study," *NovT* 15 (1973) 72–80, and *The New Testament Concept of Witness*, SNTSMS 31 (Cambridge: Cambridge University Press, 1977).

sion of the idea found in Maccabean literature that the lawless killing of God's people is a profanation of his name.

Most important for our purposes, however, is evidence from the New Testament that the social function of this communal icon—describing a mutually identified reputation between God and Israel—was at work in some Christian circles. The New Testament materials that rely on this communal icon form a bridge between the Maccabean era and rabbinic times. See, for example, Paul's adaption of Isaiah 52:2 in Romans 2:24 where he put forth the notion of Israel's profanation of the name.[64] B. Gerhardsson has cogently argued that Matt 10:32//Luke 12:8 is one among a group of sayings, e.g., Mark 8:38, Matt 10:33, 16:27, and Luke 9:26, that express a confession/denial theme wherein confession of the Lord brings reward while denial of him brings its opposite.[65] Here Christians assert the common idea that one's status with God depends on how one behaves among other human beings. The way this assertion is expressed represents a particular take on the integration of the divine and human realms, specifically with regard to the idea of mutually determined reputations. It is not so great a leap to believe that how one lives has a direct bearing on God's reputation, as is fully developed in the rabbinic doctrine of *kiddush ha-shem*.[66] That is, if what happens to God's people has a bearing on God's reputation, then how one represents one's self as a person of God among human beings determines how God is perceived by others and so has an impact on God's reputation. In Christian hands, however, this idea has a profoundly different twist from how it will be expressed by the Tannaim. Whereas, according the tannaim, the confession or acknowledgment of one's status as a member of Israel is indicated through following the Torah, the early Christians asserted that the confession of one's status as a member of God's people is revealed through identification with the Son of Man or Jesus of Nazareth.

It has been argued that the confession/denial sayings had their origins in situations of conflict or even persecution. This suggestion,

---

64. As C. E. B. Cranfield observes, Paul has adapted what originally referred "to the reviling of God's name by the oppressors of Israel on account of Israel's misfortunes . . . to the reviling of God's name by the Gentiles on account of the Jews' disobedience to His Law." This idea is echoed in 2 Pet 2:2, and as Cranfield notes, the idea will be reflected later in rabbinic writings. Cranfield, *A Critical and Exegetical Commentary on the Epistle to the Romans*, 2 vols., ICC (Edinburgh: T. & T. Clark 1980) 1:171.

65. See B. Gerhardsson, "Confession and Denial before Men: Observations on Matt 26:57–27:2," *JSNT* 13 (1981) 46–66. Indeed it has been argued that these New Testament traditions are best understood against the background of teaching involving קידוש השם and חילול השם. See Daube, "Limitations on Self-Sacrifice," 293.

66. See Ezek 22:16, 26; 36:22–33 and significantly Rom 2:24.

along with the Aramaic coloring in the syntax of the Matt 10:32//Luke 12:8 form of the saying, supports the probability that the saying had its *Sitz im Leben* in times of conflict among Jews (those who would and who would not become Christians) in Palestine.[67] The argument for the early dating of the saying rests mainly on these observations (and for some the third person use of the Son of Man title).[68]

Do the social circumstances in which the author of Revelation produced his text reflect similar conditions? Are there enough similarities in the social circumstances that gave rise to these different texts, such that one could assert that in the production of this material the various authors had recourse to the same communal icon involving the mutually identified reputation of God and the people of God? I think that we can say there are such similarities. That is, the context of the phrase both in Revelation as a whole and particularly in the letter to the Church in Sardis is one of persecution.[69] More specifically, the theology of the Apocalypse centers on the public proclamation of the Christian faith in deed before a demonic world empire. The setting of Revelation 3:5 therefore mirrors this aspect of the *Sitz im Leben* of the confession/denial sayings found in the synoptic Gospels, though in Revelation the Roman world replaces the Jewish authorities with whom the earliest Christians came into conflict. The seven letters of the Apocalypse, with their threats and promises to the churches in Asia, are pervaded by this theme. The churches are to be "tried" in the public arena by the way of life practiced by its members. Promises are made to those whose works are pleasing to God, who follow the lamb, and who do not accommodate themselves to the world empire. Prophecies of doom are pronounced against those who are unable to do so.[70]

---

67. This is the conclusion of Boring (165) and Käsemann (77–79).

68. That is, those scholars who believe that when the Son of Man is referred to in the third person it must reflect early tradition prior to Jesus and the Son of Man being identified by the Church; see J. Weiss, *Jesus' Proclamation of the Kingdom of God*, trans. and ed. R. H. Heirs and D. L. Holland (Philadelphia: Fortress, 1971), especially 114–29; and his followers, R. Bultmann, *History of the Synoptic Tradition*, trans. J. Marsh (New York: Harper and Row, 1963) 128, 151; H. Tödt, *The Son of Man*, trans. D. M. Barton (Philadelphia: Westminster, 1965) 42–43; J. Jeremias, *New Testament Theology* (New York: Scribners, 1971) 275; among others.

69. See for example the commentary by G. B. Caird, *The Revelation of St. John the Divine*, HNTC (New York: Harper & Row, 1966); or Schüssler Fiorenza, *Revelation Vision of a Just World*, Proclamation Commentaries (Minneapolis: Fortress Press, 1991). The debate on nature of the crisis reflected in Revelation need not detain us here. See Yarbro Collins, *Crisis and Catharsis*. However one interprets political events in the social world of the Apocalypse, persecution is clearly the literary setting of the book.

70. On this issue see J. P. Sweet, *Revelation*, Westminster Pelican Commentaries (Philadelphia: Westminster, 1979) 31–35; Yarbro Collins, *Crisis* 124–27; L. Thompson, *The Book of Revelation: Apocalypse and Empire* (New York: Oxford University Press, 1990) 169–70. On this theme in the seven letters see the commentaries of Ramsey, Charles, Caird, and Swete.

The church in Sardis to whom the promise in 3:5 is made seems not to have much going for it: it is called "dead" and is threatened with a *parousia* of the lord as a "thief." The denial aspect of the confession/denial theme, therefore, constitutes the first part of the letter (Rev 3:1c–3). By implication, the conqueror is one whose works are perfect, and thus is the only one who is "worthy" to walk with Christ (3:4). To be "worthy" in the Apocalypse is to have withstood the trial of persecution and/or public confession of one's allegiance through the manner of one's life.[71] Moreover, the participle Ὁ νικῶν can be taken in a conditional sense which would undergird a reading of the letter in the context of the conditions attendant upon the believer for the confession and/or denial of Jesus.[72]

At this point let us recall conclusions reached earlier. The common use of the verb ὁμολογέω is significant, but it alone cannot bear the weight of an argument establishing a direct link between Q and Rev 3:5c. When this observation is coupled with the fact that the context of the phrase in the Apocalypse implies a condition like the protasis of a saying found in Q, it allows for the conclusion that John intended for this reference to invoke the confession/denial teaching—oral or written—now extant in the body of sayings found elsewhere in the NT (Mark 8:38; Matt 10:33; 16:27; Luke 9:26). This is the main argument of this section: that there is a group of Christian sayings that have very similar *Sitz im Leben*; that all represent Christian applications of traditional Jewish teaching regarding the confession and denial of the divine name; and that all exhibit similar but not identical literary features. This does not tell us, however, anything specific about the relationship between the saying found in the synoptics and Revelation 3:5c. It is to this question that we now return.

A COMMUNAL ICON OF THE LAST JUDGMENT

There were many visualized expectations regarding the *parousia,* each dealing with various questions at issue in the lives of the early Christians: Will the dead rise before or after the Lord comes?[73] Who, if anyone, will sit in judgment with him?[74] Will all the dead rise, or

---

71. See W. C. Van Unnik "'Worthy is the Lamb': The Background of Apoc 5," in *Mélanges Bibliques en hommage au R. P. Béda Rigaux,* ed. A. Deschamps and R. P. A. de Halleux (Gembloux: Duculot, 1970) 445–61. He builds his case on the Hellenistic background of the word, yet, as can be seen it is closely tied to the rabbinic idea of sanctification of the name.

72. See BDF §417–18 (2) and §466 (4); also note that the context of the verse (Rev 3:1–4) sets up a condition juxtaposed to the promise in 3:5.

73. A question reflected perhaps in 1 Thess 4:13-18 or 1 Cor 15:52.

74. Matt 19:28; Luke 22:30.

only the righteous, and in what state?[75] Among the many questions regarding the end time, there were expectations regarding the nature of "the preliminary time of evil" or "the messianic woes," or even expectation of the eschatological adversary.[76]

The various Jesus sayings that invoke the confession/denial theme belong in this larger context of expectations regarding the *parousia*. Moreover, these confession/denial sayings contain a constellation of common elements. In order to identify the elements of the communal icon that lies behind these sayings consider the following passages:

ὃς γὰρ ἐὰν ἐπαισχυνθῇ με καὶ τοὺς ἐμοὺς λόγους ἐν τῇ γενεᾷ ταύτῃ τῇ μοιχαλίδι καὶ ἁμαρτωλῷ, καὶ ὁ υἱὸς τοῦ ἀνθρώπου ἐπαισχυνθήσεται αὐτόν, ὅταν ἔλθῃ ἐν τῇ δόξῃ τοῦ πατρὸς αὐτοῦ μετὰ τῶν ἀγγέλων τῶν ἁγίων. (Mark 8:38)

μέλλει γὰρ ὁ υἱὸς τοῦ ἀνθρώπου ἔρχεσθαι ἐν τῇ δόξῃ τοῦ πατρὸς αὐτοῦ μετὰ τῶν ἀγγέλων αὐτοῦ, καὶ τότε ἀποδώσει ἑκάστῳ κατὰ τὴν πρᾶξιν αὐτοῦ. (Matt 16:27)

ὃς γὰρ ἂν ἐπαισχυνθῇ με καὶ τοὺς ἐμοὺς λόγους, τοῦτον ὁ υἱὸς τοῦ ἀνθρώπου ἐπαισχυνθήσεται, ὅταν ἔλθῃ ἐν τῇ δόξῃ αὐτοῦ καὶ τοῦ πατρὸς καὶ τῶν ἁγίων ἀγγέλων. (Luke 9:26)

As can be seen, these sayings all contain references to "God," "glory," "my father," "the Son of Man," and "his angels" ("his" meaning either the Father or the Son of Man). Also implied in these sayings is a judgment scene or the idea of retribution inherent in early Christian eschatological expectations.

---

75. In some forms of apocalyptic speculation only the righteous will rise (*Ps. Sol.* 3:9-12), but most follow Dan 12 where both the righteous and the unrighteous will be raised, the former for blessing and the latter to judgment.

76. Hartman, 28-34; cf. Court, 43-47, and n. 43 above. The image or expectation of the eschatological adversary, popularly called "Antichrist," plays a significant role in the teaching of the Apocalypse. Yarbro Collins (*Combat Myth*, 166-67) informs us that the literature dealing with the question of the Antichrist, in both Rev and the rest of the NT, is burdened with great terminological confusion. Long ago Bousset (*Der Antichrist* [Göttingen: Vandenhoeck & Ruprecht, 1895]) argued for the existence of an independent pre-Christian Antichrist tradition. He is followed in this by Charles, *Revelation* 2:76-87. The latter, however, notes that many different myths, each with different "epithets belonging to the Antichrist" (78) need to be distinguished, and so distinguished Nero and Beliar myths from the Antichrist myth proper. Other notable studies (B. Rigaux, *L'Antéchrist et l'opposition au royaume messianique dans l'Ancien et le Nouveau Testament* [Gembloux: Ducluot, 1932], for example) tend to subsume discussion of any portrayals of Satan (or evil) under this one heading, which, however dogmatically appropriate, tends to obscure the different traditions which feed into the idea as it existed in the first century. Yarbro Collins, on the other hand, notes "if they [the terms referring to evil forces opposing God] are held absolutely, the similarities between the various myths are obscured." She therefore follows J. Ernst and uses the more general term "eschatological adversary" when dealing with the phenomenon as a whole. Ernst, *Die eschatologischen Gegenspieler in den Schriften des Neuen Testaments*, Biblische Untersuchungen 3 (Regensburg: Friedrich Pustet, 1967).

It will be recalled that the Q saying Matthew 10:32//Luke 12:8 is coupled in both Matthew and Luke with a complementary saying carrying a threat regarding those who would be ashamed of Jesus/the Son of Man (Matt 10:33//Luke 12:9). The sayings reproduced above, then, are parallel in meaning to the Q tradition Matthew 10:33//Luke 12:9. Each of these sayings includes some but not all of the elements I have noted as being present in the group as a whole. For example, as a group these sayings refer to "my Father" and "his angels," as does Revelation 3:5c, though Matthew 10:32 has only "my Father," and Luke 12:8 refers to some angels. I believe we can account for the conflation of these two elements in the Revelation passage not by recourse to a common discrete source underlying it and Q, or by John's dependence on the synoptics, but with the hypothesis that these elements were part of a communal icon of the last judgment inherited by the prophet, one that places Jesus in the role of both prosecuting and defense attorney. The role Jesus plays in this picture *vis-à-vis* the believer is a personification of a belief that would be readily acceptable to the Jewish social imagination. This Christian icon of the coming judgment appropriates and transforms the communal icon describing the mutually identified reputation of Israel and God. In the case of the icon in Christian circles, judgment is based on whether, in his or her public behavior, the Christian has acknowledged Jesus.

Instruction concerning the necessity of public witness to Jesus through proper behavior involved community promises and threats concerning the *parousia:* the coming of the Son of Man together with angels and the judgment that would then ensue. The various elements— "glory," "God" (as judge), "Father" (as judge), "the Son of Man," and "angels"—are generally scattered in sayings involving this idea, but they coalesce to create a picture of the judgment involving a heavenly courtroom scene where the Son of Man or Jesus appears as a witness. He acts as a witness for the defense for those who confessed him publicly and a witness for the prosecution against those who denied him.[77] It is this image, and the elements associated with it, that is common to the passages discussed in this study. Where Matthew and Luke may indeed be dependent on a common source, Q, the prophet of Patmos, it would seem, simply knows the icon and has used elements associated with it in creating the conclusion of the promise to the conquerors in 3:5.

---

77. In most sayings referring to the coming Son of Man at the *parousia* he brings condemnation of those who opposed him; however, only in the three texts under consideration here he acts as a witness for the defense also.

Absent in the Apocalypse is any scene where Jesus confesses the name of his followers before his Father. One must therefore hear 3:5 with some *pre*figured image which, when confronted with the configuration of symbols in the text, can be *re*figured in accordance with the world presented by the text. The hearer must already know what confession before the Father means for the promise in Revelation 3:5 to be effective. Indeed, the promise to "the one who conquers" is forceful only when the promise recalls to its hearers something like Jesus' teachings as presented in the synoptic Gospels.

The confession/denial motif is found broadly sprinkled about in early Christian literature.[78] If it is familiar, it is likely that it is precisely because the hearers know of some saying like the one preserved in Matthew 10:32–33 and Luke 12:8–9. It is impossible to prove what was familiar to the readers of an ancient work; one can only assert here that, if the readers were not familiar with something like the confession/denial theme in Jesus' teaching, the phrase in Revelation would make no sense.[79] In sum, John apprehended an image of the judgment scene, one created through a familiarity with a variety of Jesus sayings dealing with this particular issue. He wrote down the promise for "those who conquer" using elements derived from a communal icon of an image of the coming judgment of God. The promise, therefore, reflects the language generally used by early Christians regarding proper behavior in times of persecution as a result of their identification as followers of Jesus.

Most of Revelation's images are not self-explanatory. They function in association with images, ideas, and beliefs already held by the hearer. For example, the hearers must know who the Lamb is to make sense of the work at all, as Jesus is not ever expressly identified with the Lamb.[80] I would venture that the reason the Apocalypse has remained so impenetrable to later readers is that we no longer share communal icons which the author assumes on the part of his audience. The text has nothing to manipulate in us, no commonly held assumptions against which to proclaim its prophetic message. The writer's

---

78. Along with the examples from the synoptic Gospels see also Rom 10:9–10; 1 John 2:22–23; 2 Tim 2:12; 2 Pet 2:1; *2 Clem.* 3:2; *Herm. Vis.* II 2:7–8.

79. If John does have in the back of his mind a piece of tradition like the conditional statement in Q, then the reference to the name in Rev 3:5c would imply the counterpart, "He who confesses my name among human beings" to his phrase "I will confess his name before my Father and his angels." As such Jesus' name is being used in a way which mirrors rabbinic expressions involving sanctification of the divine name.

80. The hearer must know what it means "to keep one's garments" or to "be seen exposed" for the warning in 16:15 to have any effect; most important, they must know what it means "to conquer"—"as I myself have conquered" in 3:21, that is, they must know the way of the cross. These examples could be multiplied many times over.

references *are* obscure; but if the hearer is familiar with the tradition of symbolic language in which John writes, the narrative of the Apocalypse can function either to accentuate the ideas thus represented or, by radically changing them, powerfully to reshape the worldview of its recipient. The communal icons assumed by the author, or rather, held in common by both him and his readers are grist for his prophetic spirit.

5

The Sermon on the Mount as Foundational Text

More than Catechism

The Sermon on the Mount in the Gospel of Matthew and the Sermon on the Plain in Luke present the teaching of Jesus in a summary way. The sermon in both versions can be called foundational on more than one account. It can certainly be called foundational because it presents Jesus' first extended speech. In both Gospel stories the discourse holds a place of emphasis. The narrative flow comes to a halt, and the stage is set for teaching. According to Luke (6:17), Jesus descends from the mountain and positions himself on a level place, "the place of meeting with the people."[1] According to Matthew (5:1), Jesus ascends the mountain and sits down, thus taking the position of a teacher practicing his profession. In both Matthew and Luke, the narrative that precedes the sermon reports the formation of a group of disciples and the gathering of people in great numbers. With the disciples as the closer, more immediate audience and the crowds as the wider, Jesus begins to teach.

The two versions of the speech present their common material in basically the same order, starting with blessings and ending with parables of judgment. It makes sense therefore to speak of "the inaugural sermon of Jesus" already on the level of Q, the hypothetical source that Luke and Matthew both use independently of one another.[2]

---

1. Hans Conzelmann, *The Theology of St. Luke* (Philadelphia: Fortress, 1982) 44. For the significance of ascent and descent, see Exod 19.
2. John S. Kloppenborg, "The Formation of Q and Antique Instructional Genres," *JBL* 105 (1986) 451.

Of the two discourses, the Sermon on the Mount (SM) is not only the most comprehensive but also the most carefully delimited text. The biblical phrase "[he] opened his mouth" gives gravity to the introduction of the speech in 5:2. The book of Daniel and other writings of the Hebrew Scriptures attest the expression. Its predominant function is to introduce oracles or other important messages from God. Likewise the end of the sermon has a solemn ring to it: "when Jesus had finished saying these things" (7:28a). The formula resembles the stereotyped phrases that mark the end of discourses in the book of Deuteronomy. Hubert Frankemölle suggests that it is on this model that Matthew has shaped the closure formula of which 7:28a is only the first example.[3] With little variation the formula recurs at the end of other discourses. "[He] opened his mouth" thus has its counterpart in "[He] had finished saying." The narrative framing of the speech is also carefully balanced. In both 4:23–25 and 7:28–8:1 there is mention of "crowds following him," "teaching," and the "mountain." Consequently, "like . . . between two bookends, 5:3–7:27 is marked off as a distinct literary unit."[4] To my reading, a predominantly redaction-critical reading, the circumspect framing of the speech is evidence of the foundational role of the SM for Matthew's understanding of Jesus' ministry.

OF WHAT GENRE?

Augustine chose chapters 5–7 of Matthew for his full-size commentary, entitled *De Sermone in Monte*. Augustine's treatment of the Sermon on the Mount as an independent text is of some significance for Hans Dieter Betz, who in his 1995 Hermeneia commentary, and in several articles prior to that, has argued for an understanding of the SM as an early pre-synoptic, even pre-Q, collection of sayings. The Sermon on the Plain (SP) is another version of the collection. According to Betz, the internal consistency of both the SM and the SP is the result of redactional work before the Gospel writers integrated the material into their narratives. The two versions of the speech were aimed at different audiences. The addressees of the SM were Jewish; SP was directed to Gentiles. SM and SP were added at later stages of Q, the SM to Q-Matt, the SP to Q-Luke.[5]

---

3. Hubert Frankemölle, *Jahwe-Bund und Kirche Christi*, NTAbh NF 10 (Münster: Aschendorff, 1974) 340. Other scholars refer to Luke 7:1 and suggest that Matthew has developed a formula present in Q.

4. Dale C. Allison, "The Structure of the Sermon on the Mount," *JBL* 106 (1987) 429.

5. Hans Dieter Betz, "The Sermon on the Mount and Q: Some Aspects of the Problem," in *Gospel Origins and Christian Beginnings: In Honor of James M. Robinson*, ed. James E. Goehr-

As Betz sees the matter, these pre-Gospel documents belong to the ancient literary genre of *epitome,* a summary or digest of a famous teacher's doctrines (such as Epicurus or Epictetus). Among Betz's examples of epitome I find Epictetus's *Encheiridion,* the classic manual on virtue and happiness, an intriguing analogy. The SM is open to a humanistic reading that goes beyond a church-oriented interpretation of the text focused on the ethics of a Christian community. Seen in a humanistic perspective, it is a speech with conversational features (*sermo*) that speaks to a human search for what is ultimately good.[6] It is a discourse that lays open the power of anger, anxiety, and obsession, or as Richard Lischer has put it, "The Sermon takes our humanness seriously."[7] One can also say that the SM is similar to Epictetus's *Manual* in being, like that document, a treasury of action-wisdom.[8] While I recognize the epitome/manual of life genre as a possible analogy to the SM, I cannot accept it as an adequate classification of either SM or SP. Both compendium[9] and epitome, for example, evidently assume a setting-apart of the sermon both from other speeches in Matthew and from the entire story. The SM, however, is permeated by Matthean favorite vocabulary and cherished theological ideas, making it difficult to isolate the text from the Gospel as a whole.[10]

The designation *catechism* proposed by modern scholars has flaws as well. Its major drawback is that it suggests teaching rather than proclamation. The SM has a strong proclamatory character because of its close relation to the "kingdom of heaven," which is announced by Jesus in 4:17, then referred to in 4:23 and repeatedly in the sermon itself. I find, nevertheless, that the classification catechism, though inadequate, calls to our attention important aspects of SM that broaden our understanding by helping us to situate the sermon in a particular social-cultural situation.

The classification "catechism" has a long history. Observing the presence of formalized teaching material in the New Testament, Alfred Seeberg, in 1903, proposed the existence of a common catechism in the

---

ing et al. (Sonoma: Polebridge, 1990) 19–34. Recent Gospel commentators commonly suppose that Q reached Matthew and Luke in slightly different versions.

6. Hans Dieter Betz, *The Sermon on the Mount*, Hermeneia (Minneapolis: Fortress, 1995) 60. Indeed, Betz's classification "epitome" stands in a humanistic tradition: the great humanist theologian Erasmus termed the SM a "compendium" because of its summary character.

7. Richard Lischer, "The Sermon on the Mount as Radical Pastoral Care," *Int* 41 (1987) 167.

8. Epictetus, *The Art of Living*, trans. Sharon Lebell (San Francisco: Harper, 1995) x.

9. See note 6.

10. Redaction-critical scholars overwhelmingly regard the SM as a Matthean composition, a point of view which I share.

early church that has left traces in New Testament texts.[11] Seeberg also suggested that this early church catechism was dependent on a catechism for proselytes used within contemporary Judaism. Neither view is held by scholars today, but for a period of time Seeberg's views were influential; C. H. Dodd in a number of works and E. G. Selwyn in the commentary on 1 Peter make this influence manifest.[12] In our day, again, the question of catechetical classification animates scholars both with regard to the wisdom material in Q and in the framework of social scientific approaches to the New Testament.

Among the speeches in Matthew, none has had greater impact than the Sermon on the Mount. So it was already in the early church; among the uses of the synoptic tradition in the writings before Irenaeus, most show similarity with, or are derivative from, the Gospel of Matthew and particularly the SM. M. Jack Suggs is convinced that this preferential usage witnesses to the prime place of obedience in the early church's message.[13] The Gospel of Matthew indeed stresses the importance of right conduct. In the SM we read, "Not everyone who says to me, 'Lord, Lord' will enter the kingdom of heaven, but only the one who does the will of my Father in heaven (7:21)." And the Gospel ends: "teaching them to observe everything that I have commanded you (28:20)."[14] Ernst von Dobschütz noticed and defined in literary terms the prevalent ethical emphasis of Matthew: "[Matthew] aims in this Gospel to provide the Christian community with a kind of church order and catechism of Christian behaviour."[15] In more general terms, Raymond E. Brown says that of all the Gospels, Matthew was best suited to the manifold needs of the later church and the most serviceable for catechetical purposes.[16]

What precisely made the Gospel of Matthew so useful? Wolf-Dietrich Köhler points to the discourses of the Gospel and suggests that

---

11. A. Seeberg, *Der Katechismus der Urchristenheit* (Leipzig: Deichert, 1903).

12. C. H. Dodd, *The Apostolic Preaching and Its Developments* (London: Hodder & Stoughton, 1936). E. G. Selwyn, *The First Epistle of St. Peter* (London: Macmillan & Co., 1952).

13. M. Jack Suggs, "The Christian Two Ways Tradition: Its Antiquity, Form and Function," in *Studies in New Testament and Early Christian Literature: Essays in Honor of Allen P. Wikgren*, ed. David Aune (Leiden: Brill, 1972) 74.

14. While my quotations normally are from the NRSV, here I use RSV, finding it more faithful to the Greek text because τηρεῖν ("keep") combines cognitive and volitional aspects. Betz's suggestion is worth considering: "'keep' . . . should not be taken to imply total obedience to a rigid code of rules and regulations. The term *terein* should rather be interpreted as 'preserve' a legacy and this is what the Gospel of Matthew is attempting to provide." H. D. Betz, "The Sermon on the Mount in Matthew's Interpretation," in *The Future of Early Christianity: Essays in Honor of Helmut Koester*, ed. Birger A. Pearson (Minneapolis: Fortress, 1991) 270.

15. Ernst von Dobschütz, "Matthew as Rabbi and Catechist," in *The Interpretation of Matthew*, ed. Graham Stanton (London/Philadelphia: SPCK/Fortress, 1983) 25–26.

16. Raymond E. Brown, *The Churches the Apostles Left Behind* (New York: Paulist, 1984)

with their thematic and well-organized fullness of contents including practical counsel easy to apply, they attracted the churches more than the Gospels of John, Mark, or Luke.[17] Dobschütz observed that Matthew not only systematizes the material but also formalizes it by means of repeated stereotyped phrases. I mentioned above the closure formula which occurs at the end of the five major discourses: the SM, the missionary discourse in chapter 10, the parables presented in chapter 13, the "church-order" of chapter 18, and the extensive eschatological discourse in chapters 24–25. Two more examples of Matthew's preference for stereotyped expressions will suffice: (1) A dozen or so quotations from the Hebrew Bible are introduced in a circumstantial and firmly fixed way emphasizing the notion of fulfillment; and (2) We hear six times that "there will be weeping and gnashing of teeth," a phrase that underscores the theme of judgment which is a strong current in Matthean theology. Dobschütz suggests that Matthew's inclination for repetition and stereotyped phrasing is a manifestation of rabbinic style; the Talmud excels in uniformity. Research on Matthew after Dobschütz (1928) has demonstrated, moreover, that in his skillful working with sources and traditions the Evangelist manifests himself not only as a former rabbi and a devoted catechist but also as an impressive theologian.

The Sermon on the Mount, to be sure, gives a summary of Jesus' teaching. Is it justified, then, to label it "catechism"? While I am reluctant to classify it that way, I am aware of some valuable insights that this particular position offers. For my part, I prefer to call the Sermon on the Mount a *programmatic speech with catechetical features*. In what follows, I will supply my reasons for this preference and will suggest that the SM is a foundational text, not primarily because it gives basic instruction about doctrine and ethics (catechism), but because it is *programmatic*. It was so in relation to Jesus' ministry, for the early church, and for communities of believers today—for us all as we search for essential human values and wrestle with questions of social justice.[18]

As an introduction to my discussion of the content and form of the SM, let me state my reasons for my understanding of the SM as a

---

124.

17. Wolf-Dietrich Köhler, *Die Rezeption des Matthäusevangeliums in der Zeit vor Irenäus* (Tübingen: J. C. B. Mohr [P. Siebeck], 1987) 534.

18. Observing the important role of the Two Ways alternative (7:13–14) for the SM as a whole and reflecting on the fundamental desire we have as human beings to choose the way of life we consider good, Betz says, "Discipleship is not simply a call to join a small sect of devotees of Jesus. Rather, it is a call to be human beings in an uncompromising way" (*Sermon*, 61).

"programmatic speech." First, I characterize the SM to be foundational in the sense that it gives us the first extended presentation by Jesus. Its programmatic character may be illustrated by contrast with the SP. In many respects, of course, the SP (Luke 6:20-49) resembles the SM, but in the Gospel of Luke, it is not the SP, but rather the section 4:16-30, the Sermon in Nazareth with its narrative context, that is programmatic. This is so not only because Luke's Sermon in Nazareth comes before the SP but also because of the content. Empowered by the Spirit (4:14) Jesus comes to the synagogue in Nazareth where he quotes a passage from Isaiah 61: "the Spirit of the Lord has sent me to proclaim the good news to the poor" (cf. Matt 5:3 and 11:5). The initial preaching of Jesus in the Gospel of Luke is a manifestation of the Spirit, an eschatological, fulfilling event inasmuch as it realizes God's promises. The Sermon on the Mount in the Gospel of Matthew follows Jesus' proclamation of the dawning of the kingdom of heaven in 4:17. The proclamation is an eschatological event, a manifestation of the proleptic presence of the future with the appearance of Jesus.[19] The SM demands, therefore, to be read in light of the nearness of the kingdom. As Ulrich Luz asserts, "The kingdom of heaven, promised for the future, governs the whole Sermon on the Mount."[20] In the Beatitudes (5:3-12), for example, "for theirs is the kingdom of heaven" forms an *inclusio* between verses 3 and 10. Thus the blessings are pronounced in the perspective of the kingdom of God. The Beatitudes constitute the first part of the *exordium* or introduction that sets the tone for the entire discourse.[21] The Sermon on the Mount, then, is foundational because of its programmatic relation to the kingdom of heaven.

Second, the SM is programmatic in that the kingdom of God language implies a *program*. "Kingdom" in the metaphor "kingdom of God," as Krister Stendahl says, has "a concrete and social dimension, with people and community restored."[22] In the narrative context of the SM (4:23-25), a gathering takes place with an implied subscription to a pattern of life under the auspices of the dynamic sovereignty of God (εὐαγγέλιον τῆς βασιλείας, 4:23). The allusion to Sinai given through the scenic information that Jesus ascends (ἀναβαίνει) the mountain (Ex 19:3 LXX, ἀναβαίνει) strengthens this understanding: Sinai-Torah and Jesus' διδαχή are antithetically related.[23] The term "programmatic" can be used only with caution because the kingdom of God is a meta-

---

19. Wolfgang Schrage, *The Ethics of the New Testament* (Philadelphia: Fortress, 1988) 19.
20. Ulrich Luz, *Matthew 1-7* (Minneapolis: Fortress, 1989) 213.
21. Betz, *Sermon*, 59.
22. Krister Stendahl, *Energy for Life* (Geneva: WCC, 1990) 26.
23. Gerhard Lohfink, "Wem gilt die Bergpredigt?" *ThQ* 163 (1983) 264-84.

phor. We all know that we can never catch a metaphor: metaphor is "the language of semantic motion."[24] Because of the dynamic and unfinished character of the SM in its attempts to expound on the metaphor kingdom of heaven, we can rightly say, with Krister Stendahl, that what the sermon presents is a "laboratory model." [25] The program is dynamic, not static.

In content, the Sermon on the Mount presents the teaching of Jesus in a summary way. The sermon begins with a series of blessings pronounced in the perspective of the kingdom of God, followed by a word of promise directed to the disciples in their mission to the world. Then, the Teacher of the Sermon on the Mount presents a new interpretation of Torah in the Antitheses (5:21–48). The section is organized on a 3+3 principle, that is, three Antitheses following on a first group of three. The body of the parenetical teaching is concluded with a general guide to human conduct, the Golden Rule (7:12), which forms an inclusion with 5:17 through the repetition of "the Law and the Prophets." Directions regarding religious practices occupy the middle part of the speech organized on the "Three Rules" model (6:1–18, cf. Tobit 12:8). An exhortation to make the fundamental decision of what way of life to pursue introduces the epilogue (7:13–14), which heavily builds on contrasts (7:15–27). The choice is presented as one between the narrow gate/way and the broad gate/way, the former leading to life, the latter to destruction; the parable of judgment is a forceful illustration of the alternatives (the fall of the house built on sand).

The Two Ways model that informs the epilogue was widely employed in catechetical teaching in ancient Judaism.[26] We find examples of the model in Qumran (1QS 3:13-4:26) and later in early Christian writings, e.g., the *Didache* and *The Epistle of Barnabas*. The more ancient precursor of the model is found in the book of Deuteronomy where Moses says, "I call heaven and earth to witness against you today that I have set before you life and death, blessings and curses. Choose life so that you and your descendants may live, loving the LORD your God, obeying him, and holding fast to him" (30:19-20). Compare the *incipit* of the *Didache*: "There are two ways, one of life and one of death; and between the two ways there is a great difference." The text that follows this introduction in the *Didache* presents the Way of Life; it does so first summarily through quoting the

---

24. Phyllis Trible, *God and the Rhetoric of Sexuality* (Philadelphia: Fortress, 1978) 17.
25. Stendahl, *Energy*, 48.
26. "Catechetical" here is taken broadly as proposed by Betz in his SM commentary: "much of the wisdom literature of Hellenistic Judaism can be called 'catechetical' since it comes from a school milieu and serves pedagogy" (*Sermon*, 72).

double love commandment in combination with the Golden Rule in its negative form: "'First, you must love God who made you, and second, your neighbor as yourself.' And whatever you want people to refrain from doing to you, you must not do to them" (1:2).[27] The passage has, as Kurt Niederwimmer comments, "a didactic and catechism-like character."[28] Following this summary statement in the *Didache* is an insertion of material very similar to that of the SM/SP, often referred to as *sectio evangelica*. Since the material included in this section (1:3b–1:6) appears to be older than the SM according to most scholars,[29] a comparative study of this part of the *Didache* recommends itself in our efforts to understand the genre of the SM.

THE *DIDACHE* AND THE
SERMON ON THE MOUNT

Considering the predominance of instructional material in the SM and the formulaic way in which it is presented, the presence of both the Three Rules and the Two Ways model of ethical teaching, and the affinities with the *Didache*, should we not conclude with a number of New Testament scholars that the SM is an example of early Christian catechism?

We must first ask what the designation "catechism" might mean in relation to a text from the first century. It would be anachronistic to think of something as formalized as Luther's *Small Catechism* with its question-and-answer format, a novelty in its time. Let us keep in mind, however, that the SM includes the Lord's Prayer and has a section on commandments taken from the Decalogue, ingredients of catechetical instruction for centuries. Should we conceive the SM as a "catechism in the making"? Certain aspects of catechism now become especially relevant to our question.

If catechism is taken as a comprehensive summary of Christian teaching for the purpose of prebaptismal instruction, then the label does not fit the SM for both chronological and literary reasons. With respect to chronology, it is open to question whether the instruction was intentionally prebaptismal at the time of Matthew.[30] Only with Hippolytus's *Apostolical Tradition* (ca. 200–220) is there firm evidence

---

27. Translation from Cyril C. Richardson, *Early Christian Fathers* (New York: Macmillan, 1970).

28. Kurt Niederwimmer, *Die Didache*, Kommentar zu den apostolischen Vätern (Göttingen: Vandenhoeck & Ruprecht, 1989) 92.

29. Ibid., 93–100.

30. Krister Stendahl, *The School of St. Matthew* (Philadelphia: Fortress, 1968) 22.

of an instituted catechumenate. *Second Clement*, from the mid-second century, attests for the first time a technical use of the verb κατηχεῖν in relation to baptismal instruction. While the New Testament includes a few occurrences of κατηχεῖν and while some of them carry the sense of "to give instruction concerning the content of faith," the instruction is not earmarked as baptismal instruction.[31] Matthew's Gospel is the only New Testament writing to employ, once, the noun καθηγητής ("instructor"), and that in the context of polemical discussions with the teaching authorities within Judaism of his time: "Nor are you to be called instructors, for you have one instructor (καθηγητής), the Messiah" (23:10).

Betz proposes a baptismal context for the Beatitudes. He finds that the predominant function of the beatitudes as a genre was liturgical in some sense; in the SM they therefore serve "as a reminder of the ritual experience." The ritual act presupposed would naturally be initiation through baptism. "Indeed," Betz continues, "this possibility is supported by the redactional framework in Matthew, according to which Christians are to be made disciples, baptized, and taught."[32] He alludes of course to Matt 28:19–20. Attractive as this suggestion might seem, I do not think it holds up to further scrutiny. For one thing, the Beatitudes are not addressed to the disciples only, but to a large crowd of other people as well. Therefore the Beatitudes serve rather as "invitations," or better, "eschatological blessings," than as reminders of an initiation experience.[33] Furthermore, in the Great Commission the stress is on "making disciples," with "baptizing" and "teaching" as two aspects of this activity stated without any indication of order. This is not to say that baptism is without importance for the evangelist Matthew, but only that it is nowhere in the Gospel established as either more or less important than teaching. On other grounds, too, the SM fails to meet typical standards of comprehensive Christian catechism: there is no mention of Jesus' death and resurrection. Karlmann Beyschlag is right to the point when he says that the SM is strikingly lacking in central New Testament concepts such as "faith" and even "love of neighbor." "Instead of the latter," says Beyschlag, "there is the commandment of enemy love."[34]

---

31. H.W. Beyer, "κατηχέω," in *TDNT* 3:638–39.

32. Betz, *Sermon*, 59.

33. The designation "eschatological blessings" comes from Robert A. Guelich, "The Matthean Beatitudes: 'Entrance-requirements' or Eschatological Blessings?" *JBL* 95 (1976) 415–34. "The tone of these beatitudes is more that of consolation and assurance than that of parenetic exhortation" (417).

34. Karlmann Beyschlag, "Zur Geschichte der Bergpredigt in der Alten Kirche," *ZThK* 74 (1977) 297.

The *Didache*, by contrast, does provide evidence of an explicit baptismal context for teaching. The document includes a series of precepts and advice in chapters 1–6 to which the instruction regarding baptism in 7:1 refers in retrospect: "baptize in this way, having said all this before."[35] The "catechism" of the *Didache*, though, is almost exclusively ethical; chapters 1–6 do not include much of the doctrinal material we usually associate with catechism. The rest of this clearly composite document should rather be classified as liturgical manual (7–10) and church order (11–15).[36]

If, on the grounds suggested above, one would agree to call *Didache* 1–6 "catechism-in-the-making," how close is the *Didache* to the SM in form and content? The sayings included in the first part of the *Didache* are loosely organized; one might say that they are strung together. We find examples of this also in the SM. For example Matthew 5:42 is combined with verses 40–41 by the means of catchword connection: "give" of verse 42 connects with the "give" of verse 40. The connection is not thematic because verses 40–41 speak of violence and verse 42 deals with giving/lending money without any mention of an element of force in the situation. The SM also contains sayings of different kinds, such as wisdom sayings and prophetic-apocalyptic sayings. Betz therefore suggests that the *logoi* of 7:28a functions as a designation of genre. He says, "The term *logoi* ('sayings') takes up the literary category of the components of the SM from the text itself."[37] But considering that the SM is one discourse among several in the Gospel of Matthew that include the term *logoi* in formulaic closure, the *logoi* of 7:28a is probably not as specific as Betz suggests. The same Greek word can refer to thematically coherent material, even extensive parables. (See the concluding formulae of chapters 18, 24, and 25.)[38]

---

35. My translation deviates from Richardson's who takes the prepositional prefix *pro-* attached to the saying verb in the sense of "public"; Gal 3:1 is an example where the same prefix has that force of public announcement. In *Didache* 7:1, however, the temporal force must be intended.

36. Chapter 16 deals with eschatology and, admittedly, that is the note on which the SM ends. But *Didache* chapter 16 has more similarity in content with Matthew 24 than with Matthew 7. Furthermore, in the SM, eschatology is not confined to chapter 7 but rather permeates the whole sermon.

37. Betz, in Pearson, *Future*, 266.

38. For his understanding of the SM as a collection of sayings, Betz turns to the fragment from Papias preserved by Eusebius where it is said that Matthew συνετάξατο the sayings of Jesus. Betz understands the verb to mean "collected," but other scholars prefer the meaning "arranged." Few ancient Christian texts have produced a greater variety of interpretations than the Papias fragment! I find "arranged" to be the more natural meaning, taking into account that it offers a fitting contrast to Mark's account of Jesus' sayings and deeds mentioned in the preceding part of the fragment; Papias characterizes Mark's account as having been done with accuracy but "not according to order (τάξει)."

I pointed above to the presence of a few organizational principles in the SM that give coherence to the material. By contrast, although there are structural features in *Didache* 1–6 that mark off distinctive units of material, the overall impression of the *Didache* is that it is loosely organized. A redactor has been at work, but his editorial intervention is slight.[39]

A more important difference between the two texts is the proclamatory nature of the SM facilitated by the consistent presence of the speaker in the text; by contrast, there is no authoritative "I" in *Didache* 1–6. Furthermore, there is a theological structure to the SM provided by the recurrent "your heavenly Father/your Father in heaven" in 5:16–7:11, a reference which has its center in the address of the Lord's Prayer, "Our Father in heaven." The *Didache*, on the other hand, lacks a theological focus. The two last differences make it especially difficult to place the *Didache* and the SM in the same category.

When Helmut Koester discusses the Gospel of Matthew in his *Introduction to the New Testament*, he presents the SM in the following words: "The Sermon on the Mount does not proclaim eschatological ethics, but a catechism for the community."[40] I disagree with the statement in its entirety, but to different degrees with its two parts. To the first part, I briefly retort: there is more here than ethics, but the ethics that *are* here are predominantly eschatological. Betz rightly claims that an eschatological perspective characterizes the whole of the SM.[41] One recalls that in the motivational clauses of the Beatitudes, all but verses 3 and 10 use the future tense; in these verses reference is made to the kingdom of heaven, itself future. Here the proclamation of ethics is intrinsic to the kingdom since the paradigmatic manifestation of the kingdom in Jesus calls for committed obedience. In the Matthean version of the Lord's Prayer—the text at the center of the SM—the petition "let your kingdom come" is followed by "let your will be done."[42] Thus does the SM emphasize the nexus of eschatology and ethics (obedience).

Koester's insistence that the SM is a "catechism for the community" is based, in part, on his understanding that this discourse, like

---

39. Niederwimmer, 64–77.

40. Helmut Koester, *Introduction to the New Testament* (New York: Walter De Gruyter, 1987) 2:176.

41. Betz, *Sermon*, 60.

42. The passive verb in the Greek is open for an understanding of both God and the human being as agents with the result that the petition can best be understood in light of Old Testament thought where "the will of the active God is always understood as the claim on an active partner" (Luz, *Matthew 1–7*, 380).

Matthew's other four discourses (chapters 10, 13, 18, 24–25), is a "church order." Such a classification is justified to the extent that the Gospel of Matthew does focus on the church and particularly so in the discourses. For example, in the Mission Discourse in Chapter 10 the disciples are commissioned to go out proclaiming and healing. But the narrative never tells us that the disciples leave for this mission. This is one indication among many that the disciples in the Gospel are "transparent" for the church of Matthew's own time, or as Frankemölle has phrased it, "they are not to be interpreted historically as concrete followers of Jesus; rather, they have a typological and paradigmatic meaning for the community of believers in Jesus."[43] Similarly, among the parables of chapter 13, the parable of the wheat and the weeds is significant for Matthew's ecclesiology. The church before the eschaton remains a *corpus mixtum*, a mix of good and evil, vulnerable to *skandala*.[44] The problem with the presence of the weeds is not solved until the final separation by the Son of Man acting as judge. In Matthew's theology, the church "is the place of those who must prove their worth, not that of the pure."[45] Chapter 18 is called the Discourse on Church Life for obvious reasons, and chapters 24–25 comprehend a final warning addressed to the church. But notwithstanding the ecclesiological dimension of the major discourses, "church order" is hardly an appropriate label unless taken in a very broad sense.

As we have seen, scholars compare the *Didache* to the SM in terms of catechism and church order. I agree that the section comprised of chapters 1–6 of the *Didache* is "catechism-like" for two basic literary reasons: (1) it employs the Two Ways model of teaching as structural principle, and (2) it comprises a collection of precepts and counsels relative to Christian life. Considering first the precepts and counsels in the *Didache*, we observe close parallels in the synoptic tradition (particularly with *Did*. 1:3b–2:1). How, then, does *Didache* 1–6 compare to the Sermon on the Mount? An examination of a teaching common to the two texts, the imperative love of enemies, will serve to illustrate the point.

---

43. Frankemölle, *Jahwe-Bund*, 143.
44. Ulrich Luz, *Das Evangelium nach Matthäus 2*, Evangelisch-katholischer Kommentar zum Neuen Testament (Zürich and Neukirchen–Vluyn: Benzinger/Neukirchener, 1985) 341.
45. Ulrich Luz, *The Theology of the Gospel of Matthew* (Cambridge: Cambridge University Press, 1995) 107.

1. Parallel Precepts and Counsels

Both the SM and *Didache* highlight this precept. Love of enemies is the topic of the last antithesis in Matthew 5 (vv 43–48). It is preceded by the antithesis to the law of retribution, which is illustrated by "turn the other cheek." The *Didache* (1:3a) also highlights the command to love one's enemies—first by way of position, and second by combining it with the addition in 1:4, "If someone strikes you on the right cheek, turn to him the other too, and you will be perfect [τέλειος]." The consequential addition introduced by "and" gives weight to the whole commandment. Matthew 5:48 emphasizes "love of enemies" by using the same qualification, "perfect," or better "complete/integrated," as Robin Scroggs and others have suggested.[46] The *Didache* further highlights the command to love one's enemies by expressing the commandment in a formalized manner: "Bless those who curse you and pray for your enemies and fast for those who persecute you" (1:3a). The command has a triadic form which Clayton N. Jefford explains as an instance of the so-called Three Rules formula found in other Jewish and Christian sources.[47] The same triad—charity, praying, and fasting—provides the organizing structure for Matthew 6:1–18. The application of the Three Rules formula "bless, pray, fast" to the precept "love of enemies" effects a change in the exhortation from the sphere of broad-based ethics to a specific form of piety.

The *Didache* includes, however, the univocal ethical command, "love those who hate you" (1:4). The imperative is part of the text unit that immediately follows the Three Rules command regarding one's enemies (1:3a).[48] The unit begins, "what credit is it to you if you love those who love you?" (1:3b). The wording is closer to Luke 6:32 than to the Matthean parallel in 5:46. The Matthean version does not include the term "credit" used in the parallel texts; rather, it contains "reward," a word with indisputable theological connotations. This means that Matthew has "theologized" a saying that had a more conventional human wisdom flavor on the level of Q. Another example

---

46. Robin Scroggs, "Eschatological Existence in Matthew and Paul: *Coincidentia Oppositorum,*" in *The Text and the Times: New Testament Essays for Today* (Minneapolis: Fortress, 1993) 247 and 250, where the climactic nature of τέλειος in 5:48 is highlighted and compared to 19:21.

47. Clayton N. Jefford, *The Sayings of Jesus and the Teachings of the Twelve Apostles* (Leiden: E. J. Brill) 44–45. Tobit 12:8 is an early example of this form: "Prayer with fasting is good, but better than both is almsgiving with righteousness. *Didache* offers still another closely related example of the Three Rules: "Say your prayers, give your charity, and do everything just as you find it in the gospel of the Lord" (15:4).

48. I disregard the exhortation "abstain from carnal passion" in 1:4a since it has all the appearance of being a later interpolation.

from the *Didache* will illustrate the same conceptual distinction. To the imperative "love those who hate you," a result clause is added: "and you will not have an enemy." Is this an example of a later stage of reflection as Köhler suggests?[49] Not necessarily. Worldly recompense is a typical motivation of exhortations in the wisdom tradition. Compare for example Proverbs 22:11, "Those who love a pure heart and are gracious in speech will have the king as a friend." The charge given in Matthew 5:44, "love your enemies," on the other hand, is part of a theological model of ethics where God's providential and generous love serves as an example to be imitated.

In the conclusion to the catechetical section (1–6), the *Didache* reads, "If you can bear the Lord's full yoke, you will be perfect [τέλειος]. But if you cannot, then do what you can" (6:2). Here we are dealing with a later softening by *Didache* of the more radical Matthean command. While in modern times the impossibility of fulfilling the SM is often stressed, in the ancient church this was not so. The church fathers asked, rather, "Who is able to do it?" In other words, the difficulties of implementation were recognized while the legitimacy of the demand was taken for granted.[50]

In a final point of comparison, I call attention to a thoroughgoing literary difference between the two treatments of the command to love one's enemies. In the SM, "turn the other cheek" serves as the antithesis to the law of retribution, namely, "do not resist an evildoer." This frame is absent from the *Didache*. That is to say, in the *Didache* we are not faced with the radical command to forgo our natural human inclination "to give back" or to put self-protection first. In addition to the lack of a framework such as the reference to the Torah in Matthew, the uniform series "if someone strikes/forces/deprives you" in the *Didache* has a juridical character absent in the equivalent sayings in the SM. The text of Matthew 5:39–41 reads, "whoever strikes," etc., which means that a particular situation is depicted in a provocative manner. In Robert C. Tannehill's words,

> The command does not do the hearer's thinking for him; it starts him thinking in a definite direction. Its meaning for a particular situation becomes apparent not through a process of legal deduction but only through the imaginative shock felt by the serious hearer, a shock which arouses the moral imagination, enabling the hearer to see his situation in a new way and to contemplate new possibilities of action.[51]

---

49. Köhler, *Rezeption*, 53.
50. Luz, *Matthew 1–7*; and Beyschlag, "Geschichte," 297–98.
51. Robert C. Tannehill, "The 'Focal Instance,'" in *The Sword of His Mouth* (Philadelphia and Missoula, MT: Fortress/Scholars Press, 1975) 74; reprint of an article published in 1970 (the

Thus, the *Didache* text, which does not slow down to include a particular situation like the court scene in Matt 5:40 (cf. *Didache* 1:4), does not involve the reader in the same intense way as does the SM.

2. The Two Ways

The other literary justification for classifying the *Didache* as catechism is that it employs the Two Ways model of teaching as a structural principle. Again we find a point of comparison between the *Didache*, which uses the model to frame the section 1-6, and the SM, where the same model appears in Matt 7:13-14. The metaphor "way" (signifying conduct) used in these two texts witnesses to the importance of ethics for the early church. "Life" signals an eschatological perspective for this moral teaching as does its contrast "death/destruction" which implies condemning judgment.

The Two Ways model is not only a pedagogical model or a traditional pattern of ethical exhortation, but serves specifically to sum up rules for the life of a religious community as we can see in the Rule of Discipline from Qumran (1QS). It serves thereby to delineate the boundaries of the group. Hence Suggs, speaking about the Two Ways tradition, says: "The genre's function in intensifying in-group/out-group consciousness and its relation to the social myth of the elect community point to its origin in sectarian Judaism."[52]

The Two Ways section of *Didache* (1-6) does, in fact, include admonitions to behavior that distinguishes the community from the gentile world. Two examples will suffice. First, in the framework of the Way of Life, "what credit is it to you if you love those who love you? Is that not the way the heathen act?" Second, as part of the Way of Death, a personalized list of vices includes the characterizing statement: "who do not know him who made them." This is a traditional way of referring to pagans in Jewish and Christian sources. A stance of reserve toward the pagan world comes across in the SM as well: "Do not even the tax-collectors do the same? . . . Do not even the Gentiles do the same?" (5:46-47). The Two Ways model serves well the social function of demarcating a community of a particular worldview from its environment where other views and values prevail; it also is apt to strengthen the sense of community identity and to initiate recent converts to a new symbolic world, i.e., "a system of shared meaning that

_____

date explains the lack of inclusive language).
52. Suggs, "Christian Two Ways," 73.

enables us to live together as a group."[53] Thus the designation "community catechism" for the Two Ways model makes a lot of sense.

THE PURPOSE OF THE TWO WAYS
IN THE SERMON ON THE MOUNT

In the *Didache* the Two Ways model serves as an organizational principle; it introduces the positive exhortations ("Way of Life" in 1:2) and the negative admonitions ("Way of Death" in 2:1). In the SM, however, the explicit model comes in *after* the ethical teaching has been summed up in 7:12. Even so, Betz affirms that "the ethical task itself is described by the image of the Two Ways"[54] and James G. Williams has a corresponding view when he identifies verses 7:13-14 as having "a recapitulatory role."[55] It seems to me, however, that Matthew 7:13-14 does not only refer back to the ethical teaching as summed up in 7:12, but also urges for a decision and warns about pending judgment. In other words, Matthew 7:13-14 goes beyond recapitulation to active urging.

Matthew 7:13-14 introduces the epilogue of the SM. As is the case with the concluding part of other Matthean discourses, here again the theme of judgment is invoked. Günther Bornkamm has demonstrated in a now classic study that Matthew's understanding of the church lies in close relation to the expectation of the end time.[56] Hubert Frankemölle suggests a model for this thematic connection: the book of Deuteronomy. In the discourses of Deuteronomy and other writings under deuteronomistic influence, the theme of judgment is often evoked for the purpose of warning the people of Israel.[57] Likewise, in Matthew's Gospel the judgment theme is not used to separate the community from the world; rather, it is used to beseech the church to stay faithful and live in accordance with the teaching of Jesus (see e.g., 7:24 and 18:23-35). Judgment is the privilege of the church, not to impose, but to receive.[58] In introducing the epilogue, Matthew 7:13-14 so stresses the either-or nature of the alternatives—"wide"

---

53. Luke Timothy Johnson, *The Writings of the New Testament: An Interpretation* (Philadelphia: Fortress, 1986) 13.

54. Betz, *Sermon*, 60.

55. James G. Williams, "Paraenesis, Excess, and Ethics: Matthew's Rhetoric in the Sermon on the Mount," *Semeia* 50 (1990) 168.

56. Günther Bornkamm, "End-Expectation and Church in Matthew" in *Tradition and Interpretation in Matthew*, ed. Günther Bornkamm, Gerhard Barth, and H. J. Held, 15-57 (Philadelphia: Westminster, 1963).

57. Frankemölle, *Jahwe-Bund*, 341.

58. The same point is made in 1 Pet 4:17: "For the time has come for judgment to begin with the household of God."

versus "narrow" and "destruction" versus "life"—that it becomes apparent that the intent of the text is not teaching ethics, as Betz suggests ("presenting the ethical task"), but rather prodding for a decision.

Another interpretation of 7:13–14 is based on alleged "sect" terminology in the passage. The contrast between "many" and "few" seems to encourage such a reading. Inasmuch as the Two Ways model can serve as a means of demarcating a community, this passage gives the impression that it wants to strengthen the community's understanding of itself. We have seen that this is a concern discernible both in the SM and in the *Didache*. James G. Williams, in fact, understands the whole SM in this way:

> Both the form and content of the SM point to a group of committed disciples who go apart with their teacher and are instructed by him concerning the meaning of the separated or sacred community that gathers around him."[59]

The Sermon on the Mount, however, has a double audience—the disciples *and* the others—and this fact has implications for the interpretation of the text as a whole. While it is true that Matthew gives special emphasis to the disciples, he does so "because they are the first persons to enact the Sermon," not because they are the only audience.[60]

Daniel Marguerat, in his study "Judgment in the Gospel of Matthew," presents a better interpretation of the "many" and the "few" in Matthew 7:13–14.[61] Marguerat argues that in these verses Matthew interprets the traditional motif of the Two Ways by applying it to his own community. We recall that "the way" is combined with "the gate," a rather unusual combination of motifs in Jewish texts but attested in 4 Ezra. In this combination one motif interprets the other: the decision to be faithful ("gate") must constantly be renewed ("way").[62] "Many" does not denote the mass of people outside the community, nor does "few" refer to a community of the elect. Rather, the "many" refers to those *within* the community who neglect obedience to the will of God (see 7:21–22). Thus, the choice of "many" serves the purpose of warning to those already *within* the community.

The last word of Matthew in the SM, however, is not one of judgment. The key placement of Matthew 7:13–14 as the introduction to

---

59. Williams, "Paraenesis," 164.

60. Luz, *Theology*, 43.

61. Daniel Marguerat, *Le Jugement dans l'Evangile de Matthieu*, 2d ed. (Geneva: Labor et Fides, 1995); pp. 175–82 discuss 7:13–14.

62. See also Jan Bergman, "Zum Zwei-Wege-Motiv; Religionsgeschichtliche und

the epilogue suggests that these verses should guide our understanding of the rest of the text. The introduction contains the keyword "find" (v. 14); one should therefore consider the teaching that precedes 7:13 as instruction that enables the hearers to find the "narrow gate/way." The passage incorporates *gospel:* it invites hearers to the "narrow gate" which Jesus through his teaching has made possible to find. The judgment theme, then, serves the purpose of entreating the community of believers to continue to walk the difficult and demanding way of faithfulness with ever-renewed decision.

In conclusion, although the Sermon on the Mount displays certain features of a "catechism for the community" as Helmut Koester contends, I find those features, e.g., regulation of particular practices, to be toned down in the Gospel of Matthew. They are subdued, I am suggesting, for the overall purpose of proclaiming the visionary and dynamic Good News to which, according to Matthew, "eschatological ethics" belongs.

I arrive then at my understanding of the Sermon on the Mount as a "programmatic speech with catechetical features." It is programmatic because it presents a model of action-wisdom to be enacted in an exemplary way by the disciples. It is programmatic because it issues a call for obedience to the will of God. Indeed, for centuries the Sermon on the Mount has served as a programmatic resource for theology in that it has effected both new constructions of theology and new conduct. Rather than the entire speech functioning as a regulatory unit, selected sayings have had an astounding peregrination throughout church history. These sayings have been understood to contain the whole of the Christian faith expressed in abridgment. For the ancient Church, "Blessed are the pure in heart, for they will see God" was of enormous theological significance. The saying became the quintessential vehicle of Christian mysticism and asceticism.[63]

Today, in my own home country, Sweden, "Look at the birds of the air" and "Consider the lilies of the field" inspire some Christians to challenge the church to proclaim and live a "theology of contentment." This theology includes an affirmation of a simple lifestyle and of spiritual abundance. I find this programmatic use of a passage from the Sermon on the Mount to be in tune with the totality of the text. Like a mighty resounding chord, initially set in the Beatitudes and repeated throughout the Sermon on the Mount, we can hear the theme of spiritual abundance. The action-wisdom urging of the text sounds with sincerity for all times.

---

exegetische Bemerkungen," *Svensk Exegetisk Årsbok* 41–42 (1976–77) 43.
    63. Beyschlag, *Geschichte*, 304–5.

PART II

READING

THE JEWISH CONTEXT OF

EARLY CHRISTIANITY

6

Moral Dualism and Virtues
in Matthew's Gospel

Deirdre Good

Lists of virtues attributable to gods were visible, audible, and legible in the Hellenistic world. On the walls of temples, stone inscriptions displayed the virtues and deeds of the deities Isis, Asclepius, and Serapis. Their aretalogies were probably read out loud, perhaps in a liturgical context and certainly with a view to promulgating the cult.[1] Likewise, in appreciation of an individual life, Hellenistic biographies often list an individual's attributes and his or her accomplishments, singling out commendable qualities or virtues. This is surely a worthy subject for a Festschrift in which we honor a colleague's academic contribution and achievements![2]

Today, virtues characterizing the life of an individual may reflect cultural values. Such lists may appear in written or oral form. For example, yesterday's newspapers describe Bob Dole's speech at the Republican National Convention as one echoing the traditional American values of God, family, honor, duty, and country. The nominee links his personal virtues to these values: "If I am combative, it is for love of country." He issues an invitation to the electorate based on the qualities of a government he hopes to lead: "And to anyone who believes that restraint, honor, and trust in the people cannot be returned to the government, I say, follow me."[3] Traditional American values, however, although they may have the rhetorical

---

1. See the Isis aretalogy in Apuleius, *Metamorphoses* 11.5.1–3.
2. The present study is part of a larger study on the meekness of Jesus. I would like to thank Professor Celia Deutsch for very helpful observations on an earlier draft.
3. "Dole's Speech Accepting the G.O.P. Nomination for President," *New York Times*, 16 August 1996, A26.

appeal of age and endurance, do not all go back as far as the first century. Even when words such as "honor" or "family" appear in ancient texts, they are not seen as values, nor do they carry the same meaning.[4] Use of the term "value" to reflect individual or social worth is a modern phenomenon.

Within the Christian tradition there is also a legacy of teaching about virtues. Humility, for example, was the starting point for the desert monks, both because it was the first commandment (Matt 5:3) and because they knew that without the self-emptying implied by humility, the treasures for which they had come to the desert would forever elude them.[5] The desert fathers strove to incorporate the humility of Christ and the Gospels into their lives. For practitioners of that specifically Christian virtue, humility was as vital as the breath of life itself. As Amma Syncletica said, "Just as one cannot build a ship unless one has some nails, so it is impossible to be saved without humility."[6] Humility was as elusive as it was desired.

Thomas Aquinas represents virtue as a habit of the soul, either potentially or actually. Virtues are acquired either by one's own actions (the so-called cardinal virtues of prudence, justice, temperance, and fortitude) or by the grace of divine infusion (the theological virtues of faith, hope, and love). All virtues can increase and grow, and by the same token, may decrease and be lost.[7]

Interest in virtue continues well into the nineteenth century where, in the writings of Schleiermacher, there is a quartet of virtues: the power of symbolization (thought of as inspiring and struggling) and the powers of organizing, of producing love, and of fortitude.[8] Early twentieth-century Protestant ethics shows a remarkable lack of interest in a theory of virtues and a concomitant attempt to sever the meaning of New Testament lists of virtues from the meaning of similar Greek lists in biographies or aretalogies.[9] Unfortunately, this tendency has by no means disappeared. In writers exposed to Catholic religious tradi-

---

4. Carolyn Osiek, "The Family in Early Christianity: 'Family Values' Revisited," *CBQ* 58 (1996) 1–24.

5. For discussion, see Douglas Burton-Christie, *The Word in the Desert: Scripture and the Quest for Holiness in Early Christian Monasticism* (New York: Oxford University Press, 1993) 236–60.

6. Syncletica 26 in Jean-Claude Guy, *Recherches sur la tradition grecque des Apophthegmata Patrum*, Subsidia Hagiographa 36 (Brussels: Société des Bollandistes, 1962) S9;35.

7. Aquinas, *Summa Theologiae* II qq. 49–55. For discussion, see Jean Porter, *The Recovery of Virtue: The Relevance of Aquinas for Christian Ethics* (Louisville, KY: Westminster/John Knox, 1990).

8. *F. Schleiermachers saemmtliche Werke*, Dritte Abteilung: Zur Philosophie, II (Berlin, 1838) 350–78.

9. Eilert Herms, "Virtue: A Neglected Concept in Protestant Ethics," *SJT* 35 (1981) 481–95.

tions, by contrast, discussion of virtues is very much alive. In the essays of Simone Weil (d. 1943), for example, an argument is made for the centrality of humility in religious life as a sign of the recognition of limits. As well as being a transcendent quality, humility, she insists, should be the goal of all academic inquiry. It is allied to the faculty of attention.[10] Where do the New Testament writers fit within this varied history of both interest and lack of interest in virtues?

The New Testament does, of course, list virtues: "Now the fruit of the spirit is love, joy, peace, patience, kindness, goodness, faithfulness, meekness, [and] self-control."[11] In Paul's writings, such qualities become the basis of a personal appeal: "I, Paul, myself entreat you, by the meekness and gentleness of Christ . . ."[12] Sometimes the New Testament ascribes certain virtues to Christ. For the most part, however, lists of virtues have no intrinsic connection to the person of Christ. They are commendable insofar as they reflect new behavior patterns. Often they are accompanied by a list of contrasting qualities from the old way of life.[13]

Certain virtues are highlighted in Matthew's Gospel. They describe individuals in the Gospel. Joseph is called "just" or "righteous" when he does not wish to make an example of Mary; Jesus invites others to learn from him for he is "meek" and "humble in heart." These descriptions reflect individual qualities deemed valuable by the society of which Matthew was a part. By themselves they simply describe certain states. However, in the course of the narrative, cognate verbs of these states address groups of people. This indicates that Matthew understands qualities not just as modes of being but as *community* virtues. At the same time, these quiet virtues appear in a world of moral dualism juxtaposing positive and negative attributes: righteous and unrighteous, sensible and foolish, good and evil. This dualistic language reflects an apocalyptic worldview in which the world is seen as essentially divided into moral opposites. Such language is found in texts of the Second Temple period, particularly those from Qumran.

Placing the exercise of virtues within the context of apocalyptic language serves to remove the reader of Matthew's Gospel from the

---

10. Simone Weil, "Reflections on the Right Use of School Studies with a View to the Love of God" and "The Father's Silence" in *The Simone Weil Reader*, ed. George Panichas (Wakefield, Rhode Island, and London: Moyer Bell, 1977). Also to be taken into account is the work of Alasdair MacIntyre, alongside that of other philosophers ably summarized by Martha Nussbaum in "Virtue Revived: Habit, Passion, Reflection in the Aristotelian Tradition," *Times Literary Supplement* (3 July 1992) 9–11.

11. Gal 5:22; cf. Phil 4:8; 1 Pet 2:9; 2 Pet 1:3, 5.

12. 1 Cor 10:1.

13. Gal 5:2; Phil 3:18–19; 1 Pet 2:1; 2 Pet 1:9.

calm world of philosophical contemplation. It also serves to refine general discussions of Mediterranean social values.[14] In Matthew's Gospel good and bad, life and death, are all around. This context means that the consequences of exercising a virtue are seen almost immediately. Thus, Joseph's righteousness in associating with Mary becomes an occasion for terror. To avoid consequences of life and death, he must take the family and withdraw to Egypt. The meek sovereignty of Jesus entering Jerusalem foreshadows his own humiliation and death. The dream of Pilate's wife identifying Jesus as righteous occurs when he is on trial for sedition. In apocalyptic thought, time frames and life spans tend to shorten. The virtuous act itself contributes to one or the other moral absolute.

Thus, to explore the moral landscape of Matthew's Gospel one needs to know something about Jewish virtues in the Hellenistic period, virtues in Hellenistic philosophical texts and biographies, and Mediterranean social values. Most important however is the distinctive apocalyptic tone characterizing Matthew's Gospel, for it is this apocalyptic context in Matthew that frames the expression of virtues.

MORAL DUALISM

In Matthew's Gospel, God's sun shines and the rain falls indiscriminately on the just and the unjust, on the evil and the good (5:45). The good and the bad attend weddings (22:10), and in the parable of the wheat and the tares, just like that of the dragnet, both the good and the rotten (13:48) lead a generally undisturbed life until harvest time or "the close of the age" when they are sorted. God treats both sets of people apparently without distinction. This rationale is given for praying for one's enemies, as well as for greeting people other than one's brothers (and sisters; 5:44–46).

Thus, the world is full of undifferentiated good and bad.[15] But it is not that simple. Jesus himself holds to and teaches absolute distinctions: "The good person brings good things out of a good treasure, and the evil person brings evil things out of an evil treasure" (12:35). But he also recognizes a disconcerting problem: people can say good things but be evil (12:34); they can look righteous but inside be lawless (23:28). This is on the one hand a question of perception and on the

---

14. John J. Pilch and Bruce Malina, *Biblical Social Values and Their Meaning: A Handbook* (Peabody, MA: Hendrickson, 1993) is generally helpful but not specific enough since each term takes on different nuances in a particular literary context.

15. See chart at the end of this essay, p. 123.

other a flaw in the moral order, for it means that absolute distinctions do not hold. One solution to this dilemma in Matthew is fragmentation: body parts may be good and healthy or unhealthy and evil: "The eye is the lamp of the body. If your eye is healthy, your whole body is full of light, but if your eye is unhealthy, your whole body will be full of darkness. If the light in you is darkness, how great the darkness!" (6:22–23). This is an exclamatory observation and nothing more. It addresses the disciples, and through them the crowds. Elsewhere Jesus recommends the excision of a body part when it becomes an occasion for stumbling (18:8–9).[16]

Another solution to the dilemma of people who say good things but are nevertheless evil lies in the way Matthew explicitly connects moral dualism to apocalyptic thought. Jesus uses parables to teach that differentiation between good and bad is to be withheld until the day of judgment when the angels will divide one from the other. This at least temporarily contains the problem of the duplicity of those who say good things but who are in fact evil (12:36–37). It defers the conundra of the wheat and the tares and the good and rotten fish. Since these two cases appear in parables about the kingdom, it would not be difficult to argue that Matthew's community is composed of good and bad. But we can see the puzzle behind the disciples' question: "Master, did you not sow good seed in your field? Where, then, did these weeds come from?" (13:27). The parable solves the problem of their existence: they are to be left alone until the end. But then what about right and wrong? What about justice and injustice, righteousness and unrighteousness?

Behind the English words "just/ice" and "right/eousness" or the verbs "to justify" and "to make right" in Matthew's Gospel lies a single Greek root. The "many prophets and righteous people" of 13:17 gives the general meaning of the noun which designates a class of the pious in ancient Israel like the prophets. In Matthew, "the righteous" are contrasted with "the unjust" in 5:45, and in 13:49 with "evil ones." Both Joseph (1:19) and Jesus (27:19) are called "righteous" in Matthew. The narrator describes Joseph as a just man and Pilate's wife warns him about Jesus: "Have nothing to do with that righteous man for I have suffered much over him today in a dream."[17] Jesus himself speaks of the righteous (or innocent) Abel in 23:25.

A group of righteous people is vindicated in the Great Judgment for their conduct toward the hungry or thirsty or those in prison. In the judgment scene, the righteous are divided from "those on the left."

---

16. Perhaps this is a reference to any vice within an individual that leads to sin.
17. Matt 27:19. The NRSV translates "innocent man."

Thus, righteousness is linked to righteous acts not done ostentatiously.[18] But they must be done. Jesus himself is baptized by John "to fulfill all righteousness" (3:15). He warns listeners of the Sermon on the Mount that they will not enter the kingdom "unless their righteousness exceeds that of the scribes and Pharisees" (5:20). At the end of the sermon, the person who hears his words and does them is compared to a sensible man who built a house on stable foundations. A foolish person simply hears the words and does nothing.

As a consequence of their actions the righteous may expect mistreatment. This even Jesus himself mentions from the example of Abel through prophetic figures (23:35). Vindication in the form of eternal life is a future promise while "those on the left" may expect only eternal punishment (25:46).

Not only actions but also words cause a person to be justified or condemned on the day of judgment (12:37). What about actions or words during one's lifetime? Here, the parable of the laborers in the vineyard is instructive. To the laborers hired after the beginning of the day, the owner of the vineyard says: "You also go into the vineyard, and whatever is just, I will pay you."[19] Those hired first, reckoning that they would be paid more at the end of the day, grumbled against the vineyard owner. "Those last ones worked only one hour, and you made them equal to us, the ones who bore the brunt of the day and the heat." The vineyard owner replies to one of them,

> Friend, I did not treat you unjustly. Did you not agree with me for a day's wage? Take what is yours and go. For I wish to give to the last what I gave to you. Is it not lawful for me to do what I want with what is mine? Or is your eye evil because I am good? (Matt 20:13–15).

The vineyard owner holds to the principle of what is just (or right) and chides one who, on another principle (equal work for equal pay), argues against equivalent payment. The vineyard owner is accountable even as he dismisses the grumbler whose eye is evil. The world of moral alternatives (good/evil; what is right or just/what is wrong or unjust) is not bridged, but the hired laborer's perception of wrongdoing on the part of the vineyard owner causes the owner to explain his action. In the light of other parables in which no obvious explanation is given for the conduct of the chief subject, the vineyard owner's accountability in this parable is an important defense of justice.

---

18. Matt 6:1: "Beware of practicing your piety [lit. "righteousness"] before men in order to be seen by them; for then you will have no reward from your father who is in heaven."

19. Matt 20:4. The NRSV translates "whatever is right."

In the parable of the king who gave a wedding banquet for his son, after the invitations have been turned down by the invited guests, the enraged king destroys the murderers of his servants and burns their city. His servants go out and invite whomever they can find—good and bad alike—to the wedding feast. The king notices one of the guests without a wedding garment. When called to account the guest is silent. The king commands that he be bound hand and foot and cast into outer darkness.[20]

We may conclude that Matthew's community consists of good and bad, right and wrong. Individuals are accountable both for what they do and for what they say. Sometimes the standards to which they are held accountable are clear, and sometimes they are not. However, all actions form the basis of judgment.

VIRTUES IN GREEK TEXTS

The Greek word behind the English term "virtue" has a long and rich history. It connotes goodness or excellence of any kind. The same quality has different attributes in women and men: in women, excellence is more an innate quality[21] while in men it often signifies valor or brave deeds.[22] Philosophical texts like those of Aristotle and Plato laud virtues in general and in particular those virtues of self-control, meekness, justice, and courage. Praise of these quiet virtues implicitly challenges an older value system of competitive virtues found in the Homeric epics.[23]

Authors in the Hellenistic period esteem the quiet virtues. The fourth-century (B.C.E.) writer Isocrates commends the practice of meekness to the future Cyprian king Nicocles. To be meek is to be compassionate and kind: "Do nothing," says Isocrates, "in anger. . . . Show yourself stern by overlooking nothing that happens, but kind by making the punishment less than the offense."[24]

A good illustration of the juxtaposition of competitive values with quieter ones in the Hellenistic period may be seen in the encomium of Evagoras by Isocrates, a rhetorical eulogy written sometime after his

---

20. Matt 22:1–14.

21. The Greek word is ἀρετή. Homer, *Odyssey* 2.206: "And we [the suitors of Penelope, the wife of Odysseus] on our part wait here day after day by reason of her *excellence* and go not after other women whom each one might fitly wed."

22. Herodotus, *Histories* 1.176: "When Harpagus led his army into the plain of Xanthus, the Lycians came out to meet him and showed *brave deeds* fighting few against many."

23. Arthur W. H. Adkins, *Merit and Responsibility: A Study in Greek Values* (Oxford: Clarendon, 1960) 36–38.

24. Isocrates, *To Nicocles* 23.

death in 374 B.C.E. The literary convention of a eulogy is written, of course, in order to praise the achievements of the dead. But at the conclusion of this eulogy in a demonstration of the general excellence of Evagoras and in particular of his courage and his wisdom, Isocrates praises the martial achievements through which Evagoras became king, the restoration of honor to his family, the transformation of the barbarian (i.e., non-Greeks into Greeks), and the civilizing and taming of a wild and inhospitable country. That Isocrates praises Evagoras for the taming and domestication of a country alongside more traditionally competitive achievements shows that the juxtaposition of two sets of values within the life of one educated ruler is thought to be admirable during this period. Isocrates says that he cannot choose which of these accomplishments is the greatest. As well as respecting the conventions of the genre, he is saying that he esteems the life of Evagoras for both the competitive and the quiet virtues that he exemplified.

Several centuries later, in the writings of the philosopher Plutarch, we find an extensive exploration of the quiet virtues.[25] In his treatise *On the Control of Anger*, Sulla comments on the change he observes in his friend Fundanus after a year's absence, noting that his friend's temper has become "mild and subservient to reason."[26] Fundanus embarks, then, on a lengthy explanation of how his anger has become tempered and how, once his cure began, he began to observe ire in others. He marvels at the transformation of expression and the demeanor it effects. To reinforce his proposals, Plutarch attacks the value structure that reinforces anger, and it is in this attack by Plutarch that we see how the competitive virtues have given way to the quiet virtues. Contrary to those who confuse the turbulence of anger with activity, its blustering nature with confident boldness, its obstinacy with strength of character, its cruelty with magnificence, or its implacability with firm resolve, anger is in reality "not well-bred, or manly, nor possessing any quality of pride or greatness."[27] The

---

25. Here, I am concentrating in particular on meekness and humility since these adjectives describe Jesus in Matthew's Gospel. See the general discussion of Jacqueline de Romilly, *La Douceur dans la pensée grecque* (Paris: Les Belles Lettres, 1979). It is remarkable how the English term "meek" has all but disappeared from modern translations of the Bible. The richness of the English word and its use in the English-speaking world is another topic of discussion. Its gradual eclipse may be traced back to eighteenth- and nineteenth-century discussions of the term "meekness" particularly in Matthew's Gospel. See John Farrer, *Sermons on the Mission and Character of Christ and on the Beatitudes* (Oxford: Oxford University Press, 1804); and William Porcher DuBose, *The Gospel in the Gospels* (London: Longmans, Green and Co., 1906). The prominent British scholar at Oxford, William Sanday, particularly commended DuBose's work on meekness. See Sanday, *The Life of Christ in Recent Research* (New York: Oxford University Press, 1907).

26. Plutarch, *On the Control of Anger* 453c. The word "mild" here is "meek" elsewhere.

27. Plutarch, *On the Control of Anger* 456–57.

demeanor of angry persons declares their smallness and weakness, not only when they rage against inferiors such as women, children, and animals, but also in the slaughter done by tyrants.

Here, Plutarch advances his argument by identifying tyrants as weak and sick. The tyrant who assumes that his vengeful retaliation against his enemies demonstrates his virtuous courage and justice is, from the perspective of Plutarch, consumed rather by the vice of anger. Plutarch advocates another value system: one which replaces the pair "courageous and just" with the preferable virtues of "justice and meekness." In support of this system he cites numerous examples of courage and meekness in rulers. Philip of Macedon, for example, met the hostility of an enemy with kindness and so transformed his enemy's attitude that he became Philip's eulogist.

Meekness, in the writings of Hellenistic authors, is the product of conscious effort rather than an emotional state. The source of virtuous practice is education itself, which Plutarch commends because it enhances cooperative virtues. Some people are said to possess meekness naturally; in most it is the result of training. It is an inner moral condition visible in a person's appearance and bearing, in facial expression and sound of voice, in self-control, and in equanimity. Above all, meekness stems from a care for others made buoyant by awareness of a common humanity. One cannot feel compassion for others if one does not care for them. Tyrants do not care for the feelings of slaves; a humane master of the household does.

Since all these attributes oppose severity and the excesses of tyranny, and since meekness moves judges and the powerful to clemency, it became in the Hellenistic world a constant epithet for the emperor, kings, and high officials.

Of what relevance is the idea of meekness in some Greek writers to Matthew's Gospel? For scholars of an earlier generation, nurtured on the Greek classics, the meekness of Jesus in Matthew 11:29 and the blessed state of the meek in Matthew 5:5 cannot be understood without reference to Greek writings.

RECENT SCHOLARSHIP

Contemporary scholars disagree in assessing the relevance of Greek material for an understanding of the terms "meek" and "humble" in Matthew's Gospel. On the one hand, Ulrich Luz proposes that Matthew's use of the term is influenced more by "the tradition of ecclesiastical interpretation" than by "Greek usage."[28] To illustrate the former he cites Gregory of Nyssa's *Homily on the Beatitudes* and for the latter Aristotle's *Nicomachean Ethics.* He thinks that Jewish-Christian usage influences Matthew since the beatitude is a quotation of Psalm 36:11. The meek stand for the Hebrew "poor," and the term comes to mean humble. This is shown in New Testament passages like Matthew 11:29 where the terms "meek" and "humble" lie side by side. Matthew 11:29 includes the element of kindness while 21:5 includes the idea of nonviolence. Meekness, for Matthew, is thus humility demonstrated in kindness, not the renunciation of power or a political strategy of pacifism.[29]

On the other hand, Hans-Dieter Betz states that "there is no question . . . that the [Sermon on the Mount] joins with the Hellenistic world in general when it singles out meekness as a fundamental ethical standard," and he cites in support an array of Greek writers.[30]

Both perspectives indicate, of course, what each author thinks of Matthew in general: what sort of writing it is (*genre*), its environment (*milieu*), and for whom it is written (audience). For Luz, although Matthew looks like a Hellenistic biography, it is actually not a typical story of an exemplary human being but the unique story of God with the human Jesus. The Matthean genealogy of chapter 1 and the discourses within the broad context of the story of Jesus suggest rather that the Gospel is a historical proclamation modeled on Mark. Behind the Gospel lie Jewish-Christian partly scribal circles and a worshipping community.[31] This community decided to carry the proclamation of Jesus to the Gentiles. Matthew stands on the threshold in defense of this mission to the Gentiles. The Sermon on the Mount itself is a composition of architectonic symmetry shaped by Matthew himself. At its center is the Lord's Prayer. This ring composition of the sermon stretches into the wider context of the Gospel itself.[32]

For Betz, the Sermon on the Mount is a type of literature called an *epitome,* or summary, in this case a summary of Jesus' teaching. It was compiled from various (oral and written) sources in Jewish-Christian

28. Ulrich Luz, *Matthew 1–7, A Commentary* (Minneapolis: Augsburg, 1989) 236.

29. Luz, *Matthew*, 236. Luz begins his discussion by linking the semantic range of the word to the observation that it becomes a mirror of each interpreter's piety. In this way, the projection of the interpreters supplants the range of interpretations the term conveys. While not denying that interpreters could emphasize aspects of meekness to match their religious outlook, one might ask whether the semantic range of the word does not facilitate this landscape of interpretation.

30. Hans-Dieter Betz, *The Sermon on the Mount* (Minneapolis: Augsburg Fortress, 1995) 126.

31. Luz, *Matthew*, 77–78.

32. Ibid., 212–13.

circles within one generation after Jesus' death in order to instruct converts from Judaism. The sermon argues for use of the fundamental
teachings of Jesus in terms of Jewish theology.[33] Other examples of
such summaries considered essential within Jewish movements of the
time include *The Manual of Discipline* and the *Damascus Document*
from Qumran. From Rabbinic Judaism one may cite the *Pirqe ʿAbot*
and the *ʿAbot de Rabbi Nathan*. On the Greek side there are important
literary precursors in Epictetus's *Encheiridion*, a handbook compilation
of the philosopher's sayings, and its prototype, Epicurus's *Principal
Doctrines*. Within the sermon itself literary evidence such as the functional terms of sense perception (the use of verbs of seeing and knowing in 5:16 and 6:3), reflection (the use of the verb "to think" in 6:7),
and practice (the use of the verb "to do" in 7:24) point to exercises
like those in Hellenistic philosophy. All these examples are provided in
order to assist listeners in appropriating an ethical tradition; in the case
of the Sermon on the Mount, for a Jewish listener to hear and put into
practice the teachings of Jesus.

Betz's position is carefully nuanced. Such philosophical language
as exists within the sermon would be familiar to first-century Jewish
ears. His work relies on a broad understanding of Jewish movements
of the period that have already appropriated Greek concepts and language. The term "meek" for example, already familiar in Greek ethics,
was used by Greek translators of the Hebrew Bible to interpret the
Hebrew word "poor" for Greek-speaking readers. Luz's position is
exactly the opposite: the Hebrew word "poor" circumscribes the meaning of the Greek word.[34] Betz argues that Matthew understands the
virtue "mildness," "gentleness," or "meekness" as an ethical standard,
closely associated with philanthropy and underlying many passages in
the Sermon on the Mount: 5:21-26, 38-42, 43-48; 6:12, 14-15. The
opposites of meekness were brutality and untamed anger. Meekness
becomes part of the description of a Christian sage elsewhere in the
New Testament.[35]

I suggest that an examination of the uses of the Hebrew plural
עֲנָוִים (translated "poor," "humble," or "meek" in English) in Jewish
sources before or during the first century C.E. will enable us to move
beyond the alternatives of Luz and Betz. Do these Jewish texts
understand the Hebrew term more narrowly or more broadly? Such an
analysis would imply some influence from Greek ideas but not neces-

---

33. Betz, *Sermon*, 73, 80, 88.
34. Luz, *Matthew*, 236.
35. Betz, *Sermon*, 126-27; see James 3:13.

sarily literary borrowing. That is, while I will be considering in what follows specific terms and translations of terms, the *ideas* that underlie these particular terms will be my primary focus. We already know that the term עֲנָוִים appears in the Hebrew text of Psalm 37:11 (LXX Ps 36:11) and that this is translated "meek" (πραεῖς) in the Septuagint. This LXX translation of the psalm is reflected in Matthew's use of πραεῖς at 5:5. The same Greek term describes Moses in the Septuagint translation of Numbers 12:2 and occurs elsewhere in the Septuagint.[36] Are there other uses of the Hebrew term in the same period that can shed light on Matthew's understanding of meekness?

My argument here is that the use of עֲנָוִים in the *Rule of the Community* from the Dead Sea Scrolls shows that this term conveyed a broad understanding of meekness that is in line with the Greek conception of this virtue. If one Jewish community understood the Hebrew term עֲנָוִים in a wider conceptual sense than simply "the poor" or "the humble," then the Septuagint translators of Psalm 36:11 may have done so too. Thus a broader reading of Matthew's use of πραεῖς, translated "meek," would be more plausible.

THE MEEK IN THE DEAD SEA SCROLLS

The Dead Sea Scrolls refer to many manuscripts found in the ruins or caves of the Wadis of the Judean desert. Amongst them are the manuscripts of Qumran written in Hebrew, Aramaic, or Greek and found in eleven caves in the area around Khirbet Qumran either through excavation or purchase on the antiquities market. The manuscripts from Qumran are from the period before the destruction of the site in the war against Rome in the first century C.E.[37] *The Rule of the Community* (1QS) consists of regulations governing the life of the community. Descriptions of the community, its organization, its self-regulation, and indeed its self-understanding characterize the text.[38]

The Rule of the Community (hereafter *The Rule*) opens with a declaration of purpose (although there are lines missing):

> . . . in order to seek God with all (one's) heart and with all (one's) soul; in order to do what is good and just in his presence, as commanded by

---

36. (LXX) Pss 24:9; 75:10; 147:6; 149:4.

37. Florentino Garcia Martinez, *The Dead Sea Scrolls Translated: The Qumran Texts in English*, 2d ed. (Leiden: Brill, and Grand Rapids, MI: Eerdmans, 1996).

38. *The Rule of the Community* is a composite text bearing signs of continual revision. It is not possible yet to say whether the existence of several copies in different caves suggests widespread use or an originally single and continuous text. They do suggest shaping of the text over time.

means of the hand of Moses and his servants the prophets . . . in order to love everything he selects and to hate everything he rejects; in order to keep oneself at a distance from all evil . . . ; to bring about truth, justice and uprightness on earth and not to walk in the stubbornness of a guilty heart and lecherous eyes performing every evil; in order to welcome into the covenant of kindness all those who freely volunteer to carry out God's decrees. . . .[39]

Entering individuals shall establish a covenant before God to carry out commands. In a collective voice they confess sins and are blessed by priests. Curses on outsiders follow to which the initiands respond "Amen." The priests enter the rule first, followed by the Levites, and then all the people "so that all the children of Israel may know their standing in God's Community. . . ."[40] A statement about the stability of the hierarchy is followed by the rationale: "For all shall be a single Community of truth, of proper meekness, of compassionate love and upright purpose, towards each other in the holy council, associates of an everlasting society." Here, "meekness" (ענוה) describes the Community of truth. It is part of a list defining social behavior in the community.

Shortly afterward, in typically dualist language, the document describes the God of Israel and the angel of his truth assisting all the "Sons of Light," a frequent term describing members of the Community. The text sets the Sons of Light over and against the Sons of Darkness outside the company. The paths of the Sons of Light in the world are "to enlighten the heart of man" and

to establish in his heart respect for the precepts of God; it is a spirit of meekness, of patience, generous compassion, eternal goodness, intelligence, understanding, potent wisdom which trusts in all the deeds of God and depends on his abundant mercy; a spirit of knowledge in all the plans of action, of enthusiasm for the decrees of justice, of holy plans with firm purpose, of generous compassion with all the sons of truth, of magnificent purity which detests all unclean idols, of unpretentious behavior with moderation in everything, of prudence in respect of the truth concerning the mysteries of knowledge.[41]

This list of virtues is a description of the inner orientation of a member of the Community that shapes social behavior. It starts, probably in order of primacy, with "the spirit of meekness."

39. Martinez, *The Dead Sea Scrolls*, 3.
40. IQS2, 18.
41. IQS3, 24–4, 6. Cited in Martinez, *The Dead Sea Scrolls*, 6.

The next passage in *The Rule* concerns the reproof of a community member.

> Each should reproach his fellow in truth, in meekness and in compassionate love for the man. . . . No one should speak to his brother in anger or muttering, or with a hard neck or with passionate spiteful intent and he should not detest him in the stubbornness of his heart, but instead reproach him that day so as not to incur a sin for his fault.[42]

This passage is particularly interesting in that it, in a fashion much like we saw in Plutarch, contrasts anger with meekness and links the latter to "compassionate love."

The final passage is fragmentary, but it is part of a section toward the end of the text in which an individual utters a blessing to God. Presumably the individual speaks in the "spirit of meekness" described in column 4:

> I shall share out the regulation with the cord of the ages
> . . . justice and compassionate love with the oppressed,
> and to strengthen the hands of the . . .
> understanding of those with a stray spirit
> in order to instruct in the teaching those who complain
> to reply with meekness to the haughty of spirit,
> and with a repentant spirit to the men of the stick,
> those who point the finger and speak evil,
> and are keen on riches.[43]

In this passage, the purpose clause "in order" is followed by the infinitive "to instruct." The object of the instruction are "those who complain" who are taught further "to reply with meekness" to the haughty. Again, as in Plutarch, meekness is thus learned rather than innate. This would then accord with the "spirit of meekness" the individual acquires in column 1.

The interpretation of Psalm 37 in another Dead Sea Scroll text, 4Q171, simply understands "the poor" of 37:11 to describe the "congregation of the poor."[44]

Thus, four texts from *The Rule of the Community* imply that meekness is a dispositional virtue to be learned, that it is the chief characteristic of community members and the whole company, and that it is to be used in a disciplined fashion to reproach a brother. It is also thought

---

42. IQS5, 24–6, 1. Cited in Martinez, *The Dead Sea Scrolls*, 9.

43. IQS10, 26–11, 2.

44. 4Q171 cited in Martinez, *The Dead Sea Scrolls*, 203–6. IQ15, *The Zephaniah Pesher*, is too fragmentary to deduce what might have been of the use of "a meek and humble people" in 3:12.

of in contrast to anger and haughtiness. All these imply a broader understanding of עֲנָוָה than one in which it could be seen simply as being "humble," "poor," or "kind." With this broader range of meaning for the Hebrew at least possible in the first century, I now turn to Matthew.

THE VIRTUES OF MEEKNESS AND HUMILITY
IN MATTHEW'S GOSPEL

Matthew's Gospel never explains the meaning of the adjectives "meek" or "humble" as they apply to Jesus in 11:29. What makes the above material from *The Rule of the Community* particularly useful is that, unlike Isocrates and Plutarch, both Matthew and the Dead Sea Scrolls share an apocalyptic landscape of moral dualism. One cannot simply appropriate a Greek discussion of the term and conclude that this is Matthew's meaning.[45] How does the language of moral dualism affect the meaning and use of the virtues meekness and humility in Matthew's Gospel?

In Matthew's Gospel, Jesus not only commends the meek (5:5, πραεῖς), he describes himself as meek and humble (11:29, πραΰς, ταπεινός), and the narrator describes his entry into Jerusalem as that of a meek king (21:5, πραΰς). Moreover, the verb "to humble oneself" (ταπεινόω ἑαυτόν) occurs at 18:4. At least these four passages must be taken into account in discussing internal evidence to obtain a coherent explanation of the meekness and humility of Jesus within the entire context of the Gospel narrative. There may also be other places where the virtues of meekness and humility play a role even while the terms themselves do not occur in the text. At most, a coherent reading of these pieces of evidence can give a plausible reading of how Matthew or his community understood the virtues of meekness and humility.

1. "Behold, your king comes to you meek"

The third instance of the term "meek" (21:5) occurs in a composite citation from Isaiah 62:11 and Zechariah 9:9. The term "meek" derives from the Greek text of Zechariah. Matthew presents Jesus as a meek king at the point of his entry into Jerusalem.

The demeanor of other kings in the Gospel contrasts with that of Jesus. Jesus' birth takes place "in the days of Herod the king" (2:1).

---

45. Perhaps this is the force of Luz's objection. This approach as we have seen is taken by commentators on the text from the eighteenth century to the present; cf. William Barclay, *The Gospel of Matthew* (London: Mowbrays, 1947) 1:64–66.

Herod's reaction to the magis' news of the birth is fear and terror, and thereafter, he reacts deviously. Through a dream, the magis are warned not to return to Herod after they have found the object of their journey. Learning of this, Herod becomes extremely angry (2:19) and in reaction kills all the male children born at about the same time as the child of whom the magis spoke.

Two other kings are the subjects of parables. The first, wishing to settle accounts with his servants, is compassionate to a servant who cannot repay debts. Learning that this same servant showed no mercy to a fellow servant similarly indebted to him, but had the servant imprisoned, the king addresses the first servant:

> "Wicked servant! All that debt I forgave you since you implored me. Is it not necessary for you also to have mercy on your fellow servant as I had mercy on you?" Having become angry, his lord delivered him to the jailers until he should pay all that he owed. (18:32–34, au. trans.)

In the second parable, a king wishes to give a marriage feast for his son. When the invited guests make their excuses, even maltreating and killing the king's servants, the king becomes angry. He sends his troops and destroys the murderers, burning their city. He sends his servants to invite anyone they can find on the streets, good and bad alike. Gazing at the assembly, and noticing one present who has no wedding garment, the king demands an explanation. Hearing none, he commands the man to be bound hand and foot and cast into outer darkness.

In these two cases, no adjective describes either king. However, both have deferred anger. Both seem justified. In the first example, anger does not emerge until the mistreatment of the one servant by the servant to whom the king showed mercy. In the second, anger is a justifiable response to the unwarranted murder of the king's servants. These two examples of justified anger form a sharp contrast to the disproportionate rage of Herod.

That anger should occur in all three accounts of kings indicates that anger and sovereignty are linked for Matthew. Anger does not occur in regard to any other character in the Gospel.[46] Nor does it occur in regard to Jesus, either when entering Jerusalem as king or at points in the narrative where such an emotive coloring might make sense. For example, in 21:12–17, the episode recording the cleansing of the temple is remarkably devoid of emotion. In fact, Matthew alone

---

46. The NRSV translates 20:24 and 21:15 in such a way that the ten and the chief priests and scribes "become angry." The RSV translates both passages better: "became indignant." The word in both cases is not the same as the Greek verb at 22:7 and 18:34. The verb at 2:16 is different.

records that after the "cleansing," the blind and the lame came to him in the temple and he healed them. The reaction of the chief priests and scribes to this is the only emotion in the passage: they become indignant.

Thus we can conclude that some anger on the part of a sovereign is justifiable. This is particularly the case if the king figures of the parables have anything to do with God. Indeed, these parables do describe a facet of God's reign in which anger plays a part. However, the violence of Herod's response is unwarranted. Jesus, when seen as a king, is not angry but meek. He displays this characteristic in a number of ways, one of which may be seen by the "amazing things" he does for the lame and the blind in the temple shortly after he has been described as meek in the text.

Meekness and kingship go together in the Hellenistic world. Meekness indicates the self-discipline of an educated ruler who shows compassion for his subjects. Matthew's choice of Zechariah 9:9 reflects his interest in this *topos* as does his linking of kingship with anger in two different ways.

As king, Jesus enters Jerusalem in meekness. He does not show anger. Indeed, at 5:22, he eschews anger since it leads to murder and advocates instead reconciliation as the proper attitude to one's brother. Only God expresses righteous indignation. Just as a Hellenistic king from a position of influence does not advance his own household and friends, neither does Jesus. To the mother of the sons of Zebedee, he says, "to sit at my right hand and my left is not mine to grant, but it is for those for whom it has been prepared by my father" (20:23). The mode of ruling that should characterize the Matthean community is servanthood in contrast to the rulers of the Gentiles whose great ones rule or lord it over them (20:25). One should note that while members of the community are servants to one another, Jesus elsewhere describes their status: "the sons are free" in this case from tax or tribute to earthly kings (17:25–26). For Matthew, Jesus shows that such servanthood lies in his free but costly acceptance of God's will, his humble manner, and his subordinate status to God as son.

2. "For I am meek and lowly of heart"

The meekness and humility of Jesus referred to in 11:29 is not part of a list of Jesus' qualities in the way that aretalogies list the virtues and achievements of divine figures and human heroes. It is rather part of a rationale for learning from Jesus as teacher: "Take my yoke upon you and learn of me, for I am meek and lowly of heart, and you will find rest for your souls." Here, one learns from Jesus as meek precisely because he is compassionate and patient. What does this mean in the context of the Gospel? He reassures listeners that they are of great value (6:26; 10:31; 12:12); he expects no compensation (10:8); he shows compassion for others consistently whatever their response (9:36; 23:37); and he promises his presence whenever two or three are gathered (18:20). What he teaches to the disciples during their life together is "what has been hidden from the foundation of the world" (13:34–35). In the Great Commission at the end of the Gospel, he reminds the disciples of his earlier teaching as he sends them out to teach (28:20). What one learns is based on the revelation of all things transmitted within the particular relationship of son to father (11:27). If writers from the Second Temple period knows that "Many are lofty and renowned, but to the meek [God] reveals his secrets,"[47] it is also true that meekness in particular individuals is an indication of religious humility: the meekness of Moses in the Greek translation of Numbers 12:2 reflects the unique character of Moses' relationship to God.[48]

The extent of Jesus' meekness may be seen in his refusal to meet aggression with aggression; in response to the hostility of some Pharisees, he withdraws (12:14–21).[49] The addition of the words "he will not wrangle" (12:19) to the citation from Isaiah in Matthew 12:18–21 is a further interpretation of the theme of meekness.

What does he teach that exemplifies meekness? First, as we see in the antitheses, he teaches the disciples—and through them the community—to avoid anger. Slandering a sibling of the community renders one liable to judgment. Next, he advocates reconciliation rather than lasting enmity between community brethren as the precondition to offering a gift at the altar (5:23–24). In the teaching, "do not resist an evil person" (5:39), we have an anticipation of the phrase "he will not wrangle" (12:19), here interpreted for the community. What does the principle of nonretaliation mean?

Retaliation today means to exact revenge. In the realm of ethics it means to "return evil with evil." But in Matthew the issue of nonretaliation is subordinate to the issue of combating evil. Since evil results in lawlessness (7:23), the combating of evil is undertaken precisely to establish justice. Revenge does not further the cause of jus-

---

47. Sirach 3:19.

48. Dale Allison, *The New Moses: A Matthean Typology* (Minneapolis: Fortress, 1993) 218–33.

49. Deirdre Good, "The Verb ΑΝΑΧΩΡΕΩ, to Withdraw, in Matthew's Gospel" *Novum Testamentum* 32, no. 1 (1990) 1–12.

tice, for it breaks the law (5:19) and furthers injustice. Nonretaliation, on the other hand, defeats evil and furthers the cause of justice.

Moreover, nonretaliation does not mean a passive acceptance of evil, but is itself a move toward the overcoming of evil. In each of these cases, the cycle of violence is broken. Turning the other cheek or walking another mile is an active move of a nonretaliatory nature implying a different course of action. It overloads the aggression onto the aggressor by eliminating the means to extend the aggressive act while at the same time taking the initiative away from the evil perpetrator.

Each of the examples of nonretaliation describes an act of violence: being hit, being sued, being forced to accompany someone, and being appealed to for money. The responsive behavior is quite different from what might be expected: turning the other cheek, giving your cloak to one who sues you and takes your coat, going the second mile, and giving to everyone who begs or who wants to borrow from you. All the examples are in the second person singular. This indicates that their hortatory force is in direct address to the community member.

Within the Gospel, Jesus exemplifies self-conscious and deliberate nonretaliation. When the crowd of mourners "laughs at him" for maintaining that the daughter of the leader of the synagogues is not dead but sleeping, the narrative continues, "Going in, he grasped her hand and raised the young girl" (9:24–25). The mocking crowd is simply "put outside." In response to the beheading of John the Baptist, he withdraws (14:13). When some Pharisees plot to snare him in what he says, he chooses not between the alternatives of paying some or no taxes to the emperor but opts instead for paying to the emperor what is due him and likewise what is due to God (22:15–22).[50] At his arrest, Jesus tells the disciple who takes his sword and cuts off the ear of the high priest's servant: "Put your sword back into its place; for all who take the sword will perish by the sword" (26:52). He specifically says that he will not appeal to the father to summon legions of angels, and he cites the example of his teaching daily in the temple as a response to a desire to arrest him (26:53–55).

Matthew's use of the motif of Jesus' meekness and humility as conscious nonretaliation resonates within the Gospel and in other con-

---

50. The verb παγιδεύω (NRSV: "entrap") is unique to Matthew. Behind it lies a deadly aggression. In the LXX, the verb is frequently used to mean "death trap" e.g. Ps 18:5 (LXX 17:6): "The cords of Sheol surrounded me, the *snares* of death confronted me." Cf. Jer 18:22; Sir 9:13; Job 22:10 where the same word in the Greek text describes threats to the righteous.

texts as well. We have already noted that Plutarch advocates a linking of courage and gentleness rather than courage and justice in certain cases of wrongdoing.

But there is a fundamental difference between Matthew and Hellenistic authors like Plutarch and Philo over the question of the acquisition of this particular virtue. Educated men of the Hellenistic world acquire meekness through discipline and control of emotions. Philo, for example, in the first century, describes Moses' control of emotions during his adolescence. He uses philosophical language in which value is attached to control of the affective aspects of human life through reason. Beyond boyhood, Moses' good sense[51] began to appear. Using the reins of temperance and self-control, he holds at bay adolescent desires. As for the other passions "he tamed[52] and appeased and brought under due command every one of the other passions which are naturally and as far as they are themselves concerned frantic, violent, and unmanageable."[53]

Moses thus acquires meekness by means of self-discipline. This is also true of Plutarch's subjects. It is not the case with Jesus. Matthew understands Jesus' meekness to be revealed rather than acquired (11:27). As part of the revelation of "all things" from the Father, Jesus' meekness and humility in heart is part of his status as dependent and obedient son of God. Filial obedience requires forgoing all exercise of power, as can be seen in the rejection of each of the satanic temptations: to make stones bread, to jump off the temple and be rescued by angels, and to possess all the kingdoms of the world (4:3–10). Whereas the notion of obedient sonship is not foreign to other Gospels, it is Matthew alone who articulates the aspect of sonship as revealed and dependent humility and who identifies it as such within the character of Jesus himself.[54] Jesus' teaching of nonretaliation and his avoidance of anger ensures that enacting meekness is not one of those things that is hidden until revealed but is already accessible.

It is also accessible when the community speaks liturgically in the corporate voice of dependent child: in the Lord's Prayer to petition the heavenly father (6:9–13). Prominent individuals among the disciples may themselves receive a revelation of Jesus' sonship (16:15–17). In

---

51. This word has the connotation of intellect.

52. This is the verb formed from the noun "meek." Since the English verb "to meeken" is now obsolete, the verb can be translated as "to tame" or "discipline," or "subdue."

53. Philo, *Moses I*, 25–27.

54. Hence, one could say that in respect to the quiet virtues, for Matthew, Jesus' gender identity is not acquired but revealed. I have to think about this further. It means that gender is incidental to Matthew.

all these cases, the teaching now accessible is what fosters the well-being of community. The final teaching about meekness and humility comes in Jesus' teaching about the kingdom: "Whoever humbles himself like this child is the greatest in the kingdom of heaven" (18:4). Here, the verb with a reflexive pronoun, "to humble oneself," (unfortunately lost in the NRSV translation "whoever becomes humble") is very important because as an active verb it indicates action that can be taken by the individual. Prefacing this teaching is the possibility of change (18:3). Both changing ($\sigma\tau\rho\alpha\phi\hat{\eta}\tau\varepsilon$) and "becoming humble" imply volition on the individual's part.

CONCLUSION

A comprehensive examination of all instances of moral dualism and virtues in Matthew's Gospel allows the reader to interpret these ideas not abstractly but within the lives of individuals or groups. Thus, there are sensible and foolish people in the text whose conduct one can avoid or emulate. In the case of the righteous or those who say good things, matters are more complicated since one can look righteous but be hypocritical and lawless (23:28), or speak good but be evil (12:34). In the text there are those who neglect justice, mercy, and faith (23:23), and there are wicked servants or unprepared wedding guests who are consigned to prison or to outer darkness. But in the dichotomy of sensible and foolish, two cognate verbs address a prominent individual and the Matthean community to indicate a way forward: Jesus tells Peter: "You are not *setting your mind* on things of God" (16:23), which of course implies that one *can* set one's mind on things of God and thus avoid being foolish. The community is warned, "Take care that *you do not despise* one of these little ones" (18:10), suggesting that community members not disparage or look down on each other. Since this warning occurs in the context of "humbling oneself" (18:4), it is possible that people who did "humble themselves" either were or might be despised. The Greek verb ($\kappa\alpha\tau\alpha\phi\rho\nu\varepsilon\hat{\iota}\nu$) is a compound verb connected to the same root as "wise/sensible.'

To those who deem a situation unjust, accountability is offered by means of the cognate verb "I *did not wrong* you" ($\dot{\alpha}\delta\iota\kappa\hat{\omega}$, 20:13). Thus, a standard of justice different from "equal work for equal pay" is put on the lips of the divine figure in the parable. In the antitheses, the principle of retaliation is also overturned in favor of active non-resistance furthering the cause of justice. This teaching in turn supports the portrait of Jesus as meek and humble of heart (11:19). While in the immediate context these adjectives describe a patient and compassionate teacher from whom all might learn, in the broader context Jesus' humility is exemplified in his withdrawal from hostility, his refusal to meet aggression with aggression, and his death. Far from being evidence of passive servility, his own words to the servant and the crowd at the arrest and his prayers to God in Gethsemane indicate that humility is part of choosing obedient sonship and collapsing his will into that of God. Jesus' sovereign meekness is seen in contrast to the demeanor of tyrannical Gentile rulers who dominate their subjects or Herod's furious anger that causes the slaughter of the innocents.

The admonition in the active verbs to change and humble oneself (18:4) is the means whereby Matthew's community appropriates the revelation of Jesus as meek and humble of heart. The community is changed by the alteration of each individual. Material from *The Rule of the Community* demonstrates a similar use of meekness as preeminently a virtue of temperament enhancing community life within a context of moral dualism. This usage anticipates early Christian use of meekness and humility as communal virtues particularly given to promoting harmony.[55]

---

55. *1 Clement* 29-30; 48:5; 56:1: Ignatius, *Polycarp* 6.2.

MORAL DUALISM IN MATTHEW'S GOSPEL

Exhortation/ Observation	Virtue/Vice	Symptom
"If you then who are evil know how to give good gifts to your children, how much more . . ." (7:11)	**good & evil** (22:10)	How can you speak **good things**, being **evil**? (12:34)
"Friend, **I did not wrong** you." (20:13) "Beware of practicing your **piety** before others" (6:1)	**righteousness/ unrighteousness** (5:45)	look **righteous** but inside are lawless (23:28)
does not wish to make an example of a woman (1:19) "I desire mercy and not sacrifice." (9:13)	**a just man** 1:19	neglect of **justice, mercy,** and **faith** (23:23) condemns guiltless (12:7)
He will not dispute (12:19) "Unless you change and become like children . . . whoever **humbles** himself like this child . . . " (18:4)	**"I am meek and lowly of heart"** (11:29) your king is coming, **meek** (21:5)	exercises authority over (20:25)
"You are of more value than birds of the air." (6:26; 10:31)	the sons are **free** (17:26)	"fear him who can destroy both soul and body in hell" (10:28) [soul and body are of sufficient value to be preserved]
"But I say to you, everyone who is **angry** with his brother shall be liable to judgment" (5:22)	a king delays **anger** (18:34)	a king becomes very **angry** in retaliation (2:16)

7

The Transfiguration

Vision and Social Setting in Matthew's Gospel (Matthew 17:1-9)

Celia Deutsch

My purpose in this essay is to examine Matthew's transfiguration narrative in light of biblical and Jewish sources. I focus on how Matthew, by emphasizing the features of vision and revelation, heightens a Moses/Sinai typology that is already present in Mark's narrative.[1] Matthew's interest in vision and revelation corresponds with other narratives in Jewish literature, where the scribe has a vision in which he sees God or other heavenly beings. Like the transfiguration narrative, these visions are narrated in language that recalls the Sinai narrative and the figure of Moses. The purpose of these visions is to legitimate the function of the visionaries who are scribes—transmitters, interpreters, and teachers of the tradition. While authors usually focus on the figure of Jesus in the narrative of the transfiguration, Wenham and Moses have noted in passing that the text legitimates the disciples' teaching function, thus raising the question of the social setting of the

I am deeply grateful to Robin Scroggs for the generosity with which he has shared with me his keen insight into the social settings of New Testament texts, for his critique of my own work, and for his support and encouragement.

1. Commentators on Matthew's transfiguration narrative note parallels in biblical and Jewish literature, and observe the Moses and Sinai typology. They often observe that, in his redaction of the transfiguration narrative, the Evangelist heightens the apocalyptic character already present in the Markan source. See, for example, W. D. Davies, *The Setting of the Sermon on the Mount* (Cambridge: Cambridge University Press, 1966) 50–55; W. D. Davies and D. C. Allison, *A Critical and Exegetical Commentary on the Gospel According to Saint Matthew*, ICC (Edinburgh: T. & T. Clark, 1995) 2:687–88; O. L. Cope, *Matthew: A Scribe Trained for the Kingdom of Heaven*, CBQMS 5 (Washington, DC: Catholic Biblical Association, 1976) 99–102; and A. D. A. Moses, *Matthew's Transfiguration Story and Jewish-Christian Controversy*, JSNTSS 122 (Sheffield: Sheffield Academic Press, 1996). Moses's work was not yet available when this paper was written.

narrative in Matthew's Gospel.[2] I argue that, like these other visionary texts, Matthew's transfiguration narrative serves to legitimate the function of the visionaries who represent teachers in his community.

My examination of the Sinai typology and apocalyptic correspondences does not represent a thorough interpretation of the passage in question.[3] For example, I do not analyze the relation between Matthew's transfiguration narrative and Isaiah 42:1-4 or Daniel 7:13-14. Nor do I assume Matthew's literary dependence on Second Temple or tannaitic sources. The limitation of my present investigation of Matthew's religious and intellectual context allows us to test the hypothesis that Matthew 17:1-9 is a scribal visionary text, legitimating not only the teaching authority of Jesus, but also that of the scribes who exercise some of the leadership functions in the Matthean community.

SINAI AND APOCALYPTIC
IN MATTHEW 17:1-9

In the Matthean text of the transfiguration, Jesus and the disciples Peter, James, and John go up a "high mountain" (ὄρος ὑψηλόν). There, Jesus undergoes a metamorphosis, the disciples see him conversing with Moses and Elijah, and a voice proclaims from the cloud overshadowing the mountain that Jesus is "My beloved son" (ὁ υἱός μου ὁ ἀγαπητός). In Matthew's version the voice continues, commanding the disciples to "hear him" (ἀκούετε αὐτοῦ). The disciples react with eagerness—Peter proposes to construct three booths—as well as fear. In the Matthean version they fall prostrate, only to be commanded to rise by Jesus, who also tells them to "have no fear" (μὴ φοβεῖσθε).

Matthew adopts the Marcan context for the transfiguration.[4] That is, his version of the narrative follows Peter's confession at Caesarea Philippi (16:13-20//Mark 8:27-30), the first passion prediction (16:21-23//Mark 8:31-33), and the sayings about discipleship (16:24-28//Mark 8:34-9:1). The latter includes a saying about the coming of the Son of Man "in the glory of his Father with his angels" (ἐν τῇ δόξῃ τοῦ πατρὸς αὐτοῦ μετὰ τῶν ἀγγέλων αὐτοῦ, 16:27) and predicts that

---

2. D. Wenham and A. D. A. Moses, "'There Are Some Standing Here . . .': Did They Become the 'Reputed Pillars' of the Jerusalem Church? Some Reflections on Mark 9:1, Galatians 2:9 and the Transfiguration," *NovT* 36 (1994) 147.

3. Luz speaks of the passage as polyvalent (*vieldeutig*) and having many associations; *Das Evangelium nach Matthäus (Mt 8-17)*, EKKNT 1/2 (Zurich: Benziger and Neukirchener, 1990) 506-9. Luz does not really deal with the phenomenon of apocalyptic scribal vision.

4. On the relationship of Matt 17:1-9 to its context, see Luz, 505; also A. Del Agua, "The Narrative of the Transfiguration as a Derashic Scenification of a Faith Confession (Mark 9.2-8 Par)," *NTS* 39 (1993) 345-46; Wenham and Moses, 149.

event in the lifetime of some of those present (16:28).[5] In verse 28, Matthew changes the Marcan "kingdom of God come with power" to "the Son of Man coming in his kingdom." The transfiguration narrative is followed immediately by sayings about Elijah (17:10-13//Mark 9:11-13). Here, Matthew deletes the Marcan saying about the suffering of the Son of Man (Mark 9:12b), possibly because it deflects attention from Elijah. The deletion emphasizes the parallels between the violence done to "Elijah" and the suffering of the Son of Man. Matthew also adds, "Then the disciples understood that he was speaking to them of John the Baptist" (17:13).

The transfiguration narrative illustrates the assertion in 16:28 about the imminent coming of the kingdom of the Son of Man. The sayings about Elijah suggest that the coming of that kingdom will be in an unanticipated form. Matthew's redaction implies that just as those looking for Elijah did not recognize him in the person of John the Baptist, so too those looking for the kingdom do not recognize its revelation, its *apocalypsis*, in the transfigured Jesus.

1. Moses/Sinai Typology in Matthew 17:1-9

Matthew takes over Mark's parallel with Sinai which is implied first of all by time ("after six days," $\mu\epsilon\theta$' $\dot{\eta}\mu\dot{\epsilon}\rho\alpha\varsigma$ $\ddot{\epsilon}\xi$, Mark 9:2)[6] and place ("a high mountain," $\ddot{o}\rho\circ\varsigma$ $\dot{\nu}\psi\eta\lambda\dot{o}\nu$, Mark 9:2), as well as by the appearance of Moses and Elijah, who is also associated with Sinai/Horeb (Mark 9:4-5; 1 Kgs 19:1-17). There are references to ascent, leading up ($\dot{\alpha}\nu\alpha\phi\dot{\epsilon}\rho\omega$ in Matt 17:1 and Mark 9:2; $\dot{\alpha}\nu\alpha\beta\alpha\dot{\iota}\nu\omega$, Exod 24:9, 12, 13, 15), descent ($\kappa\alpha\tau\alpha\beta\alpha\dot{\iota}\nu\omega$, Exod 34:29, 35), and companions (Aaron, Nadab, Abihu, and seventy elders, Exod 24:1; Joshua, Exod 24:13-14). Peter would build a booth or tent ($\sigma\kappa\eta\nu\dot{\eta}$; cf. Exod 25:8-9, מִשְׁכָּן//$\sigma\kappa\eta\nu\dot{\eta}$). There is the cloud that overshadows Jesus, Peter, James, and John (Exod 24:16, 18), and the divine voice that speaks from the cloud (Exod 19:16-19). There is the reference to Jesus' radiant face (Exod 34:29, 35). And, finally, there is the command to those present to hear/obey the designated one (Deut 18:15, 19).[7]

---

5. This is a hint of 24:30-31 (par. Mark 13:26-27), and reflects Dan 7:13-14.

6. See F. R. McCurley, "'And After Six Days' (Mark 9:2): A Semitic Literary Device," *JBL* 93 (1974) 67-81.

7. J. Moiser, "Moses and Elijah," *ExpTimes* 96 (1984-85) 216. On the parallels between the transfiguration and Sinai narratives, see J. Gnilka, *Das Matthäusevangelium* (Freiburg: Herder, 1988) 2:92-94; R. H. Gundry, *Matthew: A Commentary on His Literary and Theological Art* (Grand Rapids, MI: Eerdmans, 1982) 342; M. Smith, "The Origin and History of the Transfiguration Story," *USQR* 36 (1980) 41-42. Luz observes that Matthew makes audition as well as vision central to the pericope (505).

Matthew takes several of these allusions to Moses and the theophany on Sinai from Mark: the reference to six days, the ascent and descent from the mountain, the tent or booth proposed by Peter, the cloud and the heavenly voice from the cloud, and the presence of companions.[8] Matthew emphasizes the Sinai/Moses typology by adding the reference to Jesus' shining face (v 2; Exod 34:29, 33–35) and by adding the adjective "bright" ($\phi\omega\tau\epsilon\iota\nu\dot{\eta}$, v 5) to describe the cloud. He also reverses the Marcan "Elijah with Moses" to read "Moses and Elijah," thereby giving priority to Moses.[9]

2. Apocalyptic Features in Matthew 17:1–9

There are apocalyptic features corresponding to the Sinai tradition already present in Mark (Mark 9:2–10):[10] the mountain as a place of revelation,[11] the seer's altered appearance,[12] and white garments,[13] the angelic or divine voice,[14] the cloud,[15] and the acknowledgment of the seer by the heavenly voice.[16] Finally, there is the presence of Moses

---

8. Exod 24:9–18; 34:29–35; see Gnilka, 2:93; T. Donaldson, *Jesus on the Mountain: A Study in Matthean Theology*, JSNTSS 8 (Sheffield, England: JSOT Press, 1985) 149–50; Davies, *Setting*, 50.

9. Davies, *Setting*, 51–52; Donaldson, 149–50; Gundry, 342–43. The Marcan order suggests that possibly the "account originally had to do only with Elijah as the eschatological forerunner of the Messiah (Mal 3:1 and 4:5);" A. J. Nau, *Peter in Matthew; Discipleship, Diplomacy and Dispraise . . . with an Assessment of Power and Privilege in the Petrine Office*, Good News Studies 36 (Collegeville, MN: Michael Glazier/Liturgical Press, 1992) 78; see E. Schweizer, *The Good News According to Matthew*, trans. D. E. Green (Atlanta: John Knox Press, 1975) 349.

10. See M. Smith, "Ascent to the Heavens and the Beginnings of Christianity," *Eranosjahrbuch* 50 (1981) 403–24, and "Origin and History," 39–44. Smith argues that the transfiguration narrative reflects, not a "misplaced resurrection story" but an experience of apocalyptic ascent during the ministry of the historical Jesus.

11. E.g., *1 Enoch* 18:6–16; *T. Levi* 2:5–6; *Apoc. Abr.* 9:9; 12:3; *2 Apoc. Bar.* 13:1; see Donaldson, 141–42. For other examples in Second Temple Jewish sources, see Ezekiel the Trajedian in Eusebius, *Prep. Ev.* 9.29.4–5; note the way in which Josephus emphasizes the forbidding terrain of Sinai (*Ant.* 3.76, 79–80).

12. E.g., Dan 12:3; *1 Enoch* 39:14; 71:11; *2 Enoch* 1:7j; *2 Apoc. Bar.* 51:1–3, 10; 4 Ezra 7:97; 10:25; *Apoc. Zeph.* 5:4; see also Josephus, *Ant.* 3.83; Philo, *Mos.* 2.70, 288; Rev 1:16.

13. E.g., Dan 10:5; *1 Enoch* 14:20; 62:15–16; *2 Enoch* 22:8–10; *Apoc. Elijah* 5:6; Rev 3:4–5; 7:9.

14. E.g., Dan 8:16; *1 Enoch* 14:8; *T. Levi* 2:5–7; 5:1; 18:6; 4 Ezra 14:1–26; *Apoc. Abr.* 8:1–4; 17:1; 19:1–3; *2 Apoc. Bar.* 13:1; 22:1; Rev 11:12.

15. E.g., Dan 7:13; *1 Enoch* 14:8; *2 Enoch* 3:1j; Rev 14:4.

16. For the acknowledgment of the Son of Man by God or the heavenly revealer, see *1 Enoch* 46:1–8; 62:1–16; 71:1–17. The last text is particularly significant because Enoch the seer actually becomes the Son of Man acknowledged by the heavenly revealer. See A. F. Segal, "Heavenly Ascent in Hellenistic Judaism, Early Christianity and Their Environment," *ANRW* II.2 (1980) 1378; C. R. A. Morray Jones, "Transformational Mysticism in the Apocalyptic-Merkabah Tradition," *JJS* 43 (1992) 26. For another view see J. J. Collins, "The Son of Man in First-Century Judaism," *NTS* 38 (1992) 455–59. In *Apoc. Abr.* Abraham is God's beloved (9:6; 10:5–7; 16:4; 19:3; 23:2; cf. 10:5; 14:2). In 14:3, Iaoel says that God, whom Abraham has loved, has chosen him. He tells Abraham to do whatever he, Iaoel, tells him against Azazel. In *T. Levi* 2, an angel commissions Levi: "You shall be his [God's] priest and you shall tell forth his mysteries to men [*sic*]" (2:10). In a vision, an angel tells Levi that he will become God's son, "as minister and priest in his presence" (4:2; see Ps 2:7). Levi stands on a high mountain. See also *3 Apoc. Bar.*

and Elijah, associated with the end time and with heavenly ascents.[17]

Matthew's editorial activity enhances the apocalyptic quality already present in Mark.[18] For example, Matthew adopts Mark's four-fold repetition of various forms of ὁράω to state the nature of the experience (16:28; 17:3, 8, 9). But he emphasizes that usage by changing Mark's aorist εἶδόν to the noun ὅραμα at the conclusion of the pericope (Matt 17:9). Matthew also emphasizes the perceptual nature of the vision by adding ἀκούω in verses 5 and 6.

Furthermore, Matthew adds to Mark's description of Jesus' metamorphosis: "And his face shone like the sun" (καὶ ἔλαμψεν τὸ πρόσωπον αὐτοῦ ὡς ὁ ἥλιος, 17:2).[19] Whereas Mark has an extended description of the whiteness of Jesus' garments, Matthew abbreviates and has simply: "His garments became white as light" (τὰ δὲ ἱμάτια αὐτοῦ ἐγένετο λευκὰ ὡς τὸ φῶς, 17:2b).[20]

Matthew's editing has two principal effects: (1) He makes a strong parallel between the shining of Jesus' face and the whiteness of his garments (ὡς ὁ ἥλιος//ὡς τὸ φῶς). (2) This, in turn, heightens the apocalyptic note already present in Mark, for brilliance of countenance and raiment was a commonplace in apocalyptic literature.[21] For example, 4 Ezra tells us that in the end time, the faces of those "who have kept the ways of the Most High" will "shine like the sun" and they will be made "like the light of stars" (7:88, 97).[22] And in 2 Enoch 22:8j, God tells Michael to take Enoch's earthly clothing and "put him into the clothes of my glory."

Matthew adds a further apocalyptic note. At God's words designating Jesus as the beloved Son, the disciples "fell on their faces and

1:3 where the angel calls Baruch "greatly beloved."

17. See G. Sellin, "Das Leben des Gottessohnes: Taufe und Verklärung Jesu als Bestandteile eines vormarkinischen 'Evangeliums'," *Kairos* 25 (1983) 244. *Apoc. Abr.* 12:1–3 associates the seer with both Moses and Elijah. Beyond the apocalyptic texts, there are other Second Temple Jewish traditions that Elijah and/or Moses will return in the final time; e.g., Sir 48:1–11; *Syb. Or.* 2.187–89, 238–48. The final redaction of the latter text is Christian; however, the citation may easily preserve an earlier Jewish tradition since the only feature which is Christian is the use of "Christ" at the end of the text. And still others associate Elijah with Moses; e.g., Philo *Quaest. in Gen.* 1.86. Philo believes that Moses, as well as Elijah, ascended into the heavenly realms since no one knows the burial place of the former.

18. Regarding the relationship of Matthew's transfiguration narrative to apocalyptic thought, see Donaldson, 141; Gnilka, 2:93–97; L. Sabourin, "Traits apocalyptiques dans l'évangile de Matthieu," *Science et Esprit* 33 (1981) 365.

19. See note 12 above.

20. See note 13 above.

21. Countenance: Of the righteous, 4 Ezra 7:97; Dan 12:3; *2 Apoc. Bar.* 51:3; of God, *1 Enoch* 14:21; *2 Enoch* 22:1–2; of Jesus, Rev 1:16. Raiment: of God, Dan 7:9; *1 Enoch* 14:20; of a heavenly visitor, Dan 10:5; of the seer, *2 Enoch* 22:8–10; the righteous, *1 Enoch* 62:15–16; Rev 3:4–5; 7:9.

22. Unless otherwise noted, I have used the translations of the pseudepigrapha found in J. H. Charlesworth, ed., *The Old Testament Pseudepigrapha*, 2 vols. (Garden City, NY: Doubleday, 1983 and 1985).

were filled with fear" (οἱ μαθηταὶ ἔπεσαν ἐπὶ πρόσωπον αὐτῶν καὶ ἐφοβήθησαν σφόδρα, 17:6). Jesus then touches them and says, "Rise, and have no fear" (Ἐγέρθητε καὶ μὴ φοβεῖσθε, 17:7). Prostration occurs as a response to visionary experience in biblical and post-biblical Jewish literature, particularly apocalyptic texts,[23] as do awe or fear.[24] Then God or a heavenly visitor bids the visionary to have no fear, reassures the visionary,[25] and raises the prostrate figure or bids the person to stand.[26] We read about Enoch who enters the heavenly palace and is overcome with fear and trembling. He falls upon his face (14:13-14). The text continues:

> And the Lord called me with his own mouth and said to me, "Come near to me, Enoch, and to my holy Word." And he lifted me up and brought me near to the gate, but I (continued) to look down with my face. But he raised me up and said to me with his voice, "Enoch." I (then) heard, "Do not fear, Enoch, righteous man, scribe of righteousness; come near to me and hear my voice" (14:24-15:1).

Finally, there are occasional references to the visionary's companions. For example, at God's command, Ezra takes with him five companions—all scribes—into the field where he will have the vision in which God will dictate the sacred texts, both public and esoteric (4 Ezra 14:23-26, 37-48). Matthew's addition, with its description of the disciples' prostration and fear and Jesus' touch and command, thus emphasizes the disciples' visionary experience, places that experience in continuity with the visionaries who have preceded them, and confirms the apocalyptic nature of Jesus' sonship.

One can, then, interpret the transfiguration narrative by an examination of the Exodus/Sinai traditions, especially Exodus 24:9-18 and 34:29-35. But a study of the passage in the context of early Jewish literature, particularly visionary texts like those cited above, sheds further light on the pericope. I suggest that all these materials—Matthew, Second Temple, and rabbinic sources—associate visionary experience with the Sinai narratives. They place the authority of those teachers who are central to the texts within a narrative "chain of tradition" that

---

23. E.g., Josh 5:14; Judg 13:20; 2 Chr 7:3; Ezek 2:1; 9:8; Dan 8:17; 10:9; *1 Enoch* 14:24-15:2; *2 Enoch* 1:7j and a; 21:2; 22:4; *Apoc. Zeph.* 6:4-7, 15; 4 Ezra 4:12; 5:14-15; 10:29-33; *Apoc. Abr.* 9:1-10; 10:2.

24. E.g., Gen 28:17; Dan 8:17; cf. Luke 1:29.

25. E.g., Gen 15:1; 21:17; 26:24; Dan 10:12, 19; *1 Enoch* 14:25-15:2; *2 Enoch* 1:7j and a; 21:3; 22:5; 4 Ezra 5:14-15; 10:29-33; *Apoc. Abr.* 10:4ff; Luke 1:30.

26. E.g., Ezek 2:1-2; Dan 10:11; *1 Enoch* 15:1; *Apoc. Abr.* 10:4-5, 15.

goes all the way back to Sinai.[27] Use of visionary experience in and of itself shows that the sage has divine sanction for his authority.

VISIONARY TEXTS IN
EARLY JEWISH LITERATURE

Is Matthew using Sinai typology to describe Jesus in such a way as to parallel Moses himself? Yes.[28] Similar parallels between an inspired teacher and Moses appear elsewhere in Second Temple texts. Both 4 Ezra and *2 Apocalypse of Baruch* describe the seer or teacher as a "new Moses." They use explicit references to the Exodus/Sinai narratives and place their central characters—and their teaching—in continuity with the prior tradition. In this way, the narrative legitimates their position as authoritative teachers.[29]

For example, in the vision in which God commissions Ezra to receive, write, and promulgate the books, both canonical and esoteric, the seer hears a voice call to him from a nearby bush. He responds "Here I am, Lord" (4 Ezra 14:1-2, 45-48).[30] The vision legitimates Ezra's authority to interpret the events surrounding the destruction of Jerusalem—the signs, dreams, and interpretations disclosed in his visions (14:8).

The author(s) of *2 Apocalyse of Baruch* also legitimate the teaching and leadership of Baruch by likening him to Moses. The parallels are perhaps clearest and most focused in chapter 84, part of Baruch's letter (chapters 78-86). This chapter recalls explicitly the renewal of the covenant by Moses in Deuteronomy 33:19-20, calling on heaven and earth as witnesses (*2 Apoc. Bar.* 84:2). Baruch instructs the people in "Babylon" to "learn my mighty commandments which he has in-

---

27. The chain of tradition is a device that traces a teacher's authority back through the "chain" of his predecessors. See E. Bickerman, "La chaine de la tradition pharisienne," *RB* 59 (1952) 44-54; A. J. Saldarini, *Scholastic Rabbinism: A Literary Study of the Fathers According to Rabbi Nathan*, BJS 14 (Chico, CA: Scholars Press, 1982) 67-78. On the function of ascent visions in the context of the chain of tradition, see N. Janowitz, *The Poetics of Ascent; Theories of Language in a Rabbinic Ascent Text* (Albany, NY: State University of New York Press, 1989) 31, 93-95.

28. Many commentators note this parallel, for example Davies and Allison, *Commentary*, 2:685-704; Donaldson, 149-50; Gnilka, 2:93-94.

29. See J. J. Collins, "The Sage in the Apocalyptic and Pseudepigraphic Literature," in *The Sage in Israel and the Ancient Near East*, ed. J. G. Gammie and L. G. Perdue (Winona Lake, IN: Eisenbrauns, 1990) 352; M. Knibb, "Apocalyptic and Wisdom in Fourth Ezra," *JSJ* 13 (1982) 62-63; J. M. Myers, *I and II Esdras*, AB 42 (Garden City, NY: Doubleday, 1974) 327-329. For a study of the parallels between Baruch and Moses in 2 Baruch, see F. J. Murphy, *The Structure and Meaning of Second Baruch*, SBLDS 78 (Atlanta: Scholars Press, 1985) 129-30.

30. Cf. Exod 3:4. In the canonical literature Ezra is already paralleled with Moses in his roles of teacher of the law and leader in covenant renewal; e.g., Neh 8:19, 38.

structed you" (84:1).[31] Like Moses, Baruch is both intermediary and intercessor. Following visionary experiences he brings instruction back to the people. In paralleling Baruch with Moses, the authors have vested Baruch the apocalyptic prophet-scribe with authority over Torah.

Moses/Sinai typology appear in another group of texts relevant for our study, and that is the rabbinic material commenting on *m. Ḥag* 2:1, which restricts the expounding or exegeting of certain biblical texts (Lev 18; Gen 1; Ezek 1 and possibly 10). This material contains several passages that show the master with one or more disciples.[32] All contain elements of the visionary, and all contain Sinai/Moses typology in reference to the sages and their disciples.

For example, in one passage, R. Johanan recounts his dream— keep in mind that "dream" is the equivalent of "vision."[33] He is reclining at a banquet on Mount Sinai. A *bat qol*, or heavenly voice, invites him and his disciples to ascend higher (*b. Ḥag* 14b). The invitation echoes God's invitation to Moses: "Come up to me on the mountain" (Exod 24:12).

In the Jerusalem Talmud, there is the story of R. Eliezer and R. Joshua, present at the circumcision of Elisha ben Abuyah. When other guests at the ensuing celebration exhibit unseemly behavior, the two sages withdraw and begin to study together. Fire descends from heaven and surrounds them. The two sages say "the words were as alive as when they were given from Mt. Sinai. And the fire shone around us as it shone from Mt. Sinai" (*y. Ḥag* 2:1). The account links the study of Torah to Sinai by naming the mountain of revelation, as well as by the fire which descended upon it (cf. Exod 19:18).

A tradition of visionary experience articulated in Sinai typology is, then, associated with R. Johanan ben Zakkai and his disciples. This serves to lend authority to Johanan ben Zakkai and his disciples in their task of interpreting Torah. It forms a narrative "chain of

---

31. See Murphy, 120–130; M. Desjardins, "Law in II Baruch and IV Ezra," *SR* 14 (1985) 28.

32. This material is found in *m. Ḥag* 2:1; *t. Ḥag* 2:1–7; *b. Ḥag* 11b–16a; *y. Ḥag* 2:1 (77b); see also *b. 'Abot* 80b, *b. Ber.* 7a; *Ḥul.* 91b; *Meg* 24b; *Gen. Rab.* 2:4; cf. A. Saldarini, "Apocalypses and 'Apocalyptic' in Rabbinic Literature," *Semeia* 14 (1979) 188. Halperin calls the material in *t. Ḥag* 2:1–7; *y. Ḥag* 2:1; *b. Ḥag* 11b, 15b–15a, the "mystical collection" and presents a fuller list of parallels in *Genesis Rabbah*; D. J. Halperin, *The Merkabah in Rabbinic Literature*, American Oriental Series 62 (New Haven: American Oriental Society, 1980) 69, n. 11. He believes it represents a collection redacted prior to these sources and used by all three; see pp. 65–105.

33. The Jerusalem Talmud attributes this to Jose ha-Cohen and Shimeon ben Nathanael. It follows directly their *merkabah* exposition; Halperin considers the account in the Babylonian Talmud to resemble more closely the original, since it resembles the account of Levi's ascent in *T. Levi* 2:5–6; *Merkabah in Rabbinic Literature*, 130–31.

tradition" and bestows the authority of Sinai on Johanan ben Zakkai and his disciples.

But what does all this tell us about the transfiguration narrative? Texts from Second Temple and early rabbinic sources suggest that descriptions of visionary experiences often draw on the Sinai narrative. The visionaries are teachers and disciples, and both the attribution of visionary experience and the description of that experience in the language of the Sinai event serve the literary function—and I think it likely the social function as well—of investing those teachers and their instruction with authority—dare we say, the authority of Moses.

THE TEACHER AND HIS DISCIPLES

Both Moses typology and apocalyptic motifs appear in the transfiguration narrative. Matthew heightens these features in ways that recall Second Temple literature such as 4 Ezra and *2 Apocalypse of Baruch*. But the transfiguration occurs on several levels. First of all, *Jesus,* described in apocalyptic terms, has a vision. He sees heavenly visitors, is overshadowed by the cloud, hears the voice that designates him as beloved Son, and tells the companions to hear him. Moses and Elijah, both associated with Sinai, disappear after the divine command "Listen to him" (vv. 5-8; Mk 9:7-8). The narrative implies that both are subordinate to Jesus the Son[34] whose authority goes all the way back to Sinai. In touching the prostrate disciples and commanding them to have no fear and to rise, Jesus performs a function usually ascribed to God or heavenly visitors in the parallel literature. All of this corresponds well to an environment in which visionary experience involves "the transformation of the visionary into an angelic or supra-angelic being,"[35] suggested by the change of countenance and garments as well as heavenly journeys.

Matthew's transfiguration narrative also corresponds to a cultural/religious context in which vision serves to commission a seer/teacher. In Enoch's vision, for instance, God sends him to the Watchers as messenger and intercessor (*1 Enoch* 15:2).[36] Moreover, Matthew's addition of the words ἐν ᾧ εὐδόκησα recalls the divine

---

34. Smith, "Origin and History," 42; see also R. Kieffer, "A Christology of Superiority in the Synoptic Gospels," *Religious Studies Bulletin* 3:2 (May 1983) 64; M. Thrall, "The Transfiguration: Elijah and Moses," *NTS* 16 (1969) 316.

35. C. R. A. Morray-Jones, "Transformational Mysticism," 22; e.g., *1 Enoch* 71; *2 Enoch* 22; *T. Levi* 8; *Asc. Isa.* 9.

36. In *T. Levi* 2:1-12, an angel commissions Levi as priest who will announce God's mysteries. In 4 Ezra 14:1-48, God commissions Ezra to proclaim repentance and to write the sacred texts.

acclamation at the baptism in 3:17, the beginning of the story of Jesus' ministry.[37] Now, Matthew understands Jesus to be his community's primary teacher. He presents instruction about the kingdom of heaven, interprets *halachah*, engages in debate with his counterparts in other Jewish teaching circles (i.e., scribes and Pharisees). In Matthew's narrative the authority of Jesus is legitimated by the divine voice from heaven that proclaims him Son (17:5) and tells Peter, James, and John to hear him.[38] The divine command "hear him," an allusion to Deuteronomy 18:15 and 19, suggests that Jesus is the prophet like Moses. In the broader context of Matthew, with its use of allusions to Moses to portray Jesus, the transfiguration dramatizes and confirms his identity as authoritative teacher of Torah. That authority is further legitimated by the presence of Moses and Elijah conversing with him, and then disappearing. Having seen the ways in which Matthew has heightened the apocalyptic motifs already present in Mark, I think it is safe to say that in the transfiguration, he presents Jesus as a seer-teacher whose authority is legitimated by the vision. That vision bestows on him the mantle of Sinai.

Matthew is quite emphatic in his dramatization. In his redaction, Jesus' transformation serves to allow him to converse with Moses and Elijah who are *heavenly* figures.[39] He is their equal. Shining countenance and white garments signal that Jesus too is a heavenly being. And there is more. The apocalyptic acknowledgment implicit in the Matthean addition "hear him" implies that Jesus is a Moses figure. Jesus addresses the prostrate disciples with the message usually spoken by a heavenly figure "do not fear." And, when they raise their eyes, they see only Jesus; the other two heavenly figures have disappeared. Jesus, in other words, is at the center of Torah and prophecy. His status as bearer of revelatory knowledge exceeds even that of Moses and Elijah. Coming as it does, after the first passion prediction and the prediction of the *parousia*, the transfiguration—the *vision*—confirms anew Jesus' authority.

On a second level, or simultaneously, the three disciples also have a vision. They see the transfigured Jesus conversing with Moses and Elijah, see the cloud, hear the voice, and Peter as spokesperson

---

37. In the baptism pericope Mark has "You are my Son, the Beloved; with you I am well pleased" (Σὺ εἶ ὁ υἱός μου ὁ ἀγαπητός, ἐν σοὶ εὐδόκησα, 1:11). Matthew has "This is my Son the Beloved, with whom I am well pleased" (Οὗτός ἐστιν ὁ υἱός μου ὁ ἀγαπητός, ἐν ᾧ εὐδόκησα, 3:17).

38. See also 3:17.

39. S. Pedersen, "Die Proklamation Jesu als des eschatologischen Offenbarunsträgers (Mt. xvii 1–13)," *NovT* 17 (1975) 248.

responds with a proposal to build a σκηνή. Matthew highlights Peter's role here as elsewhere by using ποιήσω ("I will make") rather than the plural ποιήσωμεν ("let us make"), as well as by adding the polite εἰ θέλεις, ("if you wish.")[40] All three are overtaken with fear and prostration.

Now, Matthew is not simply writing the story of Jesus and transmitting his teaching. He is, rather, speaking of and to his community. This is the narrative's second level. In the Matthean community, the teachers form the core of the leadership class.[41] They interpret *halachah*, discipline errant members, and transmit the tradition. They are sent by Jesus, and their authority is legitimated by miracles.

The transfiguration narrative illustrates a most important characteristic in this picture of the scribal role of the teachers of the Matthean community: they possess revelatory knowledge. In 11:25-30, Jesus praises God for having revealed "these things" to the little ones—i.e., the disciples. The immediate context suggests that "these things" refers to Jesus' identity as Son and, indirectly, to the apocalyptic mysteries. Again, in chapter 13 (vv. 10-17), Jesus tells his disciples that the mysteries of the reign of heaven have been given to them. In 16:17-19, Jesus pronounces Peter blessed because God has revealed to him the identity of Jesus as Messiah and Son of God. Finally, Jesus commissions the disciples in a postresurrection vision that has apocalyptic tones (28:16-20).

The immediate literary context of the transfiguration narrative highlights the importance of this vision for the disciples, and thus for the teachers of the Matthean community. Matthew indeed follows the Marcan order. This includes the confession at Caesarea Philippi (Matt 16:13-20//Mk 8:27-30), and—most immediately—the instruction about discipleship with its concluding statement about the coming of the Son of Man (16:27-28//Mk 8:37-9:1). Matthew's version, however, includes Jesus' acclamation of Simon Peter in which he declares that it is God who has revealed to him Jesus' identity as the "Christ, the Son of the Living God" (16:16-19). And the evangelist's redaction of the saying about the coming of the Son of Man heightens the apocalyptic nature of that saying and of the Son of Man who is its object.

The transfiguration narrative carries all of this yet further. It enacts in vision the revelation of Jesus as God's Son and Son of Man.

---

40. Nau, *Peter in Matthew*, 79.

41. On the leaders of Matthew's community as teachers, see my *Lady Wisdom, Jesus, and the Sages: Metaphor and Social Context in Matthew's Gospel* (Valley Forge, PA: Trinity Press International, 1996).

The disciples hear Jesus proclaimed Son by the voice, and they see the shining countenance, the white garments, and the cloud. Matthew's enhancement of the apocalyptic nature of the vision and his use of the traditional context show the audience that the transfigured Jesus is indeed Son of Man come in his glory, a glory made manifest in the transfiguration itself.

The disciples possess revelatory knowledge: they both see and hear in vision what they have been told in ordinary discourse. I believe that, for Matthew, the presence of Peter, James, and John—representing the teachers in his community—serves to legitimate the authority of those teachers,[42] just as the presence of Ezra's disciples or those of the tannaim functions to authorize them. Even the confirmation of Jesus' status as beloved son serves this purpose. That is, the disciples see the transformed Jesus and hear the heavenly voice declare Jesus as Son. The narrative points to the close of the Gospel in which, in yet another vision, the disciples are commissioned and sent forth.

Peter, James, and John participate in the vision. In other words, they undergo an experience which is that of seers and sages—transmitters of apocalyptic mysteries and Torah. They have privileged access to the understanding of Jesus' succession to the mantle of Sinai. And in their teaching the teaching of Jesus continues. Beyond the synoptic tradition there is other evidence for such a functioning of the transfiguration tradition.[43] The writer of 2 Peter 1:16-19 claims authority for his teaching on the basis of his status as eyewitness to the transfiguration:

> For we did not follow cleverly devised myths when we made known to you the power and coming of our Lord Jesus Christ, but we had been eyewitnesses of his majesty. For he received honor and glory from God the Father when that voice was conveyed to him by the Majestic Glory saying, "This is my Son, my Beloved, with whom I am well pleased." We ourselves heard this voice come from heaven, while we were with him on the holy mountain. So we have the prophetic message more fully confirmed.

Paul speaks of revelatory experience of the risen Jesus in contexts that suggest he legitimates his own teaching authority through that vision-

---

42. Wenham and Moses (147) point out the special position of authority that the early church seems to have ascribed to Peter, James, and John. They believe that the transfiguration "was seen as giving particular status to the three disciples who witnessed it, as well as being of enormous christological importance."

43. On the relationship between the transfiguration in the synoptic tradition and other New Testament texts in this regard, see Pedersen, "Proklamation," 243, 252; Wenham and Moses, 146-63; B. Chilton, "The Transfiguration: Dominical Assurance and Apostolic Vision," *NTS* 27 (1981) 123.

ary experience. In Galatians Paul says that he did not receive his gospel from a human authority, but rather "received it through a revelation of Jesus Christ. . . . God . . . was pleased to reveal his Son to me" (Gal 1:12, 15b–16). In 2 Corinthians 12:2–5, Paul speaks of his heavenly journey, thereby besting the opposing teachers of chapters 10–12. They might indeed boast of intellectual prowess, rhetorical skill, and wonder-working (11:5–6; 12:11–12). Paul, however, has received his message in apocalyptic vision, and he works corresponding signs, wonders, and mighty works (σημεῖα, τέρατα, δυνάμεις, 12:12).[44]

CONCLUSION

How would visionary experience have functioned to legitimate the authority of the teaching class in the Matthean community? I am speculating, of course. The highly sophisticated convergence of allusions to the Hebrew Bible, the knowledge of certain hermeneutical techniques and apocalyptic conventions, suggest that this passage—as indeed, Matthew's Gospel—would have originated in a learned circle.[45] But I would say that, as with other scribal leaders in this period, revelatory experience authorizes halachic interpretation as well as the interpretation of contemporary events. In this case, examples are suggested by the reference to the keys of the kingdom of heaven in 16:17–19, the pericope of the temple tax (17:24–27), and the materials on community order in chapter 18. Vision/revelatory knowledge set apart Jesus' disciples—the Matthean scribes—from the community at large (chapter 13) or opposing teachers (the "wise and understanding," 11:25).

Are these teachers—Matthew and his contemporaries—involved in the kinds of visionary experience described in 2 Corinthians as well as Second Temple Jewish literature? Are they engaged in the ascetical practices used as propaedeutic to that experience which are described in the contemporary literature?[46] We have no evidence one way or

---

44. On Paul's use of language familiar from other Jewish mystical sources, see Alan F. Segal, *Paul the Convert: The Apostolate and Apostasy of Saul the Pharisee* (New Haven: Yale University, 1990) 34–71.

45. Del Agua, 353–54. I would suggest such a provenance for Mark as well. Regarding Matthew, I suggest elsewhere, the demands of creating such a document would assume access to literary resources, to written texts which would then presuppose a certain social location—likely a large town or city, financial means, or a wealthy patron; see Deutsch, *Lady Wisdom*, 4–7.

46. Such practices include reading texts, weeping, fasting, eating special foods, special posture; see 4 Ezra 5:20, 6:31, 35; 9:23–27; 12:51; 13:1; 14:1; 2 *Apoc. Bar.* 5:6–7; 6: 9:2; 20:5–21:1; 47:2; *1 Enoch* 13:7–8. See D. S. Russell, *The Method and Message of Jewish Apocalyptic*, The Old Testament Library (Philadelphia: Westminster, 1976) 169–73; I. Gruenwald, *Apocalyptic and Kerkavah Mysticism* (Leiden: Brill, 1980) 99–102.

another. I would simply say that we cannot rule this out.[47]

There are other questions. Does the transfiguration tell us something, not only about Matthean scribes in general, but about the ways in which the redactor and his community understood Peter, James, and John specifically? Did the Matthean scribal circle include women? In what socioeconomic stratum can we locate these people? These questions require another, further essay. For the moment, I believe it wise to conclude simply in saying that the typology and correspondences with Second Temple and tannaitic texts suggest that Matthew is using the transfiguration narrative to legitimate the authority of the scribes of his own community. Those leaders can teach and interpret the tradition precisely because they are seers.

---

47. Morton Smith believes the narrative reflects an event in the life of the earthly Jesus as well as practice in the early church; "Origin," 43; "Ascent to the Heavens," 403–29.

8

The Great Cry of Jesus in
Matthew 27:50

André LaCocque

To Robin Scroggs, a great Colleague

I

I don't know if you are like me, but ever since I first read Matthew's Gospel, I have been intrigued by the last cry of Jesus on the cross. My puzzlement is compounded because there is, shortly before, another cry that is spelled out and on which every commentator dwells with the understandable relief of knowing where it comes from and with what intention it was uttered. Although said in Aramaic, Jesus' first exclamation is the first verse of Psalm 22, "My God, my God, why have you forsaken me?" What follows immediately, however, makes a lot less sense: the crowd—allegedly composed mainly of Jews, who should know better—confuses Jesus' words with an invocation of Elijah (Matt 27:47)![1] And then, after that astonishing confusion, "Jesus again gave a loud cry, and yielded up his spirit" (27:50). This time, none of the Gospels tells us what was the content of that last cry.

In this paper, I focus on that latter text of Matthew. Whether articulate or inarticulate, the last cry of Jesus is a crucial moment in the Gospel. Matthew has it coincide ("at that moment") with a series of significant events, all of which point to the eschatological era: the curtain of the temple is torn; there occurs an earthquake; tombs are opened and saints arise; the centurion and the Roman soldiers who proceeded to the crucifixion of Jesus are confessing "this man was the son

---

1. Note that the Matthean text in ηλι (vs. Mark's ελωι) introduces better the misunderstanding.

of God." In short, the whole scene is set by Matthew within an apocalyptical framework. The reading of the Passion according to Matthew makes sense only when that literary setting is taken seriously. Not only is the vocabulary affected by that setting, but the discourse, as is typical in this genre, maintains a dialectical tension between hiddenness and revelation. The Passion narrative purports to reveal a great secret, but in such a way that the revelation does not exhaust the secrecy of events and words, and that the secrecy does not render useless its revelation. This is not unique to Matthew's apocalypse, but it needs to be recalled from the outset. In short, what is said always means more than it seems.

My thesis is that the reader of Matthew is not as deprived of clues regarding the meaning of Jesus' last cry as it might appear. First, there are parallels to be considered in Mark 25:34–37; Luke 23:45–46; and the *Gospel of Peter* (hereafter, *GPet*)5:19. Second, the expression φωνὴ μεγάλη is not unknown in the Septuagint. It will be important to consider the Hebrew correspondents in the Masoretic Text. Third, the apocalyptical phenomena[2] that accompany the Great Cry are introduced by Matthew as the outcome of the cry and as becoming the cry. There is between the Great Cry and these phenomena an organic kinship.

Fourth, the way Matthew introduces the Great Cry is perfectly consistent with what we might call the "double-entendre" of that Gospel. Matthew is writing for a mixed audience and, hence, on two levels at once. Composed some ten to twenty years after 70 in Syria, the Gospel of Matthew addresses Jews and Gentiles, the former perfectly cognizant of Jewish customs and beliefs.[3] The Evangelist[4] is aware of the rules of "reader criticism." He knows that what he writes will be interpreted by one group of readers differently from the other group. He is a great deal more "Jewish" in his record of the Passion than all the other evangelists. When Matthew speaks, for instance, of "the" temple curtain, without specifying which of the two, it is assuredly to be interpreted by the Gentile audience as the curtain that used to separate Jewish males from women and non-Jews, and by the Jewish audience as referring to the veil that used to hide the Holy of Holies.[5]

---

2. See Amos 8:3; Isa 26:19; Ezek 37:12.
3. Matt 15:2; 5:17–20; 23:2; 28:15; etc.
4. Perhaps a converted rabbi, see 13:52; 23:34; see K. Stendahl, *The School of St. Matthew* (Philadelphia: Fortress Press, 1968).
5. Even if there were any doubt about the duality of Matthew's audience, Matthew's plurivocity would remain a fact, for, at a certain stage of tradition, "all the prophetic allusions are now buried under the narrative surface," as says J. D. Crossan in *The Historical Jesus: The Life of a Mediterranean Jewish Peasant* (San Francisco: HarperCollins, 1991) 386.

The Great Cry, as I shall show, is such a double-entendre as well. By not specifying the content of the exclamation, Matthew leaves room for a plurivocal interpretation. To the Gentile audience, the humanity of the martyr is underscored. Already in the garden of Gethsemane, Jesus had petitioned his Father not to submit him to the "drinking of that cup." A moribund groaning at the end is congruent with that prayer left unheard. What about those Jews who were versed in Scripture and in postbiblical Jewish traditions? How did they understand the bridging of the Great Cry and the eschatological phenomena described as a result of that cry? How did they react to the revelation that the Holy of Holies had "exploded" with the death of Jesus? For pious Jews (as they actually were), no event more ultimate, more decisive, could ever occur. True, one possible interpretation could see in the tearing of the curtain a metaphor for the destruction of the temple in 70. But this staggering historical occurrence is only one side, the negative one, of a narrative complex that receives also a positive meaning in Matthew 27: it culminates with the advent of the messianic era heralded by Elijah, the resurrection of (the) dead, a reversal of all powers, a new creation, and the integration of all nations into the Elect People.

II

1. Φωνὴ μεγάλη in the Septuagint

The usual term in the Bible for "cry," namely זְעָקָה, a cry for help,[6] is often rendered by φωνή in the LXX. It is a very general term, one that often occurs without a direct object (the what of the cry); זעקה emphasizes the exclamation itself rather than its content.[7] Hence, the Hebrew word behind φωνή in Matthew 27:50 could be זעקה. But such a reading would disregard the apocalyptic context of Matthew's Passion. As Raymond E. Brown insists (speaking of Mark's Gospel that he considers as the source of the synoptics),[8] Mark does not report a simple death rattle in 15:34, 37; the "loud cry" is one more eschatological feature. In Mark 15:37, we could understand, "having let out *that* loud cry [in 15:34], he expired" (see Luke's one cry), but Matthew 27:50 adds πάλιν![9] Furthermore, in the New Testament in

---

6. For R. N. Boyce it is "the cry of the marginal to the king for legal hearing." Boyce, *The Cry to God in the Old Testament*, SBLDS 103 (Atlanta: Scholars Press, 1988) 72.

7. See Boyce, 10.

8. R. E. Brown, *The Death of the Messiah* (Garden City, NY: Doubleday, 1994) 2:1079.

9. Already in Mark (if it precedes Matt in time) there is a doubling of Jesus' cry (15:34, 37). This J. D. Crossan sees as a reworking of Mark's on the basis of *GPet* 5:19. Crossan, *The Cross That Spoke: The Origins of the Passion Narrative* (San Francisco: Harper and Row, 1988) 224. If Crossan is right, there has been a further reworking of the motif in Matt ("again" in

general, φωνὴ μεγάλη is found in cultic and apocalyptic contexts. Matthew and Mark have Jesus scream *at the ninth hour* (= 3:00 P.M.), that is, at the time of the afternoon prayer in the temple (see Ps 30:6). In this respect, the text of Judith 9:1 comes to mind. At the time of the evening offering, when the temple was still standing, Judith cries out, *with a loud voice* (ἐβόησε φωνῇ μεγάλη). The relation between temple and "loud voice" is here again stressed. The predicating verb in Mark (βοάω) and in Matthew (ἀναβοάω) can introduce a desperate cry for help, but can also preface a proclamation/acclamation by a crowd. In Revelation 6:10, the former martyrs shout their prayer with a "loud voice" saying, "until when . . . ?" In John 5:28 the Great Cry ushers in eschatological cosmic phenomena, and in John 11:43 it makes the dead *hear*; likewise in 1 Thessalonians 4:16, where it is sounded when the Lord comes down to raise the dead.

In such contexts, the underlying Hebrew term is רוע, a word which can parallel verbs of pain like זעק and בכא,[10] but which can be also used for shouts of joy, praise, or victory.[11] See, for instance, the LXX text of 1 Kings 4:5-6 (MT 1 Sam 4:5-6): Israel shouts with a φωνὴ μεγάλη at the placing of the ark (in lieu then of the future temple) at the head of their army facing the Philistines. These latter then hear ἡ κραυγὴ ἡ μεγάλη αὐτή. Note that, at the sound of that תרועה גדולה, the earth shakes. Almost the same effect is obtained when the Israelites shout their תרועה גדולה around Jericho. The walls of the city tumble down (Josh 6:5, 20; see Exod 32:17). Here, the LXX has ἀλαλαγμῷ μεγάλῳ καὶ ἰσχυρῷ, but the verb of action in verse 10 is, as in Matthew 27:50, ἀναβοάω. The central importance of the תרועה in Israel cannot be overstated; suffice it here to recall two texts: Numbers 23:21 (ותרועת מלך בו) and Psalm 89:16 (the people are called blessed *because* they are cognizant of the "acclamation," ידעי תרועה).

2. Φωνή in Matthew

Φωνή in Matthew designates various things:

(A) The prophetic voice of John the Baptist (or rather the voice of God through his messenger) in 3:3.[12] Already at this point, the φωνή is charged with meaning. We are not surprised, therefore, to find next that the term also represents the divine voice.

27:50). The trajectory thereafter takes us to Luke 23:46, that is, a "serene cry," and to "the majestic and divine non-cry of John 19:28-30," Crossan says (ibid.).

10. See Isa 15:4; Mic 4:9.

11. See Zeph 3:14; Zech 9:9; Ezek 3:11; Jer 31:7; 50:15.

12. "A voice is calling in the desert" of Isa 40:3, see Mark 1:3; Luke 3:4; in John 1:23, the Baptist says that he *is* the voice of one calling.

(B) The divine voice: Matthew 3:17;[13] see also Matthew 17:5.[14] One recognizes here the *bath qol* of rabbinic literature.

(C) Matthew's use of the whole expression φωνὴ μεγάλη, *however, is reserved for the narrative on the Passion.* Within the apocalyptic section of Matthew, in 24:31 (various mss), Jesus announces for "that time" (of the end) the sending of angels at the sound of a trumpet *and* a Great Cry. Translators, in general, do not retain that version because they think it does not make much sense. But the "great trumpet's sound" (שופר) refers to Isaiah 27:13, which speaks of the gathering of the exiles from "Assyria" and from "Egypt"—"in that day." The trumpet is often associated by later biblical authors with φωνή. See, for example, Revelation 1:10, and especially 1 Thessalonians 4:16 where Paul adopts an apocalyptic/lyric language to announce the coming of the Lord from heaven "with command, with the archangel's φωνή, with the trumpet of God, and the dead in Christ will rise first."

The association of the trumpet and the φωνή is not only biblically logical, but it sets us on the right track for finding the Hebrew correspondent of the "voice/sound" in Matthew 27:50: it is clearly the תרועה. As a sacred warcry with the blowing of the trumpets, see Amos 2:2 (see 1:14) and Zephaniah 1:16, "a day of the שופר and of the תרועה against the fenced cities."[15] The context in all these passages is that of the holy war, a context that also fits the ethos of Matthew 24:31, where it is a question of the ultimate battle that the Son of Man will wage with the help of his angels.

(D) Matthew 27:46 and 50: Jesus' Great Cries, one spelled out, the other not. In both cases, the term φωνή with the same Hebrew *Vorlage* is used. We are obviously not any longer in the ethos of the holy war, although still in that of the cult; verse 46 proves it.[16] That is why, as a hypothesis to be confirmed by other elements of the Passion narrative in Matthew, the Hebrew term behind φωνή in Matthew 27:50 is to be seen as תרועה.

As O. Betz writes, "A very important use of [the expression] is in relation to the speech of angels, spirits, or bearers of the Spirit."[17] Jesus expels the demons, who exit with a "loud voice," for the notion is that they know better God's mysteries than humans do; hence, Jesus,

---

13. See Mark 1:11; Luke 3:22; John, most strikingly, transposes the scene of the voice coming down from heaven to a context of Passion, John 12:28; 1:51.

14. The context of transfiguration/theophany, see Mark 9:7; Luke 9:35–36; 2 Pet 1:17–18.

15. See Ps 47:6; see Jer 20:16; Ezek 21:27; Job 39:25.

16. See also Num 31:6; 2 Chr 13:12.

17. O. Betz, in *TDNT*, s.v. φωνή, 9:293.

in Mark, commands them to remain silent.[18] *A contrario,* when the mute person is freed of demons, he starts to speak up![19] It is remarkable that, when God in HB texts shouts to manifest himself, his shout is accompanied by cosmic manifestations.[20]

Φωνὴ μεγάλη as used by Matthew always announces a major revelation. As a means of revelation, it *rends* the silence of ignorance and incomprehension on the part of the *goyim,* here represented by the centurion and his men; the connection of the Great Cry with the centurion's confession is also stressed by O. Betz. He says (speaking of the Markan text), "it is probable that Mark regarded as an epiphany the loud cry with which Jesus died on the cross."[21] The author calls attention to the simultaneity of the cry and the end of darkness (Mark 15:37). In fact, it rends the protective darkness of God's secrecy and the obliterating darkness that covered the universe. It rends the veil that used to hide God's presence from all. It rends mountains and rocks, unearthing, as in Job 38, things buried, and freeing saints from the shackles of death.

If indeed Matthew came after Mark, he did not follow Mark's model for the last moments of Jesus. Instead of one cry of prayer in the words of Psalm 22, Matthew introduced the word πάλιν and thus insisted on two different cries, the latter more decisive yet than the first.[22]

III

Matthew's plurivocity must be kept in mind by the reader of the Gospel. The Evangelist came with a narrative whose details would be understandable by non-initiates, that is, by Gentiles, while constantly alluding, for the sake of the Jewish Christians of his audience, to exegetical and midrashic traditions, shedding light on a deeper meaning of the testimony. This kind of "double-entendre" in the Gospel of Mat-

---

18. Mark 1:25; 5:7; see Luke 4:33–35.
19. Matthew 9:33, see Luke 11:14.
20. See Amos 1:2; Jer 25:30; Ps 45:7; Joel 4:16.
21. O. Betz, 294. I believe that the critic who came closest to the right appreciation of the Great Cry was K. Stock. See his article, "Das Bekenntnis des Centurio: Markus 15.39 im Rahmen des Markusevangeliums," *ZKT* 100 (1978) 289-301. The cry was revelational; it was an epiphany (see p. 294). But the weakness of his demonstration is that it misses the *apocalyptic* setting in Matt, and also the Yom Kippur ethos, with the high priest entering the holy of holies and shouting the Name.
22. Donald P. Senior is doubtless wrong when he comments on Matthew 27:50 that Jesus is here again quoting Psalm 22:2 but striking a note of confidence, expressing "his confident and triumphant faith." See Senior, *The Passion Narrative According to Matthew,* BETL 39 (Leuven: Leuven University Press, 1975). R. E. Brown is right to recall that the following verse in the psalm says, "I shout by day, and you do not answer."

thew will be crucial when we turn to the Great Cry of Jesus on the cross. It is without surprise that we shall discover that the shout also has a double sense, one plain meaning for the Gentiles, one profounder meaning for the Jews.[23]

1. Why a Passion Apocalypse?

The apocalyptic section of Matthew's passion narrative is introduced in chapter 21, with Jesus entering the temple (21:12). Already on his arrival in Jerusalem, he stirs a "quake." But soon the narrative focuses on what becomes the veritable stage of the unwinding drama, that is, the temple during the preparation for Passover.[24] The temple is shown to be the "den" of Jesus' enemies, and the confrontation with them will continue until his death on the cross. The accent is on the paradoxical nature of Jesus' opponents. For Matthew it has been a protracted struggle since that conflict between Cain and Abel, even between Eve and the serpent, and throughout the history of the prophets and their killers (Matt 23:33–35). The conflict continues after the crucifixion with the disciples being persecuted in Matthew's own time.[25]

Having begun in chapter 21, the Matthean apocalypse is interrupted by the narrative of the betrayal of Jesus, followed by his Passion. The apocalypse rebounds when Jesus is nailed on the cross. Thus again the indissoluble tie between narrative and apocalypse is exemplified, the latter being always presented within a narrative frame. One remembers J. J. Collins's definition of apocalypse as "*a genre of revelatory literature with a narrative framework.*"[26]

The references to the "quake" (Matt 21:10 and 27:51) and to the "clamor" of the multitude (ἔκραζον) in 21:9 *versus* the cry and the earthquake in 27:50–51 form a double *inclusio*. We shall return to the quake in what follows, but already at this point, it is important to emphasize that the phenomenon is thematically tied with the temple. In Matthew 24:1–2, Jesus exits the temple and announces its (physical and spiritual) destruction. The time of the temple is gone; as Matthew 27 will make clear, the omphalic and centripetal temple becomes

---

23. The more one insists, as I do, on the Jewish character of Matthew's Gospel, the more doubtful become theories about the possible preexistence of an Aramean *Vorlage,* Targum, or source. The intertestamental literature is not devoid of Jewish Hellenistic works addressed to both Jews and Gentiles for apologetic purposes.

24. Hence, the expectation of the return of Elijah; see 27:47, 49: note the irony.

25. Matt 24:9–14; in chapters 24–25 there is an accumulation of terms which use the imagery of Jesus' Passion to designate the expected sufferings of his disciples: flogged, hounded, arrested, tortured, stoned, crucified. Nothing of this is metaphorical.

26. J. J. Collins, ed., "Apocalypse, The Morphology of a Genre," *Semeia* 14 (1979) 9.

centrifugal and extends to the confines of the earth.[27] In fact, Matthew presents Jesus' Passion as the result of a clash with the temple, that is, with the Jewish establishment of the time.[28] While Jesus' death should secure the triumph of the establishment, the contrary result is obtained. But, in order to prove this, Matthew must introduce an episode during the crucifixion that spells out the temple's demise. He thus brings an apocalyptic complex of words and events related to the crucifixion, a complex that culminates in the Great Cry. It is through this apocalyptic complex that Matthew communicates that the death of Jesus has rendered the former era totally obsolete.

Thus, Matthew uses an apocalyptic language, the appropriate language in fact for describing the temple's desecration and/or destruction. With this theme, we touch on the first motivation of Matthew. In chapter 24, Jesus refers to Daniel 9:27, denouncing the presence of the "desolating abomination" in the temple (verse 15), an abomination that Jesus now identifies with the *high priest* himself! P. S. Minear interprets the passage thus[29] and I believe that he is right. The urgent warning note to the reader in 24:15 gives cogency to Minear's reading, as does the whole context of the cleansing of the temple by Jesus (21:12–17). The temple has become the nest of all evil (21:13).

Matthew's second motivation for using apocalyptic language derives from the way in which such language heralds a reversal of power. This it does through mentioning two pairs of "quakes" with mutually corresponding elements. The first appears in the form of a simile on Palm Sunday (Matt 21:10) with its response in the metaphoric "quake" of the guards at the tomb on the Resurrection Sunday (28:4). The other, presented as really seismic, occurs on Good Friday (27:51); it is echoed by another tremor on Easter (Matt 28:2). Minear, accurately, writes, "an earthquake separates those who perceive a change in the balance of power from those who are quite unaware."[30]

---

27. From the beginning, the centrality of Israel and its temple is meant to radiate and reach the ends of the universe (see Isa 2; Mic 4; Isa 42:6). But the fulfillment of such purpose underscores the relativity of the promise's vessel. On the same line, when, according to Joel 4, everyone becomes prophetic, it is clear that the presence of individual prophets becomes obsolete. It is thus understandable that the establishment would be the least prepared to acknowledge its own demise. Therefore, paradoxically, the temple defiled by the "desolating abomination" becomes a historical necessity before it can be discarded; similarly, prophecy in Israel had become a hoax (see Zech 14) before it waned away. R. Johanan ben Zakkai came close to drawing the same conclusion when saying, "be not grieved [on the destroyed temple]; we have another atonement as effective as this . . . ; it is acts of loving-kindness." *The Fathers According to Rabbi Nathan*, trans. J. Goldin (New Haven: Yale University Press, 1955) 34–35.

28. See Matt 27:61; as Josephus says [in *JA* 18:63], Jesus was "accused by men of the highest standing amongst us."

29. P. S. Minear, *The Golgotha Earthquake* (Cleveland: Pilgrim Press, 1995) 87.

30. Ibid., 102. He refers to HB texts like Ps 18:1–15; 60:2; Isa 64:1–3; Jer 4:23–28; 10:10; Ezek 12:17–20; Joel 2:10; Sir 16:17–23; 2 Esd 16:8–17. (Ibid., 130 n. 8).

Furthermore, as these texts and still others show, the earthquake is an expression of God's wrath over systemic evil that must be eradicated; the earth "vomits" those who are unworthy to tread it. A new order is about to be born.

A third motivation for the Matthean use of apocalyptic language can be seen in the link that an early Christian tradition draws between Jesus' Passion and the future apocalyptic consummation, as is already attested in the Epistle of Barnabas (perhaps written before the end of the first c. C.E.). The point here is the prolepsis of Jesus' Passion as seen by the early church; hence its Matthean tallying with eschatological texts of the Hebrew Bible. J. D. Crossan makes a convincing case for the Passion narrative being the result of an original "prophetic passion" based on a "florilegium" of prophetic texts interpreted as foretelling the sufferings of the Messiah.[31] As regards Matthew, however, I would suggest that the Evangelist replaced the hypothetically original "prophetic passion" by an "apocalyptic passion." Such a realization is important on several scores, one of which is the presence of mythology in the narrative—not an "embarrassing" feature,[32] but a constitutive ingredient of apocalyptic.[33]

It is from this perspective that all the elements of Matthew's Passion are meaningful, including both the obvious apocalyptic phenomena such as darkness, earthquake, the temple veil, the open tombs, and also the less obviously apocalyptic motifs such as the Great Cry and the Gentile confession.[34] I shall return to the sequence of those elements below, but it is to be stressed that the Great Cry motif, also and especially, must be understood as apocalyptic. It "unveils" and inaugurates; it reveals and ushers in; it is an end and a beginning. A Janus-like phenomenon, it signifies that the old world sinks into darkness with the sound of a shriek, and that the new world is born at the sound of a תרועה.

2. The Different Elements in the Passion Apocalypse

I said above that the apocalyptic development of the Passion in Matthew starts in 21:12. It is interrupted by a narrative on the betrayal of Jesus. The resurgence of the apocalyptic, when Jesus is nailed on the

---

31. See Crossan, *The Historical Jesus*. According to intertestamental literature, the earthquake belongs to the חבלו של משיח (the Messiah's woes), see *T. Mos.* 10:4; *T. Levi* 4:1; 4 Esd 9:3; 2 Bar 27:7; *Apoc. Abr.* 30.

32. *Pace* Crossan, *Historical Jesus*, 389.

33. See John J. Collins's or my own work on Daniel 7.

34. Jesus' resurrection is off-limits in this paper.

cross, is inaugurated by a *mention of Elijah*. The mention of that figure here would be improbable (how could anyone hearing Jesus recite Psalm 22:1 confuse אלי אלי with אליהו?) were it not for the familiar abbreviation of his name into *"Elî"* as shown by Jewish inscriptions in Rome.[35] Clearly, Matthew wanted to conclude his Gospel the same way he initiated it.[36] The old prophet is the precursor of the Messiah.[37]

To facilitate the connection/confusion between the two referents *"eli"* (my God) and *"eli(yah),"* Matthew imagines that Jesus recited Psalm 22:1 in Aramaic, *"èlei, èlei."* At any rate, the Aramaic introduces a taut ambiguity, for one can now "hear" Jesus say, "Elijah, Elijah, why have you abandoned me (and my Messianic claim)?" So, some bystanders conclude that this might prompt Elijah to hear and intervene, and they construe the giving of vinegar to Jesus (to induce a loss of consciousness) as an unwelcome interference (27:49).

The somewhat awkward intervention of the Elijah motif in the Passion narrative (of Matthew and Mark) is important. As Jonathan Z. Smith has shown,[38] the people's expectation in the time of Jesus, and already before, was two-pronged and in mutual opposition: the restoration of the temple's purity (hence, the Jewish canon ends with 2 Chr 36:23) and the coming of a divine man, the *magus* Elijah (hence the Christian canon ends with Mal 4:5). In this perspective, the a-topic mobility of Jesus constitutes the ultimate challenge to the temple. "No matter what Jesus thought, said, or did about the temple, he was its functional opponent, alternative, and substitute," J. D. Crossan says.[39]

The figure of Elijah in "history" and in tradition, cannot be separated from the theophany on Mount Horeb reported in 1 Kings 19 (see especially verses 11–12), that falls in parallel and contrast with the *Urtheophanie* to Moses in Exodus 19 (see verses 16–19). There is a "thick cloud, . . . smoke, . . . a quake, . . . a very loud trumpet blast"

---

35. See Y. Kutscher, *The Language and Linguistic Background of the Isaiah Scroll (1QIsa*[a]*)*, Studies on the Texts of the Desert of Judah 6 (Leiden: Brill, 1964) 181–82. Another possibility is contemplated by T. Boman in 1963 and X. Léon-Dufour, developing a suggestion made earlier by H. Sahlin: Jesus spoke in Hebrew and said, אלי אתה (you are my God), a phrase present in four Psalms (22:11; 63:2; 118:28; 140:7; see Isa 44:17). But this was understood as the Aramaic *"éliya' tha"* (Elijah, come!). Finally, there exists still the possibility of "un sinistre jeu de mots," as says L. Vaganay (243). At any rate, adds X. Léon-Dufour, Jesus' saying becomes in Matthew, through its Hebraization, a liturgical quote of Ps 22:1 (672). Boman, "Das letzte Wort Jesu," *Studia Theologica* 17 (1963) 103-19; Léon-Dufour, "Le dernier cri de Jésus," *Etudes* 348 (1978) 666-82; Vaganay, *L'Evangile de Pierre* (Paris: Gabalda, 1930).

36. In 3:4, John the Baptist is dressed like Elijah (see 2 Kgs 1:8), and John is identified with the expected Elijah (Matt 17:11–12).

37. Mal 3:23; Sir 48:10–11; *m.* '*Ed.* 8:7; *m. B. Meṣ.* 3:5; see Mark 9:11–13.

38. Jonathan Z. Smith, "The Temple and the Magician," in *God's Christ and His People: Studies in Honour of Nils Alstrup Dahl*, ed. J. Jervell and W. A. Meeks (Oslo: Universitetsforlaget, 1977) 233-47.

39. *The Historical Jesus*, 355.

(Exodus), "rocks crushed . . . and [in a stark contrast with the trumpet/Great Cry] a tenuous silence" (1 Kings).[40] Matthew's choice of Elijah over Moses in the Passion story serves the purpose of affirming the messiahship of the martyr. Horeb and Calvary: the holy mountain where the divine man meets God face to face.

The *splitting of the rocks* in Matthew 27:52 is apparently the result of the earthquake. Some texts of the Hebrew Bible refer to the "earthquake" as sign of the end and of the divine presence.[41] The verb used by Matthew is the same as for the "splitting" of the temple curtain in the preceding verse. But much more is intended by that motif. In Zechariah 14:4 "YHWH's feet stand on the Mount of Olives which shall split in two from east to west by a very wide valley." The "splitting in two" (נבקע הר הזיתים מחציו) has inspired Matthew for the tearing of the curtain.[42] It is in parallel to this that he now speaks of the tearing of the rocks, that is, the eschatological splitting of the Mount of Olives of the Zecharian oracle, which according to Jewish tradition is a prelude to the resurrection of the dead.[43] Zechariah associates this yawning open of the Mount of Olives with an earthquake as well (14:5).

The tally of the apocalyptic elements found in Matthew 27 is crucial. The Great Cry, the earthquake, the resurrection of (the) dead, belong together. This is particularly clear in the *Targum of Zechariah 14*. *Tg. Zech.* 14:33–35 tells us that *God blows the trumpet* ten times to announce the resurrection. The *Targum of Song of Songs* 8:5 adds that the resurrection will happen as the Mount of Olives will be cleft.

Thus, Matthew 27:52–53 is, as it were, a further response to the disciples' inquiry in 24:3, as also 27:45 comes in fulfillment of 24:29. This latter text introduces the mysterious "Sign of the Son of Man" (see verses 29–30), at the sight of which "all the tribes of the earth" repent and understand. The sign is signaled by angels blowing the "great שופר" (24:31), a habitual accompaniment of the Great Cry, as we saw above. Matthew 27:50 comes with the actualization of the sign: the Great Cry is followed by the confessing centurion and his men.

Before we proceed with the review of other apocalyptic manifestations, a preliminary conclusion imposes itself. We readily realize that

---

40. As we shall see Matthew also collapses the festivals of Passover and Yom Kippur as he does Elijah and Moses.

41. So Isa 2:19 (LXX); 1 Kgs 19:11–12; Nah 1:5–6; *T. Levi* 4:1.

42. In the LXX of Zech, the same verb σχισθήσεται appears for the splitting of the Mount of Olives.

43. See *Pesiqta Rabbati* 31 (147a); *Tg. Song* 8:5; *Apoc. Dan.* 128; see the Synagogue of Dura Europos's fresco; Josephus, *Ant.* 9,10,4 and 20,8,6. According to *Sanh.* 92, "those who remain in Jerusalem shall be called holy," God will raise those righteous from the dead (see *t. Sanh. ad loc.*; *Midr. Ps* 42:1) and the "world to come" is then inaugurated.

the whole apocalyptic sequence in Matthew constitutes a *unit*: Elijah, the darkness, the earthquake, the split rocks, the Great Cry (= the trumpet blast). The theme of the resurrection of the righteous[44] was added on account of the topographical proximity of the Mount of Olives, a magnet for eschatological speculations on the final resurrection.[45] The Elijah figure in 1 Kings 17:17–24 and 2 Kings 2:11 also typifies resurrection/immortality.

Matthew wants to convey the idea that Jesus' death inaugurates the end of times; it is the final act that pushes history over the edge and ushers in the "world to come," the kingdom of heaven so dear to the evangelist Matthew. Whereas death reigned in "this world," the coming world is the world of life. The righteous dead arise and enter the Holy City; that is, they are enthroned in Zion with the one whose reign is still for a while hidden to many eyes. The risen righteous are the visible aspect of their Lord about to be or already risen ("many saw them"). In the Gospel, only those saints arise who are in the close vicinity of the cross, because the tradition is unanimous in stating that resurrection will start with those buried on the Mount of Olives. That tradition explains why so many pious Jews through the centuries have wanted to be buried there.[46]

Something of the same nature is expressed by the *darkness* that accompanies the earthquake on Good Friday. We are reminded of a text like Amos 5:18–20; or 8:9: "On that day, says the Lord God, I will make the sun go down at noon and darken the earth in broad daylight. I will turn your feasts into mourning." The motif is found also in Isaiah 13:9–16 (judgment), or in Jeremiah 4:5–6 (mourning), and so forth. But, especially in the intertestamental literature, the theme is eschatological:[47] darkness signals the advent of the Day of the Lord.[48] An interesting parallel is drawn in *GPet* 15, whose text comes closer to Amos than do the texts of the synoptics. *GPet* uses the term μεσημβρία (midday) of LXX Amos 8:9, rather than the ὥρα ἕκτη of the gospels. At any rate, the re-use by the Gospels of the Amos text shows that for them the eschatological day has come; it is a day when the ethos of Yom Kippur prevails over that of Passover, as we shall see

---

44. This is also a *bona fide* apocalyptic ingredient, reminiscent of Dan 7:18 ff. and 12:1; the use of οἱ ἅγιοι by Matthew is unusual.

45. In Zech 14:4–5, the text of the LXX has also οἱ ἅγιοι.

46. In *GPet* 10:39–42, the risen Jesus is followed by a procession of holy ones after Jesus went to preach to them in hell. It is the theme of the vindication of the innocent, according to the concluding development in the "innocence rescued" genre as identified by J. D. Crossan (*The Historical Jesus*, 384 ff.).

47. See *T. Mos.* 10:5; *T. Levi* 4:1; *2 Bar.* 10:12; etc.

48. On which, see 1 Cor 1:8; 2 Thess 2:2; 2 Pet 3:10.

below and as the Amos text (8:9) forecast ("I will turn your feasts into mourning").[49]

The darkness is the same as in Genesis 1:2–4 and is not to be confused with the night.[50] This absence of light (rather than being its contrast and its correspondent) is the darkness of chaos and lifelessness that precedes creation. Creation is summarized by "light," that is, by revelation, by self-disclosure of the Creator.[51] When Jesus is about to die, the cosmos reverts to chaos, and darkness shrouds the earth in the middle of the day. It lingers for three hours (27:45), as many hours as the days Jesus would remain in the grave; after which there is a new creation, with an ushering earthquake (28:2) and the presence of an angel radiating a blinding light, "like lightning, and his raiment was white as snow."[52] But this does not happen before Jesus, figuratively at least, pulls with him into his grave (or into hell) the whole world. It would stay there forever where it deserves to be; but, as death is unable to hold Jesus in its sway (see Acts 2:24), so the just come back to life (27:52–53), forerunners of all those who will share in the new world. In that respect, the reader must be attentive to the surprising use by Matthew of a very unusual Greek expression for the expiring of Jesus: ἀφῆκεν τὸ πνεῦμα (27:50). It is particularly the word πνεῦμα that is at issue. One recognizes Ezekiel 37 in the background with its announcement of re-creation through the πνεῦμα (LXX). Note that, for John as well, the gift of the Spirit depends upon Jesus' death.[53]

So, the expected "world to come" has now come according to Matthew's witness. This allows us, I believe, to be attentive to the plurivocity of the motif of darkness. Once the curtain closing up the

---

49. On the conflation of festivals, see Tob 2:1, 5 where lament prevails over Pentecost and the same text of Amos 8:9–10 is referred to. This feature is also stressed by some fathers of the church. So Irenaeus (*Ad. Her.* 4.33.12) says, "those days that were their festivals according to the law, and their songs, should be changed into grief and lamentation." And Tertullian (*An Answer to the Jews* 10) insists on an aspect of Passover that is ominous instead of joyful: the unleavened bread had to be eaten "with bitterness," in which Tertullian sees the Passion of Christ. (Quoted by J. D. Crossan, *The Cross*, 199).

50. It is no eclipse, an astronomical impossibility since Passover falls in a full-moon season. (*GPet* has been particularly sensitive to that impossibility.) When *Sib. Or.* 8.305–6 alludes to the "night" when the temple veil is rent, it qualifies this by adding "night dark and monstrous" (1.375).

51. Gen 1:3; one thinks also of the darkness that covers Egypt at the eve of the first Passover: Exod 10:22.

52. *GPet* 22 has missed that nuance present in Matthew and insists on the return of the light at 3:00 P.M. at the relief of "the Jews," who were afraid they had violated the law (in not burying Jesus before sunset; see Deut 21:22).

53. Again here, the liturgy of Yom Kippur is not far off. We read in *Pesiq. R.* 40.5, "Remake yourselves by repentance [says God] during the 10 days between New Year's Day and the Day of Atonement, and on the Day of Atonement I will hold you guiltless, regarding you as a newly made creature." (*Pesiqta Rabbati*, trans. W. G. Braude, [New Haven: Yale University Press, 1968] 2:711).

Holy of Holies (דביר) is rent, the darkness of the sacred place (see 1 Kgs 8:12) invades the whole earth[54] as also its sacredness covers the world. At the moment of contact with the sacred, the earth quakes, it looses its grip on the dead bodies of the saints, and these "enter the City after his raising (them)." So also did the revived dry bones enter the land of Israel in Ezekiel 37:13. The amphibology of darkness extends also to the holy city. For the latter can also represent the heavenly abode.[55] The interrelationship of several seats of holiness is remarkable in the Matthean development. The "Holy of Holies" is extended to the whole earth, so that the "holy ones" asleep in an unholy ground (tombs) are made alive and enter the holy city. The latter is Jerusalem but also the universal sphere of holiness, for the darkness of the דביר now covers the whole γῆ. Such a recuperation of all sorts of seats of holiness is made possible by the holy high priest entering his realm with the תרועה, the Great Cry of the universal atonement. I refer here to the *Testament of Levi* 18:10–11, which says that the last high priest "will open the gates of paradise . . . and will give to the holy ones to eat from the tree of life."

But Matthew is not the first one who believed at the foot of the cross. At the moment when Jesus shouts his Great Cry and expires, the veil of the temple is rent from top to bottom, and *the centurion* who is there with his men—those who crucified Jesus—seeing what was happening, confesses, "Truly, this was the son of God" (Matt 27:54). Here the centurion and his men function as representatives of all the Gentiles now allowed to step over through the rent curtain into the sacred precincts of the holy shrine. Again with this motif, there is another *inclusio* with Matthew 4:16 (the promise that the Gentiles would see a great light, following Isa 9:1–2). Incidentally, it is very interesting that William Farmer sees Matthew's Gospel entirely organized in accordance with the fulfillment of the prophecy of those verses of Isaiah (from Galilee to Transjordan to Jerusalem).[56] Matthew forwards the apostolic tradition of Jerusalem.

According to Matthew, the centurion's confession further forms an *inclusio* with the high priests' "wish" to see Jesus come down from the cross as King and Son of God so that they may believe (27:42–43). On this point, Raymond Brown wonders why Matthew drops the Markan

---

54. γῆ; see Mark 15:33//Luke 23:44; *GPet* 5:15 has "the whole of Judah."

55. "Holy city" designates Jerusalem in Isa 48:2; 52:1; Matt 4:5–7; *T. Levi* 11:2. Rev 21:2, 10; 22:19 speak of a heavenly Jerusalem (see Heb 13:14). *T. Levi* has the just going in paradise and cutting the fruit of life (see also *T. Dan.* 5:12). In John 1:51, the heaven is open.

56. W. Farmer, *The Gospel of Jesus* (Louisville: W/JKP, 1996) 16.

mention of "Messiah."[57] Doubtless the reason is that, to the Romans, the title was synonymous with guerrilla leader or λῃστής.[58] The most important point, however, is that the centurion saw what the chief priests did not, for their wish to see was spurious.[59] The Gentile centurion is substituted for the chief priests, a notion that is not unfamiliar to Jewish tradition. ʿAboda Zara 3a declares, on the basis of Leviticus 18:5, that, "a Gentile who occupies himself with Torah is like a High Priest, for it says 'a man', it does not say 'a priest' or 'a Levite' or 'an Israelite', but 'a man'."[60] Thus, to the high priest's question whether Jesus is "the Messiah, the Son of God" (26:63),[61] the response comes from a Gentile officer! Raymond Brown opines that the centurion's confession is "the highest Christological evaluation in the Gospel."[62] No reader of the New Testament will be surprised. The whole ministry of Jesus emphasized this through, for example, declaring the priority of tax-gatherers and harlots over "chief priests and elders" (Matt 21:23, 31–32). To John the Baptist's disciples inquiring about Jesus' mission, Jesus responded, "Go and tell John . . . the poor have good news preached to them" (a fact that seems to surpass even the resurrection of the dead! Luke 7:22).

The confession is synchronous with *the rending of the curtain*—Paul Minear translates ἰδού by "at that moment."[63] Four things occur simultaneously: the great shout, the bursting of the light, the rending of the temple curtain, and the confession of the centurion. Four powers are overcome: the temple establishment, nature, death, and Rome; that is, the religious power, the cosmic power, the ontological power, and the political power. As befits the apocalyptic discourse, what had been prophesied earlier (see the recurrent "that it might be fulfilled which was spoken by the prophet") is now "unveiled" for everyone to see, as even the most secret and sacred of all veils, the one of the temple, is removed. The verb "to see" occurs some ten times in twenty verses of Matthew 27. I shall return to this issue of revelation/accomplishment in part V below.

---

57. R. E. Brown, *The Death of the Messiah*, 2:993.

58. See below, part V. Similarly, I suggest that the anarthrous expression θεοῦ υἱός lies at some distance from the arthrous full expression ὁ υἱὸς τοῦ θεοῦ, but must, however, be translated here, with R. Brown, by "the Son of God," not "a son of (a) god."

59. K. Stock sees the opposition (see 300–301), but he reduces it by drawing a parallel with the role assigned to Pilate in contrast to the Jewish establishment during the trial (298).

60. Same opinion in *Sifra* 86b, etc.

61. Note the explicating "Son of God" to prevent any misunderstanding with a gang leader.

62. R. Brown, 1144.

63. He is right as is shown by the ms Syr^s of Matt 27:51; see also *GPet* 20 (αὐτῆς ὥρας).

The rending of the temple veil is clearly a crucial moment in Matthew's report on the crucifixion (also in Mark). The Matthean text remains vague, however, as there are two different curtains of the temple that may be referred to here, as texts like Exodus 26:1 versus 31 or 36:8 versus 35 show (see also 2 Chr 3:14). In fact, the ambiguity in Matthew is not accidental. It is already present in the Septuagint's undifferentiated designation of both veils, using the same word that we find in Matthew here, καταπέτασμα, for the outer one and the inner one.[64] But what the Evangelist had in mind is first and foremost the פרכת that separates the holy of holies from the holy place and maintains the דביר in total obscurity.[65] The term פרכת appears seventeen times in the source P;[66] etymologically it means "that which shuts off" (from the Akkadian *parrâku*) and this sense of the word says it all: Matthew wants to stress the end of an era through the "opening up" (or, apocalypse) of what used to be "shut off." A text like Hebrews 10:19-20 is appropriate here also: Christ has given us access to the temple through the veil. Another echo can be found in Revelation, which in 11:19 and 15:5 speaks of the opening of God's temple in heaven, the prototype of the earthly temple in Jerusalem.[67] The phenomenon also includes an earthquake, like in Matthew, *and the ark of the covenant is now made visible*, which was behind the veil! The association in Matthew of the Great Cry with the revelation of the inside of the holy of holies (cf. Rev. 11:15) must be strongly emphasized.[68]

In the Babylonian Talmud, *m. Yoma* 5.1-6.2 (see *Git.* 56b) has the following,

> R. Jose says, Only one curtain was there . . . [he quotes Exod 26:33 where the word "veil" appears in the sg.] . . . When he [the high priest] reached the Ark . . . he heaped up the incense on the coals and the whole place became filled with smoke . . . He then came to the scapegoat and laid his two hands upon it and made confession . . . [He recites Lev 16:30, which ends with the words:] "ye shall be clean before YHWH" [and he apparently spelled out the Tetragrammaton, for the text continues:] And when the priests and the people which stood in the temple

---

64. Same ambiguity in Jos. *B.J.* 5.5.4 and 5.5.5; or in 1 Macc 4:51, and the Heb; see *Shek.* 8:5.

65. See 1 Kgs 8:12; Ps 18:12. In the LXX, Exod 26:31-33; 30:6; 35:12; 39:34; 40:21; Num 4:5.

66. See, e.g., Exod 26:31; 35:12; 39:34; 40:21; Num 4:5; Lev 4:6; 24:3.

67. See also Matt 3:16 and, especially Mark 1:10-11 where is used the same verb as in Matt 27:51 on the model of Ezek 1 and 10.

68. See *Sib. Or.* 8.299-309, "For no longer by secret law and in hidden temple to serve the phantoms of this world, the hidden truth was again revealed."

> Court heard the Expressed Name come forth from the mouth of the High
> Priest, they used to kneel and bow, etc . . .[69]

The priestly shout is called תרועה. In fact, the Jewish tradition has it
that the high priest shouted the divine Name more than once, which,
most probably, is the origin of the Matthean use of the word πάλιν
(27:50) to speak of Jesus crying again before expiring. It has nothing
to do with an alleged repetition of Psalm 22 by the moribund.[70] The
Great Cry is immensely more important. With it, Jesus puts an end to
the priestly function in the former dispensation.[71] For *Testament of
Levi* 10, in which one can recognize a Christian addition, the rent
curtain reveals the shame of the temple priests. *Testament of Benjamin*
9 sees in the rending of the curtain not only the cancellation of the
Jerusalem priesthood but the pouring of the divine Spirit (like a fire)
upon the Gentiles.

In closing this section, one must take seriously the violence
implied in the verb "to rend." In addition, the simultaneity of Jesus
expiring and the veil being torn focuses the attention of the reader on
the Crucified himself. It is not enough to say that his death is a portent
of the temple's end. Rather, his death *is the destruction of the temple.*
An early and striking Christian interpretation identified the ruin of the
temple and the breaking of Jesus' body (see John 2:21). The opening of
Jesus' mouth for his last breath/Great Cry—that is, the tearing of his
flesh—*is the tearing of the veil* (as it is the "tearing" of the rocks, and
of the tombs). For Matthew, the destruction of the temple will not wait
until 70 C.E.; it is concomitant with the last Cry. It is so, shall we say,
because the last and ultimate Word is then pronounced at a place that
becomes the true holy of holies.[72] All the rest is either commentary or
silence.

IV
Φωνὴ Μεγάλη and Yom Kippur in Matthew 27

As seen above, the context of both Matthew 27:46 and 50 is cultic,[73]
thus making it appropriate to turn to a series of Hebrew texts where

---

69. See text in C. K. Barrett, *The New Testament Background: Selected Documents* (San
Francisco: Harper and Row, 1987) 203.

70. See Harrington, *The Gospel of Matthew* (Collegeville, MN: Liturgical Press, 1991)
1:403.

71. See Heb 6:19; 9:12, 24; 10:20.

72. See below the collapsing of Calvary with Mt. Sinai.

73. Remarkably, the Great Cry appears in the four Gospels and in *GPet*. This does not
mean, however, that they all think of the same thing. *GPet*, for instance, uses the same composite
verb (an unusual fact in *GPet*) as does Matt to introduce the cry, ἀνεβόησε λεγῶν, but the content
of the cry is the same as the first cry in Matt [here: "my power, the power has abandoned me"]

תְּרוּעָה, not just זְעָקָה or קוֹל, is shouted or blown with a wind instrument and designates a cultic cry/sound: Leviticus 25:9 and Numbers 10:5–6; Leviticus 23:24 and Numbers 29:1. Since in Matthew 27:50 we are in a cultic context, the predicating verb cannot be ἀφίεναι (to let go) as in Mark 15:37, but κράζειν as actually in Matthew (κράξας φωνῇ μεγάλῃ, to cry out, to shout).

Note that, in the Greek of the LXX, κραυή or κραυγή also render the Hebrew key-word תְּרוּעָה,[74] but most of these occurrences are irrelevant here. One New Testament text, however, deserves mention as it clearly alludes to our problem. In Hebrews 5:7 we read, "[Jesus] offered prayers and petitions μετὰ κραυγῆς ἰσχυρᾶς and with tears to the one who could save him from death, and he was heard because of his submission." At first sight, it seems that the Great Cry of Jesus here simply falls in parallel with "prayers," as "tears" corresponds to "petitions," thus keeping the whole within the frame of Jesus' supplication not to die. But the context cannot be ignored; it is one of priestly dedication and self-oblation (see 10:9–10). The term τελειωθείς in Hebrews 5:9 has this meaning in the cultic texts of Exodus 29 or Leviticus 8; see also Sirach 50:11. In other words, in Hebrews as well the Great Cry has a cultic, priestly connotation, and in Hebrews as well it is set within the framework of the Passion. There is furthermore a strange paradox in this Hebrews passage: Jesus begs not to die—and he is heard by God. Does the text mean that he did not die? Assuredly not. Then, how was he heard by God? Through his resurrection, which Hebrews (like Matthew and parallel texts) puts in relation with what Jesus utters on the cross! His utterances are "prayers and petitions" and they are presented to God with "a Great Cry," that is, with a תְּרוּעָה גְדוֹלָה.[75]

This is in direct reference to the liturgy of Yom Kippur, which Philo of Alexandria describes as "entirely devoted to prayers and supplications . . . petitions and humble entreaty in which one seeks earnestly to propitiate God."[76] In Numbers 29:1 (P), Yom Kippur is called "the day of the תְּרוּעָה." Above, we read a talmudic text (*m. Yoma* 5.1) which describes the high priest shouting the Tetragram-

and *GPet* deletes φωνὴ μεγάλη, which, I argue, would have oriented toward a different conclusion.

74. See 1 Kgs 4:6 (twice); 2 Kgs 6:15; Amos 1:14; Zeph 1:16; Jer 4:19; Ezek 21:17, 27.

75. True, one cannot infer from the theology of one document the theology of another document, but at least the possibility exists of a similar understanding of the same events by NT writers. Between Matthew and Hebrews, the difference is not in the fact that Jesus is seen by the latter as the eschatological high priest, but in what it means for him to fulfill that role.

76. See *The Special Laws*, vol. 2, LCL, 7:193–203.

maton in the holy of holies on Yom Kippur. Such a rapprochement is crucial for the thesis of this paper. Matthew sets the Passion ostensibly within the framework of Passover, but compositionally within a context of Yom Kippur! He had done the same collapsing of festivals in 21:9, for example, where, in the midst of the preparation for Passover, we encounter with surprise features of Sukkot: people shout the great *Hallel* and wave bundles of boughs. Similarly, the popular acclamation of the King-Messiah is punctuated with cries of "Hosanna" in the streets, as they used to be shouted in the temple![77] Hence, the temple motif is perfectly in place here: Jesus enters the temple and overthrows the tables of sacrifice providers and of treasurers (exchangers).[78]

It is also within the context of the collapse of festivals that the subsequent episode of the sterile fig tree is to be read. It happens when Jesus leaves the temple. Now the time for the fig tree to yield fruits was not Passover but Pentecost. The law in Exodus 23:16 is that the firstfruits be brought in at "the feast of harvest" (Pentecost), some five months from the time of Passover. In other words, Jesus behaves as if the time of פסח were the time of שבעות.

Such festival-collapsing is not without precedent in Hebrew literature. One finds the same substitution of festivals in Daniel 9–11. Clearly, the setting of Daniel 9 is Yom Kippur (see v. 20, e.g.). This is also true of chapters 10–11, although the alleged time is Passover (10:4). "Daniel, in the light of the harsh times and the interdiction against celebrating Passover [by Antiochus IV] has, in a way, transformed *Pesaḥ* into Yom Kippur."[79] More accurately, he has substituted a Jubilee, that is, a Yom Kippur falling every 7 x 7 years (and of which Daniel 9 speaks). On that day, the Israelites practice self-oblation.[80] In the time of Jesus Yom Kippur—the great atonement made by the high priest donning sacral vestments—was the main festival of the year. Note that we have a parody of this in Matthew 27:28, 31, 35, 59 as regards Jesus; even his shroud belongs to this context.[81]

Other details shed light on the Matthean development. For instance, the priest is anointed (משח). He purges the holy shrine, the tabernacle (to become the holy of holies), the altar, the priests, the people.[82] The priest puts his life at risk in the process, for it is at all

---

77. See here 21:15; see *m.Sukk* 3 on the singing of the *Hallel* of Ps 118.

78. That is, those who received the half shekel of the individual yearly contribution to the temple reserves, while taking for themselves a percentage.

79. See A. LaCocque, *Daniel* (Atlanta: John Knox Press, 1979) 209.

80. ונתתם את־נפשתיכם. See Lev 23:26–32; 16:29–34; Num 29:7–11.

81. On the day of Atonement, some pious people don a white shroud (a *kittel*) as a symbol of their repentance and contrition.

82. Lev 16:29–34; to recall, the Matthean narrative on the Passion starts with the purification by Jesus of the temple.

times forbidden to go "behind the curtain," as YHWH is present there in the cloud. The priest face-to-face with the cover is bloody; the sacrifice of animals "shields" him. When he emerges "in his glorious robe . . . in his glorious perfection," he comes out "like the morning star among the clouds and then the other priests shout, they sound the trumpets of beaten work, they make a great sound heard" while the people fall upon their faces (Sirach 50:1–24).[83]

It is of interest that talmudic traditions report strange phenomena that, allegedly, occurred in the temple forty years before its destruction. What is striking is that those premonitory signs are in relation to Yom Kippur (*j. Yoma* 43c; *b. Yoma* 39b).[84] Our interest is similarly aroused by the *Epistle of Barnabas*, which introduces Jesus' passion by tracing a parallel with the scapegoat of Yom Kippur (*Barn* 7).[85] The motif of the mocking of Jesus, for example, is prefigured in the goat being cursed, spit on, goaded (pierced), "crowned" with a scarlet ribbon, and cast in the "desert." (See also Justin Martyr, *Dialogue with Trypho*, 40.)[86] Incidentally, the *Barnabas* tradition may shed light on the striking episode of the crowd's choice between two Jesuses, one Jeshua bar Abba and one Jeshua called Christ (or: King of the Jews). Indeed, *Barnabas* 7 stresses the Yom Kippur's pair of goats being alike. One is sacrificed on the altar, the other is accursed and sent into the desert.

The Yom Kippur context also helps understand the episode of Jesus at Gethsemane (Matt 26:36–46) with its literary contrasts of sleeping and being awake. On the eve of the Day of Atonement, the high priest is kept awake the whole night by younger clergy (*m. Yoma* 1, 3–7). Such a night gathering of clergy (and other VIPs, as we shall see) introduces us into a very unsettling detail of the Passion narrative. All historians stumble on the Gospel's mention of repeated meetings of the Sanhedrin to deal with Jesus' fate.[87] At least the second meeting occurs at night (Matt 27:1//Mark 15:1//Luke 23:1), and this is another cause of surprise. The gatherings include the high priest, scribes, elders—that is, the whole Jewish establishment of the time.

Now, during the seven-day preparation for Yom Kippur in the Second Temple era, the Jewish authorities, we are told, would sit in

---

83. See here again Heb 5:9.

84. Incidentally, it is also said in *j. Sanh* that 40 years before the temple's destruction, "judgment in capital causes was taken away from Israel;" this sheds light on John 18:31.

85. R. Le Déaut (*Le Nuit pascale*, AnBib 22 [Rome: PBI, 1963] 284) mentions a rabbinic tradition (perhaps anti-Christian) stating that the Messiah will not come on a Sabbath day, or during the (eve of a) festival. (*Exod. Rab.* 3:12).

86. The abuse of the scapegoat, before being sent to "Azazel," is a Mishnaic tradition; see J. D. Crossan, *The Cross That Spoke*, 118–19.

87. Matt 26:3 and 26:57–68 in the high priest Caiaphas's house! Then, Matthew 27:1–2 and 27:7 in an unspecified place, undoubtedly the seat of the Sanhedrin.

the house of the high priest. Those leaders, according to other lists, included "the head of the court, the patriarch, the High Priest, the prefect of the priests, and the king, as well as the seventy members of the Sanhedrin."[88] As said above, they prepare the High Priest for his functions on the Day of Atonement, and they keep him awake the night before the day. When the time has come, he is led ceremoniously to the shrine. The whole scene as described by different sources is majestic, but one gets the impression of someone led to his death "like a lamb to the slaughter." The high priest, says Marcus,[89] "turns aside in tears and awe." It is understandable that, after coming out alive, he proclaims a holiday "because he had come out of the sanctuary in peace."

The insistence of Matthew that events happen on the eve of Sabbath and even during the preparation for Passover is striking.[90] To recall, Yom Kippur is the "Sabbath of Sabbaths" (see Lev 23:26–32 esp. v. 32). Furthermore, Matthew uses the term "high priest" no less than fourteen times in the crucial chapters 26 and 27![91] A close reading of those fourteen occurrences shows that Matthew used the term in places where it was not demanded by the context. This, I suggest, is meant by Matthew to create a sacral atmosphere, or rather its parody. The high priest and his cohorts become buffoons of sorts; they will be replaced by the true high priest who will offer no other sacrifice but himself and will shout the sacred Name in a most paradoxical holy of holies that reaches to the confines of the earth.

Matthew becomes more explicit on this in the scene of Jesus' confrontation with Caiaphas. To him, Jesus announces that he is the one spoken about in Daniel 7:13: the high priest will himself witness the enthronement of Jesus as Son of Man at the right hand of the "Power" (a free rendition of the Danielic "Ancient of Days") and coming [down] on the clouds of heaven (Matt 26:64). In my commentary on Daniel,[92] I have attempted to show that the scene of enthronement in Daniel 7 is one of a high priest. In light of this, Jesus' answer to Caiaphas amounts to Caiaphas's demotion, for Jesus claims for himself, as it were, the true and ultimate high priesthood. True, Jesus' position of utter weakness before the pontiff makes his words seem

---

88. So Solomon Ibn Verga (16th cent.) reporting a purported account of Marcus, Roman justice of the Jews during the Roman era. Note that King Herod does not figure except in Luke (23:6–16). But in the four Gospels Jesus is condemned as "King of the Jews."

89. See preeeding note.

90. See 27:62; 28:1 (//Mark 16:1; Luke 23:54); John 20:1.

91. See 26:51, 57, 58, 59, 62, 63, 65 (= 7 times); 27:1, 3, 6, 12, 20, 41, 62 (= 7 times).

92. A. LaCocque, *Daniel.*

nothing less than ludicrous. But that is why the apocalyptic manifestations accompanying his Passion are meant to reveal the divine power behind the human vulnerability. That they are inaugurated by a last φωνὴ μεγάλη must be seen within this context of Jesus' claim to the high priesthood.

V
Apocalypse and Cult

With the advent of the Second Temple period, deep transformations occurred in Israel's complexion. The progressive absence of prophecy created a vacuum that the temple clergy naturally filled. Thus the temple became more powerful than ever in Israel's society.

Now, spirituality and power are not good bedfellows. By contrast, power and corruption often sleep together. The history of the Second Temple Judean priesthood is nothing but appalling. Thus yawned a second-degree vacuum. It stirred reactions in which the priestly and the cultic play a major part, namely, the monasticism of Qumran and the end-time fervor of the apocalypse. In both, priests again assumed a prime position. They became the natural leaders of the various apocalyptic movements, taking, for instance, the lead in the revolt against the Syrians in the second century B.C.E.

The priests' functions and interests are squarely cultic. They promote a worldview attuned to a cultic temporality. Thus, the Qumran community lives in a liturgical rhythm. The washing of the body is baptismal; the eating of food is "eucharistic"; dialogical exchange is sacred discourse. Similarly the apocalypse "liturgizes" history/time. Universal history is the awesome and terrible struggle between the formidable powers of evil and the angelic priests/Priest of the end time.

The climax of the cultic drama is reached at the "midnight" of time, a razor-edged moment (καιρός) of paroxysmic evil and theophanic triumph. (The apocalyptic signs in Matt 27 convey that tautly tensive ambivalence.) Meanwhile, the apocalyptic fever is characteristic of a worshipping community overcome by its own fervor; מרנא תא (Come, O Lord!) easily becomes מרן אתא (Our Lord comes [now]!).

The apocalyptic language is a cultic jargon. It says that things are not just coming to an end, but that they are doing so in a certain way. The final cataclysm is more than an eventual big bang. The whole of history is cataclysmic as it is liturgical. To express this notion, the apocalyptic revives mythological images, because it claims to speak of more than meets the eye. The narrated events become images, metaphors, symbols. Antiochus IV is more than a historical, hence transient, despot. He is "such as into himself eternity changes him," that is, a monster, the monster of evil incarnate. His destruction demands no less than heavenly intervention.

In the Gospel, along the same line, Jesus' deeds, his words, his destiny and, above all, his death/resurrection,[93] are as a whole fulfillment of Scripture. "So that what the prophet said . . . " does not signal coincidence or serendipity. Jesus' life is seen by the Evangelist as the history of salvation (*Heilsgeschichte*) transformed into a cultic liturgy: every word, every move, is charged with sacred sense. That is why the Church recites the words and repeats the narrative liturgically. Jesus' "calendar" becomes her calendar, in her attempt to live at the same rhythm, to be baptized in the same water, to eat the same bread, to breathe the same air. All this amounts to participating in the cultic Christ, an apocalyptic liturgy "until he come."

The Great Cry is to be seen within that context, which is its *Sitz im Leben* and its *Sitz im Wort*. Understated as it generally is by scholars, it escapes all context and is, so to speak, a raw ejaculation. But nothing in the Gospel is of the nature of the "raw." On the contrary, the Great Cry marks the climactic "midnight" of history as cult. Concomitantly, Jesus expires and all is changed, to begin with the opening up of the holy of holies. It is the apocalyptic moment par excellence, when darkness and light, shout and silence, the same and the other, death and life, do meet.

Concomitance is the main obstacle for narrativity. The Gospel introduces a delay, a space between the poles: Jesus dies on a Friday and comes back to life the following Sunday. It is a caesura, a counterpoint. "Gapping" is the price to pay to cross over from the liturgical moment to a narrative development, or, if you want, from apocalyptic fervor to reasonable stability. First death, then resurrection.[94] But, for the apocalypse, these events do not occur in sequence. The Great Cry is concomitance: Jesus shouts something with his last breath and all is changed—history, cult, divine election, world.

The Great Cry is judgment. It is *krisis*. To some, the apocalyptic phenomena appear strictly in their negativity: darkness, earthquake, overturning of tombstones, agony and death. But, to others, to the disciples of Jesus, the same occurrences are also presence of eternity: love in the midst of hatred, hope in the midst of despair, life in the midst of death. This has been from time immemorial Israel's proclamation. The liturgy has arrived at its own accomplishment, "so that what the prophet said be fulfilled."

---

93. On this conflation, see below.
94. This even led some to the disastrous conclusion that death is a rite of passage.

VI
The Death of the Messiah

Jesus was crucified with two λῃστής. Should we see in this scene a reminiscence of two rebels, the brothers Simon and Jacob, crucified together by the Romans in 67? They were sons of Menahem of Galilee, who was assassinated on his way to Jerusalem where he was to be crowned as "King of the Jews."

It is remarkable how each of the guerrilla leaders of the time proclaimed himself Messiah. The term, as a consequence, became synonymous with rebel both for the Jews and the Romans. Although in theory it is no impropriety for a Jew to proclaim himself Messiah, the circumstances in Jesus' time gave to the title a politically subversive connotation. The "Messiah" was by definition the enemy of Rome and, consequently, of the Jewish establishment. Hence, both colluded to arrest Jesus and kill him. Here is probably the historical truth behind the slanted narrative on Jesus' trial with the active participation of the Jewish authorities. Jesus' claim to Messiahship would entail his condemnation on a political-religious ground.

As to the plot adopted by Matthew, I follow the lead of J. W. Doeve.[95] False witnesses (only in Matthew and Mark) testify about Jesus' will to destroy the temple.[96] On the basis of that testimony, the Sanhedrin condemns Jesus to death (Matt 26:66). The model text is Jeremiah 26:5 ff. [LXX 33:5 ff.] and the condemnation of Jeremiah to death (26:7–8). In the LXX, the condemning "prophets" of the Hebrew text are called "false prophets" (LXX 33:7–8). Jeremiah also is brought to the civil authorities of Judah to be executed (26:10–11) because of his declarations against the temple and the city (26:15–16). But if they kill him, Jeremiah says, they will bring innocent blood upon themselves, the city, and its inhabitants. An echo of this is found in Matthew 27:4, 24–25 (without parallel!). In Matthew, the death sentence by the Sanhedrin appears twice, on the model of Jeremiah's sentence repeated twice in the narrative (Jer 26:8, 19–20).

Thus, when the witnesses are shown perjuring themselves in Matthew and Mark, it is the Jeremiah narrative that is the literary model for this perjury. This literary motif notwithstanding, the "purification" of the temple by Jesus was truly a symbolic destruction. The subsequent cursing of the fig tree indicates that, as the useless fig tree is

---

95. J. W. Doeve, *Jewish Hermeneutics in the Synoptic Gospels and Acts* (Assen: van Gorcum, 1954) 182–88.

96. See Matt 24:1–14 and par.; 27:40; John 2:19.

destroyed, so will be the useless temple.[97] Jesus stops the temple operations, and that subversion cannot remain unpunished by the authorities for it is a politico-religious provocation. The insistence of the Gospel is that Jesus knew all along that his move would be a fatal one. My reading of the apocalypse of Matthew as starting in chapter 21 and being pursued until the end of the Passion narrative allows me to be less reticent (than Crossan, for example) to see Jesus' condemnation as the direct result of his symbolic destruction of the temple.

It is to be expected, from that perspective, that the narrative on the last hours of Jesus' life would not "forget" about the real cause of Jesus' death in the first place. On the contrary, as we saw above, the temple is omnipresent, from the moment when the name of Elijah was "heard" to the last breath of the crucified. That is, the double-entendre that pervades the Gospel of Matthew becomes at this point more complex: there is now a double perspective or focus. To the "general" audience or reader, the focus is on the person of the martyr. All the rest serves the purpose of directing the limelight upon the torn flesh of Jesus. The last cry is understood within that context. It is no fake agony, and Jesus is no stoical philosopher. He has not looked to being martyred, and death on the cross is a horrible torture, for him as for anyone else.

But to the Jewish "initiates," the Great Cry evokes still another perspective, namely, that of the high priest shouting the Name of God three times behind the veil of the temple on the Day of Atonement. It is the תרועה par excellence, the cry that, at long last, utters the unuttered and the unutterable. Matthew left his readers to fill the gap: What kind of Great Cry did the Messiah shout? Was it an inarticulate groan? A repetition of Psalm 22:1? Or was it a Word, a word that Matthew leaves unwritten in conformity with the pervasive biblical device of understatement?[98] If the latter, one remembers the gaps in narratives like Genesis 22 or Judges 3:20–23. The content of the discourse is known only through its bearing on the one(s) addressed and more broadly on the general audience or on nature as a whole (see Judg 5; 1 Kgs 19). In Matthew's Passion narrative, the effect of the Great Cry is overpowering: human witnesses confess that "this one was the Son of God," and the whole universe enters into convulsions. In the beginning

---

97. See J. D. Crossan, *The Historical Jesus*, 357.

98. Note that, as the rending of the temple veil is only mentioned without explanation of its meaning in the synoptics, so the Great Cry remains without comment. X. Léon-Dufour says that there existed a Christian tradition according to which Jesus said something with his last cry. That something was to be restored by each community; so Mark understood it one way and Luke another way (676).

was the Word and the Word was God; it is fitting that the last historical Word be the ineffable Name.[99]

The first and the last—the Semitic mind is especially sensitive to their contrast and correspondence. If one follows the New Testament scholars' consensus (I shall here credit Oscar Cullmann with such insight) and read the Gospel, as it were, retrospectively, from its end as its real beginning, the cross occupies its deserved central place, at the crossroad of the past and the future. The Passion narrative is a prolepsis of church history, "the Christ spread out," as Bossuet said. This means that the last words of Jesus on the cross are less a conclusion to a story than a prelude to history in its newness. Jesus' last words are thus inaugural, they are words of foundation, whose import cannot be overstated. To interpret them as a last inarticulate cry is hardly fitting.[100]

Matthew's preamble (ch. 1–2) and its epilogue (26:3–28.20) together frame the threefold report on Jesus' ministry.[101] Now, Matthew 1–2 are most evidently a midrashic story on Jesus' birth and infancy. A corresponding part in the epilogue expectedly displays purely Jewish characteristics, where motifs such as "Elijah," total darkness, earthquake, the rending of the temple curtain find their places naturally. This extends to the motif of the Last Cry. For there exists a Jewish tradition about martyrdom. It coalesced around the figures of the עשרה חרוגי מלכות, that is the "ten [Jewish] martyrs of the [Roman] Empire." All of them died an exemplary death. Among their number was R. Aqiba. According to the legend, the Rabbi is reported (by *Mekhilta* on Exod 15:2) to have read עלמות [maidens] in Canticles 1:3 as על מות [(love) unto death], interpreting this verse of Song with Psalm 44:23, "for Your sake we are killed all the day." Consequently, R. Aqiba died shouting the *shemaᶜ* (Deut 6:6) of which he prolonged the last word אחד (one), until his last breath (*j. Ber.* 9:5; *b. Ber.* 61b). It is my conviction that Matthew inscribed the death of Jesus within that tradition (whether or not it was already in existence as a coalesced corpus is immaterial). On the same R. Aqiba, a famous Tosephta passage (on Hag 2:3–4) says that only he left the *pardes* (paradise) safely

---

99. O. Betz writes, "In content, φωνή is also . . . the significant and authoritative word" (295).

100. Nothing can be drawn, in terms of the content of Jesus' cry, from the fact that, according to Acts 7:59–60, St. Stephen also dies with a great cry in the imitation of his Master, for, most evidently Acts wanted to show a total morphological parallel between his death and the one of Jesus: he also commits his spirit and prays God as well not to hold this against his murderers.

101. See the five occurrences of the formula concluding the main collections of Jesus' *logia* (Matt 7:28; 11:1; 13:53; 19:1; 26:1).

after being transported there mystically, in contrast to his colleagues Ben Azza' (who died), Ben Zoma (who became mad), and Elisha (who "cut the young plants" [*sic*]). David J. Halperin discusses this text and shows convincingly that, "to leave safely" means "to depart this life free of the taint of heresy,"[102] that is, the crime for which the death of Jesus was demanded by Jewish authorities. R. Aqiba's last recitation of Deuteronomy 6:4 (קריאת שמע) was sublime and personal; Jesus' cry is apocalyptic and universal.[103]

---

102. D. J. Halperin, *The Faces of the Chariot* (Tübingen/Philadelphia: J. C. B. Mohr, 1988) 33.

103. Robert Smith writes, "Mark 13 indicates that [Jesus'] death has universal significance, ultimate power, cosmic sweep . . . [It] is inaugurating eschatology." "Darkness at Noon: Mark's Passion Narrative," *CTM* 49 (1973) 333.

9

The Priest's Daughter
and the Thief in the Orchard

The Soul of Midrash Leviticus Rabbah

Burton L. Visotzky

A rabbi of the first century warned, "The spirit indeed is willing, but the flesh is weak," and so canonized a problematic distinction unique to the human condition.[1] Spirit and flesh, mind and body, body and soul, together these make up the contours of the antinomies that set us apart, apparently, from God's other creatures.[2] Elsewhere, in rabbinic literature of a somewhat later period, the soul/body dichotomy is contrasted with the relationship of the Creator to the world.[3]

> The soul fills the body just as God fills the entire universe. . . .
> May the soul which fills the body
> Come praise the Blessed Holy One Who fills the universe.
>
> The soul suffers the body just as the Holy suffers the universe. . . .
> May the soul which suffers the body
> Come praise the Blessed Holy One Who suffers the universe.
>
> The soul outlasts the body just as the Blessed Holy One outlasts the universe. . . .

---

1. Matt 26:4. I open with a New Testament quote to pay homage to Robin Scroggs—a great teacher of NT, who with spirit and flesh, soul and body, teaches students and colleagues alike through both careful exegesis and living example.

2. This is not the place to explore the fine distinctions among these varying antinomies, a topic which merits its own separate study.

3. *Leviticus Rabbah* 4:8. *Lev. Rab.* dates from the fifth or sixth century, a product of Byzantine Palestine. For basic bibliography on the text, background, forms, and polemics of *Lev. Rab.*, see B. Visotzky, "Anti-Christian Polemic in Leviticus Rabbah," *Proceedings of the American Academy for Jewish Research* 56 (1990) 83–100, reprinted in idem, *Fathers of the World: Essays in Rabbinic and Patristic Literatures* (Tübingen: Mohr/Siebeck, 1995), 93–110; esp. n. 1.

> May the soul which outlasts the body
> Come praise the Blessed Holy One Who outlasts the universe.
>
> The soul does not eat within the body just as the Blessed Holy One does not eat[4] within the universe. . . .[5]
> The soul is unique to the body just as the Blessed Holy One is unique in the universe. . . .
> The soul is pure within the body just as the Blessed Holy One is pure within the universe. . . .
> The soul sees yet is unseen just as the Blessed Holy One sees yet is unseen. . . .
> The soul does not slumber just as the blessed Holy One does not slumber,[6] "Behold, God neither sleeps nor slumbers, guardian of Israel." (Ps. 121:4)

This lovely paean to God and the soul ends a chapter of Leviticus Rabbah which expounds on the relationship of body and soul, ostensibly in exegetical service of Leviticus 4:2, "The soul which sins unwittingly. . . ."[7] There, the soul is also likened to a princess, fed dainties by her urbane husband, yet to no avail; for as a princess, she is never satisfied.[8]

The best known of the comparisons to the soul in this chapter of midrash is not to the soul alone, but in fact dilates on the relationship of soul to body—not as with God to the world but through much more mundane comparison. This text begins with a *mashal*[9] which has been much studied and doted upon, mostly by virtue of the parallels it shares in Greco-Roman literature,[10] less so for the significance of its statements on the nature of the soul. The parallels to our body/soul analogy are instructive and, for the most part, precise, and once again show how at home the rabbis were within the Greco-Roman orbit. Seneca is

---

4. Here the text literally reads, "as there is no eating before the Blessed Holy One," a standard rabbinic circumlocution to avoid the appearance of corporeality to God—emphasizing, perhaps, the comparison of God to soul rather than body.

5. The poetic construction continues through the balance of the text, omitted here for the sake of brevity.

6. As above, n. 4, our text here lit. reads, "there is no sleep before the Blessed Holy One."

7. I translate literally, most modern translations read, "If anyone sins unwittingly" (RSV) or "When a person unwittingly" (NJV). The midrashist of *Lev. Rab.* uses the literal meaning as an excuse to expatiate on the topic.

8. *Lev. Rab.* 4:2.

9. For the *mashal* see David Stern, *Parables in Midrash* (Cambridge: Harvard University Press, 1991), passim, and his exchange with Daniel Boyarin in *Prooftexts* 5 (1985). See also my review of Stern in *CBQ* 55 (1993) 183–84.

10. Marmorstein in the Hebrew journal, *Eshkol* vol. 1, p. 576; H. Malter, *JQR* 2 (1912) 453–479; L. Wallach, *JQR* 31 (1940–41), pp. 259–86; idem., *JBL* 62 (1943) 338–39; and in G. F. Moore, *Judaism* 1:487, n.1; 3:148, n. 206 (with Buddhist, Sankhya, and Islamic parallels, too); I. Ziegler, *Die Koenigsgleichnisse des Midrasch*, ad loc.; and most recently Brad Young, *Jesus and His Jewish Parables*, 64–69 at nn. 22–50.

often cited,[11] as is the *Greek Anthology,* quoting first- and second-century epigrams.[12] So, Leonidas of Alexandria offers an epigram:

> The blind beggar supported the lame one on his feet, and gained in return the help of the other's eyes. Thus the two incomplete beings fitted into each other to form one complete being, each supplying what the other lacked.

The same type is found in Antiphilus of Byzantium and a century later in a text by Philippus or, perhaps, Isodorus. It is also attributed to Plato the younger, whose date is unknown to us. Nor is our midrash found exclusively in pagan authors. The *Apocryphon of Ezekiel,* variously dated from the first century B.C.E. through the first century C.E., quotes a version of our parable,[13] explicitly likening it to the soul/body relationship. The church father and heresiologist Epiphanius, bishop of Salamis, quotes the Apocryphon in his *Panarion,* in a much fuller rendition.[14]

Epiphanius, who lived in the fourth century and was born in Palestine, quotes a text which is suspiciously like that of Leviticus Rabbah, enough so to suspect that there is borrowing from one Palestinian authority by another. But since we are focusing here on the relationship of body and soul rather than that of church and synagogue, we'll forgo close comparison and move, instead, to the text as we have it in Leviticus Rabbah. There it is quoted as a tannaitic source.[15]

An analogy may be made to[16] a king who had an orchard, within which

---

11. *ad Lucilium. Epistulae Morales,* ed. R. M. Gummere, LCL 3:21ff.

12. ed. Patton, LCL vol. 3, pp. 8–9.

13. I do not cite it here since the Apocryphon is only fragmentary and the quotation is usually lifted from later literature for inclusion in a presentation of the Apocryphon. See, e.g., J. R. Mueller and S. E. Robinson in *The Old Testament Pseudepigrapha,* ed. J. Charlesworth, 1:487–95. See also Marc Bregman's "Parable of the Lame and the Blind: Epiphanius' Quotation from an Apocryphon of Ezekiel," *JTS* 42 (1991) 125–38; and see J. R. Mueller, now in *The Five Fragments of the Apocryphon of Ezekiel: A Critical Study,* JSPSup 5 (Sheffield: Sheffield Academic Press, 1994), who responds to Bregman. Most recently see R. Bauckham, "The Parable of the Royal Wedding Feast and the Parable of the Lame Man and the Blind Man," *JBL* 115 (1996) 471–88. None of these discusses the Priest's Daughter, for which, see below. Our text is quoted in versions from Epiphanius (see below) and *b. Sanh.* 91a-b (again, below).

14. 64.70, 5–17. See the translation of P. R. Amidon (Oxford: Oxford University Press, 1990) 216–17.

15. In the name of Rabbi Ishmael, fl. early to mid–second century C.E. The tannaitic texts which redact "the school of R. Ishmael" date, quite naturally, from a somewhat later era, viz. late-second- to early-third-century Palestine. Cf. *Mekhilta Rabbi Ishmael,* Shira 2, ed. Horowitz-Rabin, p. 125; *Mekilta Shimeon ben Yohai ad Exodus* 15:1, ed. Hoffman, pp. 76–77; see *b. Sanh.* 91 a-b (mentioned above, see *Diqduqe Sopherim,* ad loc), *Tanhuma Lev.* 6 (ed. Mantua onward) and cf. *Tan. Buber Lev.* 12; and later in *Mid. HaGadol ad Leviticus,* ed. Margulies, p. 290; *Mid. Aggadah Lev.* p. 8, and below for more parallels to the second part of the midrash found in even later texts.

16. Hebrew *mashal l.....*

were beautiful young figs.[17] He set two guards therein, one lame and one blind, that they might guard it.

He said to them, Be wary of the fruit, then he left them and went on his way. The lame one said to the blind one, I see beautiful young figs.

The other one said, Let's eat.

The first one answered, Can I walk?

The blind one said, And can I see?

What did they do? The lame one rode on the back of the blind one and so they took the fruits and ate them. Then they each went and sat in their original places.

Some days later the king came and asked them, Where are my fruits!?

The blind one said to him, Can I see?

The lame one said to him, Can I walk?

Now the king, who was wily, what did he do? He rode the lame one on the back of the blind one and tortured[18] them as one. He said, Thus did you eat them!

So in the Coming Future the Holy will say to the soul, Why did you sin against Me?[19]

She will say to God, Master of the Universe, was it I who sinned against you? It was the body that sinned, for from the day I have departed it have I sinned at all?

God will ask the body, Why did you sin?

The body will say to God, Master of both worlds[20], it was the soul that sinned, for from the day she has departed from me am I not tossed down like a potsherd on a garbage heap?

What will the Blessed Holy One do? God will restore the soul to the body and torture them as one. . . .

This midrash is, at first blush, witness to the rabbinic tendency to see the soul and body as contiguous, in happy symbiosis. Here we presumably see the rabbis distinguished from their more austere Christian and even pagan brethren.[21] Yet some commentary is called for on this rabbinic text and its pagan parallels. First, it must be pointed out that while the parallels are precise—that is to say both sets

---

17. Lit. firstfruits, which biblically should belong to God. Does this imply that the king of the parable wants his just due, or that the king, of flesh and blood, recognizes his debt to a Higher Authority? Further, does it imply that the two guardians have an obligation to guard things outside themselves (e.g. commandments or perhaps moral-ethical obligations) for offering to the King? In later rabbinic usage the phrase *bikhorot* applies particularly to the succulent young figs that grew in Palestine.

18. For this meaning of Hebrew, *dan*, see S. Lieberman, *JQR* 35 (1944) 15, n. 99; idem, "On Sins and Their Punishment," in *Texts and Studies* (Ktav, 1974) 32, n. 31; and idem, *Wolfson Jubilee Volume* (Jerusalem, 1965) 521, at n. 57.

19. lit., "before Me."

20. That is to say, this world and the world to come.

21. On the ephemerality of this distinction, also see my article, "Three Syriac Cruxes," *Journal of Jewish Studies* 52 (1991) 167–75; reprinted in my *Fathers of the World*, 150–59, esp. 157ff.

of text, rabbinic and pagan, each have lame riding blind—the pagan texts do *not* invoke this trope as a parable or analogy to explain the relationship of body and soul. Indeed, in the *Greek Anthology* they are presented framed by a set of "octopus" epigrams, which also presumably illustrate the principle of symbiosis, but more so in nature's pecking order than in the realm of metaphysics on the soul. To wit, only the Jewish texts[22] relate this epigram to the soul/body problem.[23]

But even the rabbinic tendency to turn these epigrams into a *mashal*[24] on the soul/body distinction is problematic. We cannot ignore the fact that this midrash seems to contradict the lessons of the other midrashim in the same chapter of Leviticus Rabbah, as well as the distinction drawn by Jesus in the Matthean text cited at the outset of this essay. In all of these texts, and many, many more, the soul is given privilege over the body.[25]

The clues for the preference of the soul may be observed even in our own text. The soul claims that since departure from the body she has "not sinned at all." The implication of the text is that the soul is otherwise pure; she may be besmirched only in conjunction with the body. This is emphasized by the body's claim that since the soul's departure, it is "like a potsherd on a garbage heap," that is to say, just so much trash. Indeed, the tannaitic antecedent to our version opens with a colloquy between the Emperor Antoninus and Rabbi Judah the Patriarch,[26] in which the emperor asks, "When a person dies and the body is decayed,[27] does the Blessed Holy One resurrect it for judgment?" To which the pious rabbi responds, "While you are asking me about the body, which is impure,[28] why not ask me about the soul, which is pure?"[29]

Despite the apparent desire in the blind-and-lame midrash to have soul and body share and share alike, it seems that the text undermines

---

22. Here I include the Apocryphon of Ezekiel and even Epiphanius, who does no more than quote it.

23. One must invoke Rebecca Goldstein's witty novel, *The Mind/Body Problem*, at this juncture, if for no other reason than to point out that her model for the distinction is in the differences between New York City and Princeton rather than between blind and lame.

24. See Stern, *Parables,* on the process of "regularization," esp. 19–24 and 206–11.

25. This privileging is ubiquitous in the ancient world. See the NT dictionaries and encyclopedias, s.v. "soul," where Paul's expansion and refinement of the dichotomy is appropriately given pride of place. For the Roman world at large as background to later Christian anthropology and doctrine on the soul/body antinomy, see Peter Brown's magisterial *The Body and Society: Men, Women, and Sexual Renunciation in Early Christianity* (New York: Columbia University Press, 1988) passim.

26. Mekhilta Rabbi Ishmael. See L. Wallach.

27. Heb. *kaleh,* lit. "finished."

28. Heb. *tam'eh*

29. Heb. *tahor,* as in the poetic text cited above from *Lev. Rab.* 4:8.

itself, foundering on the superiority of soul to body. In case there is any doubt that the soul has a place of privilege in rabbinic thought, the continuation of our midrash,[30] also presented as a tannaitic source,[31] dispels it.

> An analogy may be made to a priest who had two wives, one the daughter of a priest, the other the daughter of an Israelite. He gave them a measure of dough[32] which was *terumah*[33] and they rendered it unfit. He took the daughter of the priest to task and left the daughter of the Israelite alone. She [the daughter of the priest] complained, Mr. priest, sir, you gave it to us as one, why do you rebuke me and leave her alone?
>
> He explained to her, You are the daughter of a priest and were schooled [in handling *terumah*] since childhood.[34] She is the daughter of an Israelite and was not schooled since childhood. That's why I hold you accountable.
>
> So in the Coming Future the Blessed Holy One will say to the soul, Why did you sin before me?
>
> She will respond, Master of the Universe, the body and I sinned as one, why do you take me to task and leave that one [the body] alone?
> God will tell her, You are from the heavenly sphere, a place where they do not sin, while the body is from the earthly realm,[35] a place where they sin. That is why I hold you accountable.

Of course, the very accountability of the soul implies a less than perfect purity. Nevertheless, it is indicative of a privileged position in God's household, one which perhaps presumes the continuity of the soul after death and even more so, the pre-existence of the soul before its placement in a corporeal, corrupt body. This does not undermine the rabbinic concept of bodily resurrection and reunification of body and soul for judgment—which our first text asserts; it does, however, clearly seat the soul in place of pride.

---

30. The continuation of our text is virtually unmentioned in all of the preceding studies cited.

31. Introduced as *tani rabbi hiyya*, normally the phrase *Lev. Rab.* uses to introduce a quote from the tannaitic commentary on Leviticus, *Sifra debei Rav*. See Margulies notes, ad loc. As he points out, this text does not appear in current versions of that midrash, but only appears in much later traditions in *Tanhuma Lev.* 6 (ed. Mantua onwards), *Tan. Buber Lev.* and *Midrash HaGadol ad Lev.* 5:1 (ed. Margulies, p. 86, ed. Steinsaltz, p. 108). In the latter text (as well as MS. variants to *Lev. R.*, see Margulies apparatus) the *mashal* is cited in the name of Rabbi Levi, a Palestinian amora of the third generation, ca. 300 C.E.

32. Heb. *'iyssah.*

33. Cf. e.g., Exod 25:2, Lev 7:32, *terumah* was the priest's portion, but had to be eaten in a state of ritual fitness or purity (*taharah*, as said of the soul, above; and in opposition to unfitness or impurity, *tuma'h*).

34. lit. "in your father's house."

35. The distinction between heavenly and earthly in Hebrew is, lit. "upper" as opposed to "lower."

These two texts, joined together as they are in Leviticus Rabbah, function as co-texts, in dialectic with one another.[36] While the parable of the thief in the orchard implies a symbiosis of body and soul, the parable of the priest's daughter teaches the superiority of the soul. This latter *mashal* forces the reader/listener to return for a more nuanced reading of the first parable. Is the implication of the "thief in the orchard" that body and soul are co-equals? Apparently not, only that at the time of resurrection they will share punishment together. But enduring torture is not the same as bearing responsibility. For that, the pure soul must accept the onus. For the rabbis of Leviticus Rabbah, it is not enough to say, "The spirit indeed is willing, but the flesh is weak." For when the flesh is weak, it is the spirit that is culpable. And, for the sake of their punishment—the expiation of sin[37]—the rabbis imagine God putting body and soul together.

---

36. See Daniel Boyarin, *Intertextuality and the Reading of Midrash* (Bloomington: Indiana University Press, 1990), esp. 57–79, and David Kraemer, *The Mind of the Talmud* (Oxford: Oxford University Press, 1990) esp. 79–138, and, idem., *Reading the Rabbis* (Oxford: Oxford University Press, 1996) esp. 33–59. Kraemer deals with the rhetoric of co-texts or countertexts in the Babylonian rabbinic tradition.

37. See S. Lieberman, "On Sins and Their Punishments," in *Texts and Studies* (Ktav, 1974) 29–57, and also B. Visotzky, "Mortal Sins," *USQR* 44 (1990) 31–53, reprinted in idem, *Fathers of the World*, 41–60.

10

The Disappearance of the Gentiles
God-fearers and the Image of the Jews in Luke-Acts

Gary Gilbert

A critical narrative and theological transition occurs in Acts of the Apostles chapter 10 when the Roman centurion Cornelius converts to Christianity (10:1-48).[1] Up to this point in the story, almost all those who had come to believe in Jesus—the apostles and the thousands in Jerusalem and the surrounding environs of Judea—were Jews (1:15; 2:41-42, 47; 4:4; 5:14; 6:7). Beginning with the Cornelius episode through to the end, the book moves gradually away from a world inhabited exclusively by Jews to one with an increasing interest in and success with the conversion of Gentiles. Acts, which commences with the Jewish apostles huddled in Jerusalem—the religious navel of Judaism—concludes with Paul preaching openly in the capital of the Gentile world. The final words reverberate beyond the closure of the narrative as Paul announces to the assembled crowd of Jews in Rome that God's salvation "has been sent to the Gentiles, they will listen" (28:28). Although he had uttered the same threat twice before (13:46; 18:6), the addition of the prooftext from Isaiah supplies a far more ominous tone. The final scene leaves little doubt that the future of Christianity will follow a missionary trajectory that, beginning with Cornelius, moves away from Jews and toward Gentiles.[2]

I am very pleased to offer this paper in recognition of the significant contributions Robin Scroggs has made to our collective understanding of formative Christianity and to my own appreciation of the ways ancient texts can speak to modern contexts.

1. Unless otherwise noted, all scriptural references are to Acts of the Apostles.
2. Joseph B. Tyson, "The Problem of Jewish Rejection in Acts," in *Luke-Acts and the Jewish People*, ed. Joseph B. Tyson (Minneapolis: Augsburg, 1988) 124-27; Ernst Haenchen,

The Cornelius episode, in chapter 10, derives its pivotal role not only from its location within the narrative geography, but also from its length—one of the longest single stories in the entire work—and its highly dramatic rendering—including a heavenly double-vision reminiscent of popular literature of the ancient world.[3] Just as the conversion story occupies an integral place in the narrative of Acts, so too can we appreciate the unique qualities of its main character—Cornelius. Although a Roman centurion, he is described as a devout man who gives alms liberally, prays constantly, and shows reverence for God (φοβούμενος τὸν θεόν, 10:2). These pious acts distinguish Cornelius as someone who, while not a Jew either by birth or through conversion, nonetheless has a strong commitment to the God of Israel. It is remarkable and, I believe, highly significant that Cornelius's behavior has earned for him the moniker of "God-fearer"—a term normally referring to non-Jews who engaged in the religious life of Jewish communities in the ancient world. Acts sets forth as the centerpiece for the justification of the Gentile mission a very distinctive type of Gentile.[4]

GOD-FEARERS:
EVIDENCE AND IDENTITY

Our information about God-fearers comes from a variety of Jewish, Christian, and Greek and Latin texts and inscriptions.[5] Their engagement with Judaism manifested itself in various ways, including the acknowledgment of the existence and potency of the God of Israel, knowledge and appreciation for Jewish sacred texts, service as benefactors of Jewish communities, participation in Jewish religious festivals, and attendance in the synagogue.

Over the past several years scholars have devoted considerable attention to the identity, indeed, the existence of God-fearers. The discussions have been fueled in large part by two powerful catalysts. The first was the provocative thesis articulated by Thomas Kraabel that the God-fearers were invented by the author of Luke–Acts.[6] Kraabel set

---

"The Book of Acts as Source Material for the History of Early Christianity," in *Studies in Luke-Acts*, ed. Leander E. Keck and J. Louis Martyn (Philadelphia: Fortress, 1966) 278; Jack T. Sanders, *The Jews in Luke-Acts* (Philadelphia: Fortress, 1987) 296–99. For a somewhat different and more optimistic interpretation, see Robert C. Tannehill, "Rejection by Jews and Turning to Gentiles: The Pattern of Paul's Mission in Acts," in *Luke-Acts and the Jewish People*, 96–99.

3. Richard I. Pervo, *Profit with Delight: The Literary Genre of the Acts of the Apostles* (Philadelphia: Fortress, 1987) 73–74.

4. Joseph B. Tyson, "The Gentile Mission and Scripture in Acts," *NTS* 33 (1987) 622.

5. For a complete discussion see my dissertation, "Pagans in a Jewish World: Pagan Involvement in Jewish Religious and Social Life in the First Four Centuries CE" (Ann Arbor: UMI, 1992).

6. A. T. Kraabel, "The Disappearance of the 'God-fearers'," *Numen* 28 (1981) 113–26.

out to refute a long-standing scholarly convention that accepted the Greek, Latin, and Hebrew terms for God-fearers[7] as technical terms for a large population of semiproselytes who could be found in practically every Jewish community in the first century.[8] The second catalyst was the discovery on the site of the ancient city of Aphrodisias of an inscription that identifies fifty-four men by the term θεοσεβεῖς—one of the Greek words most often understood as a designation for God-fearers.[9] The text, inscribed probably in the early third century C.E., records the names of those Gentiles who had donated to or somehow participated in the activities of a Jewish beneficent association that referred to itself as the δεκανία.

These two contributions to the study of God-fearers have spawned numerous other investigations.[10] Most have focused on historical questions: Did God-fearers actually exist? Do the accounts in which they appear possess reliable historical information? A near consensus has rejected Kraabel's position and has championed God-fearers as living, breathing fixtures in Jewish life and in the formation of early Christianity. These investigations have deepened our understanding of pagan association with Jews and of Jewish ways of acknowledging the pious acts of non-Jews who were not intent upon converting to Judaism. My purpose in this paper is neither to revisit Kraabel's argument nor to adjudicate between him and his opponents. Rather, I wish to shift the focus from God-fearers as ancient *realia* to God-fearers as literary characters in Acts. What does the presence of God-fearers contribute to our reading of the text and the meanings that are produced in the process?[11]

---

7. Φοβούμενος/σεβόμενος τὸν θεόν, θεοσεβής, *metuens*, and ירא שמים, respectively.

8. Kraabel, "Disappearance," 121.

9. The *editio princeps* and commentary are published by J. Reynolds and R. Tannenbaum, *Jews and Godfearers at Aphrodisias*, CPS supp. 12 (Cambridge: Cambridge Philological Society, 1987). For alternative interpretations of the text, see Margaret Williams, "The Jews and Godfearers Inscription from Aphrodisias: Case of Patriarchal Interference in Early 3rd Century Caria?" *Historia* 41 (1992) 297–310; and Gary Gilbert, "Jews in Aphrodisias," in *Ancient Judaism 8*, ed. Amy-Jill Levine and Richard Pervo (Atlanta: Scholars, forthcoming).

10. Other recent studies on God-fearers include Louis Feldman, "The Omnipresence of the God-fearers," *BAR* 12 (1986) 62–69; Louis Feldman, "Proselytes and Sympathizers in the Light of the New Inscription from Aphrodisias," *REJ* 148 (1989) 265–305; Thomas M. Finn, "The God-fearers Reconsidered," *CBQ* 47 (1985) 75–83; A. Thomas Kraabel, "The God-fearers Meet the Beloved Disciple," in *The Future of Early Christianity: Essays in Honor of Helmut Koester*, ed. Birger Pearson, 276–84 (Minneapolis: Fortress, 1991); J. Andrew Overman, "The God-fearers: Some Neglected Features," *JSNT* 32 (1988) 17–26; and Folker Siegert, "Gottesfürchtige und Sympathisanten," *JSJ* 4 (1973) 109–64.

11. In seeking to understand the narrative dimensions of these characters, I hold in abeyance any judgment as to the historical value of the stories in which they appear. I do this not because I think the issue to be unimportant. Historical figures, no matter how they are represented, can serve as vehicles for conveying ideas and meaning no less well than fictional characters, as anyone who has ever read Shakespeare's historical plays or has seen an Oliver Stone movie can attest. An analogy can be drawn from how Jews are portrayed in Luke–Acts. No one would doubt the existence of Jews when the text was written, and we might reasonably argue

GOD-FEARERS:
A SCHOLARLY CONSENSUS?

In Acts, not only does a God-fearer serve as the main character in one of the narrative's most critical scenes, but God-fearers also appear in significant numbers throughout the central third of the book.[12] A few bear names, such as Cornelius or Lydia the Thyatiran merchant (16:11–15) or Titius Justus, a neighbor of the local synagogue in Corinth (18:5–11). Countless others who attend the various synagogues of Asia Minor and Greece in which Paul preaches remain anonymous. That God-fearers represent important characters in Acts is unmistakable. What effect their presence has for understanding the text, however, is less clear.

Most discussions of the role of God-fearers in Acts from a literary or theological perspective argue that God-fearers assist in moving the narrative from a world that is predominantly Jewish to one that is primarily Gentile. Thomas Kraabel, for instance, observed that God-fearers play important literary and theological roles in the unfolding of the narrative. The significance of his analysis has unfortunately been lost in the negative reaction to his theory that God-fearers have no historical reality. In his article, "The Disappearance of the 'God-fearers,'" Kraabel claims that

> the God-fearers are a symbol to help Luke show how Christianity had become a Gentile religion *legitimately* and without losing its Old Testament roots. The Jewish mission to Gentiles recalled in the God-fearers is ample precedent for the far more extensive mission to Gentiles which Christianity had in fact undertaken with such success. Once that point has been made Luke can let the God-fearers disappear from his story.[13]

---

that the author personally knew Jews of his day. Our knowledge of the existence of actual Jews at the time of Acts, however, does not prevent us from appreciating their narrative function as well. Numerous studies focusing on the portrayal of Jews in Luke–Acts have demonstrated how these characters help to advance certain literary and theological ideas. The same can and should be said for God-fearers. For recent work on the Jews in Luke–Acts, see Robert Brawley, *Luke–Acts and the Jews: Conflict, Apology, and Conciliation*, SBLMS 33 (Atlanta: Scholars, 1987); P. F. Essler, *The Community and Gospel in Luke–Acts*, SNTS 57 (Cambridge: Cambridge University Press, 1990); Howard Kee, "The Jews in Acts," in *Diaspora Jews and Judaism: Essays in Honor of and in Dialogue with A. Thomas Kraabel*, ed. J. Andrew Overman and Robert S. MacLennan, South Florida Studies in the History of Judaism 41, 183–96 (Atlanta: Scholars, 1992); Jack T. Sanders, *The Jews in Luke–Acts*; Joseph B. Tyson, *Luke–Acts and the Jewish People*; and Lawrence M. Wills, "The Depiction of the Jews in Acts," *JBL* 110 (1991) 631–54.

12. God-fearers, whether they are explicitly referred to as such or not, appear in eight stories: Ethiopian eunuch (8:26–40), the conversion of Cornelius (10:1–48), and Paul's visits to Pisidian Antioch (13:13–52), Iconium (14:1–7), Philippi (16:11–40), Thessalonica (17:1–9), Beroea (17:10–15), and Corinth (18:5–11).

13. Kraabel, "Disappearance," 120–21 (emphasis in the original).

Jack Sanders, is his monograph on the Jews in Luke–Acts, takes a similar approach. He writes,

> Luke thinks of God's salvation as passing from the Jews to Gentiles via a periphery, a penumbra that is made up of outcasts, proselytes, and God-fearers and Samaritans. . . . We would then have a definite progression after the persecution of Acts 8: Samaritans, proselyte (the Ethiopian), God-fearer (Cornelius), Gentile mission (beginning slowly in Acts 11.19–24, then gaining momentum after chap. 12). This pattern would dovetail with the geographical scheme announced in Acts 1.[14]

Both descriptions, and the many others offering minor variations, present God-fearers as a bridge spanning the gulf that separates Jew from Gentile; they exist as an anomalous throng, the conduit through which the gospel is exported to "the end of the earth" (1:8). God-fearers, in this view, are not Jews, but they resemble Jews in their acceptance of Jewish practices; they are Gentiles, but perform acts uncharacteristic of most Gentiles. They are, in other words, a *sui generis* group which, because of its unique, medial position, can best facilitate the expansion of the gospel from its Jewish origins to its Gentile future. Once the bridge has been crossed and the Gentiles have received the gospel, the God-fearers have served their purpose and can recede from the narrative stage.

This traditional interpretation of God-fearers has much to recommend it. The God-fearers, who are among the regular cast of characters beginning in chapter 8, make their last appearance in chapter 18, and are then absent from the last third of the work. Their rather abrupt disappearance is peculiar and suggestive of a temporary role that, once having been fulfilled, obviates any need for their further presence. Moreover, the systematic progression from Jew to God-fearer to Gentile fits well with the program the Gospel of Luke describes as an "orderly" and well-structured account of events (Luke 1:3).[15]

Moreover, Gentiles rest at the theological core of the text and in large measure account for the order Luke imposes on the narrative; the discourse in Acts is suffused with thoughts and predictions about their position in the newly revealed divine economy. In the Gospel of Luke,

---

14. Sanders, *The Jews in Luke–Acts*, 142 and 151.

15. Examples of the imperative for orderliness occur often. For instance, in an effort to demarcate clearly one period of history ending with John the Baptist and another beginning with Jesus (cf. Luke 16:16), the text presents an awkward and sequentially impossible report of John's arrest occurring *before* he baptizes Jesus (3:19–22). In this case, the demand for an orderly presentation of John's activities concluding before Jesus begins his ministry takes precedence over a logical narration. For a more complete discussion of the tightly knit literary structure of the work, see Charles Talbert, *Literary Patterns, Theological Themes, and the Genre of Luke–Acts* (Missoula, MT: Scholars, 1974).

Simeon praises God for allowing him to witness the coming of the one who will be a revelation to the Gentiles (Luke 2:30–32). Jesus, in his appearance before the apostles at the beginning of Acts, announces that the gospel will spread beyond the geographic and ethnic boundaries represented by his original, Jewish followers (1:8). On several occasions, we learn how God's favor has extended to Gentiles. Peter depicts this point most dramatically during his speech in the house of Cornelius. Despite his earlier prevailing attitude that a Jew is not "to associate with or to visit any one of another nation" (10:28), he joyously proclaims that "I truly understand that God shows no partiality, but in every nation anyone who fears him and does what is right is acceptable to him" (10:33–34). Finally, Gentiles appear as the alternatives to the recalcitrant Jews as Paul thrice juxtaposes the disbelief of Jews with a reaffirmation of his mission among Gentiles. In short, the theological trajectory toward Gentiles is central to the overall structure of the work and is articulated by all its major characters.

QUESTIONING THE CONSENSUS

Initially, then, the traditional argument that conceives of God-fearers as midwives to the birth of a universal Christianity appears sound. Upon more careful scrutiny, however, the argument begins to break down. While it is true that God-fearers disappear after chapter 18, it is also true that virtually all missionary activity, whether it be to Jews, Samaritans, God-fearers, or Gentiles ceases at this point. From the time Paul returns from his "third" journey to the end of the book (chs. 21–28), no additional characters become believers in Jesus and convert to Christianity.[16] The last third of Acts does not expand its horizons from God-fearer to Gentile, but reorients the narrative's focus from missionary adventures to Paul and his legal predicament. Moreover, the traditional argument envisions a three-step progression in missionary activity—Jew, God-fearer, Gentile—but ignores the fact that a depiction of the third element in this scenario, a wide-open mission to Gentiles, is absent from the entirety of Acts. While the speeches in Acts create a tremendous expectation for a surfeit of Gentile converts, the narrative tells a different story. Whatever hopes are built up for the mass conversion of Gentiles remain largely unfulfilled at the very end of the book. The non-Jews who populate the early Christian communities are not Gentiles in the broadest sense of the term, but are

---

16. A minor exception occurs when Paul arrives in Rome and convinces some of unnamed Jews with whom he meets (28:23–24).

almost exclusively God-fearers. The few exceptions—an unnamed jailer in Philippi (16:30) and Dionysius and Damaris in Athens (17:34)— underscore the realization that in Acts God-fearers play the role of the typical Gentile recipients of the Christian message and serve as the exemplars of non-Jewish converts to Christianity.[17]

This point is made most dramatically in the stories of the non-Jews whom Paul encounters on his journeys. The typical pattern has Paul entering a city and preaching on the Sabbath to an assembled group of Jews and non-Jews (i.e., God-fearers). We witness this stylized activity as Paul arrives in Pisidian Antioch, Iconium, Philippi, Thessalonica, and Corinth. Through this narrative pattern Acts presents a picture of Jewish rejection and Gentile acceptance. In each instance, the Gentiles are almost exclusively God-fearers. The story of Paul's experience in Corinth provides a striking example of the role God-fearers play as representatives for all Gentiles. After failing to persuade the Jews of Corinth, Paul declares that he will turn his attention to the Gentiles (18:5-6). With the words hardly out of his mouth, Paul is described as living and working among Gentiles. His initial and only Gentile acquaintance identified by name, however, is Titius Justus, a God-fearer ($\sigma\epsilon\beta\acute{o}\mu\epsilon\nu o\varsigma$ $\tau\grave{o}\nu$ $\theta\epsilon\acute{o}\nu$) who lives next door to the synagogue (18:7). Paul's actions in this instance reflect the wider phenomenon in which Acts speaks often about Gentiles as a group, but presents them *individually* as characters in the guise of God-fearers.

The conspicuous absence in Acts of a widespread mission to Gentiles and in its place the ubiquitous appearance of God-fearers forces a reevaluation of the argument that envisions God-fearers as the bridge between Jew and Gentile. To the extent that God-fearers function as this metaphorical bridge, they exist as a bridge to nowhere. The narrative devotes considerable attention to Jews, one end of the span, but fails to depict the other *terminus*—a full-scale mission to Gentiles. Acts does not construct a movement that progresses from Jew to God-fearer to Gentile, but, rather, from Jew to God-fearer and no further. There is a discrepancy in Acts, then, between the theological focus on Gentiles and the literary representation of God-fearers. God-fearers help to advance the theological discussion that God's favor

---

17. The case of Sergius Paulus, proconsul of Cyprus, is somewhat ambiguous (13:4-12). While certainly a Gentile, his introduction to Paul and to Christianity comes about from his relationship with the *Jewish* magician Bar-Jesus/Elymas. Paul's triumph over Elymas can be understood as a miniature enactment of the larger-scale triumph of Christianity over Judaism. See Susan R. Garrett, *The Demise of the Devil: Magic and the Demonic in Luke's Writings* (Minneapolis: Fortress, 1989) 87. Just like Sergius Paulus, all those who have knowledge of Judaism (i.e., God-fearers) should recognize the superior power and qualities of Christianity.

has been opened to all human beings with no distinction between Jew and Gentile. They do not, however, serve the narrative as the temporary waystation for the gospel as it passes from one group to another.

From a literary viewpoint, God-fearers are not minor characters who stand between the two great pillars of Jew and Gentile. Rather, they exist as *the* alternative to the Jewish community, as the foil for Jews—the "other" against whom the Jews are compared and judged. The prominence of the God-fearers and dearth of Gentiles in Acts should make us rethink the consensus of God-fearers as innocuous mediators and have us look to the dynamic role they play as characters in their own right.

GOD-FEARERS AND THE
IMAGE OF THE JEWS

One of the common features that unites all the God-fearers in Acts is their interaction with Jewish characters and Jewish tradition. The Ethiopian eunuch shares with Jews reverence for the temple and an interest in Scripture. Cornelius performs pious acts typical of Jews and is well spoken of by the whole Jewish nation (10:22). God-fearers in Asia Minor and Greece worship with Jews in the local synagogues. As we attempt to develop a better sense of what God-fearers contribute to an interpretation of Acts, we would be well served by examining the ways in which these characters relate to Jews in the narrative text, and in particular how the stories about God-fearers help to construct an image of Jews. Scholars have long argued that Luke–Acts presents a negative image of Jews, similar to that found in the other canonical Gospels and elsewhere in early Christian literature.[18] Depictions of Jews failing to understand Jesus or actively persecuting both him and those who proclaim his messianic identity—most notably Stephen and Paul—are deeply woven into the narrative fabric. Others have suggested that Luke–Acts actually portrays Jews in a somewhat less venal light. For instance, they suggest that Luke–Acts (1) mollifies the anti-Jewish tone by having many Jews become followers of Jesus; (2)

---

18. Lloyd Gaston, "Anti-Judaism and the Passion Narrative in Luke and Acts," in *Anti-Judaism in Early Christianity*, ed. Peter Richardson (Waterloo, Ont.: Wilfrid Laurier University, 1986) 1:127–53; Jerome Neyrey, *The Passion According to Luke* (New York: Paulist, 1985); Frank J. Matera, "Responsibility for the Death of Jesus According to the Acts of the Apostles," *JSNT* 39 (1990) 77–93; Joseph B. Tyson, *The Death of Jesus in Luke–Acts* (Columbia, SC: University of South Carolina, 1986); Stephen Wilson, "The Jews and the Death of Jesus in Acts," in *Anti-Judaism in Early Christianity*, 1:155–64.

focuses the blame against specific Jewish leaders or groups or on Jews living in Jerusalem rather than on the people as a whole; (3) excuses the actions of malevolent Jews by virtue of their ignorance; (4) portrays Christians like Paul as living the life of an observant Jew; or (5) holds out hope for ultimate inclusion of the Jews despite the reality of their current rejection.[19] Given the various positions espoused, one conclusion is clear—the presentation of Jews in Luke–Acts is extremely complex. Unlike Jews in the Gospel of John, Jews in Luke–Acts are not the demonized opponents of Jesus (John 8:44), nor do they appear before Pilate and condemn future generations, as they do in the Gospel of Matthew, by asking that the blood of Jesus be on them and their children (Matt 27:25).[20]

In attempting to negotiate the narrative's multifaceted presentation of Jews in Luke–Acts, scholarly analysis has traditionally focused on the ideas expressed by its main characters, Jesus, Peter, Paul, and other apostles, and the reaction to these ideas by Jewish characters. The approach is straightforward and has produced a significant amount of valuable information. I wish to add another dimension to this discussion: Rather than focusing on the words and deeds explicitly by and about Jews, I turn to the God-fearers and the contribution they make to the representation of Jews in Luke–Acts.

To reiterate my findings to this point: Acts sets before the reader a Gentile Christian world in which God-fearers exist as its primary inhabitants. In so doing, Acts provides a highly distinctive and exemplary portrait of Gentile Christians whose superior moral qualities are demonstrated by their reverence for the God of Israel and their observance of those rituals that distinguish them as pious individuals—prayer, almsgiving, and synagogue worship. The agreement brokered at the Jerusalem conference creates a context in which the reader can observe that Gentiles who wish to become Christians in the future will maintain these high standards. They will have to abstain from idolatry, sexual immorality, ritually unclean meat, and blood (15:20). James points out that this decision differs in no way from what Jews have

---

19. See Robert Brawley, *Luke–Acts and the Jews: Conflict, Apology, and Conciliation*, SBLMS 33 (Atlanta: Scholars, 1987); Hans Conzelmann, *The Theology of St. Luke* (London: SCM, 1982) 145–48; Augustin George, "Israël dans l'oeuvre de Luc," *RB* 75 (1968) 481–525; Jacob Jervell, *Luke and the People of God: A New Look at Luke–Acts* (Minneapolis: Augsburg, 1972); Frank Matera, "The Responsibility for the Death of Jesus in Acts," *JSNT* 39 (1990) 77–93; Robert Tannehill, "Israel in Luke–Acts: A Tragic Story," *JBL* 104 (1985) 69–85; Etienne Trocmé, "The Jews as Seen by Paul and Luke," in *"To See Ourselves as Others See Us": Christians, Jews, "Others" in Late Antiquity*, ed. Jacob Neusner and Ernest S. Frerichs (Chico, CA: Scholars, 1985) 157–60.

20. In Acts Paul uses similar language against the Jews of Corinth (18:6).

always required of Gentiles. The apostles merely reiterate those conditions established since the time of Moses—requirements that have been written in Scripture and are known to all through its recitation in the synagogues. In essence, Acts depicts a Christianity in which all members of the Gentile community are of the highest moral character as judged by Mosaic standards. The unwashed masses of the pagan world are not wanted, nor, for that matter, do they show much interest in Christianity's message.[21]

THE DIVIDING EFFECT OF BELIEF IN JESUS AS THE MESSIAH

Having recognized the way in which the Gentile Christian world in Acts is dominated by God-fearers, we can begin to appreciate the profound effect this presentation has on our understanding of the Jewish characters in the text. Acts constantly presents the juxtaposition of Jews and God-fearers. A comparison of the two is inevitable. In many respects the two groups share some basic religious tenets: both worship God, both acknowledge the revelatory truth of Scripture; both abide by those precepts set down for them by God. The numerous congruencies between Jews and the Gentiles depicted in Acts allows the reader to focus on the one fundamental issue dividing them: Is Jesus the Messiah? As depicted in the central portion of Acts, the Gentile God-fearers generally affirm this proclamation while Jews largely reject it. Having God-fearers represent the Gentile world reduces the ideological distance between the Jews and Gentiles, and thereby intensifies the failure of the Jews to share with the God-fearers their belief in Jesus. Not only do the God-fearers pose a serious challenge to Jews for their failure to accept Jesus as the Messiah, but they also expose the Jews as being especially irrational in their rejection of Gentiles as members of God's people. Jews do not reject Gentiles *per se*, but Gentiles who exhibit behavior that is considered by Jews to be ethically proper—they worship God, give alms, pray in the accepted fashion—and who are thought of quite highly by the Jewish people. Moreover, the position of these Gentiles as members of God's people is verified by the texts that the Jews themselves hold sacred.

---

21. For the most part, non–God-fearing Gentiles either misunderstand the words and actions of the apostles (e.g., the inhabitants of Lystra, 14:8–18) or work to subvert their activity (e.g., Demetrius, the silversmith of Ephesus, 19:23–41). The most notable exceptions, Dionysius and Damaris of Athens, become converts based on Paul's declaration that biblical revelation shares with philosophical rationalism the same truth of God's existence and purpose (17:22–31).

The characteristics of disobedience and obduracy are honed even more sharply through the encounter that Jews and God-fearers have with the sacred texts. Not surprisingly, the Jewish characters are well-acquainted with Scripture. The same also applies to God-fearers. The Ethiopian eunuch represents the most obvious example of this trait. While returning home from his pilgrimage to Jerusalem, he is found by Philip seated in his chariot reading from the scroll of Isaiah (8:28). In addition, the many anonymous God-fearers who attend the synagogues visited by Paul also are portrayed as knowledgeable in Scripture. Indeed, in Luke–Acts the synagogue and Scripture are inseparable; the synagogue serves as the primary venue for Scripture reading and inter-pretation. While preaching in the synagogue in Nazareth Jesus reads from the book of Isaiah (Luke 4:17–20); Paul visits the synagogue in Pisidian Antioch where the reading of the law and prophets takes place (13:15), and James specifies that Scripture is read every Sabbath in the synagogue (15:21). Acts creates a world in which not only Jews but God-fearers as well possess both a familiarity with and an appreciation for Scripture.

Scripture joins Jews and God-fearers together; it also bitterly divides them. Acts presents two peoples who honor scriptural tradition, but who respond to the Christian message based on this authority in dramatically different ways. The preaching by Jesus, Stephen, Paul, and apostles from and about Scripture yields opposing reactions from Jews and God-fearers. Beginning in chapter 7 where Stephen delivers his impassioned speech castigating the Jews for their stiff-necked nature, most Jews in the story reject the gospel while the God-fearers are often seen as eager recipients of its message. In most instances it is the preaching from Scripture that induces the God-fearers such as the Ethiopian eunuch and the God-fearers in Pisidian Antioch, Iconium, Philippi, Thessalonica, and Corinth to convert to Christianity.[22] In vivid contrast, Jews in those same places listening to the same texts demonstrate an overwhelming rejection of the gospel. By basing the proclamation on a source common to Jews and God-fearers, Scripture, Acts forestalls the claim that jews did not receive authentic proof that Jesus is the Messiah (18:28). Not only were they presented with this proof, the response by the God-fearers provides the model for how Jews should have acted, but did not. The failure of the Jews to respond

---

22. Scripture is often a catalyst for conversion, though hardly the only one. Elsewhere in Luke–Acts miraculous events (e.g., Paul on Cyprus [13:4–12] or in Ephesus [19:11–20]), and epiphanic experiences (Luke 24:13–35) play a similar role in conversion accounts. On the impor-tance of Scripture as the means toward conversion, see Tyson, "The Gentile Mission and the Authority of Scripture in Acts," 619–31.

positively to the proclamation of the gospel in and of itself fosters an image of them as ignorant and disobedient. This negative portrayal is magnified by the presence of another group of people, God-fearers, who acknowledge Jesus as the Messiah and all humanity as God's people and do so on the basis of the texts that Jews claim as authoritative. The Scripture that should serve as the basis for bringing all people, Jews and Gentile alike, to God instead functions as a divisive wedge that darkens a depiction of Jews that is already highly critical.

The portrayal of Gentile Christians in Acts places Jews in a defensive posture. The Christian asks of the Jew, "What's wrong with Gentile Christians? They are pious people who, like Cornelius, observe many of your customs. They read Scripture and understand it to confirm Jesus as the Messiah. You Jews whose traditions and sacred texts have led others to the true understanding of God and Jesus should know better and do likewise." The imaginary Jewish interlocutor is left speechless, disturbed, or both, not unlike the way many Jews respond to the speeches of Stephen, Peter, and Paul. By presenting God-fearers as typical of Gentile Christianity, the text heightens its censure of Jews for not accepting Jesus and rejecting the inclusion of Gentiles in this new religious order. The refusal of most Jews to recognize Jesus is tragic. But the presence of so many non-Jews who derive their understanding about Jesus from the very texts that Jews claim to be authoritative and sacred transforms a tragedy into a drama of condemnation.[23]

CONCLUSION

Literary analysis of Luke–Acts suggests, then, that God-fearers are not the neutral way station between Jew and Gentile that most commentators suggest. Rather, the generally receptive and committed response of these pious and Scripture-savvy Gentiles to proclamations about Jesus is meant as a foil to the increasingly antagonistic reaction

---

23. Jews, it must be said, do not appear in the work as a monolithic unit. Some readily convert to Christianity; others, like the Pharisee Gamaliel, are willing to take a wait-and-see attitude (5:38–39). Far more typical of Luke–Acts, however, is a highly negative image of Jews. They are the ones who are responsible for the murders of Jesus and Stephen. They are the ones who instigate riot and trouble in the cities of Greece and Asia Minor, who persecute and plot to kill Paul, who are castigated by Stephen, Peter, and Paul as being stubborn and disobedient toward God, who falsely accuse Paul of impiety. Even reports of positive reaction by Jews (e.g., 17:11–12) are often followed immediately by more encompassing negative depictions (e.g., 13:43–46 and 17:13). The God-fearers on the other hand are unassailable representatives of Gentile Christianity, and provide the measure by which the Jewish rejection of Christianity is judged. Their presence in the narrative adds greater weight to the predominantly negative portrayal of Jews in Acts.

of most Jews. Depicting a wider array of Gentiles rather than focusing on God-fearers would not have produced the same result. The mass of Gentiles does not stand upon the same religious foundation as do God-fearers and Jews. Instead, Acts presents two groups, Jews and God-fearers, who confront the gospel from a similar religious vantage point but respond to it with opposite results. The presentation of two groups who share much of a common tradition but differ radically in their ability and willingness to acknowledge God's plan reinforces an image of Jews as obdurate and disobedient toward God.

Thomas Kraabel's observation of "the disappearance of the God-fearers" after the middle third of Acts led him to conclude that these accounts serve a theological and literary purpose only and should not be read as having any historical value. While Kraabel overstated his conclusion, his discernment of the critical theological and literary roles played by the God-fearers in Acts is correct and should make us extremely wary of accepting God-fearers as ubiquitous members of ancient Jewish communities. While the existence of God-fearers is beyond question, their numbers and their role in facilitating the expansion of Christianity remain unsettled issues.

What I find even more striking than the disappearance of the God-fearers is the *non-appearance* of Gentiles. Despite constant references to Gentiles and the universal perspective of Christianity articulated in Acts, the text presents a steady stream of God-fearers, Gentiles to be sure, but Gentiles with a difference. We do not witness the grand inclusion of Gentiles of all sorts. Rather, we are confronted with one very specific type of Gentiles—those who possess a ready-made knowledge of God and Scripture and who are in many respects very similiar to Jews. Because of the numerous similarities, the differences in the way Jews and God-fearers respond to the gospel become magnified. The image of the God-fearer in Acts serves as a powerful device to condemn Jews for their failure to believe in Jesus and the gospel and for their rejection of those, particularly Gentiles, who do. Understanding how the representation of God-fearers functions in Luke–Acts reinforces a perspective that Luke–Acts presents a largely negative, indeed anti-Jewish, portrayal of Jews.

11

Jews, Jewish Christians, and Judaizers in North Africa

Claudia Setzer

I am pleased to contribute to this volume in honor of Robin Scroggs. He consistently points us to the human dimensions, individual and social, of the ancient dramas we study, he explores the transformative powers of religious loyalties, and he insists on clarity. I hope that this study will show some of these features as I express my thanks to him as a mentor and fellow scholar.

Can we say anything about social relations between Jews and Christians in and around Carthage in the formative period of the North African church, the late second to the fourth century? At present, most scholars say no. In spite of evidence of a Jewish community in Carthage as early as the second century, evidence of an intense, if numerically slight Christianity at the same time, and severe statements made by Christians about Jews from this period, the recent trend has been to deny significant relations between Jews and Christians or to deny that we can know much about them.[1] While individual works or

My thanks to the National Endowment for the Humanities for supporting a period of study in this area, and to the American Academy of Religion and Manhattan College for supporting a trip to Carthage in June 1996, and to Thomas Ferguson for his reading and helpful comments on this article.

1. See T. D. Barnes, *Tertullian* (Oxford: Clarendon, 1971, reissued with corrections and postscript, 1985) 90–93, 273–75, 330; D. Scholer, "Tertullian on Jewish Persecution of Christians," *Studia Patristica* 17:2, ed. E. Livingstone (Oxford: Pergamon, 1982) 821–27; and C. Bobertz, "'For the Vineyard of the Lord of Hosts was the House of Israel': Cyprian of Carthage and the Jews," *JQR* 82 (1991) 1–15. For a later period, see P. Fredriksen, "Excaecati Occulta Justitia Dei: Augustine on Jews and Judaism," *JEarlyChrSt* 3 (1995) 299–324. These works serve as important correctives to earlier scholars. They sometimes assume a questionable dichotomy, however: that Jews in the sources are scriptural and symbolic or are real, flesh-and-blood Jews known to the authors. The Jews may be both. Early Christian martyrologies, for example, show how scriptural typologies and real people and events are interwoven and understood in light of one another.

pieces of archaeological evidence taken in isolation may not be proba-
tive, the accumulation of evidence suggests that Jews in and around
Carthage interacted with Christians and that the presence of Jews had
an impact on the developing church. I do not attempt to resolve the
question of social relations here, but I would like to re-open the discussion, and hope that this essay will lend some clarity to the conversation
by delineating what kinds of Jews we are talking about.

In discussing social relations among Jews and Christians in North
Africa, there has been little focus on what kinds of Jews populate the
evidence. In general, scholars have rejected the principle of ancient
Judaism as a monolith, but see in antiquity multiple Judaisms.
Likewise, in North Africa, the many complaints about heretics and
struggles over self-definition in the church testify to multiple
Christianities. In this essay, while I will differentiate the Jews we
encounter in the literary and material sources from North Africa, especially those associated with Carthage, I wish to caution that the
categories I use are neither rigid nor exclusive. Some references could
fit into more than one category. The ambiguity is a function of the
fragmentary nature of the evidence, but also suggests an ambiguity and
porousness among the actual groups in the early centuries.

JEWS

I define Jews as people distinguished by Jewish birth or conversion,
who identify themselves as Jews, and who do not see themselves as
having any other religious loyalties.[2] The question of method is
obvious. How much does the presence of Jews in texts imply about the
reality of flesh-and-blood Jews in the early communities?[3]

Any work that considers competing claims between Jews and
Christians presents this problem, but in the North African writers it is
especially acute. For these writers often equate Judaism with heresy,[4]
present Jews as symbolic types, and generally transmit the standard
adversus Judaeos themes about Jews as hard-hearted and willfully

---

2. The problem of answering the question "Who is a Jew?" in ancient and contemporary
contexts is well known. For my purposes, I will use this definition, while acknowledging the
problems behind it.

3. D. Satran illustrates the problem of extrapolating social context from anti-Jewish writing
in "Anti-Jewish Polemic in the *Peri Pascha* of Melito of Sardis: The Problem of Social Context,"
paper delivered at the SBL annual meeting, November 1993. This is now published in *Contra
Iudaeos: Ancient and Medieval Polemics between Jews and Christians*, ed. O. Limor and G.
Stroumsa (Tübingen: Mohr Siebeck, 1995), but only the earlier paper was available to me.

4. See D. Efroymsen, "Tertullian's Anti-Jewish Rhetoric: Guilt by Association," *USQR* 36
(1980) 25-37.

blind to the meaning of their own Scriptures. P. Fredriksen calls these symbolic types "biblical Jews" or "hermeneutical Jews."[5] References that seem purely typological or that spring solely from the *adversus Judaeos* tradition are excluded from this present study.

I will consider rather both archaeological and literary references that seem to point to contemporary situations and also the more slippery examples where references to biblical Jews and contemporary Jews are woven together. For the early authors, I contend, there is no either-or view of biblical Jews or of contemporary Jews, but rather a tendency to project one on top of the other, or to understand one in the light of the other.

The earliest archaeological evidence comes from the late-second- or early-third-century Jewish necropolis at Gamart, north of Carthage, excavated by A.-L. Delattre at the end of the nineteenth century.[6] He unearthed 103 catacombs, each with about fifteen to seventeen graves. A number of Latin inscriptions and some Hebrew ones were found, as well as one with a *lulav,* menorah, and the word "shalom."[7] The inscriptions have been removed, as well as numerous lamps decorated with menorahs, now at the National Museum in Carthage.[8] Two ostensibly Christian inscriptions were found at Gamart, but most recent scholars are reluctant to make too much of them, arguing that they are not really Christian,[9] or not really early, perhaps scratched on later to counteract Jewish magic,[10] or that the cemetery may not be Jewish. The other early Jewish site is the synagogue at nearby Hammam Lif, whose inscriptions Y. Le Bohec dates to the end of the fourth century.

Many shadowy traditions suggest the presence of Jews in and around Carthage in the first century. They are largely legendary, often

5. P. Fredriksen, "Excaecati Occulta Justitia Dei," 321.

6. A.-L. Delattre, *Gamart ou la nécropole juive de Carthage* (Lyons: Mougin–Rusand, 1895). See also J. Ferron, "Inscriptions juives de Carthage," *Cahiers de Byrsa* 32 (1951) 194–206.

7. I was fortunate to be allowed into a catacomb, now on the grounds of the French military cemetery in Gamart.

8. My thanks to Dr. A. Ennabli of the National Museum, who allowed me to see artifacts from Gamart in storage, two inscriptions, as well as some beautiful lamps from Gamart. Decorated in the same style as other lamps of the period, these are distinguished by menorahs. Most of the menorahs had seven branches, some had six, and one had four branches. See J. Lund, "A Synagogue at Carthage? Menorah Lamps from the Danish Excavations," *JRA* 8 (1995) 244–62. Thanks to Leonard Rutgers for this reference.

9. T. Barnes, *Tertullian,* 274.

10. Y. Le Bohec, "Inscriptions juives et judaïsantes dé l'Afrique romaine," *Antiquités Africaines* 17 (1981) 168–69. Le Bohec introduces some doubt, saying the menorah was not an exclusively Jewish symbol, though the location and style of the cemetery suggest it was a Jewish necropolis.

associated with much later sources.[11] Jews in North Africa, as elsewhere, used the same names, objects, and funerary decorations as the surrounding culture, so a good deal of Jewish presence is invisible to us.

The earliest literary evidence of Jews in the vicinity of Carthage comes from the tenth-century writer Josippon, who said Jews were deported after the disaster of 70 to work the Roman estates in Africa: "And Vespasian gave his son Titus the country of Africa, and he settled 30,000 Jews in Carthage, besides those he settled in other places." Although this source is extremely late, there is plenty of evidence for Jews in nearby Cyrene, Libya, and Egypt from the first century.[12] If Josippon's tradition is correct, then it suggests an element within the population that would share not only Semitic language and culture with the native Berbers, but also a natural and permanent grudge against Roman occupation.

Scattered references to rabbis from Carthage appear in the Talmuds, but tell us little except that the rabbinic orbit included some authorities from Carthage (*b. Ber.* 29a; *b. Ketub.* 27b; *b. B. Qam.* 114b; *y. Kil.* 1.9; *y. Yoma* 1.3). A tradition that Rabbi Akiba visited Africa does not mention Carthage specifically (*b. Roš. Haš.* 26a; *b. Zebaḥ.* 37b; *b. Menaḥ.* 34b). An early tradition from the Tosefta responds to the idea that the Jews seized *Eretz Israel* from the Canaanites by extoling the beauty of Africa and presenting an unusual view of the Amorites: "Rabbi Simeon ben Gamaliel says: there is no more gentle people than the Amorites. Also we have found that they believed in God, for they went into exile in Africa and God gave them a country as beautiful as theirs, and the land of Israel was called after

---

11. For example, the tenth-century Jewish source Josippon says that after the revolt of 70, Vespasian gave North Africa to Titus, who settled 30,000 Jews there. Ibn Khaldun, a fourteenth-century Muslim writer, says that at the time of the Muslim conquest, they encountered Berber tribes who had converted to Judaism. M. Simon speculates that Zealots emigrated to North Africa after the disaster of 70, the philo-Semitism of the Severan emperors allowed Judaism to gain a foothold in North Africa and the Jewish Berber tribes are the remaining evidence of this influence; "Le Judaisme Berbere en L'Afrique Ancienne," *Recherches d'Histoire judéochrétienne* (Paris: Mouton, 1962) 30–87. A. Chouaqui cites legends as early as Josephus that the Berbers are Canaanites; *Between East and West: A History of the Jews of North Africa* (Philadelphia: JPS, 1968). Their Semitic language and culture suggest a closeness to Jews, but the tradition that North African Jews are descended from Berbers does not appear in Jewish sources until the sixteenth century. Feldman notes that Jews are associated with the legendary founding of Carthage as a Phoenician trading post; *Against Apion* 2 § *16. Jew and Gentile in the Ancient World* (Princeton: Princeton University Press, 1993) 181.

12. Philo reports a million Jews in Egypt, into Libya and to the boundaries of Ethiopia (*Flaccus* 6 § 43). Josephus reports Ptolemy's settlement of Jewish garrisons in Cyrene and other Libyan cities (*Against Apion* 2 § 44, 53). Acts 2:10 refers to a community of Jews from Cyrene and surrounding Libya. The second Jewish revolt in 115–117 started in Alexandria and spread to Cyrene (*Ant.* 12.5 § 45; *Ant.* 14.7.2 § 114–116).

them" (*t. Šabb.* 7.6). A later tradition recognizes that the rabbinic reach extends as far as Carthage: "From Tyre to Carthage, they know Israel and their Father in Heaven" (*b. Menaḥ.* 110a). While these references support the claim of some rabbinic presence in Carthage, the Jews with whom Tertullian and church writers came into contact were not necessarily rabbinic Jews.

Tertullian provides more concrete evidence of a Jewish presence in Carthage. "Hebrews of old they were, who now are Jews" (*Apol.* 18.6).[13] He refers to both biblical and contemporary Jews and distinguishes them by name. This is one of several examples where he seems to show a grudging respect for Jews, underscoring their antiquity and the antiquity of their Scriptures, a pedigree not incidentally shared by the Christians as their heirs. Both groups can therefore claim a superiority to any teachings of Greece and Rome: "I say, add your very gods, temples, oracles, rituals and all—the book of a single prophet notwithstanding beats them all, with centuries to spare, the book in which is seen summed up the treasure of the whole Jewish religion, and in consequence of ours as well" (*Apol.* 19.2).

Similarly, he assumes the shared heritage of Jews and Christians in refuting the potential charge of ass-worship current in his time, based on "the assumption that we too, standing so near the Jewish religion, are devoted to worship of the same image" (*Apol.* 16.3). Other examples of such underscoring of the Jewish origins of Christianity appear in the final section of this study.

Tertullian also refers to some customs and habits of the Jews: daily immersion or washing (*Bapt.* 15.3, CCSL 1.290; *Orat.* 14, CCSL 1.265), fast days (*Jej.* 16.6, CCSL 2.1275), use of a different calendar (*Jej.* 13.6, CCSL 2.1272), observance of Sabbaths and festivals (*Idol.* 14.6, CCSL 2.1115), circumcision (*Apol.* 21.1), and veiling of Jewish women (*Cor.* 4.2, CCSL 2.1043; *Orat.* 22.8, CCSL 1.270). He knows about the Jewish tax, which he links to Jewish access to the Scriptures (in reference to the translation of the Septuagint):

> To this day in the temple of Serapis, Ptolemy's library is displayed together with the Hebrew originals. Why, yes! and the Jews openly read the books. They have that freedom in return for a tribute. Every Sabbath day there is common access to those books. (*Apol.* 18.8)

_____

13. All translations of Tertullian's *Apology, De Spectaculis,* and Minucius Felix's *Octavian* are from the edition by T. R. Glover and G. H. Rendel, LCL (Cambridge, MA: Harvard University Press, 1984). Translations of all other references in Tertullian are from *The Ante-Nicene Fathers,* vols. 3–4, ed. A. Roberts and T. Donaldson (Grand Rapids: Eerdmans, 1978–79).

Tertullian also claims to know something about contemporary Jews and their habits. At times he may be wrong or confused, but unlike the slanders of Apion or Apollonius Molon, his statements about Jewish customs are not outlandish. Nor are all these observances biblical, information that could be gleaned simply by reading the Scriptures. Daily immersion is not biblical,[14] nor is the veiling of Jewish women.[15] The Jewish tax was probably common knowledge. Tertullian claims an acquaintance with Jews of his own time and knows some things he could not gather from Scripture. He speaks of them as if they are highly visible to his readers, since they provide convenient examples for his arguments. If he did not always have the details right, that is no proof he is fabricating. How many non-Jews today live in proximity to Jews and only partially understand their customs?

The references above are neutral, either imparting information about Jewish customs or arguing the shared heritage of Jews and Christians. Other statements, however, imply rancorous relations. In talking about the classic themes of Jewish rejection of Jesus and misreading of the prophets, Tertullian implies they are part of a current dispute: "Even now the Jews look for his coming, nor is there any other greater cause of clash between us than that they do not believe he has come" (*Apol.* 21.15).

In a famous passage, he cites Jewish objections to the resurrection and the charge that Jesus' body was stolen. While the origin of this charge is clearly the Gospel of Matthew (28:15), Tertullian adds information not found elsewhere, that Jews claimed it was a gardener who took Jesus' body to avoid damage to his lettuces.[16] In his vision of the triumphant return of the Lord on the day of judgment, Tertullian visualizes Jesus taking vengeance on the Jews for their slanders against him: "This is he whom the disciples secretly stole away, that it might be said he had risen—unless it was the gardener who removed him, lest his lettuces should be trampled by the throng of visitors" (*Spect.* 30.105).

---

14. Tertullian might infer immersion from Mark 7:3-4, but those verses refer specifically to hand-washing and purification of vessels.

15. Barnes finds the observation that Jews veil their women "almost comic"; *Tertullian,* 92. But the North African context showed Oriental attitudes to the body that were decidedly more modest than the Greeks. See S. Raven, *Rome in Africa* (Routledge: London, 1969) 30. Combined with Jewish interest in feminine modesty, Tertullian's suggestion seems quite possible.

16. The resurrection as a continuing sore point between Jews and Christians appears earlier in Justin and also in Celsus. For the resurrection as a point of argument between early Jews and Christians, see my article, "'You Invent a Christ!': Christological Claims as Points of Jewish Christian Dispute," *USQR* 44 (1991) 315-28. W. Horbury argues that this reference points to Carthaginian Jews of Tertullian's time arguing against Christianity, since this tradition shows up in later Jewish sources; "Tertullian on the Jews in Light of *De Spectaculis* 30.5-6," *JTS* 22 (1972).

Tertullian also argues with Jews about the resurrection in *De Resurrectione Mortuorum* (30, CCSL 2.959-60) where he disputes the Jewish claim that Ezekiel's vision of the dry bones (37:1-14) is really about the nation of Israel, saying that it refers rather to Jesus' resurrection and the resurrection of the Christian faithful. He talks about it as if it is a debate going on in his own time and he knows Jewish interpretation of Scripture firsthand: "I am well aware how they torture even this prophecy into a proof of the allegorical sense." He alludes to disputes with Jews over other passages of Scripture, especially those pertaining to virgin birth.[17]

One example of Jewish libel of Christianity is quite unlike anything else. An apostate Jew carries a caricature of a Christian that includes a picture of a donkey's head, which he labels "Onocoetes," literally "begotten by a donkey," a reference to the god of the Christians and the pagan libel of both Jews and Christians as ass-worshipers. Tertullian claims this happened "not so long ago," and says it illustrates the Jews as "the seed-plot of all the calumny against us" (*Nat.* 1.14.1, CCSL 1.32-33). This seems a particularly pathetic and desperate example to bring as proof, however, since even Tertullian claims this person is no longer a Jew and can hardly represent the people. His purpose, however, is to somehow place Jewish persecution of Christians in the recent past.

Finally, Tertullian talks about general Jewish persecution of Christians, linking their own suffering under the pagans to the apostles' suffering under the Jews: "Will you plant there both synagogues of the Jews—fountains of persecution—before which the apostles endured the scourge, and heathen assemblages with their own circus, indeed where they readily take up the cry 'Death to the third race'" (*Scorp.* 10.10, CCSL 2.1089). The chronology is vague here, probably by intention, and it is not clear if the synagogues are fountains of persecution in Tertullian's time also, or only in the time of the apostles. But in another work he distinguishes quite clearly for his own time: "If we are apprehended, we shall not be brought into Jewish councils, nor scourged in Jewish synagogues but we shall certainly be cited before Roman magistrates and judgment seats" (*Fug.* 6.2, CCSL 2.1142).

Tertullian presents a more varied attitude toward Jews than is generally appreciated, and he implies an acquaintance with Jews of his own time. Cyprian, by comparison, in the mid-third century, presents

---

17. These are two of three problematic christological issues between Jews and Christians that surface as early as the Gospels. See my article, "'You Invent a Christ!'" 322-24.

a standard supersessionist theology of Jews and Judaism. C. Bobertz has shown that the Jews to whom Cyprian refers are usually biblical or typological, that he merely expands on a received *adversus Judaeos* tradition, bypassing opportunities to refer to contemporary Jews in Carthage.[18] For Cyprian, Jews function as types, to emphasize the totality of the opposition to Christianity: "Menaced we are not only by Gentile and Jew, but by heretics as well; for all those whose hearts and minds have been seized by the devil daily manifest their envenomed and raving madness" (*Ep.* 59.2, CSEL 3.667).[19] Including the Jews is a way of saying "everyone." Similarly, Augustine will say "Heretics, Jews and pagans . . . they form a unity against our Unity" (*Sermo* 62, *PL* 38.423).

JEWISH CHRISTIANS

Problems of definition get even murkier as we move from "Who is a Jew?" to "Who is a Jewish Christian?" For our purposes, a Jewish Christian is someone who is Jewish by birth or conversion, whose self-identification and practice are Jewish, who believes in Jesus, and whose belief in Jesus and Christology are rooted in Jewish belief.[20] A useful criterion is the implication of continued Jewish practice and belief, rather than the taking on of new practices.

Archaeological evidence for Jewish Christians around early Carthage is scant. An inscription in Greek and Hebrew was found at the early Christian basilica at Damous el Karita. It reads,

'Αννιανὸς/'Αννιανοῦ/υἱειος ἐν εἰρήνῃ/בשלום/אנינא

Annianos, son of Annianos/in peace/Anniana/in peace

Le Bohec argues that the inscription must have come from the Jewish necropolis at Gamart,[21] but this merely solves the discrepancy of an apparently Jewish inscription found in an early Christian basilica. A plausible explanation is that the person buried there is a Jewish Christian. We know of at least one baptized Jew from the inscription Sitifis 8640, found in Ksour Ghozlan, to the west of Carthage,[22] where

---

18. Bobertz shows that Cyprian's early work *Ad Quirinium* contains classic anti-Jewish material, but is cited little in his later works. When he does talk about Jews, it is usually in a biblical context ("Vineyard").

19. All translations of Cyprian are from *Ancient Christian Writers*, 4 vols., trans. G. Clarke (New York: Newman, 1984–89).

20. See S. Wilson, *Related Strangers* (Minneapolis: Fortress, 1995) 143–59 for a discussion of definition and sources related to Jewish Christians.

21. Le Bohec, "Inscriptions juives," 179, inscription 18.

22. Le Bohec, "Inscriptions juives," 192, inscription 75.

a man sets up a grave for his dead brother that incorporates the *chi-rho* and refers to both brothers as "de Iude[is]," "of the Jews."

Two other inscriptions discovered at Gamart appear to be Christian. One is reconstructed by Delattre as

> NIS . . . /Fortunatia b [L]ocus/ [. . . a]edis u[b]i <e> sunt/ [beati ste]fani marturi/ [ossa et ?] filius," . . . Fortunatia . . . place of the shrine where [the bones and ?] of the blessed Stephen the martyr, son (CIL viii, 14100).

While the reconstruction is disputed, some believe it contains a reference to a martyr named Stephen, or more likely to St. Stephen, the proto-martyr who was extremely popular in North Africa.[23]

Another inscription from Gamart contains an epitaph inscribed to one *"Longeia Flavia Laurentia, virgo sancta,"* Longeia Flavia Laurentia, holy virgin (CIL viii 24941a). The identification and reverence due one who died a virgin is in line with Christian attitudes of the second century, although Philo reports Jewish virgins among the Therapeutae near Alexandria in the first century (*De vita contempl.* 68-69). Frend accepts both epitaphs as Christian.[24] Others dispute whether or not they are Christian, whether or not Gamart is a Jewish necropolis, when the inscriptions were made, and how they got there.[25] Parkes cites legends of Christian martyrs buried in Jewish cemeteries in other places.[26]

While these references are fragmentary and cannot support unaided a theory of cordial relations, they invite speculation that Jews and Christians (probably Jewish Christians) may have been buried together near Carthage and that relations may not have been entirely acrimonious.[27] In light of this, Tertullian's complaint about those who refused Christians burial is tantalizing, "for when there had been some agitation about places of sepulture for our dead, and the cry arose, 'No *areae*—no burial grounds for the Christians,' it came that their own *areae*, their threshing floors were wanting, for they gathered in no har-

---

23. Stephen is called "the perfect martyr" as early as the second century. In North Africa he is frequently cited, his relics venerated, and numerous miracles are associated with him. See F. van der Meer, *Augustine the Bishop* (London: Sheed and Ward, 1961) 475-76, 547-53. My thanks to J. Patout Burns and Maureen Tilley for help on this point.

24. W. Frend, "A Note on Tertullian and the Jews," *Studia Patristica* 10 (1970) 292.

25. Le Bohec suggests they were scratched on later by Christians to counteract Jewish magic, "Inscriptions juives," 168-69.

26. J. Parkes, *The Conflict of the Church and Synagogue* (New York: Atheneum, 1969) 145.

27. This the suggestion of P. Monceaux a hundred years ago; *Histoire littéraire de L'Afrique Chrétienne* (Paris: Ministre de L'Instruction Publique et des Beaux-Arts, 1901) 1:9, is seconded by Parkes, *Conflict*, 145, and M. Simon, *Verus Israel*, 456, nn. 99-101.

vests" (*Scap.* 3.1, CCSL 2.1129). Is it possible that the Jews of Gamart allowed a few Jewish Christians (or even Gentile Christians) to be buried in their catacombs because they were refused burial elsewhere? The difficulty of distinguishing Jewish, Jewish Christian, and Christian burials is profound, since, as Rutgers has shown, Jews, Christians, and pagans all drew on the same funerary art and were often buried in the same areas.[28]

Literary evidence may be more helpful in pointing us to the existence of Jewish Christians. The African bishop Commodian presents, according to J. Danielou, evidence of a popular Latin Jewish Christianity that preceded Tertullian. Little is known about Commodian, but Danielou suggests he was a pagan who entered Christianity by way of Judaism. In his writings he denounces Judaism and Jewish Christianity, he retains a Christology, a reverence for the Law, and a millenarianism that Danielou attributes to an intermediate stage as a Jewish Christian.[29]

Tertullian complains that some Christians seem to be posing as Jews to avoid persecution because Judaism is a *religio licita* and the pagans would not distinguish them. Yet it is possible they are not posing and really are Jews who are also Christians. As such they would understandably argue for their protected status as Jews, a status they had never given up. Tertullian claims that Christians have nothing to do with the Jews, but he protests too much, since he argues in the same passage that Christianity rests on the ancient books of the Jews, and in many places argues the shared heritage of the Jews and Christians, "lest people think we are insinuating our ideas under cover of a famous religion . . . because (waiving all questions as to age) as regards forbidden foods, sacred days, the bodily seal, or common designation, we have nothing to do with the Jews, as should surely be the case, if we were servants of the same God" (*Apol.* 21.1–2).

Although Bobertz has shown convincingly that Cyprian says little about other Jews in his own time, Cyprian's correspondence provides some hints of Jewish Christianity. When he argues "Circumcision of the flesh ought not to block the way to circumcision of the spirit" (*Ep.* 64.5, CSEL 3.720), he is using Pauline categories of flesh and spirit, but does not make them antithetical to each other as Paul does in

---

28. L. Rutgers, "Archaeological Evidence for the Interaction of Jews and Non-Jews in Late Antiquity," *AJA* 96 (1992) 101–18. See also G. Snyder, *Ante Pacem* (Macon: Mercer, 1985), who shows that in matters of daily life, dress, food, burials, Christians were indistinguishable from their neighbors before the end of the second century.

29. J. Danielou, *The Origins of Latin Christianity* (Philadelphia: Westminster, 1977) 99–138.

Galatians. Rather he argues that fleshly circumcision has the potential to interfere with circumcision of the spirit. This could be a recognition that there are people already circumcised (i.e., Jews) within the church and a warning that their ideas are potentially troublesome. Judaizing, (i.e., Gentiles taking on circumcision) seems a less likely possibility, since it would probably evoke a stronger response.

Firmilian, the bishop of Caesarea, in his letters to Cyprian refers to "the synagogue of the heretics," which "is by no means one with us, because the bride is neither adulteress nor whore—hence the synagogue is unable to produce children of God" (*Ep.* 75.14.2, CSEL 3.819). The bride is the church, and Firmilian is trying to draw a clear line between it and a group with heretical ideas that might be confused with the church. Similarly Firmilian writes, "Egregious is the error and profound the blindness of one who declares that forgiveness of sins can be given in the synagogues of the heretics and who does not remain within the foundation of that one church" (*Ep.* 75.16.1, CSEL 3.820). In both cases, the term "synagogue" is meant to discredit on the basis of these being Jewish groups. Clearly these are groups in competition with other Christian groups, with pretensions to belonging to the church and performing the same functions as other churches. Some Jewish practice or belief sees itself as legitimately Christian, but is labeled heresy by others.

A council of Carthage in the middle of the third century provides the clearest suggestion of the presence of Jewish Christians in North Africa. It expelled from the church "those clinging to Jewish superstitions and festivals" (*IV Canon* 89).[30] "Clinging" implies a continuance of Jewish observance, rather than the sudden taking on of practices, and so points to Jewish Christians more than Judaizers.

In light of these hints of Jewish Christians in the church, a later remark by Augustine about "Christians who call themselves Jews" makes sense. They should avoid doing so, "even though they are the true Israel" (*Ep.* 196; *PL* 33.3. 894). While in this instance Augustine may refer either to Jewish Christians or Judaizers, the need to avoid confusion between Jews and Christians arises from the continued annoyance of Jewish Christians in the church, a problem that began several generations earlier. The *Caelicoli,* a group about whom we know little, are called "heretics who tried to force Christians to adopt the name 'Jew'" (*Cod. Theod.* 16.8.19). Perhaps they used that name because some of them were Jews.

---

30. J. Parkes, *The Conflict of the Church and Synagogue* (New York: Atheneum, 1969) 203.

Finally, Jews, Christians, and pagans mingled in their use of magical names (such as Iao, Sabaoth), amulets, and incantations. A third-century inscription from Hadrumetum, south of Carthage, is an incantation to compel a certain man to marry "in the name of the God of Abraham, Isaac and Jacob and in the name of the God of Israel."[31] Amulets from Carthage contain the Hebrew names for God, as well as the archangels.[32] H. Z. Hirschberg reminds us that the blurring of boundaries among groups happened as much through magic as theology.[33] Augustine, for example, complains about a Jew selling an amulet for healing (*De Civitate Dei* 22.8.21, CCSL 48.824–25).

In these examples from Carthage are concerns about the name "Jew," some evidence of Jewish practices, struggles over legitimacy, and the labeling of Judaism as heresy, a label that implies some closeness. "Heretics" are troublemakers within one's field of vision, not adherents of a separate religion.

JUDAIZERS

The definition of "Judaizer" varies, as S. Wilson has shown, but he points us to its ancient and technical sense: "non-Jews who chose to live like Jews."[34] A Judaizer is a person of Gentile birth, who remains a Gentile, but takes on certain Jewish practices. It can be very difficult to distinguish references to Gentile Christian Judaizers from references to Jewish Christians. One key is whether new Jewish practices are being taken on by Gentiles or whether Jewish practices simply remain in place even after the professing of belief in Jesus.

The inscription at Damous el Karita in Greek and Hebrew discussed above in the section on Jewish Christians could also belong to a Judaizer. A second inscription from Carthage likely refers to a child of a Judaizer:

DMS/ Sabbatis pia uix(it)/ anno (uno) diebis(us) (viginti uno)[35]

Into the hands of the gods/ dear Sabbatis lived/ one year twenty-one days (CIL viii 24976).

---

31. H. Z. Hirschberg, *A History of the Jews in North Africa* (Leiden: Brill, 1974–81) 1:85.

32. Le Bohec, "Inscriptions juives," 198–99.

33. Hirschberg, *Jews in North Africa*, 1:82–86. For examples of this mixing of magical names in nearby Egypt, see M. Meyer and R. Smith, *Ancient Christian Magic* (San Francisco: Harper, 1994).

34. S. Wilson, *Related Strangers*, 160–61.

35. Le Bohec, "Inscriptions juives," 179, inscription 17.

The combination of a pagan abbreviation for "into the hands of the gods" and a name that incorporates the word for Sabbath (as opposed to Saturn) leads Le Bohec to assume this is the infant child of a Judaizer.[36]

Tertullian provides some curious evidence of Judaizing as a continuing vexation. He complains about others Judaizing, but also stands accused of it himself, perhaps because of his stringencies about food and fasts and abstention from blood, "Others charge us with Galaticizing because we observe seasons, days, months and years" (*Jej.* 14.1, CCSL 2.1272). He also speaks of the "abstention from blood, including strangled things, or things that die of themselves . . . even that (blood) buried in the meat" (*Apol.* 9.13). Minucius Felix also refers to Christians abstaining from eating blood (*Oct.* 30.6). These practices could be gleaned entirely from Acts 15:20, 29 or directly from the Hebrew Bible (Gen 9:4; Lev 17:10–16; 19:26; Deut 12:23–25).

Furthermore, some Christians act in ways that make outsiders think they are Jews or posing as Jews. Since their school (Christians) rests on the ancient books of the Jews, " . . . perhaps some question may be raised as to the standing of the school, on the ground that, under cover of a very famous religion (and one certainly permitted by law), the school insinuates quietly certain claims of its own" (*Apol.* 21.1–2). Tertullian protests that the two, Judaism and Christianity, have nothing to do with each other, regarding food laws, festivals, and circumcision, a protest that is unnecessary unless the two groups look somewhat alike. I have already suggested that some may not be posing as Jews, but may actually be Jewish Christians. Tertullian also talks about the heresy of Judaizing, a heresy associated with Hebion (possibly Ebionites), saying these present heresies are descended from "the circumcisers in Galatia" (*Praescr. Haer.* 33.5, CCSL 1.214). Perhaps he takes aim at the same group when he cites the devil imitating "the well-known moroseness of Jewish law" (*Praescr. Haer.* 40.6, CCSL 1.220).

The possibility of Judaizing is ever present in a church that accepts the Hebrew Scriptures. As early as Paul's letter to the Galatians and in the letters of Ignatius sixty years later, the temptation for Christians to take on food laws, fasts, even circumcision is powerful. M. Simon argues that Judaizing is often a reaction against official orthodoxy and a constant tendency in the church.[37] Possibly Firmi-

---

36. Le Bohec, "Inscriptions juives," 167. Le Bohec records a number of lamps from Carthage signed with the names "Sabbati" or "Sabbatis."

37. Simon, *Verus Israel*, 307.

lian's and Cyprian's complaints against the "synagogue of the heretics" are references to Gentile Judaizers and not Jewish Christians. Firmilian seems to take aim against Judaizing when he assumes no one would claim that since Christ's coming "their most ancient customs have proved to be of some benefit to the Jews, seeing that they have rejected the new way of truth and have clung to hoary antiquity" (*Ep.* 75.19.1, CSEL 3.822). The implication is that since the coming of Christ, these customs are useless for Jews as well as for Christians.

Commodian, the North African bishop, who may have come to Christianity as a convert to Judaism or a Judaizer,[38] turns his back on Judaism. He writes two works that employ standard prophetic critiques against the Jews. Twice he rails against those who combine Judaism and Christianity, "Are you half a Jew? Then you are half profane" (*Instructions* 1.37, CSEL 15.49). This does not seem to be against Judaism, but rather against someone who is neither fully a Jew or a Christian, probably a Judaizer. He counters with some standard images of Judaism's blindness and leading astray. Similarly he chides some who are attracted to the synagogue, "Why do you run in the synagogue to the Pharisees,[39] that he may be merciful to you, whom of your own accord you deny?" (*Instructions* 1.24, CSEL 15.31).

A lamp from Carthage shows Christ treading on a menorah, which Simon takes to be an anti-Judaizing statement.[40] It could also be mere *adversus Judaeos* material, showing the supersession of Christianity over Judaism. Similarly, the expulsion from the church of "those clinging to Jewish superstitions and festivals" at the Council of Carthage in the mid-third century could point to Judaizing, though the image of "clinging" sounds more like Jewish Christians continuing to observe Jewish practices.

JEWISH IDENTIFIERS

In this last group, I include people I call "Jewish Identifiers," Christians who are not Jews and have no ambitions to be Jews or take on Jewish practices, but who stress the Jewish elements and origins of Christianity. They struggle with the challenge of early Christian theology to affirm Christianity's roots in Judaism, while freeing itself from Judaism. How could they hold on to the authority of the Hebrew Bible,

---

38. Danielou makes much of Commodian as a testimony to the Jewish roots of Latin Christianity in his low Christology and use of Jewish Christian symbolism, *The Origins of Latin Christianity* (Philadelphia: Westminster, 1977) 111–38.

39. A variant reading is *bifarios.*

40. Simon, *Verus Israel*, 354.

a book that speaks to and about biblical Israel, while affirming it is the rightful possession of Christianity, a predominantly Gentile group? In some way, every early Christian thinker had to struggle with this question. Some had to respond to people like Marcion, who wanted to sever Christianity from its Jewish roots. While present in other Christian thinkers, the affirmation of Judaism in North African thinkers has a particular resonance. Even when statements about Jews and Judaism are abstract and typological and do not reflect actual relations, in some way the association with Judaism carries the stamp of authenticity.

Tertullian, for example, defends the practice of Christian baptism and other laws and customs that lack scriptural support by likening them to the unwritten laws of the Jews (*Cor.* 4.1–4, CCSL 2.1043–44). He defends Jesus' Jewishness (*Ad. Marc.* 4.7.5–7, CCSL 1.554). In his *Apology* he assumes and argues from the shared origins of Judaism and Christianity: "I think, the assumption that we too, standing so near Jewish religion, are devoted to worship of the same image (of an ass' head)." He argues that since no image was found by Pompey in the Jewish temple, such an accusation is a slander against Judaism, and therefore against Christianity. In this way Tertullian exonerates Christians by exonerating Judaism (*Apol.* 16.3).

Tertullian also refers to the shared heritage of Scripture, "that book in which is seen summed up the treasure of the whole Jewish religion, and in consequence of ours as well" (19.2). In defending against the idea that some Christians pose as Jews, he argues they have nothing to do with each other, but admits it would be an understandable mistake for outsiders to make, since their religion "rests on the very ancient books of the Jews" (21.1). Finally, he claims that Christians are bound up with the fate of Israel, looking not for its downfall, but its restoration and conversion. He reverses the usual interpretation of the Prodigal Son, claiming the elder son represents Christians and the younger one represents the Jews, "The Jew, at the present day, having squandered God's substance, is a beggar in alien territory, serving the princes of this world. . . . For it will be fitting for the Christians to rejoice, and not to grieve at the restoration of Israel, if it be true (as it is) that the whole of our hopes is intimately united with the remaining expectation of Israel" (*Pud.* 8.8–9, CCSL 2.1295–96).

That some Christians identified with Judaism through stressing the Jewish elements within Christianity may also be seen in the enthusiasm for martyrdom in North Africa, which resonates with a strain in Judaism evident in Maccabean literature, the Zealots, and the followers of Bar Kochba. In *The Martyrdom of Montanus and Lucius* (Carthage, mid-third century) the mother of a martyr Flavian is called "a true daughter of Abraham, a mother of the race of the Maccabees."[41] Frend cites a work by Donatists showing the "kings of this world" in eternal opposition to the righteous: "A king persecuted the brethren of the Maccabees. . . . And the Lord Jesus Christ was slain by a king's most wicked judge . . . nor indeed does the hand of the butcher glow save at the instigation of your (the Catholics') tongue."[42] Frend describes the "terror-squads" of the Donatists in the fourth century who attacked the rich and powerful, reminiscent of the Zealot λῃστής who terrorized the countryside at the time of the first Jewish war.

CONCLUSION

In sometimes extreme forms, North African Christian writers exhibit an ambivalence toward Judaism that grows out of the basic dilemma that Christians owed their origins to Judaism but also needed to free themselves from it to assert their own distinctive character. As others have noted, the way out of this dilemma has often been to denigrate Judaism.[43] In this process, writers like Tertullian seem to reject Jews and Judaism with one hand, while grasping them with the other. In this process, they have revealed the presence of some real Jews in their field of vision: They have shown some knowledge of their practices, have hinted at struggles with them over scriptural interpretation and Christology and over who is the true Israel, and have shown occasional respect for them. As in other church writers, the real threat for Tertullian seems to be those who blurred the boundaries, Jewish Christians and Gentile Judaizers.[44] Nevertheless, these writers do not relinquish entirely a sense of Israel's place in history, the power of her Scripture and symbols, or the hope for her restoration.

---

41. H. Musurillo, *The Acts of the Christian Martyrs* (Oxford: Clarendon, 1972) 215–39.

42. W. H. C. Frend, *The Rise of Chistianity* (Philadelphia: Fortress, 1984) 655.

43. Recently S. Wilson has shown how early patterns of Christian worship illustrate this dependence on/differentiation from process and its anti-Jewish consequences (*Related Strangers*, 222–57).

44. Wilson makes this point for the second century in *Related Strangers*, 143, 165.

PART III

UNDERSTANDING

PAUL

12

A Formula for Communal Discord
as a Clue to the
Nature of Pastoral Guidance

J. Louis Martyn

In Galatians 5:17 Paul speaks of the dynamic relationship between the Impulsive Desire of the Flesh and the Spirit of Christ, identifying that relationship as an apocalyptic war that has been raging since the advent of the Spirit:[1]

> For the Flesh is actively inclined against the Spirit, and the Spirit against the Flesh. Indeed these two powers constitute a pair of opposites at war with one another. . . .

In the context set by Galatians 5:13–24 (see also 3:2, 5; 4:6, 29) this statement is both clear and understandable. In formulating the promise of Galatians 5:16, for example, Paul has just portrayed the Spirit and the Flesh as powers that are actively opposed to one another in the corporate life of the Galatian churches. Far from transparent, however, is the final clause of 5:17, in which Paul describes the result of the war between the Spirit and the Flesh:

---

1. With consistency Paul uses the term πνεῦμα in Galatians to refer to the Spirit of Christ, and the Galatians are very likely to have noted this consistency, for from their baptism onwards, the identity of the Spirit will have been essentially clear to them. It is not a natural part of themselves, a spirit with which they were born, corresponding to the body they were given at birth. Nor is it one of the amorphous spirits abroad in the world. It is the Spirit of the Son, drawing its characteristics from him, and being sent by God into their hearts (Gal 4:6). In Gal 5:13–24 Paul consistently employs the word σάρξ (5:13, 17 [twice], 19, 24) as an abbreviation for ἐπιθυμία σαρκός (5:16), the Impulsive Desire of the Flesh, the יצר as an apocalyptic power arrayed against the Spirit of Christ. See J. Marcus, "The Evil Inclination in the Letters of Paul," *IBS* 8 (1986) 8–21.

. . . the result being that you do not actually do the very things you wish to do.[2]

What are we to make of this surprising clause? If Paul intends the Galatians to rest assured in the promise of 5:16—a community that leads its daily life guided by the Spirit can know that it will not end up carrying out the Impulsive Desire of the Flesh—how can he follow that promise—indeed how can he ground it (note the word "for" [γάρ] at the outset of v. 17)—with the apparently discouraging assertion that the war between the Spirit and the Flesh leads to a failure to do what one wishes to do? After the promise, we could expect Paul to speak with a confidence that is contagiously enthusiastic:

> In contradistinction to the Teachers,[3] I, Paul, make you a solemn promise: Lead your daily life guided by the Spirit, and, in this way you will not end up carrying out the Impulsive Desire of the Flesh. For the Flesh is actively inclined against the Spirit, and the Spirit against the Flesh. These two powers constitute a pair of opposites at war with one another, and the result of this war is precisely the positive basis of my promise: The Spirit is in the happy process of liberating you from the destructive power of the Flesh!

Why does Paul portray instead an apparently negative result to the war between the Flesh and the Spirit? Faced with this question, interpreters have elected in general one of three readings.[4]

First, Paul has been thought to refer mainly to the Spirit's role in the war, thus striking precisely the positive note mentioned above. Far

---

2. Grammatically the ἵνα clause can be taken to state either result—on ἵνα as a substitute for the infinitive of result, see BDF §391.5, and add to the Pauline passages listed there 2 Cor 7:9—or purpose, the latter reflecting the goal had in mind by one or the other of the two combatants (or by God? cf. J. M. G. Barclay, *Obeying the Truth: A Study in Paul's Ethics in Galatians* [Edinburgh: T. & T. Clark, 1988] 115 n. 23). The strongest argument for the purposive reading is the thesis that in 5:17 Paul intends to warn the Galatians against libertinism. Taking the clause to speak of the purpose of *the Spirit* in its war against the Flesh, and translating the relative pronoun ἄ with the word "whatever," Barclay, e.g., finds just such a warning: In its war, the Spirit's purpose is to see to it that "the Galatians are not in the dangerous position of being *free* to 'do *whatever* you want' . . . " (*Obeying*, 115; emphasis added). But does not this reading import the motif of dangerous freedom into 5:17? Together with virtually the whole of 5:13–24, the clause ἵνα μὴ ποιῆτε is almost certainly descriptive rather than purposive. Paul *describes* the result of the warfare: Given the war between the Flesh and the Spirit, the Galatians *are not doing* what they wish to do.

3. With the expression "the Teachers" I refer to the Christian-Jewish evangelists whose coming into Paul's Galatian churches provoked the writing of the Galatian letter. See Martyn, "A Law-Observant Mission to Gentiles," *SJT* 38 (1985) 307–24; idem *Galatians* (Garden City, NY: Doubleday, 1997), Comment #6.

4. Cf. Barclay, *Obeying*, 113–14. In addition to Barclay's own interpretation (note 2 above), see the reading proposed by J. C. O'Neill: Gal 5:17—where "spirit" and "flesh" refer to the two complementary parts of every human being—is one of the Jewish moral aphorisms included in 5:13–6:10, a section inserted into Paul's letter by a later hand. See O'Neill, "The Holy Spirit and the Human Spirit in Gal 5:17," *EphTheolLov* 71 (1995) 107–20; cf. J. Smit, "The Letter of Paul to the Galatians: A Deliberative Speech," *NTS* 35 (1989) 1–26, esp. 25.

from intending finally to portray a paralyzing stalemate between the Flesh and the Spirit, Paul announces in Galatians 5:17 itself the encouraging news that the Spirit successfully frustrates the desires of the Flesh. R. Jewett, for example, finds in this verse a decided imbalance. The human being is paralyzed only if "he identifies his own will with that of the flesh." If he walks by the Spirit, the Flesh has no success in its attempt to lure him away.[5] One can indeed find the essence of this thought in 5:16, and in 5:18 as well. But to read the promise of 5:16 into 5:17 is to beg the question, thus giving no genuine explanation for the fact that Paul *ends* the latter verse on the note of an emphasized failure. And 5:18 is introduced by a contrastive instance of the expression εἰ δέ ("if, however"), indicating that in speaking there of the successful leading of the Spirit, Paul pictures a state of affairs different from that portrayed in 5:17.[6] This first reading is unconvincing.[7]

Second, Paul has been taken to speak equally of the Flesh and the Spirit, thus formulating an anthropological theory true of every human being: The individual self experiences a wrenching inner dualism that produces impotence of will because of an essential parity between the Flesh and the Spirit. In the battle each of these powers has as its successful intention the frustration of the other one. Paraphrasing E. D. Burton, R. N. Longenecker comments, for example:

> The flesh opposes the Spirit with the desire that people not do what they want to do when guided by the Spirit, and the Spirit opposes the flesh with the desire that people not do what they want to do when guided by the flesh.[8]

---

5. R. Jewett, *Paul's Anthropological Terms* (Leiden: Brill, 1971) 106–7. It is significant, of course, that Jewett holds Paul to have turned his attention in Gal 5:13 from nomists to libertinists (*Terms*, 101).

6. The adversative reading of εἰ δέ in 5:18 is strongly suggested by 5:24, where Paul refers to the victory over the Flesh that is characteristic of a community belonging *exclusively* to Christ.

7. Note the form of this reading proposed in Chrysostom's commentary on Galatians. Knowing some who find that Paul has divided the human being into two parts (διεῖλεν εἰς δύο τὸν ἄνθρωπον ὁ ἀπόστολος)—meaning body and soul in conflict with one another—Chrysostom is concerned to offer a refutation: When Paul speaks here of "flesh" and "spirit," he does not refer to body and soul, but rather to two reasoning powers that are opposed to one another, virtue and vice (περὶ δύο φησὶ λογισμῶν . . . ἥ ἀρετὴ καὶ ἡ κακία). Then, having found in this text a reference to virtue and vice, and concluding from other texts that it is the soul that willfully lusts (and taking ἵνα to indicate purpose), Chrysostom can offer a happy interpretation of the final clause of 5:17: The flesh and the spirit are opposed to one another, "in order that you *not allow* the soul to proceed in her evil desires" (ἵνα μὴ συγχωρήσῃς τῇ ψυχῇ πορεύεσθαι ἐν ταῖς ἐπιθυμίαις αὐτῆς ταῖς πονηραῖς; PG 61.672).

8. R. N. Longenecker, *Galatians* (Dallas: Word, 1990) 246; E. D. Burton, *The Epistle to the Galatians* (Edinburgh: T. & T. Clark, 1921) 302.

Third, Paul has been thought to refer mainly to the role of the Flesh in the life of the Christian. The intention of the Flesh in its war against the Spirit is revealed in the fact that it always stands ready to mislead the Christian, often frustrating his wish to be guided solely by the Spirit. On the one hand, while the tense conflict between willing and doing is the fate of all human beings, in the case of the Christian the Spirit can neutralize that conflict (Gal 5:16). On the other hand, however, still living *in* the Flesh, even the Christian can fall back into the conflict at any moment, thus experiencing impotence of will. Whereas he wishes to do the good, he actually does the evil (Rom 7:19).[9]

GALATIANS 5:17
AND
THE STANDARD READING OF ROMANS 7

Calling for analysis is the fact that most interpreters who propose the second and third readings do so by drawing explicitly or implicitly on a common interpretation of Romans 7. Longenecker represents numerous commentators when he says—following the statement quoted above—"In effect, Galatians 5:17 sets out in rudimentary fashion what is later spoken of more fully in Romans 7:14–25."[10] And the interpretation offered by H. D. Betz—for the most part a form of the second reading—is a particularly interesting case in point. To be sure, Betz mentions some of the differences between Galatians 5:17 and Romans 7. In the final analysis, however, his interpretation of the verse in Galatians is heavily indebted to his reading of Romans 7:15, as one can see from his use of the pronoun "I," a word that plays a prominent role in Romans 7, while being absent from Galatians 5:17. Having identified the Flesh and the Spirit in Galatians 5:17 as "impersonal forces acting within man and waging war against each other," Betz finds in that verse an anthropological theory focused finally on the impotence of the individual's will.

> Man is the battlefield of these forces within him preventing him from carrying out his will. The human "I" wills, but it is prevented from carrying out its will (ταῦτα ποιῆτε) because it is paralyzed through these dualistic forces within. As a result, the human "I" is no longer the subject in con-

9. The last two sentences are virtual quotations from U. Borse, *Der Brief an die Galater* (Regensburg: Pustet, 1984) 196.
10. Longenecker, *Galatians*, 246; cf. Borse, *Brief*, 195–96.

trol of the body . . . the human will is disabled from carrying out its intentions.[11]

When we place Galatians 5:17 and Romans 7:22-23, 15 (cf. 7:19) in parallel with one another, we can easily see how this reading of the former text has arisen:

Galatians 5:17	*Romans 7:22-23, 15 (19)*
[17a]For the Flesh is actively inclined against the Spirit, and the Spirit against the Flesh. [17b]Indeed these two powers constitute a pair of opposites at war with one another,	[22]I delight in the Law of God in my inmost self, [23]but what I see is a different Law, operative in my members. This different Law is in conflict with the Law of God to which I adhere in my intentions, and in this conflict the different Law keeps me imprisoned to itself, thus being the Law that controls me, the Law that has fallen into the hands of Sin.
[17c]the result being that you do not actually do the very things you wish to do.	[15]I do not recognize my own actions. For what I wish—the good—is not what I do; on the contrary, what I hate—the evil that I do not want—is what I actually do.[12]

The standard reading of Romans 7 credits Paul with centering his attention on two motifs, a split internal to the individual self and the resulting impotence of the self actually to carry out its own will. Regarding the first of these motifs, O. Michel, for example, identified what is distinctive about Romans 7:7-25 as "its description of the cleavage of the human self"; and H. D. Betz now echoes Michel with his assertion that in Romans 7 "the 'I' is split up into two."[13] For many interpreters, the

---

11. H. D. Betz, *Galatians* (Philadelphia: Fortress, 1979) 279-81. In offering this reading of Gal 5:17, Betz proposes that its anthropological theory of human paralysis is basically pre-Pauline (280). The fullness of Paul's own view emerges in 5:18, where he tells the Galatians that, for Christians, the battle between the Flesh and the Spirit does not issue in a stalemate. On the contrary, "the Spirit takes the lead, overwhelms, and thus defeats evil" (281).

12. Basically this interpretive translation of Rom 7:22-23, 15 (19) is drawn from P. W. Meyer, "The Worm at the Core of the Apple," in *The Conversation Continues: Studies in Paul and John in Honor of J. Louis Martyn*, ed. Robert T. Fortna and Beverly Gaventa, 62-84 (Nashville: Abingdon, 1990).

13. O. Michel, *Der Brief an die Römer*, 5th ed. (Göttingen: Vandenhoeck & Ruprecht, 1978) 225 n. 7; Betz, *Galatians*, 280.

second motif, the impotence of the human will, seems so obvious in Romans 7 as to need no demonstration. Often, however, certain "parallels" are offered, such as Ovid's "I see the better and approve; the lower I follow" (*Metamorphoses* 7.21) and the reference of Epictetus to the man who "is not doing what he wishes, and is doing what he does not wish" (*Diss.* 2.26.4; cf. 2.26.1).

From this reading of Romans 7 it would seem a short step back to the earlier passage in Galatians 5:17. To be sure, as Betz points out, Paul does not speak in Galatians of a split in the self.[14] Does he not refer, however, as Betz says, to the human body as a battlefield between two contesting forces? And does he not identify the result of this state of affairs as the disabling of the human will to carry out its intentions?

Pondering this apparently Romanesque reading of Galatians 5:17, we are faced with three questions: (a) In Romans 7:15 (19) Paul says that the self *does not* do what it wishes to do—and does what it does not wish. He could have spoken explicitly of an impotence of the will, saying that the self is *unable* to do what it wishes (οὐ γὰρ ὃ θέλω τοῦτο δύναμαι ποιῆσαι)[15]—and is unable to avoid doing what it does not wish. Is it really Paul's intention in Romans 7 to refer to an impotence of the will? (b) Given the absence of an explicit reference to that motif, is the standard interpretation of Romans 7 in need of significant correction? (c) If so, would that corrected interpretation of Romans 7 play a role in leading us to a different reading of Galatians 5:17?

A NEW INTERPRETATION OF ROMANS 7

A phenomenal advance in the interpretation of Romans 7 was made in 1990 by Paul W. Meyer.[16] Agreeing with the dominant view that in Romans 7 Paul describes the human situation apart from Christ, Meyer nevertheless offers an analysis in which both of the motifs that charac-

---

14. *Pace*, e.g., the comment on Gal 5:17 by J. Rohde, "Dementsprechend will Paulus also ausdrücken, dass nach Gottes Absicht der Wille derer, in denen Fleisch und Geist miteinander im Kampfe liegen, sowohl im Guten wie im Bösen in seiner Ausführung gehindert wird, so dass also gerade auch bei den Christen oft das Tun des Guten durch die Macht des Fleisches verhindert [wird], ebenso aber auch die Ausführung des bösen Willens durch den Geist. Dadurch, dass sich im Menschen entgegengesetzte Willensrichtungen geltend machen, wird es ihm unmöglich, allen Regungen zu folgen die sich in ihm erheben. Dadurch wird es zu einem *Kampf mit sich selbst* genötigt." Rohde, *Der Brief des Paulus an die Galater* (Berlin: Evangelische Verlagsanstalt, 1989) 234–35; emphasis added.

15. Both with the negative and without it, the locution δύναμαι ποιῆσαι—and its equivalents—is, of course, very common. In early Christian usage see, e.g., Matt 9:28, and in Paul's letters cf. 1 Cor 15:50.

16. "The Worm."

terize the standard interpretation are laid aside, the supposed split internal to the individual self and the resulting impotence of the self actually to carry out its own will.

First, in Romans 7 "both 'inmost self' (v. 22) and 'members' (v. 23) are but two aspects of the same self that is 'sold under sin.'"[17] The tragic element in Romans 7 does not arise, then, from a divided self, but rather from the self's enslavement to the power of Sin, precisely as Sin has wrested the Law out of the hands of God. That is to say, rather than speaking of two parts to the self, Paul refers to *two Laws* (7:22–23, 25; 8:2), which prove to be the Mosaic Law functioning as the Law of God and the Mosaic Law as it has fallen into the hands of Sin.[18] The terrifying *fundamentum* to the whole of Paul's argument is the fact that the Mosaic Law is not only God's Law, but also Sin's Law, a tool of Sin. One can see, then, that Romans 7 culminates in a cleavage, but that cleavage "is in the *Law* and not in the self."[19]

Second (continuing with Meyer), the result of this terrifying cleavage in the Law—the result of the fact that God's Law has fallen into the hands of Sin—is far more serious than a mere impotence of the human will. In Romans 7:15 (19) Paul's major accent lies not on inaction, but rather on action and result. Indeed, in the first clause of 7:15 Paul speaks explicitly of the result of his actions, saying that it is a mystery to him; he himself does not recognize it. Clearly something much more sinister is involved than an impotence of the will. A menacing actor other than the self is on stage, and that actor uses for its deadly purposes precisely God's holy and just and good Law. In short, Paul speaks of Sin's power to deceive him via the Law, the result being that he *accomplishes* the *opposite* of what he intended.

The subject of the discourse in Romans 7, then, "is not simple frustration of good intent, but good intention carried out and then surprised and dumbfounded by the evil it has produced."[20] And the form

---

17. Ibid., 76.

18. In this reading Meyer takes τῆς ἁμαρτίας to be a genitive of possesion, an interpretation supported by Rom 7:8–11 (seizing *the* Law, Sin used it to kill me). For an alternative reading see M. Winger, *By What Law? The Meaning of Nomos in the Letters of Paul* (Atlanta: Scholars, 1992). There τῆς ἁμαρτίας and its equivalents are taken as genitives of source, "identifying the power whose control is in turn identified by the term νόμος" (195). This interpretation is related to Winger's finding in Rom 7:21—with numerous other interpreters—a metaphorical use of νόμος (force, rule, controlling power) that then sets the precedent for a metaphorical use of νόμος in 7:22–23 (186 and 186 n138). Meyer, on the other hand, taking τὸν νόμον in 7:21 to be an adverbial accusative of respect, arrives at a paraphrase in which Paul refers in that verse itself to the Mosaic Law: "So then, as far as the (Mosaic) law is concerned, the outcome (of the above experience) is that for me, the very one who wishes to do the good, evil is what I find at hand" (79).

19. Meyer, 78.

20. Ibid., 76.

in which this good intention is carried out is precisely that of observance of the Law. Thinking of the Law as God's Law, and of his own clearly willed, altogether admirable and blameless observance of it (Rom 7:12; Phil 3:6), Paul takes as his subject the power of Sin to corrupt the highest good. For in Christ he now looks back on the demonic power of Sin "to use the Mosaic Law to effect just the opposite of what its devoted adherents expect, even and especially when it is obeyed."[21] In short, Paul's argument attaches impotence not to the human will, but rather to the Law. The Law itself is the actor who proves to be disabled vis-à-vis the sinister power of Sin. Indeed it is for that reason that God sent his own Son in behalf of all, "to deal with Sin as the Law could not (Rom 8:3–4)."[22]

A NEW INTERPRETATION OF ROMANS 7
AND A NEW READING OF GALATIANS 5:17

Does Galatians 5:17 read differently when taken in light of Meyer's interpretation of Romans 7?[23] That is a question we can consider by noting both similarities and differences between these two texts.

1. The Bifurcated Law

The picture of a bifurcated Law in Romans 7 has its earlier form in Galatians, where Paul considers the Law to have two distinct voices, one could almost say two modes of existence.[24] Transparent is Galatians 4:21, where Paul speaks of a tension *internal* to the Law.

> Tell me, you who wish to live under the power of the Law! Do you really hear what the Law says [when it speaks of children begotten by the power of the promise]?

---

21. Ibid., 80.

22. Ibid.

23. Reading the earlier letter, Galatians, in light of the later—a common if usually unconscious procedure—can lead to serious misinterpretation. With caution, however, we can make comparisons, honoring the specifics of the Galatian setting (see below) and noting significant differences between the two letters.

24. See Martyn, "The Crucial Event in the History of the Law (Gal 5:14)," in *Theology and Ethics in Paul and His Modern Interpreters: Essays in Honor of Victor Paul Furnish*, ed. E. H. Lovering Jr. and J. L. Sumney (Nashville: Abingdon, 1996) 48–61. Cf. D. Lührmann's perceptive comment on Gal 6:2, "The new teachers in Galatia may have used the expression 'the Law of Christ' to indicate that the Law of Sinai is still valid in the Christian church . . . [Paul, however, sees a] splitting of the Law into the Law of Sinai and the Law of Christ, a view that is later completed in the opposition between 'the Law of the Spirit of life' and 'the Law of Sin and death' in Rom 8:2. The 'Law of Christ' is possible only through liberation from the Law that was given on Sinai" (author's translation of *Der Brief an die Galater* [Zürich: Theologischer Verlag, 1978] 96–97).

Here the Law as enslaving overlord stands in contrast to the Law as promise. Indeed, an essential part of Paul's point in Galatians 4:21–5:1 is that the Law has two voices. The Galatians can come *under* the Law, thereby being enslaved by the power of its subjugating and *cursing voice* (4:21a; cf. 3:10), or they can *hear* the *promising voice* with which the Law speaks of the birth of circumcision-free churches among the Gentiles, thereby sensing their own true identity as children of God's promise (4:21b, 22, 27, 31).[25]

Elsewhere in Galatians Paul draws the same contrast between these two voices (or modes of existence) of the Law. There is, first, the original Law, consisting not of commandments, but rather of the promise spoken by God himself to Abraham. This is the Law that blesses, as it prophesies the birth of circumcision-free churches among the Gentiles (Gen 12:3; Galatians 3:8, 14; Isa 54:1; Gal 4:27). It is also the Law that provides daily guidance for the life of those churches, being the Law of neighbor love that has been brought to completion by Christ (Lev 19:18; Gal 5:14).[26] There is, second, the later-arriving Law of Sinai, ordained by angels acting in God's absence, and consisting of many commandments (Gal 3:19–20; 5:3).[27] This is the Law that curses, being one of the enslaving elements of the cosmos, the Law that is observed by some and not observed by others (Deut 27:26; Gal 3:10; 4:1–5; 4:24–25). It is also the Law that has no pertinence to the church's daily life, being the Law that can be in no way combined with Christ (Gal 5:3–4). In Galatians no less than in Romans, Paul portrays a cleavage in the Law.

2. The Human Will

As we have noted above, in Romans 7:15 Paul does not say that he is *unable* to do what he wishes to do, but rather that he *does not* do what he wishes to do. Similarly, in Galatians 5:17 Paul does not say that the Galatians *cannot* do the very things they wish to do (ἵνα μὴ ἃ ἐὰν θέλητε ταῦτα δυνήθητε ποιῆσαι), but rather that they *do not* do those things. Romans 7:15 and Galatians 5:17 are similar, in that neither contains an explicit reference to an impotence of the will.

---

25. See Martyn, "The Covenants of Hagar and Sarah," in *Faith and History: Essays in Honor of Paul W. Meyer*, ed. J. T. Carroll et al. (Atlanta: Scholars, 1990) 160–92.

26. In Martyn, "The Crucial Event," grounds are given for translating πεπλήρωται in Gal 5:14 with the expression "has been brought to completion (by Christ)."

27. Here and subsequently I use the expression "the Law of Sinai" (= "the Sinaitic Law") because of Paul's references to Sinai in Gal 4:24–25.

3. The "I" of Romans 7 and the "you (plural)" of Galatians 5:17

The form of the texts, however, shows them to be in one regard significantly different. Romans 7 is marked by Paul's repeatedly speaking *of* an *"I,"* whereas in Galatians 5:17 he speaks *to* a *"you* (plural),*"* the Galatians. In his Galatian letter, then, Paul does not speak anthropologically *of* a general failure to act on one's intentions. He speaks specifically and pastorally *to* the Galatian Christians about their failing to do something they corporately wish to do. This simple observation suggests the possibility that Paul intends the Galatians to hear a reference to a development that is to some degree peculiar to *their* corporate life. We can profitably ask, then, how Galatians 5:17 will have been heard by the Galatians when Paul's messenger read it aloud.

4. The Law and Christ

Posing that question, we note first that in the context of Galatians 5:17 Paul has emphatically referred to the Law—specifically in its bifurcated state—and to the relationship between this bifurcated Law and Christ. In 5:14 he has spoken of the original voice of the Law of God, the blessing and guiding Law that is altogether pertinent to the daily life of the church, being, as noted above, the Law of neighbor love that has been brought to completion by Christ (Lev 19:18). In 5:3, however, he has referred to the voice of the cursing Sinaitic Law, warning the Galatians who are commencing its observance that that Law has no pertinence to the daily life of their churches, being the Law that can be in no way combined with Christ (Gal 5:3-4). He also makes an indirect but clear reference to the Sinaitic Law in the verse immediately preceding 5:17, the promise of 5:16. For there he warns the Galatians that the Teachers are deceiving them with the claim that—as the God-given, fully potent antidote to the Impulsive Desire of the Flesh—the Sinaitic Law is the guide for their daily life. And finally, Paul speaks explicitly of the Sinaitic Law in the verse following 5:17, telling the Galatians that, when led by the Spirit, they are not under the authority of that Law (5:18). In a word, the Galatians will have heard the statements of 5:17 in a context heavy with Paul's insistence that the Sinaitic Law cannot be added to Christ.

From this observation we return to the form of Galatians 5:17, and thus to the simple fact that in Paul's "you (plural)" the Galatians will have heard a corporate reference to themselves, and thus neither to the individual human being in general—as though Paul were describing a pre-Christian anthropology—nor to all Christians everywhere—as

though Paul were speaking in general of "the Christian situation."[28]
Just as the Galatians will have sensed in 5:16 a promise Paul believes
to be pertinent to their own corporate life, so they will have heard in
5:17 Paul's statement that *they* are corporately not doing what they
wish to do.

The Galatians' understanding of 5:17 will have been affected,
then, by their having just listened to 5:15 ("But if you snap at one
another, each threatening to devour the other, take care that you are
not eaten up by one another!"). That is to say, hearing that earlier
verse, they will have been reminded of the almost animalistic dissensions currently raging in their churches. That pattern of communal life
was something the Galatians surely wished to cease. As things pre-
sently stand, however, they are continuing it. Indeed, intending to live
in harmony, they are accomplishing the opposite, intensifying their
communal conflicts. From the context, then, one can surmise that in
the last clause of 5:17 the Galatians will have heard Paul referring to
their failure to cease their internal strife, and we can suppose that Paul
intended them to hear that reference.[29]

But what does Paul mean when he says that this failure is the
result of the war between the Flesh and the Spirit? That is a question
best approached by recalling Paul's practice of speaking to the Galatian
churches as a whole, when in fact he is thinking of the numerous members who are in the process of accepting the Law-observant theology of
the Teachers (see, for example, 1:6; 3:1). In 5:17, that is to say, Paul
is thinking of the fact that many of the Galatians are commencing
observance of the Law, confident that, by adding that observance to
their allegiance to Christ, they will find the guidance in daily life they
sorely need (Gal 5:3-4). But how, exactly, does Paul think that failure
to cease dissensions is characteristic of the Galatians who are commencing observance of the Law? And how can he say that that failure
is the result, for them, of the war between the Spirit and the Flesh?
Two observations may prove helpful.

On the one hand, throughout 5:13-26 Paul presupposes a war that
has been commenced only with the coming of the Spirit. Addressing
the Galatians who have experienced the Spirit's advent in baptism, he
portrays quite specifically the situation of the Galatian churches as
communities that have been called to the battlefield by the Spirit.

---

28. As we will see below, Käsemann's statement that Gal 5:16-17 describes "the Christian
situation" does not take the Galatian setting sufficiently into account. E. Käsemann, *Romans*
(Grand Rapids: Eerdmans, 1980) 208. Note also Meyer's reservation, "The Worm," 69.

29. Note that in 5:26 Paul draws the word φθόνος, "grudging envy of the neighbor's success," from the list of the effects of the Flesh (5:21), thus relating it specifically to the situation in
the Galatian churches.

On the other hand, the failure to avoid undesired acts, as it is portrayed in 5:17, can be characteristic neither of the Christian freedom Paul has so compellingly pictured in 5:1 and 5:13, nor of the loving communal life that is the fruit of the Spirit (5:22–23a). We return, then, to the hypothesis that in 5:17 Paul is speaking to the Galatians about the stance being taken on the battlefield by those among them who are trying to direct their allegiance both to Christ and to the Sinaitic Law. In this attempt at a dual allegiance, they have, in Paul's view, nothing more to do with Christ, having fallen out of the realm of grace (5:4). Baptized persons summoned to the war by the victorious general, the Spirit, they are looking elsewhere for their guidance!

Read in the light of this hypothesis, the puzzling final clause of Galatians 5:17 proves to be an instance of Pauline abbreviation. Here Paul is able to use a kind of shorthand because, addressing the Galatians in their own setting, he can presuppose (1) their having been called by the Spirit to their place in its war against the Flesh, (2) their incipient observance of the Law, (3) the continuance of communal strife in their churches, and (4) the cause of that continued strife, not the paralyzed impotence of their will, but rather the impotence of the Sinaitic Law to curb the power of the community-destroying Flesh.[30] What the Sinaitic Law promises it cannot produce.[31] With the result clause of Galatians 5:17c, then, Paul describes the effect of the Spirit-Flesh warfare on those who, in its midst, look to the Sinaitic Law for their guidance. When they desire and expect the good—harmonious communal life—they find its opposite, without being aware of the reason.[32]

---

30. Two supplementary comments: (a) A fifth presupposition hovers in the background. The impotence of the Sinaitic Law to curb the Flesh is related to the yet more distressing fact that the Law and the Flesh are, in effect, secret allies! Via the nomistic circumcision of the flesh, the Flesh has the capacity to draw the Law to its side in its battle against the Spirit. See Gal 3:3; 4:23, 29. (b) The major accent in Paul's list of the effects of the Flesh (Gal 5:19–21a) lies on the ways in which the Flesh destroys the *communal* life that is created by the Spirit.

31. In Galatians Paul does not hesitate to say that the promise spoken by the Sinaitic Law is false. Gal 3:12 can be paraphrased as follows: "Not having its origin in the benchmark of faith, the (Sinaitic) Law speaks a false promise when it says 'The one who does the commandments will live by them'" (Lev 18:5). See Martyn, "Paul's Understanding of the Textual Contradiction Between Hab 2:4 and Lev 18:5," in *From Tradition to Interpretation: Studies in Biblical Intertextuality in Honor of James A. Sanders*, ed. C. A. Evans and S. Talmon (Leiden: Brill, 1997).

32. Along with the striking similarities between Gal 5:17 and Romans 7, there are also significant differences, one of which demands at least brief comment. In Galatians the split in the Law lacks the complex profundity characteristic of that motif in Romans 7. In Galatians, that is, the Sinaitic Law—far from being holy, just, and good (Rom 7:12)—is the product of angels who, in ordaining it, acted in God's absence, thereby establishing that Law as one of the enslaving elements of the cosmos (Gal 3:19–20; 4:3); cf. Martyn, "Christ, the Elements of the Cosmos, and the Law in Galatians," in *The Social World of the First Christians: Essays in Honor of Wayne A. Meeks*, ed. L. M. White and O. L. Yarbrough, 16–39 (Minneapolis: Fortress, 1995). Paul does not describe the deception of the Law-observant Galatians, then, by speaking of their admirable

With this reading, we can sense the line of thought that runs through the whole of Galatians 5:16-18. Speaking to the Law-observant Galatians—and to others tempted to follow them into the same cul-de-sac—Paul first issues the corrective promise of 5:16. Shortly thereafter, he explicates that promise *positively* in the confident statement of 5:18. Before doing that, however, he grounds the promise *negatively* in 5:17, speaking in such a way as to imply that Christ plus the Sinaitic Law is a formula for communal discord:[33]

> (5:16) *But*, in contradistinction to the Teachers, I, Paul, say to you: Lead your daily life guided by the Spirit rather than by the Sinaitic Law; and, in this way, you will not end up carrying out the Impulsive Desire of the Flesh. (5:17) *For*, to find a negative proof of this promise, consider carefully the war between the Flesh and the Spirit. In your case the outcome of that war is nothing other than your failure to do what you wish to do. When you wish, that is, to end the dissensions that plague your communities, you succeed only in intensifying them. Why? Because, even though you have received the perfectly potent Spirit (cf. 4:6; 5:16), you are now turning to the Law for your guidance. But, unlike the Spirit, the Law is impotent to provide the guidance that actually curbs the Flesh, and that impotence leads to the continued discord in your churches. (5:18) *If, however*, in the daily life of your communities you are consistently led by the Spirit, then you are not under the authority of the Law, the weakling that cannot deliver you from the power of the Flesh.

Finally, this reading of Galatians 5:17 provides us with a clue to the nature of Paul's positive pastoral guidance in his Galatian letter, a section of the epistle that consists of two paragraphs, 5:13-24 and 5:25-6:10. A close reading of the first paragraph reveals that Paul's conviction of the impotence of the Sinaitic Law (5:16-17) is a presupposition of all of his pastoral guidance. For that conviction is reflected in the fact that nowhere in 5:13-24 does Paul achieve pastoral specificity by making the daily life of the Galatian churches a matter of morals vis-à-vis the Law as an ethical code.[34]

At its root, behavior in the church of God is a subject Paul takes up in the first instance, not by giving a hortatory prescription of "what

---

and blameless devotion to what Paul himself knows to be the highest good. Contrast Meyer's comment about Romans 7: "[In the hands of Sin] God's own good Law takes on a quality and character opposite to that which a person knows to be true. . ." ("The Worm," 80). In Galatians Paul views Law-observant deception in simpler terms. Rather than the result of Sin's beguiling use of God's Law (Rom 7:11), the Galatians' deception is the work of the Teachers (Gal 3:1); and it consists of the Galatians' turning to what the Teachers *falsely* define as the highest good.

33. It should now be clear that this interpretation does not truly fall under any of the three readings catalogued near the beginning of this essay.

34. Cf. R. Scroggs, "New Being: Renewed Mind: New Perception. Paul's View of the Source of Ethical Insight," in *The Text and the Times*, 167-83 (Minneapolis: Fortress Press, 1993). Regarding 1 Cor 7:19 and Rom 13:8-10, see Martyn, *Galatians*, Comment #48.

ought to be," but rather by providing an indicative description of "what is," now that, by sending the Son and the Spirit of the Son, God has commenced his invasive—and ultimately victorious—war against the Flesh. "What is" proves, therefore, to be the result of that invasive action of God, the war that Paul *describes* in 5:13–24. Given the real existence of anti-God powers in the cosmos, it is necessarily in this war that God is calling into existence his new creation, the community that is marked by mutual, loving service of one another (Gal 5:13–14, 22; cf. 1 Cor 13:13; Rom 13:8–10). But that means that this community of mutual love is itself born, nurtured, and directed *in* the Spirit's war against the powers of the present evil age, the curse of the Sinaitic Law (3:10), Sin (3:22), the elements of the old cosmos (4:3, 9), and not least the Flesh (5:13). In this war, the church is God's cosmic vanguard, the company of soldiers who receive their behavioral bearings in the midst of and from the contours of this war. By describing the Spirit's victorious war against the Flesh, and by portraying the Galatians' place in this war—naming both the communal effects of the Flesh and the communal fruit borne by the Spirit (5:19–23a)—Paul speaks with pastoral specificity in 5:13–24 of the behavior for which the church is fully inspired, to which it is summoned, and for which it is responsible.

Pursuing, then, the motif of responsibility, Paul turns from the essentially descriptive paragraph of 5:13–24 to a series of imperative and hortatory verbs in the second pastoral paragraph, 5:25–6:10. He is free to do that, however, only because in 5:13–24 he has portrayed the activity by which God has graciously created *an addressable community*, a church that, led by the Spirit, is able to hear the imperative and to be thankful to God for it.

13

Freedom and the Apostle

Paul and the Paradoxes of Necessity and Choice

Michael Winger

The problem of freedom arises from our efforts to make sense of our experience. Everyone feels free; everyone feels constrained. At this point or that point we had a choice; here, however, we could hardly have done otherwise than we did; and there, we seemed at the time to be choosing; but, in hindsight we can see that all the circumstances made our choice inevitable. This last case sums up the problem, for once we acknowledge that our own choices can be illusory, what assurance could there be that *all* our choices are not illusory—every one of them? And if our experience of choosing is false, then of what use is the idea of freedom?

In Christian thought the problem has centered on the question of whether God's omnipotence leaves room for human freedom. Although this issue could have arisen in a strictly theoretical way, it is probably the case that those most vexed by the problem have been troubled by their experience, not by their theory. At any rate, this seems to have been so for Paul, with whom the Christian discussion begins. Thus, when Paul tells the Corinthians that "the word of the cross is . . . the power of God to us who are being saved" (1 Cor 1:18), he is surely speaking from his own experience. When Paul writes to the Galatians that "when it pleased the one who formed me in my mother's womb and called me through his grace to reveal his Son in me, so that I

In both his teaching and his writing Robin Scroggs has built his scholarship around the central tasks of reading biblical texts for their theology and for what they say about the problems that concern us, now. In this essay I try to follow Robin's example; I offer it here as a gesture of thanks to Robin for what I have learned from him about these tasks.

should proclaim his good news among the Gentiles, immediately I did not consult with flesh and blood . . . but went away into Arabia and returned again to Damascus" (Gal 1:15–17), the contrast between God and "flesh and blood" tells us that the journeys to Arabia and Damascus were no whim of Paul. Most directly, we have Paul's testimony in 1 Corinthians 9:16:

> For if I should preach the gospel, that is no boast for me. For necessity is laid upon me: for woe to me if I should not preach the gospel![1]

And yet all of this testimony has the ambiguity that is inherent in our experience of both freedom and constraint. Paul notes in 1 Corinthians 1:18 that the word of the cross is experienced in two ways: it is "the power of God to us," but also "foolishness to those who are perishing." From what we know of Paul's history, surely he testifies to *both halves* of this proposition from his own experience—foolishness according to his experience before God's son was revealed in him; power according to his experience afterwards. So the one word may be encountered in two ways, even by the same person. The power of God may be—ignored? Rejected? Misunderstood? Paul's experience appears to be ambiguous. In 1 Corinthians 9:16 Paul affirms that necessity is laid upon him, and yet he presents the question of whether or not he will preach as though it is a genuine question for him. He selects out of the various forms for a Greek conditional sentence not the unreal one ("If I were not to preach . . ."), but the subjunctive form ("If I should fail to preach . . ."), which always implies that a real question is presented for consideration. Apparently the issue of whether or not to preach is real enough for Paul to think about it.[2]

These ambiguities do not encourage us to look for a simple systematic solution to the problem of freedom; but they invite us to explore further Paul's remarks on the subject—to try to tease out what he thought, what concerned him, even what happened to him. Any of the texts we have noted could be used for this project, but I will focus on 1 Corinthians 9, some 27 verses which include a confusing array of assertions related to the theme of freedom: an acknowledgment (or is it an invocation?) of necessity, a rhetorical question asserting freedom, as well as an insistence that he is "enslaved to all."

---

1. Unless otherwise noted, all translations are mine.
2. See further n. 21 below.

"AM I NOT FREE?"

Different levels of experience lie behind this passage, none of them directly accessible to us. There is not only Paul's experience since the Lord was revealed in him, but the experience of the Corinthian community, whose relations with Paul have evidently prompted the whole discussion. We should be alert for clues about their experience as well as Paul's.

The chapter begins abruptly.

> [1]Am I not free? Am I not an apostle? Have I not seen Jesus our Lord? Are you not my work in the Lord? [2]If to others I am not an apostle, at least I am to you; for in the Lord it is you who are the proof of my apostleship.

"Am I not free?" asks Paul in 9:1, but he moves immediately to another question: "Am I not an apostle?" Paul then pursues this second question with two more rhetorical questions, phrased (like the first two) with the οὐ which expects a positive response.[3] The fourth question appeals to the Corinthians' experience of Paul ("Are you not my work in the Lord?"), a theme Paul pursues in the next verse. Thereafter, as we shall see, Paul treats the apostle question as settled.[4] Evidently he has raised it as a way of answering the first question: if he is an apostle, must he not therefore be free?[5]

So far, then, Paul's argument presumes that an apostle is free. But whose presumption is this? Paul will say, in 9:16, that it is precisely as an apostle that necessity is laid upon him; but there is an apparent contradiction even closer to hand, for he has just declared that "if food causes my brother or sister to stumble, I will certainly not eat meat, ever, so that I may not make my brother or sister stumble" (8:13).[6] If one takes freedom to mean that one does whatever one pleases, or if one thinks specifically of freedom from certain constraints about eating, then Paul seems to be disclaiming this sort of freedom.

A clue to Paul's argument lies in his careful choice of vocabulary in these chapters. In chapter 8, two terms are applied to the issue of eating meat which may have originated with the Corinthians. "We

---

3. BDF § 427(2).

4. Paul has already applied the term to himself in 1 Cor 4:9, and used the verbal form in 1:17.

5. When Paul multiplies rhetorical questions in this way they usually all make the same point (e.g., Rom 3:1; 8:35; 9:20–21, 21–22; 1 Cor 1:13; 9:11–12; 10:16; 14:7–8; 2 Cor 1:17; 11:29; Gal 1:10; 3:2–3; 4:9). Here, the leap from 1a to 1b is otherwise inexplicable.

6. The first negative here is οὐ μή followed by an aorist subjunctive, the emphatic future denial (BDF § 365).

know that we all have knowledge," Paul writes in 8:1, and most scholars agree that "We all have knowledge" is a Corinthian slogan.[7] Since we know that there are no idols (8:4-6), we know that meat is not really sacrificed to them (8:7)—hence we may eat such meat. When Paul refuses (emphatically and eternally) to eat meat, this might put his knowledge in doubt; yet that is not suggested. Apparently the Corinthians concede Paul's knowledge, but knowledge is not enough. There remains the other Corinthian term, found in 8:9: "Take care lest this liberty of yours become a stumbling block to the weak." The term "liberty" here (so NRSV, REB, NAB) translates ἐξουσία, not ἐλευθερία ("freedom'). Ἐξουσία is probably a Corinthian term, as Paul's phrase "this liberty of yours" (ἡ ἐξουσία ὑμῶν αὕτη) suggests.[8] Ἐξουσία most often means "authority'; it implies an element of power.[9] We may surmise that in the Corinthians' experience, whatever its details may have been, the ἐξουσία to act as they chose was of great importance. From the Corinthian perspective, Paul's power and authority—his ἐξουσία—is called into question if he submits to someone else's view on any point, and in chapter 9 Paul will claim (with some hyperbole) that he does so on *every* point.

This claim that Paul lacks authority is the charge that he anticipates in 9:1. But he changes the language from *having* ἐξουσία to *being* ἐλεύθερος, a term not particularly associated with power. Paul evidently expects, however, that the Corinthians will follow his shift from ἐξουσία to ἐλεύθερος; their suspicion that he lacks ἐξουσία translates into a suspicion that he is not ἐλεύθερος. He also expects them to accept that an apostle is free—or at least is likely to be, or ought to be. If they do not think so, the argument of 9:1-2 is wasted.

"FREEDOM" AND "RIGHT"

The next step in Paul's argument is more puzzling. In verse 3 he announces, "My defense to those questioning me is this."[10] With this

---

7. For example, Gordon D. Fee, *The First Epistle to the Corinthians* (Grand Rapids: Eerdmans, 1987) 365-66; C. K. Barrett, *The First Epistle to the Corinthians* (New York: Harper & Row, 1968) 189.

8. So Fee, 384-85.

9. As in Romans 13:1, "Let everyone be subject to the governing authorities." See also Rom 9:21; 1 Cor 7:37; 2 Cor 10:8; 13:10.

10. "This" (αὕτη) could refer to what precedes, as it tends to do (BDF § 290[2], [3]). But the position of "this" at the end suggests a connection with what follows (so Fee, 401 n. 21), and what follows certainly reads like a defense. Its sense would not be different if v. 3 were missing. Verse 3 chiefly confirms what v. 1 implies: that Paul here deals with a charge afloat among the Corinthians.

A second issue is whether the questioning referred to is actual, or only attempted, or only anticipated. Paul uses a present participle (τοῖς ἀνακρίνουσιν), which could be conative ("trying

formal introduction we would expect a statement of the charge against which Paul defends himself.[11] Yet none appears. At any rate, he proceeds in an elaborate way, in an argument with many interesting rhetorical features.[12] These verses do not seem to be phrased casually.

In verses 4–14 Paul seems to be establishing his right—for now he takes up the term ἐξουσία—to material support from those to whom he preaches. He does so by appealing first to the practice of other apostles (vv. 4–6, also 12a), then to examples taken from secular society (v. 7, also 11), then to the law (vv. 8–10; this incorporates another example like those of vv. 7, 11), then to priestly practice (v. 13). Paul's final—and one would think conclusive—appeal is to an explicit command of the Lord (v. 14).[13]

Yet as we near what appears to be the end of this multibarreled defense, Paul mentions (v. 12b) that he makes no use of the right in question, and he repeats this most emphatically in verse 15, just after his invocation of the Lord. "But *I*,"[14] he says "*I* used none of these things, and I have not written this in order that I could do so." This is clear, if surprising. But Paul is just getting started. He continues, "For I would rather die than"—and here he breaks off. His language has

---

to question," or the like); so Barrett, 201–2, NJB ("those who want to investigate me") and NRSV, REB, NAB (all using "would," evidently in the sense "would like to"); but contrast the more literal AV ("them that do examine"). Another suggestion is Wendell Willis's that the participle be translated as future. See Willis, "Apostolic Apologia? The Formal Structure of 1 Corinthians," *JSNT* 24 (1985) 33–48, at 34. All of these suggestions are doubtful. The participle is in fact tenseless, like all participles, but the sentence has a main verb, which is in the present tense: "my defense *is*. . . ." I do not know what distinction is made by insisting on a conative sense; since Paul feels compelled to reply it would seem that the questioning is real. Of course it may be that Paul is only imagining what he thinks the Corinthians say among themselves, or will say when they receive this letter, not what anyone has yet said. But there is no warrant for translating Paul as though he himself states any of these things. He presents the questioning as real, as real as is his reply.

11. As Aristotle observed, "In [forensic] speeches . . . the introduction provides a sample of the subject, in order that the hearers may know beforehand what it is about . . . for that which is undefined leads astray. . ." (*Rhet.* 3.14.6). The history of the interpretation of 1 Cor 9 could be used to illustrate Aristotle's remark.

12. Note how Paul alternates between personal terms (vv. 1–6 // 11–12 // 15) and general terms (// vv. 7–10 // 13–14), and also his alternation between rhetorical questions (1a, b, 2a, b // 4, 5, 6, 7a, b, c, 8 // 9b–10a // 11, 12a // 13 //) and statements (// 2c, d, 3 // 9a // 10b // 12b // 14, 15a, b, c).

13. ὁ κύριος διέταξεν τοῖς τὸ εὐαγγέλιον καταγγέλουσιν ἐκ τοῦ εὐαγγελίου ζῆν. Although ambiguously stated, this command at least means that communities are commanded to support those who preach the gospel, and could mean that those who preach are commanded to accept that support. The verb διατάσσω commonly takes a personal object in the dative case (e.g., Matt 11:1; 1 Cor 16:1), and it also takes an infinitive (e.g., Luke 8:55; Acts 18:2; Josephus *Ant.* 4.205); dative and infinitive are found together, with the personal object commanded to do what the infinitive describes, in Acts 24:23; *Herm. Vis.* 3,1,4. This would be the natural reading of v. 14, except that it would mean Paul directly disobeys the Lord's command. The problem is mitigated if the dative here is a dative of benefit, "commanded *for* those proclaiming the gospel that they live by the gospel" (so Barrett, 208; Fee, 413 n. 96).

14. Here Paul uses a doubly emphatic "I," opening the sentence when grammatically it was not necessary at all.

become rather strong—he would rather die than do as the Lord commanded? He pauses, as it were for breath, before bursting out: "No one shall make my boast empty!"

What are we to make of this? Paul asserts his freedom (ἐλεύθερος, 9:1) and his right (ἐξουσία, 9:4–14) as an apostle. Yet he insists with extraordinary strength that he has *not* used any of "these things" and that he has no intention of doing so. Against what, then, has Paul been defending himself? Evidently not some charge that he was accepting support for which he had no ἐξουσία. Then was the charge, conversely, that his failure to accept such support showed that he had no ἐξουσία, and thus that he was not an apostle? So most interpreters have thought.[15] But, although in 9:1 Paul raised the issue of whether he was an apostle, he also disposed of it rather quickly, in fact by the end of verse 2; the argument of vv. 4–6 takes Paul's apostleship for granted. Moreover, to a charge that Paul is no apostle, verses 4–14 are no defense—they rather lay the basis for the charge.

Verses 4–12a and 13–14 show how reasonable, natural, and indeed universal is the practice of a worker being supported by his work. By no means is this limited to apostles. It is not even solely a question of ἐξουσία (vv. 4–6), but also of practice (v. 7, perhaps v. 8). Verses 12b and 15 at any rate focus us directly on Paul's practice, and with these verses, the whole of verses 4–15 seems calculated to establish that *Paul's practice is extraordinary*. It is contrary to the practice of the apostles; it is virtually contrary to nature.

Let us go back and consider the "defense" of verse 3 in light of Paul's question in verse 1a: "Am I not free?" If Paul states anywhere the charge he means to answer, it is here. By the time we get to verse 15 it is clear that the actual topic is *not* Paul's acceptance of support, but his rejection of it. Paul's ἐξουσία is established. The question is: is he free to refuse it?

THE EXPERIENCE OF NECESSITY

We come now to the verses that drew us into this chapter, Paul's account, embedded in this discussion of freedom, of his own experience of the necessity of preaching.

> [15]But *I* used none of these things, and I have not written this in order that I could do so. For I would rather die than— No one shall make

---

15. E.g., Hans Conzelmann, *1 Corinthians*, Hermeneia (Philadelphia: Fortress, 1975) 153; Barrett, 201–2; Fee, 398–99.

my boast empty! [16]For if I should preach the gospel, that is no boast for me. For necessity is laid upon me: for woe to me if I should not preach the gospel! [17]For if I do this willingly I have a reward; but if I am unwillingly entrusted with a commission, [18]then what is my reward? Just this: that in preaching the gospel I should make the gospel without charge, that I not use my authority in the gospel.

In verse 15 Paul—declaring that this is a matter of life and death to him—vows that no one will deprive him of his "boast" ($\kappa\alpha\acute{\upsilon}\chi\eta\mu\alpha$). What is this "boast"? Paul does not say in so many words, but implies that it depends on his "using none of these things," referring evidently to all of those precedents and examples, and the Lord's command, which he has shown in verses 4–14 authorize him to claim support.[16]

The term $\kappa\alpha\acute{\upsilon}\chi\eta\mu\alpha$ carries us into verse 16: "For if I should preach the gospel, that is no boast for me.[17] For necessity is laid upon me: for woe to me if I should not preach the gospel!" Here the context is dominated by "necessity," ($\dot\alpha\nu\acute\alpha\gamma\kappa\eta$) standing at the center of verse 16.[18] The repetition of *for* ($\gamma\acute\alpha\rho$), which continues into verse 17, serves to bind together the clauses from 15b through 17a.[19] Each thought follows breathlessly here, reflecting the force described by Käsemann in his study of these verses:

> It is an eschatological happening which is being depicted here. . . .
> "*Ananke* lies upon me" is said of destiny which lays hold on a man. . . .
> His commission, and the compulsion rising out of it, originate with his Lord.[20]

The general sense of verse 16 is clear: Paul cannot boast because of his preaching, for he is forced to preach. And, as he explains in

---

16. This need not mean that the renunciation of support is *itself* Paul's boast, however; it may rather be (in some way) a condition of the boast, yet not the sole condition.

17. Or—since the Greek lacks "that"—"I have no boast" ($o\dot\upsilon\kappa\ \check\epsilon\sigma\tau\iota\nu\ \mu o\iota\ \kappa\alpha\acute\upsilon\chi\eta\mu\alpha$, with dative of possession); cf. AV, RV. However, this translation suggests that Paul *would* have a boast if he did *not* preach, which does not seem to have been his thought.

18. Some translations give $\dot\alpha\nu\acute\alpha\gamma\kappa\eta$ a weaker rendering, such as "obligation" (NRSV, NAB), which, at least nowadays, fails to suggest the compulsion implied. The best gloss here is Paul's next sentence: woe to him should he oppose this $\dot\alpha\nu\acute\alpha\gamma\kappa\eta$! In other contexts $\dot\alpha\nu\acute\alpha\gamma\kappa\eta$ is often translated "distress" (e.g., 1 Cor 7:26, AV, RV, RSV, NAB), although probably the sense is still "necessity," with the idea of "distress" supplied by the context. The context here makes it plain that distress would result from resisting $\dot\alpha\nu\acute\alpha\gamma\kappa\eta$; distress is not itself the $\dot\alpha\nu\acute\alpha\gamma\kappa\eta$.

19. The relationship between the clauses is not specified. As Robertson says, "That must be gathered from the context if possible." A. T. Robertson, *A Grammar of the Greek New Testament in the Light of Historical Research* (Nashville: Broadman, 1934) 1191; a succeeding clause may explain the preceding one, or carry it forward. See generally J. D. Denniston, *The Greek Particles*, 2d ed. (Oxford: Oxford University Press, 1934) 58–73. Compare Rom 8:18–24, where (as Robertson notes) every sentence is introduced with $\gamma\acute\alpha\rho$.

20. Ernst Käsemann, "A Pauline Version of the 'Amor Fati,'" in *New Testament Questions of Today* (Philadelphia: Fortress, 1969) 229.

verse 17a, he may claim a "reward" ($\mu\iota\sigma\theta\acute{o}\varsigma$) only for what he does by choice. So he has no choice; so much for freedom in the gospel.

Yet Paul is vehement that he *does* have a boast; so he must have done *something* voluntarily. Moreover, we have already noted that Paul claims freedom in 9:1, and will assert his freedom again in 9:19. We have also noted evidence closer to hand of ambiguity about whether Paul does, or does not, choose to preach. This evidence lies in the way Paul describes the issue.

Careful translation is essential here. I have translated the two conditional sentences of 9:16 in the form, "If I should . . . ," to convey the sense of the subjunctive form Paul uses ($\dot{\epsilon}\grave{\alpha}\nu$ $\epsilon\dot{v}\alpha\gamma\gamma\epsilon\lambda\acute{\iota}\zeta\omega\mu\alpha\iota$ . . . $\dot{\epsilon}\grave{\alpha}\nu$ $\mu\grave{\eta}$ $\epsilon\dot{v}\alpha\gamma\gamma\epsilon\lambda\acute{\iota}\sigma\omega\mu\alpha\iota$ . . .). Translators and commentators sometimes feel compelled to insert into this sentence the undoubted fact that Paul *does* preach.[21] But, in describing his own experience, Paul leaves this fact aside. It could be argued that the use of the subjunctive conditions in verse 16 is just a manner of speaking; that Paul does not mean by these grammatical forms to retract the statement (which he makes simultaneously) that necessity is upon him. And yet he does choose these grammatical forms when he might have chosen others—no necessity was on him here!

What these subjunctive conditions do is to give the setting in which "necessity" is felt. Necessity does not permit Paul to avoid the question of what he will do. If it did, it would not be felt as necessity. Paul's expressions thus exclude the third case described in the first paragraph of this paper, the case in which one seemed to be choosing freely but in hindsight discovers that powerful forces moved one in a certain direction. For Paul, the powerful force is always unmistakable. Paul's presentation of necessity in 1 Corinthians 9:16 has nothing in common with a modern conception of humans as constrained by social forces beyond their control—not only because the nature of the forces is utterly different, but because they are experienced in a different way. Where "social forces" are felt to operate beyond our consciousness, and thus scarcely to be experienced at all, Paul knows precisely how he

---

21. Thus NJB, "preaching the gospel gives me nothing to boast of," and, surprisingly, AV, "though I preach the gospel. . . ." Robertson and Plummer (*A Critical and Exegetical Commentary on the First Epistle of St. Paul to the Corinthians* [Edinburgh: Clark, 1911] 175) paraphrase, "It is quite true that I do preach"; and Fee, (418, emphasis added), "If I preach the gospel, *which I do all the time*. . . ." Fee (418 n. 24) justifies his inserted phrase as "an attempt to capture the nature of the present general condition," but "present general" is an unfortunate misnomer for any condition expressed in the subjunctive mood. The subjunctive inherently looks to the future; a condition in the subjunctive is "undetermined, but with prospect of determination" (Robertson, *Grammar*, 1016; BDF § 371). The present form of the first condition in 9:16 conveys (as present forms generally do outside the indicative mood) aspect and not tense—the idea of preaching as a continuing activity.

is compelled, and by whom.[22] We might say: necessity does not obliterate Paul's choice; rather, Paul's choice is the field in which necessity operates.[23]

In 9:17–18a Paul restates his situation, again with a pair of conditional sentences, but sentences of a different form. "For if I do this willingly I have a reward; but if I am unwillingly entrusted with a commission, then what is my reward?"[24] These conditions are in the indicative mood, relating them to what in fact is happening, rather than to what may yet happen. That Paul "does this"—preaches the gospel— is the premise of both conditions. The conditions pose the issue of whether or not he "does this" voluntarily. Why has Paul not used the unreal conditional form to specify which condition is unfulfilled? Once again, some translations make him do so;[25] but if we are interested in Paul's own understanding of his experience we should be cautious about excising his ambiguities. According to my analysis of verse 16, the line between voluntary and involuntary action is indistinct; verses 17–18a maintain this view. Even though the flow of Paul's argument depends on the fulfillment of the second condition in verses 17–18, logic does not determine perception. When Paul presents the possibilities of voluntary and involuntary action as equally real, he implies that this is how things seem to him.

The logic of Paul's argument nevertheless does determine its conclusion. This logic turns on the terms "boast" and "reward," which refer here to the same thing. "Reward" cannot mean material support

---

22. In Gal 5:16–25, and again in Rom 7:13–26, Paul refers to a different kind of force which impedes choice, or rather, impedes us from carrying out our choices. "For I do not do what I want, but I do what I hate" (Rom 7:15); "for the flesh desires against the spirit, and the spirit desires against the flesh; these oppose each other, to prevent you from doing what you want" (Gal 5:17). This force too—"the flesh"—is apparent to us. In this case the force may be overcome by "walking by the Spirit" (Gal 5:16; cf. Rom 8:2). The implication, however, is not that the Spirit then tells one just what to do, but that it frees one to carry out one's choice.

23. Think of someone commanded to act at gun point: the command can be refused, although the consequences of refusal are such that we say obedience to the command was not free. That is a negative case, demand enforced by threat; a positive case is someone whose lover demands an act of unusual commitment. Paul's case is a version of this.

24. Most translations end the second condition at the end of v. 17: "But if unwillingly, I am entrusted with a commission." This is possible, but it leaves the sentence in an anticlimax. Even if the beginning words of v. 18 are not formally part of v. 17's second condition, they still state the real conclusion of this condition (with Barrett, 210). I think it most natural to read this real conclusion as part of the sentence. Fee's objection (420 n. 39) that Paul would have been more likely to use εἰ . . . ἄρα than εἰ . . . οὖν to join 17b and 18a is of little weight. This is essentially a stylistic point, and our evidence for such details of Paul's style is insufficient to rule out his use of a particular expression in a particular sense. Οὖν is found in the apodosis of conditional sentences in classical Greek (Denniston, *Greek Particles*, 428), and it has the same force here whether or not there is a period at the end of v. 17.

25. NJB: "If I did it on my own initiative"; REB, not only "If I did it of my own choice," but "*since* I have no choice"; similarly, Robertson and Plummer, 176. On the other hand, some interpreters have taken the first condition to describe the actual case (Fee, 419 n. 35).

from Paul's congregations, for this does not depend on voluntary action; even slaves are entitled to material support. Rather, the reference to voluntary action invokes the natural idea that, as Aristotle says, "Only for voluntary actions are praise and blame given"[26]—or, in Paul's equivalent language, only such actions provide ground for a "boast." Verses 16–18 are thus an explanation of that "boast" which, according to verse 15, is so essential to Paul.

According to verse 18 Paul's "reward," or "boast," is "that in preaching the gospel I should make the gospel without charge, that I not use my authority in the gospel."[27] This verse does not yet show that this failure to charge—this relinquishment of authority—is itself worthy of praise or an occasion for boasting.[28] What the verse does do is to establish Paul's relinquishment of authority as *voluntary*. In light of verses 16–17, it is only because this relinquishment is voluntary that it can serve here as a basis for boasting. The whole argument of verses 4–14, with its puzzling demonstration of an authority Paul refuses, can now be seen as the background for establishing that this refusal is voluntary: it is free.

GAINING SLAVERY

Thus "freedom" and "authority" are severed; and to "freedom" Paul now returns, in verse 19. Note how verses 19–23 complete the thought of verses 15–18 by establishing Paul's "boast" and "reward'—

> [19]For being free from all I enslaved myself to all, in order to gain the more. [20]And I became to the Jews as a Jew, in order to gain Jews; to those under law as one under law—not being myself under law—in order to gain those under law; [21]to those without law as one without law—not being without God's law, but in the law of Christ—in order to gain those without law. [22]To the weak I became weak, in order to gain the weak. I became all things to all people, in order that by all means I should save some. [23]I do everything for the sake of the gospel, so that I may be a fellow-sharer with it.

The issue here is not one of authority, but rather a development of the idea of freedom in relation to its opposite, slavery. The key term in

---

26. Aristotle, *NE* 3.1.1 1109b.31.

27. I take the ἵνα clause and the εἰς clause of v. 18 to be parallel. They are parallel in meaning, and it is hard to work out a consequential relation between them.

28. At this point I take issue with Käsemann, who, interpreting Paul's service (no doubt correctly) in terms of love, writes, "What is the distinguishing mark of this love? Just this, that it loves and therefore does not insist on its own rights—not out of disinterest, but out of involvement. This mark of love Paul is neither willing nor able to renounce. . . . It is his boast and his reward" ("Pauline Version," 234). On the contrary, this is the *means* to Paul's reward.

this paragraph is "to gain" ($\kappa\epsilon\rho\delta\alpha\acute{\iota}\nu\omega$, vv. 19, 20a, 20b, 21, 22a), whose cognate noun $\kappa\acute{\epsilon}\rho\delta\sigma\varsigma$ is a synonym for $\mu\iota\sigma\theta\acute{\sigma}\varsigma$ ("reward").[29] The answer to Paul's question of verse 18—"What then is my reward?"—is that his reward is all of those whom, by serving, he gains. His renunciation of authority does not in itself entitle him to boast. His boast, without which he would rather die, is the fruit that this renunciation bears for the Lord.[30]

Paul describes this renunciation in terms of both freedom and slavery, which are opposed, but in another sense not opposed.[31] In each of the cases identified in verses 20-22 Paul shows himself not to be free: he is slave to the Jews, slave to those under the law, slave to those without the law, slave to the weak. Yet though these cases demonstrate Paul's servitude, Paul's servitude demonstrates his freedom. Paul is deliberately paradoxical. He has not paired freedom and slavery at random, as though the usual contrast between them did not exist. He suggests that the *purpose* of freedom is slavery—or at least, the purpose (or the use) of a particular freedom, his freedom as an apostle, is a particular kind of slavery: his enslavement to those to whom he preaches.[32] There are other paradoxes as well. It would be natural to think that when A is enslaved to B, B has gained A—a slave. Here, however, it is just the reverse: the putative slave, Paul, gains the putative master.

---

29. For the general similarity of the terms, see LSJ, BAGD, and MM, s.vv. A close link is suggested by David Daube's contention that Paul uses $\kappa\epsilon\rho\delta\alpha\acute{\iota}\nu\omega$ in 7:19-21 to match a Hebrew idiom employing שׂכר (usually in the *niphil* or *hithpael*) to speak of God winning back Israelites, sometimes by submission or service (*The New Testament and Rabbinic Judaism*, 348-49, 355-61). שׂכר is generally rendered in the LXX by $\mu\iota\sigma\theta\acute{\sigma}\varsigma$ rather than $\kappa\acute{\epsilon}\rho\delta\sigma\varsigma$. See Daube, 358; Hatch and Redpath, s.v. $\mu\iota\sigma\theta\acute{\sigma}\varsigma$, $\kappa\acute{\epsilon}\rho\delta\sigma\varsigma$. But note Eccl 4:9: $\mu\iota\sigma\theta\acute{\sigma}\varsigma$ in LXX, $\kappa\acute{\epsilon}\rho\delta\sigma\varsigma$ in Symmachus. For an argument that the background to Paul's usage is not rabbinical but Greek "philosophical discussion of support," see R. F. Hock, *The Social Context of Paul's Ministry* (Philadelphia: Fortress, 1980) 100 n. 114.

30. These verses also raise anew the question of whether some concrete dispute underlies 1 Cor 9. We connected the introductory question in v. 1—"Am I not free?"—with the issue of eating meat discussed in chapter 8; but this link need not describe the full scope of the issue. Is Paul's real purpose the defense of his missionary strategy, as now described in vv. 19-23? See G. Bornkamm, "The Missionary Stance of Paul in 1 Corinthians 9 and in Acts," in *Studies in Luke-Acts*, ed. L. E. Keck and J. L. Martyn (Philadelphia: Fortress, 1980), 194-207, 197. On the other hand, Käsemann concludes from "the depth and radical nature of the self-recollection which the apostle has been carrying on" that "he is not defending himself against reproaches from members of the community; he is giving account to himself of the truth of his apostolic existence" ("Pauline Version," 231). But these are not alternatives. I think Käsemann correctly interprets the evidence of Paul's personal involvement in the matter under discussion; yet why does that discussion appear here? Something has touched a nerve in Paul, prompting this "defense" (his own term). The terms of the defense suggest that this is likely to have been some criticism which seemed to reach (however obliquely) to "the truth of his apostolic existence."

31. The standard opposition between "slave" ($\delta\sigma\tilde{\upsilon}\lambda\sigma\varsigma$, $\pi\alpha\iota\delta\acute{\iota}\sigma\kappa\eta\varsigma$) and "free" is found frequently in Paul's letters. See Rom 6:18, 20, 22; 1 Cor 7:21, 22; 9:19; 12:13; Gal 3:28; 4:22, 23, 26, 30, 31.

32. There is a similar thought in Gal 5:13: "Only do not let your freedom be an opportunity for the flesh, but through love be slaves to one another."

A particular idea of slavery underlies these paradoxes. When Paul says he "enslaves himself" to others he means that he becomes *like* the others—not the same as them, he is quick to explain, but *as though he were the same*: a Jew, or under law, or without law, or weak, as the case may be. This is not very close to literal slavery.[33] Nevertheless the analogy with slavery does clarify Paul's understanding of freedom, for to be all these different things to different people requires freedom. To enslave *oneself* requires freedom, and to enslave oneself *successively*, to different people, requires continuing freedom. But this freedom is precisely the freedom to refuse: above all, the freedom to refuse the ἐξουσία which seems to have been so valued by the Corinthians. What seems, in the Corinthians' eyes, to show Paul's lack of ἐξουσία actually demonstrates his freedom. We have here Paul's answer to our question about the relation of freedom and authority. At the same time, it appears that the slavery which coexists with—or depends on—this kind of freedom is a kind of free servitude.[34]

THE NECESSITY OF CHOICE

Self-enslavement, then, is a kind of freedom. Paul uses this paradoxical description partly as a rhetorical device of a kind described by Aristotle: "For it becomes more evident that one has learned something when the conclusion turns out contrary to one's expectations, and the mind seems to say, 'How true it is! But I missed it'" (*Rhet.* 3.11.6). Also, using the term "self-enslavement" evokes the real servitude to which Paul alludes (although without using any term for "slavery") in verse 16, and which underlies verses 19–23: his servitude to the Lord. It is as a slave of the Lord that Paul appears "as all things to all people, that by all means I should save some," but Paul implies that he has *chosen* this manner of serving the Lord. Here is a sense in which "*self*-enslavement" may be taken almost literally. If Paul does not choose his enslavement, at least he chooses its manner; this, the Lord has left him free to do.

---

33. Although a slave would live according to the pattern *dictated by* the master, that is not the same as the pattern *of* the master, as in vv. 20–22a.

34. For a different interpretation of the way slavery functions in Paul's argument, see Dale B. Martin, *Slavery as Salvation: The Metaphor of Slavery in Pauline Christianity* (New Haven: Yale University Press, 1990). Martin argues (134) that in calling himself a slave of all Paul borrows a Hellenistic rhetorical device used in "appealing directly to the people," which yields an authority based on "the strength given the populist by popular support itself." But Paul's leadership is not the issue here. While Martin draws together a great deal of valuable material on slavery, whether this material is decisive for the interpretation of 1 Corinthians 9 is another question. It is symptomatic that Martin's bibliography does not include Käsemann's theological treatment of this passage.

Even here, though, there is an element of ambiguity beneath the surface. "Freedom" may conceal an element of compulsion that Paul must have felt. Why does Paul choose this mode of service? "To gain the more," as he says. But once Paul saw that he could thus gain the more, did he then consider himself free to refuse the Lord this service? Or is self-enslavement one of those things required by "the necessity which was laid upon him"? And woe to him if he should not!

Yet Paul *has* chosen; he will claim his reward. In 9:23 he goes so far as to call himself a "fellow-sharer" ($\sigma \upsilon \gamma \kappa o \iota \nu \omega \nu \acute{o} \varsigma$) with the gospel itself.[35] He has his contribution to make; he is never a passive instrument of the gospel, or of the Lord; the risk of being found unqualified ($\mathring{\alpha} \delta \acute{o} \kappa \iota \mu o \varsigma$, 9:27) remains with him. Necessity is upon Paul; yet he must choose. In Paul's own experience of the necessity that lies upon him, the necessity of choice is not the least element.

---

35. Most translations take this to mean sharing in the "blessings" (NRSV, REB) or "benefits" (NJB) of the gospel, supplying a concept not in the text. With Judith Gundry Volf, *Paul and Perseverance* (Louisville: Westminster/John Knox, 1990) 248–51, I think it more likely that Paul here personifies the gospel.

14

No "Race of Israel" in Paul

Calvin J. Roetzel

> *A whole mythology is deposited in our language.*
> —Ludwig Wittgenstein

I feel privileged to share in this effort to honor Robin Scroggs who has done much to renew a tired discipline, and whose scholarship has enriched my own. From the publication of his first book until now he has dealt imaginatively and provocatively with gender issues, sexual concerns, and community matters; he has used social science methodologies to uncover fresh meanings hidden in ancient texts; and he has offered evidence aplenty that a scholar can engage the ancient world on its own terms without disengaging from the modern scene. The title of this collection, *Putting Body and Soul Together*, deals with self-understanding, the construction of identity, and the organization of world. I trust the relevance of this essay for that consideration will be obvious as the argument unfolds.

INTRODUCTION

Occasionally, seminal essays appear that permanently change an academic discipline. In Pauline studies few essays have been more

I acknowledge my great debt to my colleagues in New Testament, World Religions, Classics, and Spanish—Lloyd Gaston, James Laine, Anthony Pinn, Andrew Overman, and Juanita Garciagodoy—for reading this essay and offering many valuable suggestions, and my colleague, James B. Stewart, a nineteenth-century American historian, who kindly assisted with the development of this essay from the beginning. If the essay has any strengths it is due in large measure to their valuable suggestions. Any weaknesses of the thesis or development of the argument, and any errors of fact are, however, my own.

influential than Nils Dahl's "The One God of Jews and Gentiles (Romans 3:29-30)," written for the Festschrift presented to Ernst Käsemann on his seventieth birthday in 1976.[1] There Dahl challenged the universalistic-particularistic dichotomy widely used by Christian scholars to distinguish Christianity from Judaism. He proved that dichotomy was historically false and furthermore that first-century Judaism was more universalistic than usually alleged and that early Christianity was more particularistic than normally allowed. In spite of the cogency of Dahl's essay and the acclaim it justifiably earned, the dichotomy he challenged survives to this day in various forms. For example, the contrast of Paul's inclusive gospel with a Jewish exclusiveness that limits God's covenant mercy to the "race of Israel" is still all too common. The term "race" is often carelessly used with little thought given to either the history of the term or the mythology embedded within it. Sometimes the term is deliberately used to distinguish Judaism and early Christianity. But, whether its use is careless or deliberate, its usage carries a bias that deserves interrogation, and suggests further reflection on the genesis and function of the word.

One need not launch an exhaustive search in studies on Paul to find uses of the word. One finds it in the venerable *Theological Dictionary of the New Testament*, for example, in Georg Bertram's discussion of ἔθνος and in Hermann Strathmann's discussion of λαός.[2] One finds it in translations of the New Testament, for example, in the *New International Version* of Romans 9:3-4.[3] One finds it in commentaries like those of Harrison[4] and Dunn on Romans;[5] in journal articles on

---

1. Now available in *Studies in Paul* (Minneapolis: Augsburg, 1977) 178–91.

2. See Bertram (*TDNT* 2:364) who suggests that in ἔθνος, "There is no emphasis on the particular marks or bases of fellowship or relationship, on political or cultural connections, as in such words as ארץ, לשׁן, משׁפחה (Gen 10:31), which can be used for 'people' *in a more racial, linguistic or geographical sense*" (emphasis mine). Strathmann, (*TDNT* 4:55) in his article on λαός, says of Paul's Christianity, "For the existence of this λαός the biologico-historical or national element is of no significance [implying that it is for Israel]. It is a third race, as was said later." [Strathmann here refers to Harnack's "Christians as a Third Race"]. Strathmann appears to be following Harnack who refers to Jews as a second race (see below).

3. "For I could wish that I myself were cursed and cut off from Christ for the sake of my brothers, those of my own race, the people of Israel."

4. Harrison, *Romans* in the Expositor's Bible Commentary (Grand Rapids: Zondervan, 1976) 101–3.

5. See J. D. G. Dunn, *Romans 1-8* (Dallas: Word Books, 1988) 118. Dunn compares Paul's views expressed in Rom. 2:17-20 to Ezekiel and Isaiah, noting that "as the exile showed the consequences of such pride then, so the transgression of particular Jews now make the same pride an occasion of Gentile gibes at the God who has chosen *such a race*" (emphasis mine). While Dunn usually emphasizes an exclusiveness based on ethnicity, here he uses the term "race" and in doing so introduces an absolute category with profound implications for Pauline exegesis. See the critique of that terminology also by Jacob Neusner, "Was Rabbinic Judaism Really 'Ethnic'?" *CBQ* 57 (1995) 281–305.

Paul;[6] and in older studies such as Jeremias's *Jerusalem zur Zeit Jesu*
on which several generations of scholars have relied for information
about the culture and religion of Judaism.[7] And one finds it most fla-
grantly in the recent monographs of scholars like N. Thomas Wright to
be discussed below. In these works we see both careless and deliberate
uses of racial categories which we shall later maintain do special
violence to first-century realities.

Before turning to a consideration of Pauline scholarship, we must
attend to the history of the term "race" itself, and the way it came to
inhabit Pauline studies and to distort our understanding of the Judaism
of Paul's day.

THE EMERGENCE OF THE
CONCEPT OF RACE

Could it be that this is much ado about nothing and that the construction of racial categories is the inevitable result of constructing the
"other," that is to say that the use of the term "race" legitimately
recognizes the way groups define themselves in opposition to others?
At one level it might appear so. A long time ago, Robert Redfield
taught us that the us–them dichotomy has been basic to group definition for millennia:

> It is probably safe to say that among the groupings of people in every
> society are always some that distinguish people who are my people . . .
> from people who are not so much my people.[8]

---

6. See John L. White, "God's Paternity as Root Metaphor in Paul's Conception of Community," *Forum* 8, 3–4 (1995) 281. While at one level one may agree with White's estimation of
the expansiveness of Paul's Gentile mission, the positing of a "racially limited conception of the
law" introduces a category that needs interrogation.

7. I am thinking especially of the work of Joachim Jeremias, *Jerusalem zur Zeit Jesu, Eine
kulturgeschichtliche Untersuchung zur neutestamentlichen Zeitgeschichte*, 2d ed. (Göttingen:
Vandenhoeck & Ruprecht, 1958), which retains the references to race of the prewar edition. See
especially chapter 6, "Die Israeliten reiner Abstimmung," in which Jeremias says, "Die *reinras-
sigen* Familien, nur sie, stellten das wahre Israel dar" (145). Much more offensive is the first
English translation of the third edition, *Jerusalem in the Time of Jesus*, trans. F. H. and C. H.
Cave (London: SCM Press, 1969), part 4, with the title "The Maintenance of Racial Purity," that
includes such statements as the following found on p. 270, "Up to the present, it has not been
sufficiently recognized that from a social point of view the whole community of Judaism at the
time of Jesus was dominated by the fundamental idea of the *maintenance of racial purity*"
(emphasis mine). See also p. 352 and the reference to the Samaritans as a "*mixed* Judaeo-Gentile
race" (emphasis added), and p. 302 where we find, "Although the question of *racial purity*
determined to a large extent the social position of the Jew of New Testament times within his own
community."

8. Robert Redfield, *The Primitive World and Its Transformations* (Ithaca: Cornell
University Press, 1953) 92.

That being so, one might argue that the term "race" simply shares in this aspect of world construction and is a common if not inevitable category.

The ancient world yields ready evidence of this human propensity. J. Z. Smith has noted how the Sumerians contrasted themselves with the Amorites "who do not know barley," "who do not know city life," who eat "uncooked meat," and who do not bury their dead.[9] From the Bible we learn how the Hebrews saw the Canaanites as sexually perverse, the Egyptians as oppressive for enslaving the Israelites, and the Moabites as unspeakably cruel in warfare and the products of the incestuous relationship of Lot's daughters with their aged father.[10] The Greeks viewed non-Greek speakers as barbarians because their speech sounded like "bar, bar, bar." Egyptians of the Middle Kingdom period described nomadic peoples as "other," and both the Romans and Christians of the second century found the wandering tribes of the Turko-Mongolic steppe as fiercely other:

> They have no fixed abode, their life is rude, their lust promiscuous. . . . They devour the bodies of their parents. . . . Their climate, too, exhibits the same rude nature. . . . The whole year is winter. . . . Nothing is hot except ferocity.[11]

Even the apostle Paul shared this tendency as shown by his segregation of believers from unbelievers, "saints" from "pagans," worshippers of the God of Israel from idol worshippers, and the children of light from the children of darkness (1 Thess). Even though ambiguities were concealed in these dichotomies and a vital reciprocity often existed across those divisions, group identity was significantly influenced by the construction of the "other."[12]

While these acts of fabrication almost always caricature the "other," this caricature reinforces group identity even though it may at points remain open to the surprise and opportunity for newness presented by the "other." Although these dichotomies were widespread in

---

9. See Jonathan Z. Smith, "Differential Equations: On Constructing the 'Other'," the Thirteenth Annual University Lecture in Religion at Arizona State University (1992) 3, in the version circulated to members of the AAR.

10. Derived in Genesis 19 from the Hebrew for Moab meaning "from the Father."

11. Tertullian, *Adversus Marcionem* 1.1.

12. See William Scott Green, "Otherness Within: Toward a Theory of Difference in Rabbinic Judaism," in *"To See Ourselves as Others See Us": Christians, Jews, "Others" in Late Antiquity*, ed. Jacob Neusner and Ernest S. Frerichs; literary editor Caroline McCracken-Flesher (Chico: Scholars Press, 1985) 50. Green saw that the "other" contains a dimension of the group self, and it may also offer a vital reciprocity that may surprise. "The most critical feature of otherness thus presupposes familiarity and reciprocity, and perhaps resemblance, between and among groups."

the Ancient Near East, this fabrication of the "other" was not exactly he same thing as the creation of a racial category. The category of the "other," for example, is open and pliable, whereas the category of race is absolute, and ineradicable. For example, barbarians may overcome their status as "other" by learning the language and ways of Greece. Through her love of and loyalty to Naomi, Ruth becomes more to Naomi than "seven sons" (Ruth 4:15) and in giving birth to Obed, the grandfather of David, she becomes one of the most important figures in Israel's sacred story. These acts solidify her not as Moabite "other," but as one of the most important of Israel's ancestors. Through participation in Christ unbelieving children of darkness may become children of light. The category of the "other" is, therefore, open to change. Racial categories, on the other hand, are socially constructed as permanent and irrevocable. One cannot change one's race by any act of faith, any singular act of devotion, any acquisition of knowledge, any human work, or even by religious conversion.

Yet the relationship between the categories of race and otherness in the seventeenth and eighteenth centuries in the United States was much more complex than the discussion above suggests. Even while the category of race was being formed, missionaries turned the discussion to advantage by making race a category that invited change. One cannot change the absoluteness of the category of race, they granted, but through conversion and education one could change the inhuman attributes and brutishness, and could tame the primal, destructive impulses and superstitions that other races embody. While there are different races, they held that Christ's kingdom has no boundaries, and in that kingdom races exist but racism does not. This subtle distinction—while being open to change, hopeful, and humanistic— nevertheless allowed for a view of race that was quite insidious precisely because of its attractiveness.

If the construction of racial categories is not exactly synonymous with the construction of the "other," might "race" nevertheless be an objective reality that enjoyed broad acceptance in the first century? With such evidence in hand then one could make a case for Paul's use of racial categories. Harnack did much to convince scholars that such an objective category did exist in the first centuries of the Common Era.[13] In his famous 1902 excursus, "Christians as a Third Race, in

---

13. E. P. Sanders, *Paul, the Law, and the Jewish People* (Philadelphia: Fortress Press, 1983) 173, vigorously and correctly challenges the validity of the concept of a "third race" without specifically mentioning Harnack by name, but evidently it is Harnack's essay that he has in mind.

the Judgment of Their Opponents," he cited early primary historical documents for support of his view.[14] He noted how Pliny (23–79 C.E.) referred to the Jews as a *gens contumelia numinum insignis,* which Moffatt translated "a *race (gens)* distinguished by its contempt for deities" (emphasis mine).[15] Elsewhere, Harnack pieced together Minucius Felix's record of Caecilius's reference to the Latin *gentilitas* which he takes to mean "race': *Judaeorum sola et misera gentilitas unum et epsi deum* rendered "The lonely and wretched *race* of the Jews worshipped one God" (emphasis mine).[16] Citing Tertullian, Harnack argues that as early as the second century the popular mind construed Christianity as a third race (*genus tertium*), Jews a second race, and Romans the first race (*gens*).[17] A close reading of these texts, however, shows that Harnack's translation of *gens, genus,* and *gentilitas* as "race" and his fabrication of Christianity as a "third race" that implicitly supersedes the "second race" enjoys little historical support. *Gens* (from which come *genus* and *gentilitas*) in its root sense refers to that which belongs together by birth, i.e., clan, family, tribe, people.[18] The inclusion of race in the range of meanings for *gens* reflects the nineteenth-century obsession with racial theory, and so it remains until now.[19] *Gentilitas* means clan, not race, and *genus* refers to descent, descendant, or species. Harnack's translation and construction of Jews as the second race and Christians as the third race is a reflection of the philosophical and anthropological currents in his own time, not the isolation of a demonstrable historical fact from the first century. In this translation Harnack mixes pliable with absolutely set categories. One may, for example, change clans, families, or tribes through marriage, expulsion, or renunciation. One cannot, however, change one's socially constructed race by any such means. Harnack's error was usually corrected by T. R. Glover, his contemporary, in Glover's translation of

---

14. See this essay in Adolf Harnack, *The Mission and Expansion of Christianity in the First Three Centuries,* ed. and trans. James Moffatt (Gloucester, Mass.: Peter Smith, 1972 [first German edition 1902]) 266–78.

15. See his "Christians as a Third Race," 266, n. 1.

16. See Minucius Felix, *Octavius* x.4, which Harnack mistakenly assigns to viiif. Harnack's citation as well as his translation is fraught with difficulty. He strings together random phrases from viii.2 to x.4 to construct a paragraph that is artificial and misleading. See his essay, "Christians as a Third Race," 268–69.

17. See his "Christians as a Third Race," esp. 269–77.

18. See Charlton T. Lewis and Charles Short, *A Latin Dictionary* (Oxford: Clarendon Press, 1879), in the entry for *gens.* Note, however, that the nineteenth-century interest in race theory has led Lewis and Short to include race as a possible meaning, though in its root sense race is excluded.

19. See Lewis and Short, *A Latin Dictionary,* for a good example of the way the nineteenth-century discussions of race influenced judgments about meanings of Latin terms in the first century.

Tertullian and Minucius Felix in the Loeb series.[20] Nevertheless, it was Harnack's essay and not Glover's translation that was to influence later theological discourse so profoundly.

Since World War II both historians and anthropologists have almost unanimously agreed to points made earlier by only a few, namely that race is not an objective reality but a social product. Thomas Gossett has skillfully traced the genealogy of modern racial constructs, showing how they made their debut in the sixteenth and seventeenth centuries, became a topic of importance in the eighteenth century, and assumed powerful significance in the nineteenth century. He has proven that the concept of race is primarily and fundamentally a modern construction of the West whose discourse is rooted in philosophy, natural history, and contact "of the English with Indians, and soon afterward with Negroes in the New World."[21] While a French physician, François Bernier, first had the idea of a geographical division of the world by race rather than by nations a couple of centuries earlier,[22] the tide of scholarly interest and opinion rose steadily until this theory of "racial division" reached its climax in the nineteenth century.[23] In that age physical anthropologists worked tirelessly to construct and defend racial theories that they hoped would explain human origins. Under the influence of Darwin, anthropologists related races to each other as lower species to higher, and almost universally the Caucasian race was viewed as the highest.[24] Although such a theory was given legitimacy by science, philosophers of the Enlightenment from France, Germany, and America had earlier argued for a racial hierarchy that located blacks at the bottom and whites at the top.[25]

This nineteenth-century current was running so strongly that no criticism could divert or redirect it. The idea of race was so real that

---

20. See Tertullian, *Apology*, trans. T. R. Glover (Cambridge, Mass.: Harvard University Press, 1910), and Minucius Felix, *Octavius* viii, 4; 1x, 2.

21. Thomas F. Gossett, *Race, the History of an Idea in America* (New York: Schocken Books, 1965) 17.

22. In 1684, for example, Bernier was apparently the first to offer a conceptual map of the world based on physical features. He classified the peoples of the world as conforming to four types or races—European, Far Eastern, blacks, and Lapps. The Indians of North America, he believed, were not a separate race, though he did not specify their race. For a fuller discussion see Gossett, *Race, the History of an Idea*, 32–33.

23. For a brilliant philosophical analysis of this development see Cornel West, "A Genealogy of Modern Racism," in his *Prophesy Deliverance! An Afro-American Revolutionary Christianity* (Philadelphia: Westminster Press, 1982) 47–65.

24. Gossett, *Race, the History of an Idea*, 34.

25. See West, *Prophesy Deliverance*, 61–63, for references to this construction by Montesquieu and Voltaire (France), Hume and Jefferson (Scotland and America), and Kant (Germany).

the rejection of racial theories by such luminaries as John Wesley Powell, the director of the Bureau of Ethnology at the Smithsonian, or by the French anthropologist Topinard was widely condemned, and their work did little to diminish the popularity of current racial theory. These scholarly trends penetrated every level of society itself, and even after damning reservations were expressed by distinguished scholars, race continued to be a powerful intellectual force. Once science became the ally of racism, race became something that blacks and Jews had to deal with in new ways. Almost inevitably, these forces also influenced theological study.

John M. Efron has recently shown how the nineteenth-century race theory in the hands of nationalists led to a vicious and violent anti-Semitism, and it is ironic that the same theory was co-opted by Jewish scholars to foster solidarity and to instill pride in the Jewish tradition.[26] Marginalized and threatened by assimilation, Jewish scholars argued that cultural traits and history, not biology, were the distinctive marks of this special race.[27] Efron observes that while Jewish scholars were quite willing to acknowledge that Jews were a race, from the beginning they recognized the danger of a chauvinism based on race.[28] But these Jewish scholars were bucking a powerful tide, for influential physical anthropologists believed genetics was the key to racial definition. To be a race, so it was believed, a people must be physically or psychologically different, temperamentally or creatively distinctive. Against those arguing that history and culture were the key ingredients in the definition of race,[29] physical anthropologists countered that higher fertility rates among Jewish women proved that biological factors played an important, if not decisive, role in defining the race of the Jews.[30] Predictably, these scholarly trends were reflected almost exactly by a broad-based popular opinion that included women and men, young and old, peasant and noble, illiterate and educated, academics and manual laborers.[31] And, even where there was agreement that cultural and environmental factors played an important role in defining Jewishness, the popular mythology persisted that the Jewish race was in some fundamental way different.

Increasingly, however, these racial theories came under attack. In an about-face, anthropologists like Ignaz Zollschau categorically

---

26. See the recent, excellent treatment by John M. Efron, *Defenders of the Race, Jewish Doctors and Race Science in Fin-de-Siècle Europe* (New Haven: Yale University Press, 1994).

27. Ibid., 7–9, 179.

28. Ibid., 179.

29. Ibid., 177–78.

30. Ibid., 178.

31. Ibid., 176.

rejected the concept of race. Scholarly challenges plus the historical scourge of Naziism and its death camps made it impossible for any anthropologist or historian to claim that "race science" was scientific.[32] Increasingly, after the war when the carnage visited on the "Jewish race" became common knowledge, scholars questioned the value of the category of race itself.

In the fifties, the changes in European intellectual opinion came to the United States, which faced its own form of virulent, bigoted, strident, and intractable racism. And while this racism was tragic and stubbornly resilient, and in the minds of some, quite other than the anti-Semitism of Germany, both were related to the nineteenth-century perceptions of race. In light of these experiences and continued study historians came gradually to recognize race as a social construction. Once the category of race was fabricated and sanctioned by generations of use, its legitimacy came from the air the society breathed, and no one needed to defend its veracity; it was simply taken for granted.

While such categories were real, they were, nevertheless, contingent; they possessed reality only at certain historical moments, and they had power only so long as the society lent them authenticity. In other words, it was clear that they were social constructions. Once that was recognized, scholars more and more acknowledged that it was historically false to give race an objective and transcendent meaning outside of those social constructions.

The historian Barbara J. Fields has played a key role in this discussion. She has exposed the lie of a common scholarly move: "the assumption that race is an observable fact, a thing, rather than a notion that is profoundly and in its very essence ideological."[33] While Fields concerns herself with the concept of race in the American context, her work is germane to our consideration. She suggests that "ideas about color, like ideas about anything else, derive their importance, indeed their very definition, from their context. They can no more be the unmediated reflex of psychic expressions than can other ideas."[34] By recalling anecdotally Papa Doc Duvalier's view that in Haiti any person with any white blood was considered white, whereas in the U.S. any person with any black blood was considered black, she notes the irrationality, the arbitrariness, the ideology, and the contradictory and contextual character of such categories. In the U.S., for example, the

---

32. Ibid., 178.

33. See her "Ideology and Race in American History," in *Religion, Race, and Reconstruction: Essays in Honor of C. Vann Woodward*, ed. J. Morgan Kousser and James M. McPherson (New York and Oxford: Oxford University Press, 1982) 144.

34. Ibid., 146.

dominant white view of race is that white women can bear black children, but black women cannot bear white children.[35] While such ideologies at one level may strike us as silly, at another level they offer "a ready-made interpretation of the world, a sort of hand-me-down vocabulary with which to name [and control] the elements of every new experience."[36] As Fielding notes, even when the ideologies die, their language and symbols, like the demons of New Testament times, occupy new bodies and take on a new capacity to dominate without ever being noticed.[37] And, it appears that this is precisely what has happened in Pauline scholarship—i.e., that an ideology with roots in the recent past has inhabited the vocabulary of Pauline scholarship and influenced the discourse in quite unpredictable ways. Ideologies have a history, and as such they have a beginning point and various configurations before coming to an end. The concept of race has its origins largely in the eighteenth and nineteenth centuries, and the concept of the "race of Israel" is a product of racial theories of that recent period and not a historical product of the first century.

We are left, however, with the question of whether we might have the "thing" of race in Paul's letters, even if we do not have the word, or whether we might have at least implicitly the concept of race in Paul's vocabulary and discourse even when it is not explicitly articulated. The scholar who makes the strongest case for that reality is N. Thomas Wright.

"RACE OF ISRAEL"
IN PAULINE SCHOLARSHIP

Because of the intentional way that Wright applies the category of race to Israel in his treatment of Paul's theology, and because of the implications of that application, it is important to note it.

While references to Israel as a race are sprinkled throughout Wright's work, his book *The Climax of the Covenant* develops them best. There, commenting on Romans 9:30–33, he makes Israel "guilty of a meta-sin, *the attempt to confine grace to race.*"[38] This presumption was based on the traditions of election and monotheism which were made to serve "as symbols of *national and racial* solidarity."[39]

---

35. Ibid., 146, 149.
36. Ibid., 152–53.
37. Ibid., 153.
38. See N. T. Wright, *The Climax of the Covenant: Christ and the Law in Pauline Theology* (Minneapolis: Fortress Press, 1991) 240.
39. Ibid., 13–14.

This presumption was reinforced by a religion of law observance which, according to Wright, Paul totally rejected. It was not, he states, that Paul failed to recognize that certain individual Jews did indeed observe Torah fully, but that even such faithfulness of the few could not alter the failure of "Israel as *a race.*"[40] In Paul's view, the "law is therefore to be understood not as a restriction of the Abrahamic promises *to one race*—that is the mistake Paul's opponents are making— but as a temporary measure. . . ."[41] Noting how Paul attacks this presumption of being a privileged race, Wright adds categorically, "we must note that Paul has made it clear beyond any doubt . . . that there is no covenant membership *for Israel on the basis of racial or "fleshly" identity.*"[42] While there is a remnant *"chosen by grace, not by race or by the "works"* that were the badges of Jewish privilege," the promise that "all Israel will be saved" cannot be read to imply a two-covenant doctrine which is "in fact clinging to a scheme of religion *based on race, which is exactly what Paul is renouncing and opposing with his whole theology of the new humanity in Christ.*"[43] By "two-covenant doctrine" Wright is referring to the view of Lloyd Gaston that two separate and equally valid covenants exist between God and Israel and between God and the church. In a more recent succinct summary of this position, Wright offers as a statement of fact that "the symbolic world of Judaism focused upon Temple, Torah, Land *and racial identity*" (all emphases above are mine), and in contrast Paul's symbolic world focuses on Christ for all peoples.[44]

Wright thus argues that while Paul recognizes Israel's special status as the people of the covenant, it surrendered its place by relying on race rather than grace mediated by Christ. Thus, he believes, Paul "systematically transferred the privileges and attributes of 'Israel' to the Messiah and his people."[45] With the loss of its favored place, Israel's only hope is to "be brought back in . . . 'by your [Christ's] mercy.'"[46]

---

40. Ibid., 155.

41. Ibid., 167.

42. Ibid., 245f.

43. Ibid., 247, 254.

44. See N. T. Wright, "Romans and the Theology of Paul," in *SBL 1992 Seminar Papers* (Atlanta: Scholars Press, 1992) 184–213. In his book *The New Testament and the People of God* (Minneapolis: Fortress Press, 1992) 230–32, Wright charges that after the Babylonian Exile Judaism had focused on "racial purity," that writings from the Roman period concentrate on race as a touchstone of belonging to the People of God, and that the temple institutionalized this racial ideology into policy. See discussion of this issue by Paula Fredriksen, "What You See Is What You Get: Context and Content in Current Research on the Historical Jesus," *Theology Today* 52 (1995) 88–93.

45. Wright, *The Climax of the Covenant*, 250.

46. Ibid., 249.

Wright recognizes the challenge posed to this reading of Paul by Romans 11:26 ("all Israel will be saved"). Here Paul appears to suggest that Israel's hardening is only temporary, opening the door to salvation for Gentiles, but after this interim "all Israel will be saved" when a "Deliverer" will come out of Zion (Isa 59:20-21). By his Scripture citation Paul refers to the salvation of all Israel that will come perhaps at the *parousia* of Christ, but we are not told exactly when and by whom. It is altogether possible that Paul intended to leave the identity of the Deliverer ambiguous, up to God's choice.[47] Apparently, Paul means that the inclusion of Gentiles through his Gentile gospel does not mean that God will renege on promises made to historic Israel.

Wright, however, thinks that 11:26 refers not to historic Israel but to a spiritualized Israel, i.e., the Christian church: it "is preferable," Wright argues, "to take 'all Israel' in v. 26 as a typically Pauline polemical redefinition."[48] For support Wright cites Romans 9:6 where Paul uses the term Israel in two different senses ("For not all who are descended from Israel belong to Israel"). And he summons Galatians 6:16 in which he believes Paul's reference to "the Israel of God" refers to the Christian church. Finally, he refers to Philippians 3:3 where Paul spiritualizes circumcision to refer to Christians. In reading "Israel" in 11:26 as "spiritual Israel," Wright goes with a tradition that stretches from Irenaeus to Whiteley and from Augustine through Calvin to Cerfaux; but he remains in the minority, nevertheless, in taking "all Israel" to refer to the church rather than historic Israel.[49]

While Wright observes that Paul does elsewhere spiritualize historic Israel, there is little support for the view that Paul is doing so in this context. Joseph Fitzmyer has shown that in the Hebrew Bible the phrase "all Israel" always refers to "historic, ethnic Israel" and that the phrase carried the same meaning into the rabbinic period.[50] Moreover, 11:26 is bracketed by references to Israel (11:25c) and to the beloved elect (11:28-29) that unquestionably refer to historic Israel. The sense of the passage as a whole argues for reading the reference to "all Israel" as a reference to historic Israel. It strains credulity to suggest that Paul is here arguing for the replacement of "race" with

---

47. See the commentary of Charles D. Myers Jr., on the "Epistle to the Romans," in the *Anchor Bible Dictionary*, ed. David Noel Freedman et al. (New York: Doubleday, 1992) 5:824.

48. Wright, *The Climax of the Covenant*, 250. One almost feels compelled to ask, "Preferable for whom?"

49. For a full discussion see Joseph A. Fitzmyer, *Romans, A New Translation with Introduction and Commentary* (New York: Doubleday, 1992) 623-24.

50. Ibid., 623.

"grace," that is, interpreting the promise that "all Israel will be saved" as a promise dependent upon the condition of conversion to faith in Messiah Jesus.[51]

Wright's triumphalistic reading of 11:26 dissolves the mystery (μυστήριον) which Paul introduces us to in 11:25. An inclusion by conversion would be no mystery at all, but if Paul is asking how two things that seem logically incompatible can be held together—how the gospel to the Gentiles can be entirely valid and God's promises to historic Israel entirely valid, how winners (Gentiles) do not require losers (non-messianist Jews)—then the answer would seem to be beyond human imagining. If the answer must be hidden in the mystery of the Godhead itself, then the soaring benediction Paul offers in 11:33–36 is an entirely apt expression of his wonderment at this mystery. By thus extending human logic to its breaking point Paul argues that God can find a way to be faithful to promises made to historic Israel and at the same time to include Gentiles in the *oikoumene*.[52] In an interesting if not perverse *tour de force*, Wright dismisses Gaston's two-covenant doctrine as a "scheme of religion based on race," and in its insistence that Christianity is for non-Jews, "it actually agrees in form with the German Christian theology of the 1930s."[53]

However one solves the problem of 11:26 is not the point of this paper. The point is to show how references to the Jewish race give a nuance to the text that it could not have carried in Paul's time. Wright, along with other Pauline scholars, uses an absolute category like race and assumes the power to assign Israel to this category, thereby assigning a marginality to Israel that would have been revolting to Paul. To

---

51. Wright's recognition of Paul's renunciation of [Gentile] Christian arrogance is entirely appropriate, but his coupling of that statement with his argument that *"Paul regards precisely as anti-semitic"* the "non-evangelization of the Jews" is clever, but reactionary (*The Climax of the Covenant*, 253). At one level one may view Wright's argument in tandem with that of missionaries of the seventeenth and eighteenth centuries in America who occupied a superior place because of their religious privilege. The blacks and Native Americans, in their view of a different race, were deprived environmentally and religiously; so to withhold the gospel from them, they believed, would be bad faith and inhumane. Through their evangelization they were able to make the "savage" or "uncivilized" and "uncultivated" more like them, and thus create bonds of similarity. They recognized that race is real and ineradicable, but at some level incidental. The missionaries believed all were involved in the same human nature.

What is different then about Wright's view? The difference is that the missionaries were in on the front end of a discussion about race and the gospel in which the concept of race was being defined and relationships between races being negotiated when the outcome of those discussions and negotiations could not be anticipated or predicted. We, however, are at a very different point in the discussion and have the benefit of centuries of experience and an awareness of where that discussion led. In a word, we should know better.

52. See my *"Oikoumene* and the Limits of Pluralism in Alexandrian Judaism and Paul," in *Diaspora Jews and Judaism, Essays in Honor of, and in Dialogue with, A. Thomas Kraabel*, ed. J. Andrew Overman and Robert S. MacLennan, 163–82 (Atlanta: Scholars Press, 1992).

53. Wright, *The Climax of the Covenant*, 254.

suggest that Paul assigned Israel to an absolute race category while reserving the sphere of grace for Christians comports more with our ideology than Paul's. Such an assignment ignores the complexity and tension in Paul's thought, offers a ready-made interpretation of Paul and his world that is historically false, risks imposing a caricature of Judaism on Paul, oversimplifies the Judaisms that Paul would have known, and implies an irrevocability that Paul himself vigorously contested.

The confusion is compounded by Wright's own vagueness about what he means by the term "race." Sometimes he uses it as a biological category, sometimes as a national one, and sometimes as an ethnic one.[54] The different implied meanings, however, are not interchangeable. Each category is distinct, and each has problems unique to itself. That race is a biological fact or physical attribute can, strictly and scientifically speaking, no longer be defended. To make race and nationality synonymous is little better, for from 63 B.C.E. (when Pompey invaded Palestine) until the modern period, there was no state of Israel, and without a state of Israel it is difficult to speak of a nation of Israel. The system of sovereign states as we know it is a product of the modern period as well and depends for its existence quite heavily on certain market structures emerging from modern capitalism.[55] And, as Wallerstein has noted, "it is debatable how deep a root 'nation' [or nationalism] as a communal sentiment took before the actual creation of the state."[56] More acceptable is the allusion to Israel as an ethnic people. Ethnicity is a cultural, sometimes even a religious, category that can be passed on from generation to generation and is not confined to, but may be related to, a physical place. So it would appear more appropriate to refer to Israel as an *ethnos*, a people, than as a race or a nationality.

In summary, we have seen that the category of race is not the same as the construction of the "other." It had its origin in the philosophical and scientific views of the Enlightenment, and the discovery of the New World by Western Europeans, and then was read back onto the first century, first by Harnack and then by others. Not surprisingly, theological discourse was profoundly influenced by race theory or "race science" in the nineteenth and early twentieth

---

54. Ibid., 253.

55. See Joseph R. Strayer, *On the Medieval Origins of the Modern State* (Princeton: Princeton University Press, 1970) 3–11.

56. Immanuel Wallerstein, "The Construction of Peoplehood: Racism, Nationalism, Ethnicity," in *Race, Nation, Class, Ambiguous Identities*, ed. Etienne Balibar and Immanuel Wallerstein, trans. E. Balibar and Chris Turner (London and New York: Verso, 1991) 81.

centuries, and even now vestiges of that older discussion continue to inhabit our vocabulary and distort our views of Paul. Robin Scroggs is an excellent model of a New Testament scholar who has skillfully appropriated the approaches of other scholarly disciplines to uncover nuances of ancient texts. If we can learn also from our colleagues in history and anthropology, we may see that the concept of race has no valid place in the discussion of the salvation of God's people unless we are talking about the human race or a foot race. (Interestingly, the only references to race in the KJV of 1611 are to foot races, which is what one would expect historically from that early period when the very concept of race was present only in embryonic form.) The point of this essay is a simple one: There was no concept of a Jewish race or of a race of Israel in the first century. The construction of race is a social phenomenon from the post-Enlightenment period. The category of race is one that denotes inferiority, and even unintentionally when a Christian refers to the "race of Israel," Christianity is assumed to be normative, and the Jewish "race," by implication, radically defective and inferior in its religion. If we choose to use the term, we do well to recognize the mythology concealed in the language of race and its capacity to marginalize, to assign place, and to attempt control. Such a usage, whether intentional or not, makes Paul say just the opposite of what his letters appear to say.

15

An (Un)Accomplished Model

Paul and the Rhetorical Strategy
of Philippians 3:3-17

Frederick W. Weidmann

Paul's letter to his Christian community at Philippi is one of the most personal letters in the Pauline corpus. Whether discussing his own plight or the Philippians', that of his co-worker Timothy or their representative Epaphroditus, Paul's love and concern for the members of his first mission community in the region of Macedonia is evident throughout the letter. Indeed, many recent studies have engaged external as well as internal data in understanding Philippians as a friendship letter,[1] perhaps even a "family" letter.[2]

In an article written for the Festschrift of J. Louis Martyn,[3] Robert Fortna offers a challenge—evident, to some degree, in the article's title—to much of the current understanding of Paul's letter: "Philippians: Paul's Most Egocentric Letter."[4] The study below will

---

1. See Gordon D. Fee, _Paul's Letter to the Philippians_, NICNT (Grand Rapids: Eerdmans, 1995); Ben Witherington III, _Friendship and Finances in Philippi: The Letter of Paul to the Philippians_ (Philadelphia: Trinity Press International, 1994); Wayne A. Meeks, "The Man from Heaven in Paul's Letter to the Philippians," in _The Future of Early Christianity: Essays in Honor of Helmut Koester_, ed. Birger A. Pearson, 329-36 (Minneapolis: Fortress Press, 1991); L. Michael White, "Morality between Two Worlds: A Paradigm of Friendship in Philippians," in _Greeks, Romans, and Christians: Essays in Honor of Abraham J. Malherbe_, ed. David L. Balch, Everett Ferguson, and Wayne A. Meeks, 201-15 (Minneapolis: Fortress Press, 1990).

2. Loveday Alexander, "Hellenistic Letter Forms and the Structure of Philippians," _JSNT_ 37 (1989) 87-101. For fuller bibliography, see Gordon D. Fee, _Philippians_. For discussion of these and other letter forms see Stanley K. Stowers, _Letter Writing in Greco-Roman Antiquity_, Library of Early Christianity (Philadelphia: Westminster Press, 1986).

3. Prof. Martyn preceded Prof. Scroggs in the chair of the Edward Robinson Professor of Biblical Theology on the faculty of Union Theological Seminary in New York.

4. Robert Fortna, "Philippians, Paul's Most Egocentric Letter," in _The Conversation Continues: Studies in Paul and John in Honor of J. Louis Martyn_, ed. Robert Fortna and Beverly Gaventa, 220-34 (Nashville: Abingdon Press, 1990).

consider Fortna's approach and others in order to develop an understanding of Paul's rhetorical use of himself within this fascinating letter, particularly in chapter 3. Neither egoism nor, for that matter, altruism can explain the concerns for both self and others evident in Philippians. Paul's agenda is other and larger.

PAUL'S AGENDA

According to Fortna, Paul's agenda in Philippians is to "work out a theology of his own approaching death."[5] The "issue" in chapters 3 and 4, he says, is the same as that in chapters 1 and 2: "the question of [Paul's] own standing before God and the world."[6] Formal analysis would appear to confirm Fortna's assertion. As Loveday Alexander observes: "Paul's first subject after the Thanksgiving section (1.3–11) is himself and his own welfare."[7] Further, the introduction of this "first subject" is marked by the use of the disclosure formula, "But I want you to know" (γινώσκειν δὲ ὑμᾶς βούλομαι). Such marked phraseology is significant, Alexander goes on to show, because "by the Roman period the formal opening of the body of the letter, marked by the disclosure" formula, had become the standard position for "the explicit explanation of the reason for writing."[8] So, following his thanksgiving to the community, Paul takes up the subject of Paul. That much is clear; or is it?

As I see it, the disclosure formula betrays a much different agenda. First, the translation I provide above, even though it includes the particle "but" (δέ), is arguably flat and, given the structure of the sentence as a whole, misleading. Following the "but" and preceding the true focus of Paul's remarks is the Greek μᾶλλον (often translated "rather"). In its use of "actually," the NRSV captures fairly well the significance of Paul's rhetoric, particularly the use of μᾶλλον: "I want you to know . . . that what has happened to me has actually helped to spread the gospel."[9] Paul's subject is seemingly Paul, but Paul's agenda is something else.

---

5. Ibid., 226.

6. Ibid. It should be noted that Fortna accepts Philippians "as more or less a single letter, however jarring the shift in mood and subject matter at 3:1b" (221). On this matter, he is in agreement with a growing consensus. See Meeks, "Man from Heaven," 331 n. 6. For an argument in favor of unity which considers formal and structural matters, see Alexander, "Hellenistic Letter Forms," 95. The assumption herein is that Philippians is one letter.

7. Alexander, "Hellenistic Letter Forms," 95.

8. Ibid. Alexander is quoting (in part) J. L. White, *Light from Ancient Letters* (Philadelphia: Fortress Press, 1986), 207.

9. Translations are from the NRSV unless noted otherwise.

What is marked as Paul's agenda, following the μᾶλλον, is "[the] spread of the gospel" (προκοπὴν τοῦ εὐαγγελίου). The term προκοπή ("spread," "progress," or "advancement") is, within the New Testament, unique to the Pauline corpus, and with the exception of 1 Timothy 4:15 its only uses are at the beginning of the body of this letter, first at 1:12 and, shortly thereafter, at 1:25. More precisely, Paul's concern, as he states it following the μᾶλλον, is not simply "[the] spread of the gospel" but that "what has happened" is "*for*" (εἰς) the spread of the gospel.[10] The use of προκοπή invites consideration of 1:25-26, while this particular use of εἰς suggests a glance back to 1:5-11.

Within the thanksgiving section of Philippians, Paul expresses thanks for, among other things, the Philippians' "sharing in the gospel from the first day until now" (Phil 1:5). Such language of "sharing" or "partnership" (κοινονία) is typical of Philippians. It is stated of the Philippians both here at the beginning of the letter, and again near the letter's close (Phil 4:15):

> You Philippians indeed know that in the early days of the gospel, when I left Macedonia, no church shared with (ἐκοινώνησεν) me in the matter of giving and receiving, except you alone.[11]

One notices immediately that besides specific language of sharing or partnership, these passages have in common with each other (and with 1:12) explicit mention of "the gospel."

L. Michael White observes that "Paul saw his relationship with the Philippian congregation as one of contractual reciprocity grounded in their common goal of spreading the gospel and in their common experience of salvation in Christ."[12] That Paul shares—really shares—the "common goal of spreading the gospel" is evident throughout this letter, and is not surprising at all, particularly in light of Paul's correspondence with the nearby community at Thessalonica. One recalls Paul's words in the thanksgiving section of his early letter to that com-

---

10. Emphasis mine. There is no one-to-one correspondence of an English word to the Gk. εἰς in the NRSV translation above. Rather, the NRSV supplies "has . . . helped to"; cf. RSV, "has . . . served to." For a closer correlation to the original Gk., the NRSV translation might be amended: ". . . what has happened . . . is actually for the spread of the gospel." The definite article before the noun "spread" is not visible in the Gk., but is supplied with integrity in English translations (See BDF 255, 257 [2], [3]).

11. For similar consideration of the description of individuals within this letter, such as Epaphroditus (2:25-30) and Euodia and Syntyche (4:2), see recently Meeks, 334.

12. White, 210. White is himself following J. Paul Sampley, *Pauline Partnership in Christ: Christian Community and Commitment in the Light of Roman Law* (Philadelphia: Fortress Press, 1980).

munity, 1 Thessalonians 1:6–8: "And you became imitators of us and of the Lord . . . so that you became an example to all the believers. . . . For the word of the Lord has sounded forth from you . . . in every place."

The particular partnership that Paul and the Philippians share vis-à-vis "the gospel" is made all the more explicit in Philippians 1:5 through the same use of the preposition εἰς, which was noted regarding 1:12 above. In other words, the Philippians "sharing in the gospel" is a partnership "for" the gospel. As noted by Gordon D. Fee, in his recent commentary, Paul's usage of εἰς here is "telic, pure and simple."[13] That is, the preposition is used to indicate the goal for which something is done.[14] Fee can write, therefore, of Philippians 1:5 that "the advance of the gospel . . . is the goal of their "participation."[15]

Paul's early comment in 1:5 makes clear what he believes (or wants) to be the case: he and the Philippians share a partnership "for" the gospel. In 1:12, at the beginning of the body of the letter, the overall agenda for spreading the gospel, as we have seen, remains intact while the immediate focus turns to Paul's circumstance. What of 1:25–26?

In the transitional verses of 1:24–25 Paul shifts attention to the plight of his Philippian addressees, and their "progress (προκοπήν)[16] and joy in faith." Indeed, the same prepositional usage is operative here as has been discussed above, making it evident that the matter discussed in 1:24–25a is "for your progress. . . ." What has happened to Paul's agenda for spreading the gospel?

As with the consideration of Paul's plight (1:12ff.), so with the Philippians' here—both the form and the content of the rhetoric are in service of Paul's agenda. First, as Paul and the Philippians are partners "for" the gospel, one might assume that what is true of Paul's plight, namely, that it is in service of the greater agenda (1:12), is also true of theirs (1:25ff.). Second, the repetition of (what is for Paul) the very rare term προκοπή hearkens back to 1:12 and its concern for the centrality of the gospel, while the use of εἰς . . . προκοπήν evokes reconsideration and remembrance of both 1:5 and 1:12. Finally, as the content of 1:25ff. unfolds, Paul twice mentions "the gospel" (1:27). Indeed, though their respective, immediate plights are very different,

---

13. Fee, *Philippians* 83 n. 51.

14. See BAGD, 229a.

15. Fee, *Philippians*, 83 n. 51. See also Fee's comment on Phil 1:12: "for this kind of telic use of this preposition see v. 5 (cf. vv. 15, 19, 25)"; idem, *Philippians*, 111 n. 19.

16. The same Gk. word which the NRSV translates as "spread" in 1:12.

the imprisoned Paul can even refer to his struggles and those of his Philippian partners as simply "the same" (τὸν αὐτὸς ἀγῶνα, 1:30) since both are in service of the common agenda on behalf of the gospel.

We now begin to see that the beginning of Philippians—including the thanksgiving section, as well as the first paragraphs of the body itself—is about much more than recognizing, as Fortna concedes, "that adversity as such . . . may in fact have a positive effect."[17] These paragraphs are about setting—or better, reinforcing—an understanding of partnership for, or on behalf of, the gospel.

HIERARCHY

Concerning 1:24–25, Fortna writes, "What is clearly implied here is that Paul, as appears often in this and other early letters, views his relation to his followers as set in a God-given hierarchy."[18] Paul's role, given his station at the top human level of that hierarchy, is one of "mediation" from Christ to others.[19] That Paul operates with some such understanding of "hierarchy" is beyond doubt, and one should be greatly surprised, given the social-historical context in which the letter was drafted, were it otherwise. What is fascinating is the degree to which that hierarchy is seemingly absent in Philippians and, when it is engaged, subverted.

According to Epictetus, true teachers are aware that they have been "sent" (ἀποστέλλω) by God.[20] As we have already seen, 1 Thessalonians 1:6ff. suggests just such a hierarchy: "you became imitators of us and of the Lord, . . . so that you became an example to [others]." Several lines later, in considering his "gentle" manner with the Thessalonians, Paul reminds them that he and his inner circle "might have made demands as apostles" (ἀπόστολοι); a kind of backhanded reminder of his status.[21] In Philippians, Paul uses no verb or noun form of "apostle" with regard to himself.[22]

We see in 1:5 that the standard hierarchy is operative in Philippians: the Philippians became partners with Paul "from the first day"

---

17. Fortna, "Egocentric Letter," 222.
18. Ibid., 231 n. 17.
19. Ibid., 233.
20. Epictetus 3.22.23. Text and translations of Epictetus contained herein are from *Epictetus: The Discourses as Reported by Arrian, the Manual, and the Fragments*, 2 vols., ed. W. A. Oldfather, LCL, 1925–28 (Cambridge: Harvard University Press, 1978–79).
21. Cf. 2 Cor. 11:12–13 for another roundabout assertion of "apostle" status.
22. See, however, 2:25 for a description of Epaphroditus; the only one marked as "apostle" in Philippians is a Philippian who is sent to Paul!

that he brought the gospel to them. In (at least) that sense, he is the greater or the more primary figure in the hierarchy. Further, as observed below, Paul's call in 3:17 that he be viewed as a "model" (τύπον) is also consistent with the standard hierarchy.[23]

PAUL, THE PHILIPPIANS, AND THE "PRIMORDIAL APPREHENSION OF REALITY"

In the classic Marx Brothers movie *Horsefeathers* (1932), Groucho, in the role of a professor (!) newly appointed to the presidency of a college, delivers a simple message to his colleagues: "whatever it is, I'm against it." According to Robin Scroggs, Paul has a similar sentiment as regards Sin: "to borrow from Coolidge, he is against it."[24] And Sin, according to Paul, covers a multitude of human states and aspirations. Indeed, writes Scroggs, "Sin is a matter of existence which permeates the total self in all its realities."[25] Further, and by extension of the previous comment, "The Pharisee is not a sinner when he fails to fulfill the law; somehow he is a sinner precisely when he does fulfill the Law."[26] How can this be?

A way of understanding this strange state of affairs and its resolution in Paul's thought involves a key term borrowed from the Scroggs corpus, namely, "world-switching." Conversion, for Paul, involves a "transformation" or a "world-switching"; that is, the "change from one perceived world to another, the false to the true (at least in faith), involving *a change of one's primordial apprehension of reality*, which leaves no part of the self or its world untouched or unchanged."[27] It is in chapter 3 of Philippians that Paul makes his "primordial apprehension of reality" clear to the letter's addressees, his Philippian partners on behalf of the gospel. And, as the structure of the letter reveals, this is quite by design.[28]

---

23. For further discussion of "apostle" and "teacher" as "model" (τύπος) in the Pauline corpus and other Greco-Roman literature, see Abraham J. Malherbe, *Paul and the Thessalonians: The Philosophic Tradition of Pastoral Care* (Philadelphia: Fortress Press, 1987), esp. 52–60, and idem, "Paul as Paradigm for the Community"; and Frederick Weidmann, "The Good Teacher: Social Identity and Community Purpose in the Pastoral Epistles," *Journal of Higher Criticism* 2, no. 2 (1995) 100–114, esp. 101–7.

24. Robin Scroggs, *Paul for a New Day* (Philadelphia: Fortress Press, 1977) 5. Coolidge may well be the ultimate source of both Groucho's and Scroggs's phraseology.

25. Ibid., 6.

26. Ibid.

27. Robin Scroggs, "The Theocentrism of Paul," in *The Texts and the Times: New Testament Essays for Today* (Minneapolis: Fortress Press, 1993) 189; emphasis mine.

28. In agreement with Meeks who says "the section on the whole is not polemical but hortatory" (332); see also Fee, *Philippians*, 289–95.

The chapter begins with the notorious phrase τὸ λοιπόν, incorrectly translated by NRSV and others as "finally." As explained by Fee, "what it means here is exactly what it meant in 1 Thessalonians 4:1 and 2 Thessalonians 3:1, namely, "as for the rest," or "as for what remains to be said."[29] The imperative form "rejoice" which follows, is, likewise, not a mark of closure.[30] "Paul is not saying "farewell" but repeating the exhortation to "rejoice" which is so much a feature of this letter."[31] Finally by way of directing (and calling for) attention, Paul is explicit in announcing that this particular message to his "brothers and sisters" (ἀδελφοί) is "for you" (ὑμῖν).

Paul situates his description of a "safe" (ἀσφαλές)[32] "apprehension of reality" between two depictions of wrongheadedness (3:2, 18–19). As noted by Fee, "at issue for Paul is Christian existence itself. The concerns are therefore expressed ultimately in experiential and theological language, as the alleged 'opponents' fade into the background rather quickly."[33] Whereas early and late (1:5, 12ff., 25ff.; 4:15–16) in the letter Paul was sure to confirm a partnership and concern for the gospel, here in 3:3–17, he means to model for his Philippian partners a human life lived on behalf of the gospel. Paul's concern is not Paul; his gospel-focused agenda remains intact.[34]

From the standpoint of Pauline and Greco-Roman rhetoric, Philippians 3:4–16 is unusual. Ostensibly, the verses provide the content and context for the simple charge in 3:17: "join in imitating me." That much appears normal and is to be expected. As indicated in the quotation from Epictetus above, the true teacher is one "sent" by god. And why is the teacher sent? "In order to show [humans] that in questions of good and evil they have gone astray, and are seeking the true nature of good and evil where it is not. . . ."[35] In large measure, the content of 3:4–16 meets the purpose of the teacher as espoused by Epictetus. And, to the degree Paul sets himself up as model, he is engaging or displaying neither "outrageousness"[36] nor "audacity"[37] (at least no more than would be expected of a teacher). He is simply doing his job.

---

29. Fee, *Philippians*, 291.

30. This point is argued persuasively based on analysis of actual usage of the form; Alexander, "Hellenistic Letter Forms," 97.

31. Ibid.

32. RSV; see BAGD 119a for "sure" or "certain."

33. Fee, *Philippians*, 295.

34. For a very different interpretation of the rhetoric here, see Helmut Koester, "The Purpose of the Polemic of a Pauline Fragment (Phil III)," *NTS* 8 (1961–62), 317–32, in which these verses, considered separately from the rest of Philippians, are understood primarily as "polemical" (against the group[s] identified in 3:2 and 3:18–19) rather than hortatory (*i.e.*, modeling a life lived on behalf of the gospel).

35. Epictetus 3.22.23. See also above, n. 20.

36. Fortna, "Egocentric Letter," 227.

What is striking is the manner in which the task is carried out. As Meeks writes (in a comment on Phil 4:11): "The competitive values of Greek rhetoric are tacitly reversed both here and in the inverted boasting of 3:4-16."[38] That is not to say that several of the hallmarks of Greek rhetorical structure are absent; one is struck by the extent of antithesis and irony contained herein.[39]

Given its context in Jewish self-definition and symbolism, Philippians 3:3 stands as perhaps the most audacious statement in the letter: "For it is we who are the circumcision, who worship in the Spirit of God and boast in Christ Jesus and have no confidence in the flesh." Notice, however, that here Paul is not speaking of himself alone, but is including his Philippian partners (and perhaps all with whom he is in community) in contrast to others.[40] In this verse, Paul is not interested in engaging that notion of "hierarchy" in which he stands above or before his partners as a teacher; rather he is making a general statement rooted in his "primordial apprehension of reality" in which "confidence in the flesh" is, at best, worthless.

It is at this point that Paul, somewhat abruptly, shifts the focus to Paul, and Paul the teacher and "model" (3:17) comes to the fore. Paul wants it to be clear that he has "reason for confidence in the flesh" and "if anyone else has reason to be confident in the flesh, [Paul] has more" (3:4). According to Fortna, these verses are Paul's "most grandiose"; "he dares to enumerate the grounds for [his] confidence: validly circumcised, a member of God's Chosen People and of no mean part of it . . . , a pure Hebrew, . . . belonging to the most illustrious party as to loyalty to God's will."[41] And all the while that he is listing these attributes, suggests Fortna, Paul is "violating what he has just said" in 3:3.[42] Of course! Paul is well aware of that. Paul develops this impressive resume only to throw it away, in 3:8, "as so much garbage."[43] But why? Paul states, "in order that I may gain Christ" (3:9). And what is Paul left with? What does he have to show for himself

---

37. Ibid., 228.

38. Meeks, "Man from Heaven," 334.

39. As noted also by Fortna, "Egocentric Letter," 228: "The irony here is unmistakable, but perhaps not entirely apparent to Paul himself." Contrary to Fortna, I believe Paul is quite aware of what he is doing rhetorically.

40. See Fee, *Philippians*, 298. Ernst Lohmeyer comments that this "is the first time" in Philippians that Paul gathers himself and the Philippian community together under the common "we." *Der Brief an die Philipper*, Kritisch-exegetischer Kommentar über das Neue Testament (Göttingen: Vandenhoeck and Ruprecht, 1954; first pub. 1929) 127.

41. Fortna, "Egocentric Letter," 228.

42. Ibid., 234 n. 52.

43. Leander Keck, "The Quest for Paul's Pharisaism: Some Reflections," in *Justice and the Holy: Essays in Honor of Walter Harrelson*, ed. Douglas A. Knight and Peter J. Paris, Homage Series (Atlanta: Scholars Press, 1989) 164.

now? Meeks writes, "Paul as τύπος" is not a simple *Vorbild* . . . ; there is not some heroic virtue or set of cognitions that the Philippians ought to copy."[44] What sort of model, then, is Paul? And what is it that he is modeling?

Philippians 3:12 is a complicated sentence marked by an abundance and variety of verb forms (specifically, five verb forms, among which are exhibited three tenses, two voices, and two moods). That such is the case is particularly striking (and problematic!) because there is neither a noun nor any other substantive present within the sentence to function as a grammatical object. Paul writes (literally): "Not that I took[45] already or have been perfected already, but I am pursuing if even I might seize, inasmuch as also I was seized by Christ Jesus."

The sentence is framed by two aorists, one active and one passive, acting as the simple past tense to describe the nonoccurrence and occurrence which have brought Paul to his present "reality."[46] The nonoccurrence is described in the active voice, the occurrence in the passive: Paul has been "seized by Christ."

In this current "reality" Paul has "not been perfected." It has long been assumed in Pauline scholarship that in engaging this notion of "perfection" here, and again in 3:15, Paul is consciously adopting a "slogan"[47] from some group of opponents who consider themselves to be "perfect" (τέλειοι). Mixing sarcasm with irony, Paul as model Christian admits that he has not attained what others (claim to) have attained.

The significance of the missing object of 3:12 and, for that matter, 3:13a, is its very absence. In leaving the object out, Paul is engaging his Philippian partners in the pursuit in which he is currently engaged. In 3:13b–14 following the particle "but" (δέ), which contrasts that which he is about to describe with a notion of having already been seized (3:13a),[48] Paul discusses "one thing" (ἕν), a metaphorical athletic contest,[49] in which he casts himself as a runner who is "forgetting what lies behind" while at the same time undertaking to

---

44. Meeks, "Man from Heaven," 332.

45. Or, "received." Translation mine.

46. As per Scroggs's phrase, "primordial apprehension of reality."

47. "Schlagwort," Martin Dibelius, *An die Thessalonicher I, II; an die Philipper*, HNT 11 [3rd ed.] (Tübingen: J.C. B. Mohr [Paul Siebeck], 1937) 92; "Stichwort," P. Ewald, *Der Brief des Paulus an die Philipper*, Kommentar zum Neuen Testament, 11, 3rd ed, rev. G. Wohlenberg (Leipzig: A. Deichert, 1923).

48. See BAGD 171b for the use of δέ "to emphasize a contrast."

49. For similar descriptions and imagery, see 1 Cor 9:24–27; for further discussion of such passages as these, see Victor C. Pfitzner, *Paul and the Agon Motif: Traditional Athletic Imagery in the Pauline Literature* (Leiden: E. J. Brill, 1967).

"press on (διώκω) toward the . . . prize." The introductory participle, "forgetting," as well as main verb, "press on," indicate process and action. Even the modification/description of the prize (". . . of the upward [ἄνω] call of God in Christ Jesus") suggests action.[50] Paul as athlete is currently on the course and in the race; the "emphasis" is "on the pursuit of the prize itself."[51]

In 3:15, Paul again employs irony and sarcasm in his reference to "perfect ones" (τέλειοι).[52] What is problematic is the introduction of the object τοῦτο in both the first and second parts of this verse: Literally, "think this[53] . . . God will reveal this."[54] A glance ahead provides little help in providing a clear referent, since 3:16 itself includes two pronouns and no noun. A glance back to 3:14 (and, if one is inclined, prior verses) suggests Paul's rhetoric of pursuit as the content of "this."[55]

Paul closes out this section with a final command (3:16). Though there is little, if any, consensus on its precise meaning or even a suitable translation, commentators may agree that this is "the most difficult of all" verses in Philippians.[56] Despite its difficulty, however, the verse does yield important clues to the meaning of the chapter as a whole.

First, this is Paul's punch line, bringing to a conclusion the several verses which focus on himself and precede the call for imitation in 3:17. That he wants this sentence to be understood as such is evident

---

50. And may hearken back to the Christ hymn, 2:5–11.

51. Fee, *Philippians*, 346.

52. NRSV, "mature."

53. The use of "think" (φρονέω) is significant, particularly in light of Paul's introduction to the Christ hymn at Phil 2:5 where it involves consideration of the portrayal of (the action of) Christ as model. See Meeks, 333–34; Fee, 354–55; also Wm. S. Kurz, "Kenotic Imitation of Paul and of Christ in Philippians 2 and 3," in *Discipleship in the New Testament*, ed. F. F. Segovia, 123–26 (Philadelphia: Fortress Press, 1975).

54. Translation mine. The whole of 15b is, of course, problematic in its bald assertion that "God will reveal." In fairness to Fortna's charges of audacity and grandiosity, such an assertion seems, at the very least, overconfident. For example, if Paul is merely invoking God's aid here (so Ralph P. Martin, *Philippians*, NCB [Grand Rapids: Wm. B. Eerdmans, 1985] 141) then why does he state the revealing as a certainty? On the other hand, one does well to remember that Paul's own (spiritual) autobiography in light of Alan Segal's warning "the scholarly reticence to ascribe spiritual experience to Paul may be rooted in theological embarrassment with the nonrational aspects of the human soul. . . " (in *Paul the Convert: The Apostolate and Apostasy of Saul the Pharisee* [New Haven: Yale University Press, 1990], 12). Perhaps the contents of Phil 3:15b are born of an experience of . . . and humility before . . . the Divine, such as is recounted in Gal 1:15–16: "[God] was pleased to reveal (ἀποκαλύπτω) . . . to me" (NRSV).

55. The immediate antecedent of the pronouns in 3:15 is the noun + definite article in 3:14, "the prize" (τὸ βραβεῖον). Though a grammatically possible referent (a neuter, singular noun), it makes little sense here, except by extension, i.e., Paul's understanding of the self in pursuit of the prize. More plausible, if one must locate a precise referent, is the neuter, singular noun "one thing" in 3:13b (discussed above).

56. Gerald F. Hawthorne, *Philippians*, WBC 43 (Waco: Word Books, 1983) 157.

in the use of the adverb πλήν at the top of the verse.[57] The NRSV's use of "only" adequately captures Paul's use of this small, but significant, term. Second, as explained by Hawthorne, "the main verb of the sentence is really an infinitive, στοιχεῖν, used with the force of an emphatic imperative."[58] Ralph Martin's translation, "let us walk,"[59] or Fee's, "let us live up to,"[60] are preferable here to the NRSV's "hold fast." The verb assumes and calls for activity and movement. Particularly in a military context, which is very apt for the Philippians,[61] the word means "move in line"[62] or to "go in battle order."[63] Metaphorically, the contents of a call to battle (3:16) are quite pointedly a call to action.

The verb φθάνω, translated by the NRSV and others as "attain," is used four other times by Paul,[64] once in a context analogous to this one. In Romans 9:31, Paul's point is fairly clear: "But Israel, who did strive (διώκω) for the righteousness that is based on the law, did not succeed in fulfilling (φθάνω) the law." Like Paul himself in Philippians 3, the subject of this sentence "strives" or "presses on"; unlike Paul in Philippians 3, this subject does not succeed or attain. Romans 9:31 marks failure, where Philippians 3 announces success. But in what has Paul succeeded? Just what has Paul attained? According to Philippians 3:12-13, Paul has not "seized," nor does he "consider" (λογίζομαι) himself to have done so. Unlike the occurrence in Romans 9:31b, φθάνω has no definite object in 3:16a, only a neuter, singular pronoun. And, as noted above regarding the pronouns in 3:15, there is no clear antecedent. That which Paul has attained is, at best, unclear.

Such is Paul's final "reversal" in this sketch of himself as model. There is no thing nor status nor symbol which he embodies—none, that is, except for the recognition that he "has been seized by Christ Jesus" (3:12) and set upon a course (3:13b-14). There is, however, action

---

57. See BAGD for the description of usage as "breaking of a discussion and emphasizing what is important," 669b.
58. Hawthorne, 157, citing BDF, 389. Robertson 1092 notes that while instances of the imperatival or absolute infinitive are fairly rare in the NT, the form "flourishes in the Greek prose writers"; see Rom 12:15.
59. Martin, *Philippians*, 141.
60. Fee, *Philippians*, 352.
61. In his recent study, "Military Language and Metaphors in Philippians," Edgar Krentz shows both that "the history of Philippi suggests that military language was peculiarly appropriate for the Christians there" and that Paul engaged such a semantic field in Philippians. Unfortunately, Krentz does not comment on 3:16 in particular. In *Origins and Method: Towards a New Understanding of Judaism and Christianity. Essays in Honour of John C. Hurd*, ed. Bradley H. McLean, JSNTSS 86, (Sheffield: Sheffield Academic Press, 1993) 111.
62. LSJ 1647b.
63. LSJ (intermediate ed.) 747b.
64. 1 Thess 2:16, 4:15; 2 Cor 10:14, Rom 9:31.

described (3:14) and action called for (3:16b). Apparently that action is
the "that" which Paul and his partners have attained[65] and are to keep
engaging in.

One of the weightier assertions advanced by Fortna is that the
immature Paul of Philippians, with an "outlandish theology of
do-it-yourself resurrection," will give way in later letters to the Paul
who recognizes "the free gift of God" by which "anyone . . . who is
'in Christ' has died with him."[66] I wonder, however, if the Paul of
Philippians 3, a model of one who runs (3:14) or marches (3:16),
having been "seized by Christ Jesus," is not, in fact, consistent with
the (mature) Paul of later letters.

In Romans 6:4–5 the action word is "walk" ($\pi\epsilon\rho\iota\pi\alpha\tau\epsilon\omega$), a verb
commonly used in contexts of moral exhortation.[67] The "reality"
described in Romans 6 is much the same as that described in Philippians 3. The aorist passive "were buried," the subjunctive "might
walk," and the future "will . . . be united with [Christ]," suggest a
"reality" in which current human action is called for in light of both a
past action of Christ and a future fulfillment.[68] As in Philippians 3, so
in Romans 6, those for whom Christ's past action is relevant are
engaged in a process.

Scroggs's discussion of "transformation" or "world-switching" is
of help on this matter. The "world" or "reality" into which the convert
is ushered, says Scroggs, is

> a world where all people are equal because all are equally graced. In this
> new creation, the self is founded on the deepest perception that life is a
> pure gift, thus that all action is response to that gift.[69]

What Fortna opposes as an "outlandish theology of do-it-yourself
resurrection" is neither immature nor outlandish by comparison with—
nor is it inconsistent with—the later Paul who recognizes "the free gift
of God."[70] The Paul who models the forfeiture of confidence in the
flesh (3:3), the discarding of status and accomplishment (3:4–8), and
the attainment of process (3:16) is the Paul who means to act in

---

65. Lohmeyer, commenting on the "we" explicit in the verb form in 16a, writes that the
"stress" is on the "commonality of the 'walk'." Recently Fee comments more generally that it is
usual for Paul "to shift . . . to the inclusive first person plural whenever the point shifts to some
soteriological reality that includes him as well as his readers." Fee, *Philippians*, 298. See Fee,
360–61 for 3:16a in particular.

66. Fortna, "Egocentric Letter," 229.

67. And, indeed, used by Paul in Phil 3:17. As we have seen, the verbs in 3:14 and 3:16
are consistent with the athletic and military metaphorical contexts adopted by Paul in Philippians.

68. Contra Col 2:12, with its multiple aorist passive forms.

69. Scroggs, "The Theocentrism of Paul," 189.

70. Fortna's phrase; Fortna, "Egocentric Letter," 229.

response to the gift of God through Jesus Christ which has transformed him (and those whom he addresses, and all those with whom he is in partnership on behalf of the gospel) into a *new* "primordial apprehension of reality." And as for anything having to do with the *old* "primordial apprehension of reality," whatever it is, Paul's against it.

16

Honor and Shame in the Argument of Romans

Robert Jewett

Among New Testament theologians, our honoree has broken with tradition to become a leading proponent of incorporating insights from the social sciences. His lecture "The Sociological Interpretation of the New Testament: The Present State of Research"[1] at the 1978 meeting of the Studiorum Novi Testamenti Societas argued against the tendency to approach the theology of the early church "as if believers had minds and spirits unconnected with their individual and corporate bodies."[2] He concluded that this research showed "how the New Testament message is related to the everyday lives and society needs and contexts of real human beings, how the texts cannot be separated from social dynamic without truncating the reality of both speaker and reader."[3] This essay is an effort to carry these ideas forward, stimulated by the increasingly wide-ranging discussion of honor and shame in the Mediterranean world.[4]

On the basis of sociological, anthropological, and historical information, Bruce Malina has defined the ancient view of honor as "the value of a person in his or her own eyes . . . *plus* that person's

---

1. Published in *NTS* 26 (1979–80) 164–79; reprinted in R. Scroggs, *The Text and the Times: New Testament Essays for Today*, 46–68 (Minneapolis: Fortress, 1993).

2. Scroggs, *Text and the Times*, 49.

3. Ibid., 67–68.

4. See David D. Gilmore, ed., *Honor and Shame and the Unity of the Mediterranean* (Washington: American Anthropological Association, 1987); Bruce J. Malina, *The New Testament World: Insights from Cultural Anthropology* (Atlanta: Knox, 1981) 25–50; idem, *Christian Origins and Cultural Anthropology: Practical Models for Biblical Interpretation* (Atlanta: Knox, 1986); Jerome H. Neyrey, *Paul in Other Words: A Cultural Reading of His Letters* (Louisville: Westminster/John Knox, 1990); Victor H. Matthews and Don C. Benjamin, eds., *Honor and Shame in the World of the Bible*, *Semeia* 68 (1966); Robert Atkins, "Pauline Theology and Shame Affect: Reading a Social Location," *Listening* 31 (1996) 137–51.

value in the eyes of his or her social group. Honor is a claim to worth along with the social acknowledgement of worth."[5] In the competitive environment of the Mediterranean world, such honor was gained "by excelling over others in the social interaction that we shall call challenge and response."[6] This occurs only within persons of the same class, since superiority over those of lower status was assumed and did not have to be proven. The goal of a challenge, in arenas ranging from political power to religious reputation, was

> to usurp the reputation of another, to deprive another of his reputation. When the person challenged cannot or does not respond to the challenge posed by his equal, he loses his reputation in the eyes of the public. . . . Every social interaction that takes place outside one's family or outside one's circle of friends is perceived as a challenge to honor, a mutual attempt to acquire honor from one's social equal. . . . Anthropologists call it an *agonistic* culture.[7]

The honor-shame culture reflected in the New Testament, according to Malina, produced a personality type that was very different from modern, Western "individuals" whose self-identity is allegedly internal and self-directed. Mediterranean people had a "dyadic personality" (derived from the Greek word meaning "pair"), in that they understood themselves exclusively "in terms of what others perceive and feed back" to them.[8] This is visible in the New Testament, Malina contends, where people are defined by their family and cultural group: Paul speaks to Jews and Gentiles, Greeks and barbarians, not to individuals. This has an important bearing on biblical exegesis:

> If you were a student of psychology and were to evaluate the people presented in the New Testament, you would probably say that they were rigid and highly controlled personality types, or that they were fearful of others, or that they interacted in standardized and conventional ways almost all the time. . . . The whole point is that in this aspect of their culture, they are not like we are at all.[9]

The recent publication of *Portraits of Paul* by Bruce Malina and Jerome Neyrey advances this analysis by incorporating evidence in the Book of Acts and some of the Pauline letters.[10] Although important insights are developed about Paul's ethic, vocation, and personal

---

5. Malina, *New Testament World*, 27.
6. Ibid., 29.
7. Ibid., 32.
8. Ibid., 55.
9. Ibid., 59.
10. Bruce J. Malina and Jerome H. Neyrey, *Portraits of Paul: An Archeology of Ancient Personality* (Louisville: Westminster, 1996).

values, his theological argument, particularly in Romans, is hardly touched. The goal in this essay is to begin filling in this gap by examining the cultural resonance of the language and argument of the opening chapters of Romans. By taking the work of Malina, Neyrey, et alia in a heuristic manner, I want to investigate how early Christian recipients would have understood the language related to honor and shame that plays so prominent a role in this letter. I need to begin with the pathbreaking work of the Norwegian scholar Halvor Moxnes.[11]

INTERACTING WITH THE WORK
OF HALVOR MOXNES

In "Honour and Righteousness in Romans," Moxnes places the argument of the letter in the ancient cultural context of an "honour society" in which "recognition and approval from others" is central, which means that the "group is more important than the individual."[12] This contrasts with the dominant concern of Western theology and interpretation of Romans, "in which guilt and guilt-feeling predominate as a response to wrongdoing."[13] He notes that the word fields of honor and shame play important roles in the argument of Romans, with τιμή ("honor") in 2:7, 10; 9:21; 12:10; ἀτιμία ("dishonor") in 1:26; 9:21, ἀτιμάζω ("to dishonor") in 1:24; 2:23; ἀσχημοσύνη ("shameless") in 1:27; to ἐπαισχύνομαι ("be ashamed") in 1:16; 6:21; καταισχύνω ("put to shame") in 5:5; 9:33; 10:11; δόξα ("glory") in 1:23; 2:7, 10; 3:7, 23; 4:20; 5:2; 6:4; 8:18, 21; 9:4, 23; 11:36; 15:7; 16:27; δοξάζω in 1:21; 8:30; 11:30; 15:6, 9; ἔπαινος ("praise") in 2:29; 13:3; ἐπαινέω ("to praise") in 15:11; καύχημα ("boast") in 4:2; καύκησις ("boasting") in 3:27; 15:17; κανκόομαι ("to boast") in 2:17, 23; 5:2, 3, 11. This focus on honor and shame relates to the central purpose of the letter as Moxnes understands it, "to bring together believing Jews and non-Jews in one community."[14]

To these references, I would add the socially discriminatory categories that Moxnes overlooked such as "Greeks and barbarians, educated and uneducated" in 1:14, the twenty-eight appearances of the

---

11. See Halvor Moxnes, "Honour and Righteousness in Romans," *JSNT* 32 (1988) 61–77; "Honor, Shame, and the Outside World in Paul's Letter to the Romans," in *The Social World of Formative Christianity and Judaism: Essays in Tribute to Howard Clark Kee*, ed. Jacob Neusner et al., 207–18 (Philadelphia: Fortress, 1988); "Honor and Shame," *BTB* 23 (1993) 167–76.

12. "Honour and Righteousness in Romans," 63.

13. Ibid., 62.

14. Ibid., 64.

potentially shameful epithet "Gentiles"[15] and the categories "weak" and "strong" employed in 14:1-15:7. Even more prominent are the twenty-five references to social gestures of honor in the form of "welcome" and "greeting" that dominate the last three chapters. The word field of "righteousness/unrighteousness," which plays such a prominent role in the argument of Romans, is also closely related to Jewish and Greco-Roman concepts of honor and shame: δίκαιος ("righteous") appears seven times, δικαιοσύνη ("righteousness") thirty-four times, δικαιόω ("make righteous") fourteen times, δικαίωμα ("righteous decree") five times, δικαίωσις ("being made right") twice, ἀδικία ("unrighteousness") seven times, and ἄδικος ("unrighteous") once. When compared with the single allusion to pardon in Romans 3:25, it is clear that a mainstream has been confused for a minor current in the tradition of interpreting Romans.

Moxnes concentrated on two areas of characteristic concern in honor societies that he believes play a role in the letter: power structures and gender roles. Moxnes finds the link of power to honor acknowledged in Romans 13:1-7 where the power of the state is acknowledged, and Christians are called upon to be subject to it, to render honor that is due. Subordinates could also receive honor in the form of the "praise" from the ruler (13:3), which is "a technical term referring to a specific form of public recognition, for instance in the form of inscriptions, granted by rulers to clients, cities or citizens."[16] This recognition of the public sphere, in which honor and shame rule, stands in contrast with the critique of the society and its lifestyle in Romans 1 and 6 where glory is reserved exclusively for God and human desire to honor themselves leads to idolatrous bondage. Sexual shame is seen as the result of such idolatry. In Romans 6 the former life of the Roman Christians, prior to their conversion, is viewed as a life of shame (6:21) which stands in contrast to the "holiness" they now enjoy (6:19, 22). This results in a classic "two-kingdom" understanding of Romans, that "Paul accepted the system of honour operating on the public world of Greco-Roman society but rejected this society as shameful in the area of 'private life', gender roles and sexuality."[17]

---

15. In the recent study of ἔθνός by James M. Scott, *Paul and the Nations: The Old Testament and Jewish Background of Paul's Mission to the Nations with Special Reference to the Destination of Galatians* WUNT 84 (Tübingen: Mohr [Siebeck], 1995), the reversal of shameful status is submerged by a theological argument that Paul's usage is entirely dominated by prophetic expectations.

16. Moxnes, "Honour and Righteousness in Romans," 66.

17. Ibid., 67.

There are serious difficulties in this argument, caused by Moxnes's indebtedness to the traditional style of interpreting Romans 13 and by the failure to take the rhetorical structure of the letter into account. The contrast between Romans 1, 6 on the one hand and Romans 13 on the other is caused by taking the latter first and decontextualizing it in a traditional manner. This causes the "strong contrast between this acceptance of civic obligations in Romans 13 and the rejection of the outside world and its lifestyle in Romans 1 and 6."[18] If we were to follow the rhetorical development of the letter,[19] the contrast would disappear because the societal claims of honor are radically challenged in Romans 1, which shows that the perverse desire for honor results in a claimed apotheosis that challenges the honor of God and leads to human depravity. So the honor due to the state in Romans 13 is solely due to its being established by divine authority, and not at all due to the claims of honor and divinity by the state itself, which have already been shown to be perverse and dishonest. No state or ruler is to be honored for his own sake, according to this wording, which undercuts the Roman civic cult in a decisive manner.[20]

The contrast Moxnes draws between the public system of honor and the private sphere of "gender roles and sexuality"[21] is derived from the sexual references in Romans 1. But this is a false dichotomy, on several grounds. The area of sexual relations is not specifically related to holiness in Romans (as it is in 1 Thess 4:1–8); there is no sexual ethic advanced in Romans 12–16; and the social perversion of public life described in Romans 1 is not restricted to the private sphere. Moreover, holiness is more than "distinction and separateness from society at large"[22] as defined by Moxnes. It relates to a restoration of righteousness as ordained by the creator and perverted by the prideful actions of the human race. To privatize this is to reduce the impact of conversion to the sphere of individual conscience, leaving social relationships untouched. This is inconsistent with the rest of the argument of Romans, because Romans 6 makes it plain that Christians are freed from sin and bound to holy, righteous relationships that are spelled out in social terms relevant for house and tenement churches in chapters 12–16. Romans 8 clarifies the cosmic paradox of a community of faith

---

18. Ibid., 66.

19. See Jewett, "Following the Argument of Romans," *WW* 6 (1986) 382–89; rev. and expanded, in *The Romans Debate: Revised and Expanded Edition*, ed. Karl Donfried, 265–77 (Peabody: Hendrickson, 1991).

20. See Dieter Georgi, *Theocracy in Paul's Praxis and Theology*, trans. D. E. Green (Minneapolis: Fortress, 1991) 81–104.

21. Moxnes, "Honour and Righteousness in Romans," 67.

22. Ibid.

honored by the gift of the spirit and sonship and awaiting their future glorification while their disgraceful current sufferings participate in the groaning of the whole creation. Their honorable status is grounded in the "love of God in Christ Jesus our Lord" (Rom 8:39) which no social or cosmic power can successfully assail because it derives from a transcendent source rather than from the accidents of birth and achievement.

E. A. Judge helps us understand that Paul is reversing a broad cultural tradition that viewed the earning of honor as the only suitable goal for life. "It was held that the winning of honor was the only adequate reward for merit in public life. . . . It therefore became a prime and admired objective of public figures to enshrine themselves, by actually defining their own glory, in the undying memory of posterity" by publishing memorials of their accomplishments.[23] Most of the audience of Romans, whether in Rome or in Spain, were persons with no prospects of gaining such glory. In the hierarchical context of Roman society they would have been demeaned from birth on prejudicial grounds, not because of what they had done but because of their identity, whether it be racial, cultural, sexual, or religious. The rhetoric of shame in New Testament usage includes both shameful deeds and shameful status imposed by others.[24] In fact the most damaging form of shame is to internalize prejudicial assessments that persons or groups are worthless, that their lives are without significance. Most traditional theological readings of Romans concentrate on individual guilt and on the offering of forgiveness for failing to live up to the law. In contrast the thesis of this study is that there was much more explicit argument in this letter that offered an antidote to shameful status, conveying that in Christ's ministry, those held in contempt by society were raised to a position of righteousness and honor. A primary location where this thesis should be tested, from a rhetorical perspective, is the early part of Romans where the relationship with the audience is established and the basic theological argument first articulated.[25]

---

23. E. A. Judge, "The Conflict of Educational Aims in New Testament Thought," *Journal of Christian Education* 9 (1966) 38–39; he cites Sallust, *Bellum Jugurthinum* 85.26, "Reticence would only cause people to mistake modesty for a guilty conscience."

24. See A. Horstmann, "αἰσχύνομαι be ashamed," *EDNT* 1:42–43, which lifts up the public sense of persons "being put to shame" by others in contrast to the subjective meaning of "be ashamed" of what one has done, found especially in the use of ἐπαισχύνομαι.

25. See Jewett, "Following the Argument of Romans," *The Romans Debate*, 265–77, esp. 272–74; "Ecumenical Theology for the Sake of Mission: Rom 1:1–17 + 15:14–16:24," in *Pauline Theology*, vol. 3, ed. D. M. Hay and E. E. Johnson, eds., 3:89–108 (Minneapolis: Augsburg Fortress Press, 1995; volume actually published in 1996).

HONOR AND SHAME IN THE NARRATION AND THESIS
OF ROMANS IN 1:14–17

While Moxnes offers an innovative treatment of the "paradoxical identity of the Christians" in Romans 2–12, he does not explain how chapter 1 provides a critique of the Greco-Roman and Jewish systems of gaining honor. The narration (Rom 1:13–15) and *propositio*/thesis (Rom 1:16–17) sections that introduce the formal argumentation of Romans contain some remarkable references to honor and shame. In announcing his desire to visit Rome, Paul describes his hope to "reap some fruit also among you as among the rest of the Gentiles." This is the second reference in Romans to non-Jewish peoples by the epithet used by Jews to distinguish shameful non-Jews, ἐθνός ("Gentile").[26] The ethnically discriminatory potential of this formulation is enhanced by the next verse, which employs some of the most explicitly discriminatory language in the Pauline corpus: "Greeks and barbarians . . . wise and foolish" articulate the social boundaries of Greco-Roman culture in a thoroughly abusive manner. As studies of βάρβαρος by Dauge and others have shown,[27] this is the "N-word" in Greco-Roman culture. When paired with its ideological opposite, "Greeks," it denotes the violent, perverse, corrupt, uncivilized realm beyond and at times within the Roman Empire that threatens peace and security. Similarly, the terms σοφός ("wise") and ἀνόητος ("unwise/uneducated") depict the educational boundary between citizens of the empire and the shameful masses. But it is not just Paul's use of these epithets of honor and shame that jars the reader; he undercuts the moral premise of the Greco-Roman world in proclaiming his indebtedness to the shameful as well as to the honorable representatives of the antitheses. Only Käsemann among modern commentators catches the revolutionary implications of Paul's formulation: "all earthly barriers are relativized. . . . [A]s a messenger of the gospel he can uninhibitedly stride across the conventions and prejudices of the divided cosmos."[28]

---

26. See Ulrich Heckel's discussion of the pejorative use of "Gentile" in "Das Bild der Heiden und die Identität der Christen bei Paulus," in *Die Heiden. Juden, Christen und das Problem des Fremden*, ed. R. Feldmeier and U. Heckel, WUNT 70, 269–96 (Tübingen: Mohr [Siebeck], 1994), esp. 270–72. This is downplayed by Scott in *Paul and the Nations*.

27. Yves Albert Dauge, *Le Barbare. Recherches sur la conception romaine de la barbarie et de la civilisation*, Collection Latomus 176 (Brussels: Latomus, 1981) 393–810, showing that the term barbarian in Roman materials serves to depict outsiders as irrational, ferocious, warlike, alienated, chaotic, and in all respects the opposite of the civilized Roman.

28. Ernst Käsemann, *Commentary on Romans*, trans. G. W. Bromiley (Grand Rapids: Eerdmans, 1980) 20.

When the remarkable formulation of the narration is followed by the antithetical formulation "to the Jew first and also to the Greek" in the thesis concerning the righteousness of God in Romans 1:16-17, which reverses the claim of ethnic priority that was probably being expressed by the Gentile Christian majority in Rome,[29] the stage is set for redefining sin as an untruthful distortion of social systems in 1:18-32. The reference to not being "ashamed of the gospel" (1:16) sets the tone for the entire subsequent letter.[30] As one can see from the parallel text in 1 Corinthians 1:20-31, the gospel was innately shameful as far as Mediterranean cultures were concerned. The message about a messianic redeemer being crucified was a "stumbling block to Jews and foolishness to Gentiles." A divine self-revelation on an obscene cross seemed to demean God and overlook the honor and propriety of established religious traditions, both Jewish and Greco-Roman. Rather than apppealing to the honorable and righteous members of society, such a gospel seemed designed to appeal to the despised and the powerless. To use the words of 1 Corinthians once again, "God chose what is foolish in the world to shame the wise; God chose what is weak in the world to shame the strong. God chose what is low and despised in the world . . . so that no one might boast in the presence of God" (1 Cor 1:27-29). There were powerful social reasons why Paul should have been ashamed of this gospel; his claim not to be ashamed signals that a social and ideological revolution has been inaugurated by the gospel.

At the center of the thesis of Romans in 1:16-17 is the paradox of power, that in this shameful gospel that would seem to lack the capacity to prevail, the power of God is in fact revealed. The gospel *is* the "power of God," Paul contends, in that it shatters the unrighteous precedence given to the strong over the weak, the free and well-educated over slaves and the ill-educated, the Greeks and Romans over the barbarians. If what the world considers dishonorable has power, it will prevail and achieve a new form of honor for those who have not earned it, an honor consistent with divine righteousness. All who place their faith in this gospel will be set right, that is, be placed in the right relation to the most significant arena in which honor is dispensed: divine judgment. Thus the triumph of divine righteousness through the gospel of Christ crucified and resurrected is achieved by transforming the system in which shame and honor are dispensed.

---

29. See James C. Walters, *Ethnic Issues in Paul's Letter to the Romans* (Valley Forge: Trinity Press International, 1993) 68–79.

30. See the provocative study by Gregory M. Corrigan, "Paul's Shame for the Gospel," *BTB* 16 (1986) 23–27.

UNIVERSAL SIN AND THE DISTORTION OF
HONOR AND SHAME IN ROMANS 1:18-32

While Paul employs the standard arguments of Jewish apologists in denouncing pagan culture as wicked, idolatrous, impure, boastful, inclined toward dishonorable bodily relations, and driven by passion,[31] he extends the charge to "all impiety and unrighteousness of humans who by unrighteousness are suppressing the truth" (1:18). Despite a later reference to characteristically pagan failures (1:23), the formulation with "all" indicates that Paul wishes to insinuate that Jews as well as Romans, Greeks as well as barbarians, are being held responsible.[32] This eliminates the presumption of honor claimed by Jewish religionists in their controversies with Gentiles, who are viewed as inherently shameful. Any such system of honorific exemption from Adam's fall participates in the universal human attempt at "suppressing the truth," according to this verse. In claiming glory and wisdom for themselves, all humans participate in assaulting the glory of God (1:21-23), "venerating and worshipping the creature rather than the creator" (1:25) who alone deserves honor. It is this distortion of social systems prevalent in the ancient world, claiming glory for oneself or one's group, that leads to moral impurity and dishonor (1:24, 26). This in turn leads to the shameful moral chaos described in 1:29-31.

The opening word in the catalogue of evils (1:29-31), which is carefully organized on rhetorical principles for the sake of effective oral presentation,[33] is πεπληρωμένους ("having been made full"),[34] implying the divine deliverance to a social orientation incapable of doing the right thing.[35] The connection with the following word "all" and the reiteration of this motif with μεστούς ("full") later in the

---

31. See the classic study by Heinrich Daxer, *Römer 1.18-2.10 im Verhältnis zu spätjüdischen Lehrauffassung* (Naumburg: Patz'sche, 1914).

32. These details appear to be overlooked by commentators who construe 1:18-32 as a denunciation of pagans alone. Cranfield is closer to the goal of Paul's argument when he says in *Romans* (106): "So we understand these verses as the revelation of the gospel's judgment of all men, which lays bare not only the idolatry of ancient and modern paganism but also the idolatry ensconced in Israel, in the Church, and in the life of each believer." C. E. B. Cranfield, *A Critical and Exegetical Commentary on the Epistle to the Romans*, 2 vols., ICC (Edinburgh: T. & T. Clark, 1980). For a comprehensive argument that Paul attacks the wickedness of both Jews and Gentiles in this passage, see Rolf Dabelstein, *Die Beurteilung der "Heiden" bei Paulus* BEvT 14 (Bern and Frankfurt: Lang, 1981) 73-79.

33. While recognizing the rhetorical rationale of the catalogue, some scholars refer to the chaotic sequence of vices as symbolic of the chaos of evil itself; see Käsemann, *Romans*, 49.

34. Gerhard Delling, "πλήρη κτλ.," *TDNT* 6:291 shows that the term πληρόω ("fill") sometimes "implies that a man is completely controlled and stamped by the powers which fill him. . . . There is in the term a strong element of exclusiveness or totality."

35. See Leon Morris, *The Epistle to the Romans* (Grand Rapids: Eerdmans, 1988) 95: "*filled with* wickedness, showing that he does not think of them as half-hearted about their sin. They were wholly given over to it. Their exclusion of God left room for nothing else."

sentence indicates Paul's intention to create an exclusively shameful view of humankind, which eliminates any claims of honorable exemption. The literary model for Paul's catalogue is from Greco-Roman ethics, particularly in its Stoic form,[36] though Hellenistic Judaism, Qumran, and early rabbinicism developed such catalogues as well.[37] Paul's catalogue fuses elements from these several traditions in combining a comprehensive list of nine vices with a list of twelve kinds of evil persons. Emulating the Greek tradition of four cardinal vices that stand as the opposites of the cardinal virtues,[38] paralleled by the four passions in Stoicism,[39] Paul commences with four vices defined as broadly as possible by the term "all" which qualifies all four. Grammatically, the first four vices are subordinate to the participle "having been filled" in the accusative plural, which in turn stands in apposition to the accusative plural pronoun αὐτούς ("them") in 1:28. The next series of five vices is subordinate to the accusative plural μεστούς ("full"), which stands in apposition to the same pronoun "them" in 1:28. The same can be said of the rest of the vices, all twelve of which are accusative plurals standing in apposition to the same pronoun.[40] This means that in contrast to the Greek tradition, Paul makes no effort to base the first four vices in a theory of virtues or of the individual human psyche. Nor are the additional vices coordinated as derivative from a foundational group of four, as in the Greco-Roman catalogues.[41] The source of all twenty-one evils is the human race as a whole, dominated by the "unfitting mind." Here we have a social pathology that is oriented not to the character flaws of individuals or groups but to the collective experience of the human race since Adam's fall, now seen in the radical new light shed by the gospel. It undercuts in the most sweeping manner any potential claims of individual, group, or national exceptionalism. No group can claim a position of superi-

---

36. For general orientation, see R. Hauser, "Lasterkatalog," *HWP* 5:37–39, and Burton Scott Easton, "New Testament Ethical Lists," *JBL* 51 (1932) 1–12.

37. See esp. Ehrhard Kamlah, *Die Form der katalogischen Paranese im Neuen Testament* (Tübingen: Mohr–Siebeck, 1964) 39–175; Siegfried Wibbing, *Die Tugend- und Lasterkataloge im Neuen Testament und ihre Traditionsgeschichte unter besonderer Berücksichtigung der Qumran-Texte,* BZNW 25 (Berlin: Töpelmann, 1959) 14–78.

38. Wibbing, *Lasterkatalogue,* 15–17 lists ἀφροσύνη ("foolishness"), ἀκολασία ("intemperance"), ἀδικία ("wickedness"), and δειλία ("cowardice") as the cardinal evils, as found in Stobaeus, *ecl* 2.59, 4.20, only one of which is exactly replicated by Paul.

39. Wibbing, *Lasterkatalogue,* 17 lists ἐπιθυμία ("desire"), φόβος ("fear"), λύπη ("grief") and ἡδονή ("pleasure") as the four passions, according to Zeno in J. von Arnim, *Stoicorum veterum fragmenta* (Leipzig: Teubner, 1903) 3:382–83.

40. See Cranfield, *Romans,* 129; Heinrich August Wilhelm Meyer, *Critical and Exegetical Handbook to the Epistle to the Romans* (New York: Funk and Wagnalls, 1884) 95 suggests in contrast that the last seventeen vices are all in apposition to the participle πεπληρομένους.

41. See Wibbing, *Lasterkataloge,* 16–20.

ority with regard to honor. Pursuant to this aim, the twenty-one evils are drawn from Greek, Latin, and Jewish catalogues, no one of which tallies completely with Paul's scheme.[42] Paul's effort to find common ground between competitive cultural groups in Rome is eloquently expressed by the composite nature of his catalogue of evils.

It is the shocking exclusivity of evil that emerges most strongly from the catalogue of vices in 1:29–31, with the first four sources of evil resulting in the next five expressions of social pathology. Since the first four of the second series are joined by parechesis in the repetition of the "o" sounds, with $\phi\theta\acute{o}\nu o\nu$ $\phi\acute{o}\nu o\nu$ . . . $\delta\acute{o}\lambda o\nu$ making a particularly deadly wordplay, the fifth item $\kappa\alpha\kappa o\eta\theta\epsilon\acute{\iota}\alpha$ springs out of the series by rhyming with the preceding series of four vices all ending in $-\iota\alpha$. This not only serves to reinforce the link with the first series that had been forged by the repetition of the "filled" motif, but by breaking out of the traditional pattern of fours that are characteristic for Greco-Roman vice catalogues, it gives the impression that the series could go on and on, documenting *ad infinitum* the scope of social pathology since the fall. It is not just a few bad types that are in view here, the allegedly vicious enemies of Israel or Rome, for instance, or even the antagonists of the churches in Rome, but the entire human race. The social systems of honor and shame in the Greco-Roman world are revealed as suppressions of the truth by this argument. The competition for human honor that assaults the honor and glory of God leads to shameful behavior by the entire human race. Sin is therefore redefined to refer to the universal human involvement in distorted, prevaricating systems of honor and shame.

EQUALITY IN SIN AND RIGHTEOUSNESS THROUGH FAITH AS A REVERSAL OF SYSTEMS OF HONOR AND SHAME IN ROMANS 3:9–31

While the material in Romans 3 that claims universal involvement in sin is easy to correlate with 1:18–32, the links with ancient systems of shame and honor have not been noticed. The claim that "Jews as well as Greeks are all under sin" (3:9) is followed by a catena of scriptural citations that repeat no less than eight times that "no one" can claim honorable or righteous status or performance. Dunn observes that the Psalm citations at the beginning of this catena "presuppose an anti-

---

42. See esp. Daxer, *Römer*, 48–55; for similar assessments that do not proceed word by word through Paul's catalogue in 1:29–31, see Wibbing, *Lasterkataloge*, 86–108, and Hauser, "Lasterkatalog," 37–38.

thesis between the righteous (the faithful members of the covenant) and the unrighteous. The implication is that when that presupposition of favored status before God is set aside, the Scriptures serve as a condemnation of *all* humankind."[43] In the light of the parameters established in 1:14 and developed in 1:18–32, this undercuts the superiority claims of every system of gaining honor through performance or inherited status.

It follows that "from works of the law no flesh will be set right before God" (3:20). James Dunn has moved the discussion of this verse beyond the denunciation of Jewish law popularized by the interpretative tradition undergirded by the Reformation to what he has recently called "the function of the law as an identity factor, the social function of the law as marking out the people of the law in their distinctiveness." The problem is that "works of the law" served as an identity marker for those "whom God has chosen and will vindicate," providing a method of "maintaining his status within that people."[44] However, Dunn does not link these insights with the systems of gaining honor and avoiding shame in the Mediterranean world, which would allow a broader grasp of Paul's argument. It is not just the Jewish law that is in view here, but law as an identity marker for any culture. Σάρξ in this verse was not selected by Paul to expose "the equation of covenant membership with physical rite and national kinship,"[45] but because it includes the entirety of the human race. In the face of the impartial righteousness of God, no human system of competing for glory and honor can stand.

The climactic formulation in 3:23, that "all have sinned and fallen short of the glory of God" also has a bearing on the Jewish and Greco-Roman systems of shame and honor that has not been noticed. That Adam and Eve were originally intended to bear the glory of God, but lost it through the fall, is widely acknowledged. Adam's words in *Apocalypse of Moses* 20:2 are frequently cited: "Why have you done this to me and deprived me of my glory?"[46] But the use of the verb ὑστερεῖν has not been sufficiently explained, since an equivalent term

---

43. James D. G. Dunn, *Romans 1–8*, Word Biblical Commentary 38a (Dallas: Word, 1988) 145.

44. Ibid., 159.

45. Ibid., 160.

46. Dunn, *Romans*, 168 claims that Paul refers here *"both* to the glory lost in man's fall *and* to the glory that fallen man is failing to reach in consequence." Joseph A. Fitzmyer properly repudiates such a direct reference; it would be better to speak of the Jewish references (1QS 4:23; CD 3:20; 1QH 17:15; 3 *Apoc. Bar.* 4:16) to humans participating in the "glory of God" as general background of Paul's reference. Fitzmyer, *Romans: A New Translation with Introduction and Commentary* (New York: Doubleday, 1993) 347.

is not employed in any of the Jewish parallels. This is a comparative term relating to the failure to reach a goal, to be inferior to someone, to fail, to come short of something.[47] The basic connotation is that of "deficit, which consists either in remaining below the normal level, or in being behind others,"[48] hence placing one in a position of deserving shame. An important parallel in Pauline usage is 2 Corinthians 11:5; 12:11, "to be inferior to someone," used in connection with the competition between Paul and the superapostles.[49] To fall short is an honor issue; it resonates with the competition for honor within and between groups in the Greco-Roman world; and it echoes the wording of 1:18–32 in terms of refusing to grant honor to God by choosing to worship the creature rather than the creator. Despite the claims of Jews and Greeks to surpass each other in honor, and despite their typical claims that the other groups are shameful because of their lack of wisdom or moral conformity, Paul's claim is that *all* fall short of the transcendent standard of honor. Dunn comes close to seeing this issue: Paul "reduces the difference between Jew and Gentile to the same level of their common creatureliness."[50] If all persons and groups fall short of the ultimate standard of honor that they were intended to bear, i.e. "the glory of God," then none has a right to claim superiority or to place others in positions of inferiority.

Although it has not yet been articulated in Pauline research, so far as I know, to be "set right through a gift by his grace through the redemption that is in Christ Jesus" (3:24) could also be understood in terms of shame and honor. "Righteousness," "honor," and "glory" can be used as virtually synonymous terms, a point whose relevance can be grasped only if the traditional English translation for δικαιούμενοι, "being justified," is replaced with its more adequate verbal equivalent, "being set right." To be "set right" in the context of the "righteousness of God" (3:21), and with reference to humans who have fallen short of the "glory of God," is to have such glory and honor restored, not as an achievement but as a gift. This perspective follows up on Käsemann's contention about the "correspondence of δόξα and δικαιοσύνη τοῦ θεοῦ. . . . To put it more precisely, the δόξα τοῦ θεοῦ is δικαιοσύνη within the horizon of the restoration of paradisaical perfec-

---

47. See BAGD 849.
48. See Fréderic Godet, *Commentary on St. Paul's Epistle to the Romans*, trans. A. Cusin; rev. and ed. T. W. Chambers (New York: Funk & Wagnalls, 1883; repr. Grand Rapids: Kregel, 1977) 148.
49. Paul's word choice reflects common Greek usage as found in Plato *Rep.* 7.539E.
50. Dunn, *Romans*, 168.

tion, while conversely δικαιοσύνη is the divine δόξα within the horizon of controversy with the world."[51]

Paul is not suggesting that believers gain a comparative form of honor, so that they can continue to compete with others who remain shameful. Rather, in Christ they are given an honorable relationship that results in what 2 Corinthians 3:18 refers to as an actual trans-formation derived from the mirror image of Christ in which believers change "from one degree of glory to another." In being honored by God through Christ who died for all, the formerly shamed are integrated into the community of the saints where this transformation process occurs, under the Lordship of Christ. This could be correlated with the recent work of Stuhlmacher, Dunn, and Hays, stressing that the righteousness given to the converted Jews and Gentiles is understood "primarily in terms of the covenant relationship to God and membership within the covenant community."[52] Rather than the largely theological construct elaborated by biblical theologians, Paul has in mind a new social reality: within the community of the shamed made right by the death and resurrection of Christ, there is no longer the possibility of any "distinction" (Rom 3:22) in honor. Redefining the theological issue in terms of shame and honor avoids the pitfalls of the ethical theory of justification, that humans are made righteous so that they come to deserve divine approbation; it avoids the artificiality of imputed justification, in which believers are treated as righteous although they remain sinners; it avoids the narrow scope of forgiveness as acquittal from charges arising against individual sins, or the indivi-dual experience of relief from guilty conscience, which limits being set right through Christ to those whose problem is guilt; it moves past the existentialist limits of merely providing a new self-understanding for believers as accepted by God despite all evidence to the contrary; it takes account of the actual makeup of the audience of Romans, consist-ing largely of the urban underclass experiencing a wide range of deprivations deriving from shameful status.

Paul's crucial contention is that in Christ, rightful status is not achieved on the basis of any human effort. The threefold reference in Romans 3:24 to divine "grace," to the "gift," and to "redemption" through Christ makes it plain that no one gains this honorable, righteous status by outperforming others or by privilege of birth or

---

51. Käsemann, *Romans*, 95.

52. Richard B. Hays, "Justification," *ABD* 3:1131; see Peter Stuhlmacher, *Paul's Letter to the Romans. A Commentary*, trans. S. J. Hafemann (Louisville: Westminster/John Knox, 1994) 31.

wealth. In contrast to the hypercompetitive environment of the Greco-Roman world, including its Jewish component, this new status is granted by Christ only to those who have failed, to those whose shame is manifest. By its very nature, honor granted through grace alone eliminates the basis of human boasting, which Paul explicitly states in 3:27: "Where is the boast? It is excluded!" In Moxnes's words, the result is "to exclude false claims to honour."[53]

CONCLUSION

In Robin Scroggs's most widely read book, *Paul for a New Day*, he concurs with a premise of this paper, that

> justification is not to be equated with forgiveness for sin. . . . What Paul is describing is not simply an order, a world, in which people fail, are forgiven, and then try harder. Justification throws one into an entirely different order or world, which lives out of a totally different reality. There is, in fact, a kind of condemnation involved in the eschatological judgment as Paul sees it. It is not a condemnation of persons, but a condemnation of the reality which these persons had accepted as, somehow, ontologically true.[54]

The evaluative "reality" that the gospel overturns, I would now suggest, was the system of ascribing honor and designating shame that most groups in the Mediterranean world of the first century devised with various cultural forms.

The competitive center of the ancient systems of shame and honor was what Paul called "boasting," which poisoned relations not only between individuals and ethnic groups in the ancient world but also between the "weak" and "strong" in the congregations in Rome, as the later chapters go on to show. Such tensions have a profound theological implication, for as Romans 3:29–30 shows, boasting threatens the oneness of God. In his earlier study of this material, Halvor Moxnes showed that the doctrine of monotheism in Romans 3 addressed the "problem of divisions between Jews and non-Jews within Christian communities. . . . In this context, "God is one" served as an argument for the inclusion and co-existence of both Jews and non-Jews in the

---

53. Moxnes, "Honour and Righteousness in Romans," 71. Unfortunately Moxnes goes on to claim that "it is the particular boasting of the Jew, not something which is common to Jews and Gentiles, which Paul attacks. . . . Paul sees a direct connection between boasting and the Jewish Law." This overlooks the clear implication of the earlier argument of Romans, which makes it plain that all humans are involved in seeking honor that belongs to God alone, and that they all thereby forfeit their share of the "glory of God."

54. Robin Scroggs, *Paul for a New Day* (Philadelphia: Fortress, 1977) 18.

same community, on the basis of faith."[55] Moxnes pointed out that the argument in these verses concerning God as the God of the uncircumcised as well as the circumcised constitutes "a conscious effort to include" the less popular Jewish Christians in a hostile Gentile Christian majority in Rome. In sum, "The Confession that 'God is one' was meant to serve as a bond of unity between Christians."[56] Moxnes's more recent studies of honor and the analysis of this study may help to elucidate the link between monotheism and unity. As long as the competitive system of honor prevailed, claims of superior status entailed competing assertions of divine approbation. God was in effect divided up and reduced to a function of social systems. Unity and equality between groups and persons was possible only if the entire system of competing for honor was abandoned, following the logic of the gospel. Since Paul moves on to devote the final chapters of his letter to the question of mutual welcome and honor between competing groups in the Roman church, this theme clearly stands at the center of the theology and ethic of the letter. It deserves similar emphasis in contemporary efforts to articulate the theology of Paul's most important and influential writing.

---

55. Halvor Moxnes, *Theology in Conflict: Studies in Paul's Understanding of God in Romans* (Leiden: Brill, 1980) 223.
56. Moxnes, *Romans*, 224.

PART IV

INTERPRETING

THE NEW TESTAMENT

FOR A NEW DAY

17

Whither Critical New Testament Studies for a New Day?

Some Reflections on Luke 17:11–19

Daniel Patte

Luke 17:11–19 is a most appropriate text for this essay in honor of Robin Scroggs, especially when it is critically interpreted "for a new day." We too often neglect to give thanks for the work of colleagues, especially when we are indebted to them for freeing us to pursue interpretive tasks appropriate to ever-changing situations. Now is the time to stop, turn back, praise God, and thank Robin Scroggs for his scholarship and his transforming influence on me and many other interpreters of the New Testament.

Robin Scroggs and I never had the opportunity to work closely together. Yet I owe much to him. As I retrace my steps, I find myself at the time of my Th.D. exams at the Chicago Theological Seminary in the Center for Jewish-Christian Studies. The questions he raised in those circumstances remained with me. It was shortly after the publication of *The Last Adam*[1] and when the issues raised in *Paul for a New Day*[2] were already in his mind. He confirmed for me that critical New Testament studies should not conceive of early Christianity apart from formative Judaism, and taught me that we, biblical scholars, should not hesitate to allow hermeneutical questions to structure our exegetical endeavors. As a good teacher, Robin Scroggs exemplified this teaching in each of his publications, raising existential questions following Bultmann, then taking the lead and raising feminist, social,

---

1. Robin Scroggs, *The Last Adam: A Study in Pauline Anthropology* (Philadelphia: Fortress Press, 1966).

2. Robin Scroggs, *Paul for a New Day* (Philadelphia: Fortress Press, 1977).

and sexuality issues before they became popular topics in critical biblical studies. Thus, his work takes the form of "essays for today" that open new questions for exegetes: such were his essays on "Paul and the Eschatological Woman"[3] already in 1972, on homosexuality[4] in 1983, and more recently *The Text and the Times: New Testament Essays for Today*.[5] In sum, Robin Scroggs constantly keeps in front of us the question: Whither critical New Testament studies for a new day? Turning back and looking at my own trajectory I cannot but acknowledge how much I owe him for constantly reminding me that critical New Testament studies must ever be "for a new day." Indeed, I am surprised. Why did I not acknowledge earlier my indebtedness to him? Why did I wait so long to express my thanks? Luke 17:11–19 gives me an answer.

"Then one of them, when he saw that he was healed, turned back, praising God with a loud voice. He prostrated himself at Jesus' feet and thanked him" (Luke 17:15–16). In the present context, for me— *pro me*—the pertinent teaching is not a call to imitate Jesus, even though this passage and many others in the Gospel of Luke can certainly be read as offering Jesus as a model of discipleship. It is rather a call to imitate the grateful healed leper. More precisely, for me the teaching of this text is neither the revelation of a duty that I must perform by giving thanks to those to whom I am indebted, nor a call to become "like a Samaritan" (a "foreigner," ὁ ἀλλογενής, 17:18) in order to have the proper attitude toward God, Jesus, and people to whom I owe something. Rather Luke 17:11–19 teaches me that the problem that prevents people from giving thanks to those to whom they should be grateful is that they did not recognize that they have received a precious gift from them. Like the nine and unlike the one, I did not see that I was healed—freed from the stickiness of the status quo—and thus did not turn back and give thanks to Robin Scroggs, until I was prompted to stop and assess what he had contributed all along to me. Thus, for me—*pro me*—Luke 17:11–19 is a call to "faith" (17:19); a call to open my eyes and to recognize around me those whom God has sent as bearers of good gifts (cf. Acts 7:2–53), so that in a more timely fashion I might turn back and express my thanks to them, rather than doing so belatedly.

---

3. Robin Scroggs, "Paul and the Eschatological Woman," *JAAR* 40 (1972) 283–303.

4. Robin Scroggs, *The New Testament and Homosexuality: Contextual Background for Contemporary Debate* (Philadelphia: Fortress Press, 1983).

5. Robin Scroggs, *The Text and the Times: New Testament Essays for Today* (Minneapolis: Fortress Press, 1993).

A CRITICAL NEW TESTAMENT STUDY
THAT BRINGS TO CRITICAL UNDERSTANDING
A *PRO ME* INTERPRETATION

Does this personal note—a *pro me* interpretation of Luke 17:11–19— belong to a critical study of this text? Traditionally, it would not. I want to argue that it does. In the present case, one might think that it is merely an extravagant addition to a Festschrift essay. It is a sincere expression of gratitude. Yet, it is not an artificial addition to this essay. It is not required by the literary genre for a Festschrift. A few discrete signals, such as the use of the phrase "for a new day," or an epigraph should suffice to show that it is dedicated to Robin Scroggs. Rather, by introducing this critical study of Luke 17:11–19 with a *pro me* inter- pretation regarding the way in which this text helps me express my gratitude to Robin Scroggs, I already make one of the points I want to underscore in this essay. I observe that in practice, consciously or not, critical New Testament studies have always brought to critical understanding existing *pro me* (or *pro nobis*) interpretations. I simply want to suggest that exegetes should acknowledge this aspect of our practice by making explicit at the outset the *pro me/pro nobis* inter- pretation that our critical work seeks to refine and to elucidate. In sum, my expression of gratitude to Robin Scroggs also introduces my critical study of Luke 17:11–19 by presenting the *pro me* interpretation that I propose to bring to critical understanding in the rest of this essay. Some explanations of this suggestion are in order.

Whither critical New Testament studies? My point is that if they are to be "for a new day," as indeed they should be, such studies must acknowledge and make explicit the role of the interpreter in the inter- pretation. Usually, even though one is aware that no interpretation is presuppositionless, one seeks to elucidate preunderstandings and hermeneutical circles in an effort to free one's interpretation from them. Thus, in traditional practices, it seems that a critical study starts and ends with the text; a critical study seeks to establish what the text is and says—a one-dimensional, universally true interpretation—by striving to purify the interpretive process until it becomes transparent and thus invisible. By contrast, I want to argue that this is not what a critical study actually achieves. *Today*, in a time when post-Holocaust, feminist, African American, and postcolonial perspectives as well as rapid travel and communication make it impossible to ignore the role of religious, social, political, and cultural contexts in interpretations, we have to acknowledge that critical studies bring to critical understanding existing *pro me/pro nobis* interpretations. Whether acknowledged or not, *a critical New Testament study starts and ends with interpretations*. Since a text is always encountered as interpreted, and since any interpretation reflects the interpreter's interests, concerns, and perspectives, we should make "bringing to critical understanding a *pro me/pro nobis* interpretation" the explicit goal of our practice of critical biblical study.[6] This involves making explicit (a) the specificity of the choices this interpretation reflects, (b) the legitimacy, epistemology, and value judgments it involves, and (c) its conclusions about what the text is and says, about the teaching of the text to a specific audience, and about the relative value of (a teaching of) the text.[7] The results of such critical New Testament studies do not confront us with an imperative, "you must adopt the proposed interpretation," as traditional critical practices did, but with an ethical and religious question: "Why did you choose a given interpretation rather than another one?" Such a comparative and multidimensional practice of a critical New Testament study shows that readers have a real choice, because it elucidates the polysemy of the text, and thus makes clear that several interpretations are equally legitimate and plausible.

These suggestions can be illustrated through a rapid sketch of a critical study of Luke 17:11-19. It is appropriate to begin such a study by a *pro me* (or *pro nobis*) reading, such as the one I proposed above, and then to proceed to bring to critical understanding the interpretive process that led to the choice of this particular interpretation.

BRINGING TO CRITICAL UNDERSTANDING MY *PRO ME* INTERPRETATION OF LUKE 17:11-19

The process of bringing to critical understanding my *pro me* interpretation has already begun, when I clarified it above by contrasting it briefly with three other possible interpretations. These contrasts meant to signal that I have made a choice among several legitimate and plausible readings of this text. My choice reflects *value judgments* (i.e., for me at the present time this reading is better than others). These value judgments, moreover, presuppose that I have at least tenta-

---

6. As I have argued in *Ethics of Biblical Interpretation: A Re-evaluation* (Louisville, KY: Westminster/John Knox, 1995).

7. As I have explained and illustrated in *Discipleship According to the Sermon on the Mount: Four Legitimate Readings, Four Plausible Views of Discipleship, and Their Relative Values* (Valley Forge, PA: Trinity Press International, 1996). For a detailed discussion of critical biblical studies as bringing to critical understanding an existing interpretation, see especially pp. 1-28.

tively ascertained through implicit *epistemology judgments* that this teaching and the three others "make sense of the text" and through implicit *legitimacy judgments* that there is appropriate textual evidence for these four sets of conclusions regarding the teaching of the text. It does not take long to recognize the respective roles of these three kinds of judgments in each kind of interpretation.

1. Luke 17:11-19 as a Call to Recognize the Good Gifts Others Bring to Us from God

Value Judgment. As suggested, this interpretation has a greater value for me in the present situation, because of my sense that I should have thanked Robin Scroggs long ago and that my failure to do so was due to a lack of recognition of what I received from him. My value judgment is therefore closely linked with a concrete situation and my perception of it.[8] As a consequence I read this text as a call to become like the Samaritan by striving to overcome the blindness that prevents me from recognizing those to whom I owe so much and their gifts to me. When one notes that it is a matter of "faith" (Luke 17:19)—and not merely of self-consciousness—it becomes clear that this passage cannot be isolated from the rest of the Gospel of Luke. It is by receiving the gospel as a whole that one has faith.

Legitimacy Judgment. Even though my interpretation of Luke 17:11-19 as *a call to recognize* bearers of good gifts from God was certainly informed by my study of this Gospel and of the commentaries I happen to have read, my *pro me* interpretation was formulated without full awareness of the way in which it could be grounded in this specific passage. Yet, I was confident it would be, because the text says that one of the lepers returned "when he *saw* that he was healed" (ἰδὼν ὅτι ἰάθη, Luke 17:15). Reviewing my own work, I found that my structural exegetical studies of other passages of Luke and Acts had provided evidence for the conclusion that this Gospel seeks to overcome its readers' lack of recognition (lack of faith) of the present manifestations of the divine in Jesus (cf. Luke 24) as well as in other

---

8. It should be noted that this perception of the concrete situation is filtered by my basic convictions, here regarding what is good and bad in it, i.e., the specific thymic category concerning what is felt as euphoric and dysphoric that I spontaneously use. See A. J. Greimas and J. Courtès, *Semiotics and Language: An Analytical Dictionary*, trans. L. Crist, D. Patte, et al. (Bloomington: Indiana University Press, 1982) 346. On "convictions" and fundamental semantics see D. Patte, *The Religious Dimensions of Biblical Texts: Greimas's Structural Semiotics and Biblical Exegesis* (Atlanta: Scholars Press, 1990) 111-28.

people sent by God.[9] This structural exegetical reading involves paying close attention to the explicit narrative oppositions. Here we note as particularly significant that the text contrasts the "one who *saw*" he was healed with the nine others, who presumably did not recognize their healing right away. Aletti, with his narrative approach, reaches the same conclusion.[10] This is also the conclusion of Danker, even though he emphasizes the contrast between the one who has faith and the nine who do not by taking note of the literary genre of the passage—an aretological account that calls for the recognition of the deity or person who acts as a benefactor.[11] Fitzmyer reaches a similar conclusion on a very different basis. From his redaction-critical study he concludes that 17:11–19 is a pronouncement story to which Luke has added the concluding verse. "In adding v. 19, Luke has further related Jesus' pronouncement to faith and salvation. . . . The point in the story is, in the long run, the contrast between ingratitude and gratitude . . . but also between Jews and Samaritan, and above all between the miracle of healing and the eyes of faith. . . . The contrast stresses the seeing. . . . Jesus' words in v. 19 (the Lucan appendage) relate the Samaritan's 'seeing' further to faith and salvation."[12] In sum, each of these several critical methods provides adequate justification for viewing the "seeing/faith" of the healed leper who came back to thank Jesus as particularly significant in this text.

Epistemology Judgment. Then how should we conceive of the teaching of this text for its readers (now and originally)? I implied in my *pro me* interpretation that these verses make us aware of our lack of faith: our failure to recognize the good gifts that others have brought us from God. This makes sense when one performs a typological reading of the Gospel according to Luke. From this epistemological perspective, the Gospel provides for us the corrective lenses that allow us to see what God does around us, and thus to recognize those who bring God's gifts, to rejoice and glorify God, and also to thank God's servants for what they bring us. This is to say that my epistemological judgment also reflects my convictions about biblical authority: the

---

9. See my *Structural Exegesis for New Testament Critics* (Valley Forge, PA: Trinity Press International, 1996) 99–128, and on Luke 24, "Structural Criticism," in *To Each Its Own Meaning: An Introduction to Biblical Criticisms and Their Application*, ed. S. L. McKenzie and S. R. Haynes, 153–70 (Louisville, KY: Westminster/John Knox, 1993).

10. See the brief comment of Jean-Noël Aletti, *L'art de raconter Jésus Christ* (Paris: Seuil, 1989) 116.

11. Frederick W. Danker, *Jesus and the New Age: A Commentary on St. Luke's Gospel* (Philadelphia: Fortress, 1988) 289–91.

12. Joseph A. Fitzmyer, *The Gospel According to Luke X–XXIV: A New Translation with Introduction and Commentary*, AB 28A (New York: Doubleday, 1985) 1150–51.

Scriptures present types and promises that point toward their fulfillments in the present as well as in the future. From this perspective,
this story condemns me—I am like the nine who fail to see, rather than
like the one who sees. Yet it also calls me to faith. Similarly, for Aletti
this text is designed not so much to help the readers "see" but to raise
the question of their lack of recognition and its reasons.[13] Yet, for
Aletti, this is part of the subtle typological role of Luke's story as a
narrative that retells the story of Jesus even as it follows the traces of
his presence in the community of the believers/readers.[14] Along the
same line Fitzmyer suggests that this text makes sense when one views
faith as a "seeing" (that which is in front of us and is hidden except for
the eyes of faith) that enables one to turn (convert) and to glorify
God.[15]

Taking note of the value, legitimacy, and epistemology judgments
involved in my own interpretation is necessary for bringing it to critical understanding. But this is not sufficient. I also need to acknowledge
and make explicit that I repeatedly chose among equally legitimate and
plausible options, so as to clarify my reasons for choosing this interpretation. For this purpose I need to examine other interpretations with
the positive presupposition that, until proven otherwise, they are both
legitimate and plausible. This amounts to *reading with*[16] other people,
whoever they might be, even though their interpretations are different
from the one I chose for contextual reasons. The ongoing process of
reading with others and of noting the differences between our interpretations again and again confronts me with the question: Why did I
choose this interpretation rather than another one?

Actually, among the interpretations that have similar conclusions
about what the text says (as a result of their legitimacy judgments),
there is one, Danker's, which conceptualizes the teaching of the text
through an epistemology judgment that is different from mine. According to Danker, for Greco-Roman auditors who perceive this story as an

---

13. Aletti, *L'art de raconter*, 116.

14. Thus Aletti says regarding the Gospel of Luke as a whole: ". . . pour lui [Luc],
raconter Jésus Christ, 'tout ce qu'il a dit et fait,' c'est suivre les traces de sa présence jusque dans
la communauté qui s'en recommande." *L'art de raconter*, 215.

15. Fitzmyer, *The Gospel According to Luke X–XXIV*, 1151. This interpretation which
presupposes, I believe, prototypal categories rather than archetypal ones, concerns what Fitzmyer
calls Stage I of the gospel tradition (indeed the meaning of this saying as a saying of the historical
Jesus). Yet, he believes that in Stage III of the gospel tradition (as understood by Luke) πίστις in
v. 19 carries the connotation of "Christian faith" (1152), which he seems to understand in terms
of "archetypal" categories, that is, as Danker does (see below).

16. See Musa Dube and Gerald West, ed., *"Reading With": An Exploration of the Inter-
face between Critical and Ordinary Readings of the Bible. African Overtures.* Semeia 73 (Atlanta:
Scholars Press, 1996).

aretological account and thus identify as particularly significant the seeing/faith of the healed leper, this passage is an unmistakable call to acknowledge that "Jesus is God's unique gift." In other words, this seeing/faith is, for Danker, exclusively directed toward God's past intervention in Jesus and his ministry—and not beyond it, today. This conclusion makes as much sense as mine. My point is that Danker's conceptualization of the significant data in terms of his christocentric archetypal semantic categories is as plausible as Aletti's and my conceptualization of it in terms of typological prototypal semantic categories. Indeed, as suggested in note 15 above, Fitzmyer seems to use both conceptualizations, as he distinguishes between two stages of the gospel tradition. Thus, because of Danker's interpretation, I can recognize that my interpretation involves the use of specific epistemological categories; I read the text as a prototype rather than as an archetype. Reading the Scriptures as prototypes is reading them with the hope that God will do and already does what is impossible to human beings. The choice of these epistemological categories has important implications. For instance, as Elisabeth Schüssler Fiorenza underscores by making the distinction between archetype and prototype, this choice reflects a value judgment, which makes an interpretation appropriate or inappropriate from the perspective of a feminist hermeneutics of liberation,[17] and indeed of any hermeneutics that is concerned with the humanly insurmountable plight of oppressed people, whatever might be the nature of their oppression. This choice of interpretation also reflects my convictions about the Scriptures. While this choice challenges a view of Scripture as "unique" revelation (for me, a "dead letter"), it reflects a strong view of Scriptures as living Word of God that ever point toward new fulfillments of the promises of the gospel.[18]

In sum, the elucidation of the differences that separate my interpretation from that of Danker has sharpened my awareness of the choices I have made. I have progressed in the critical understanding of my interpretation, even as I acknowledge the plausibility of this other interpretation that I do not retain because of my value judgment which has now become apparent. Identifying the differences between other interpretations and mine becomes a fascinating quest for self-understanding and for the Word of God conveyed for us by Luke 17:11–19.

---

17. Elisabeth Schüssler Fiorenza, _In Memory of Her: A Feminist Theological Reconstruction of Christian Origins_ (New York: Crossroad, 1983) 26–36.

18. See my extended discussion of this point regarding my choice of an interpretation of the Sermon on the Mount in _Discipleship_, 362–67.

2. Luke 17:11-19 as a Model of Gratitude to Be Emulated: Another Reading That Further Clarifies Mine

Bultmann's interpretation helps me to recognize other choices that my interpretation involves and to assess their relative value.

Legitimacy Judgment. As form-critical scholars have argued, Luke 17:11-19 can be read as a pronouncement story—or, in Bultmann's words, a miracle story transformed into a biographical apophthegm—which "is a reminder of gratitude" through its focus on the pronouncement in 17:17-18.[19] In such a case, 17:19 is not taken as a pronouncement, but rather as the closing scene of the miracle story. The legitimacy of this conclusion about what the text is and says cannot be doubted; it is a reading focused upon the form of the story. The pronouncement, i.e., the teaching of the apophthegm, is to be found in 17:17-18: a reminder of the duty of gratitude.

Recognizing the legitimacy of this other type of interpretation shows that Aletti, Fitzmyer, and I have chosen to focus our interpretation on a specific dimension of the text. We view as particularly significant in this text not so much Jesus' pronouncements (as Bultmann does), but the overall narrative or thematic "transformation." This is what Fitzmyer says, even though he also speaks of pronouncements, when he underscores that "the point in the story" is ultimately "the contrast" between "the miracle of healing"—presented in the beginning of the story—and "the eyes of faith"—mentioned in the last clause of the passage.[20] This narrative transformation also becomes the focus of the interpretation when one pays close attention to the way in which Luke's story divides itself in narrative sub-units, as Aletti does.[21] Similarly, in retrospect I can recognize in my own interpretation that I spontaneously focused my interpretation on the "thematic transformation": what is most significant is the way in which the view of a situation is transformed by the end of the passage.[22] Here, the view of the situation of the ten lepers expressed in Luke 17:11-13—they are unclean, in need of the "mercy" of a master (ἐλέησον) and of

19. Rudolf Bultmann, *History of the Synoptic Tradition*, trans. J. Marsh (New York: Harper and Row, 1968) 56-57, 60, 220. See also Hans Dieter Betz, "The Cleansing of the Ten Lepers (Luke 17:11-19)" *JBL* 90 (1971) 314-28. Yet neither Dibelius nor Thiessen classifies Luke 17:11-19 as an apophthegm (or pronouncement story). See Martin Dibelius, *From Tradition to Gospel* (New York: Scribner's, 1935) 120; and Gerd Theissen, *The Miracle Stories of the Early Christian Tradition*, trans. F. McDonagh (Philadelphia: Fortress, 1983) 187.

20. See again Fitzmyer, *The Gospel According to Luke X–XXIV*, 1151.

21. See Aletti, *L'art de raconter*, 112-23.

22. This is the dimension of the text upon which I focus my interpretation of the entirety of Matthew in *The Gospel According to Matthew: A Structural Commentary on Matthew's Faith* (Valley Forge, PA: Trinity Press International, 1996).

cleansing—is transformed in 17:19, where we learn that the leper actually needed salvation by means of faith—by "seeing" what God had done for him through Jesus.

Epistemology Judgment. Bultmann's interpretation which is focused on Jesus' pronouncements as particularly significant is not only legitimate; it also makes sense. According to his interpretation, the teaching of the text is a reminder of the duty of gratitude that Jesus' followers are to implement in their lives. This understanding of the teaching of the text makes sense if one envisions readers who are already believers ("have faith" in an undetermined sense) and for whom the Samaritan leper can be a model of behavior to be emulated. Such conclusions can easily be justified. For instance, the prologue (Luke 1:1–4) can be read as a sign that the implied readers are Christian believers.

Recognizing the plausibility of Bultmann's conclusions about the teaching of the text clarifies that Fitzmyer, Aletti, and I have made sense of the teaching of the text in a very different way. This different epistemological judgment is due in part to our respective ways of envisioning those to whom this teaching is addressed. By underscoring that the teaching of Luke 17:11–19 is a call to faith/recognition of the good gifts brought by people from God, we presuppose readers who lack appropriate faith, rather than readers who have faith. Both possibilities are equally plausible, in the sense that among Luke's actual readers there certainly are people who belong to each of these two groups, but also in the sense that while the implied readers are clearly "Christian" believers Luke might still see them as people whose faith needed to be strengthened. In other words, as interpreters we actually have a choice concerning the way in which the audience is to be envisioned.

These divergent epistemological judgments also reflect contrasting conceptions of the basic problem that needs to be overcome. In this interpretation Bultmann presupposes that what prevents people from doing good (here from expressing gratitude) is a lack of knowledge of their duty (or eventually, a lack of motivation). Thus, the fitting teaching of the text is to show readers what is their duty (and to motivate them to do it). By contrast, Fitzmyer, Aletti, and I presuppose that the basic problem the text seeks to address is a lack of faith, that is, a lack of seeing what are the good things that other people provide for us in the name of God.[23] Thus, in our respective interpretations, we have

---

23. "La non-reconnaissance et ses raisons" as Aletti puts it, *L'art de raconter*, 116.

chosen to make sense of the teaching of the text with very different semantic categories, categories which, though different, are equally appropriate alternatives.

Value Judgment. The interpretation proposed by Bultmann and the legitimacy and epistemology judgments it involves reflect a value judgment based upon his basic convictions as well as his interests and concerns. For some reasons, Bultmann perceived this teaching as valuable. If I were to investigate Bultmann's value judgment I would need to discuss (and second-guess!) his motivations for pursuing the study of the "history of the synoptic tradition" in the overall context of his hermeneutical quest—something which is much beyond the scope of this short essay.[24] Yet without going into such a detailed study, the preceding observations have the effect of elucidating characteristics of the value judgment involved in the choice of interpretation I made together with Fitzmyer and Aletti. Speaking for myself, it becomes clear that I adopted the preceding reading because it fits my convictions concerning the basic human predicament. Contrary to many contemporary (usually conservative Protestant) interpreters of Luke, for whom the basic human predicament is a lack of knowledge of the will of God, including our duty of gratitude, for me the basic human predicament is related to our failure to recognize the manifestations of God in our present. Thus, while for these contemporary interpreters Bultmann's interpretation of Luke 17:11–19 is readily acceptable, *for me* this interpretation is *useless and valueless*, because it emphasizes something that, especially today, Luke's readers do not really need to hear.

In sum, I can recognize one of my very fundamental reasons for not choosing Bultmann's reading; for me, it is valueless. Conversely, my choice of the reading which emphasizes a call to have a faith like the Samaritan leper reflects my perception that this reading is more valuable from the perspective of my convictions. My convictions that human beings constantly lack faith/seeing were reinforced by the present situation in which I discover that I have failed to express in a timely fashion my gratitude to Robin Scroggs because, like the nine healed lepers, I failed to recognize the gifts that I received through the agency of someone intervening in my life in the name of God. I lacked faith. The most forceful reminders of the duty of gratitude (Bultmann's

---

24. See for instance, the book that Bultmann himself viewed as a remarkable presentation of the "intention of [his] theological work" as he expresses in his preface to André Malet, *Mythos et Logos: La Pensée de Rudolf Bultmann* (Geneva: Labor et Fides, 1962). See also René Marlé, *Bultmann and Christian Faith*, trans. Theodore DuBois (Westminster, MD: Newman Press, 1968).

interpretation) do not help me to be grateful if I do not recognize that I have reasons for being grateful! A call to faith might help me to be grateful in a timely manner in the future.

As I encounter other readings of Luke 17:11–19, the characteristics of my own interpretation and the choices it involves become more apparent. Let us consider another set of interpretations, which at first sight is much closer to mine.

3. Luke 17:11–19 as a Call to Become like a Samaritan in Order to Be Faithful and Grateful

Legitimacy Judgment. Several interpreters conclude that the emphatic identification by the narrator of the grateful healed leper as a "Samaritan" (17:16b, καὶ αὐτὸς ἦν Σαμαρίτης) and as a "foreigner" by Jesus (17:18, "except this foreigner?" εἰ μὴ ὁ ἀλλογενὴς οὗτος;) is the most significant feature of Luke 17:11–19. Such are Tannehill's[25] and Meynet's[26] interpretations. Instead of finding the most significant features of the text in the narrative or thematic transformation represented by this story (Aletti, Fitzmyer, Danker, and I), or in the form of the text as pronouncement story (Bultmann, Betz), Tannehill finds it in what he calls the "controlling images" that "repeatedly asserted themselves in the process of writing" and "control what readers will find in the text."[27] Similarly, Meynet finds as particularly significant the rhetorical dimensions of the text. He reaches conclusions that are comparable to those of Tannehill because his rhetorical analysis is focused upon the figures, including both tropes and stylistic figures (of the *elocutio* or of the *ornatus*) constructed and emphasized by the text.[28] Thus, Tannehill and Meynet show me that I could have selected as a focus for my interpretation still another of its textual dimensions, namely its (rhetorical) figures. Why did I not choose this dimension?

Epistemology Judgment. Tannehill makes sense of the text by combining this emphatic identification of the grateful leper as a

---

25. Robert C. Tannehill, *The Narrative Unity of Luke–Acts: A Literary Interpretation. Volume One: The Gospel According to Luke*, Foundations & Facets, New Testament (Philadelphia: Fortress, 1986) 118–20.

26. Roland Meynet, *L'Évangile selon Saint Luc: analyse rhétorique, Volume 2, Commentaire* (Paris: Cerf, 1988) 171.

27. Tannehill, *The Narrative Unity of Luke–Acts*, 3–4.

28. Meynet, *L'Évangile selon Saint Luc*, 9–11. By reading Luke 17:11–19 as a transformation of Mark 1:40–45, Theissen studies how Luke "shaped" the story and ends up focusing on the same dimension of the text—the figure of the Samaritan as foreigner—that Luke constructed. See Theissen, *The Miracle Stories*, 187.

Samaritan with Bultmann's interpretation which reads the text as a model of gratitude to be emulated. Yet this model is not in itself the main teaching of the text. Rather, according to Tannehill's interpretation, the text presupposes readers who would regard as appropriate the healed leper's expression of gratitude, but are surprised that it is a Samaritan who exhibits this good behavior, while the other healed lepers, presumably Jewish, fail to exhibit it. In sum, the teaching of this text is that "the scene jars the stereotypes of readers or hearers of Jewish background." This passage attacks stereotypes and prejudices, by presenting the despised Samaritan as the only one among the ten cleansed lepers who is grateful, has faith and salvation.[29] Thus, the teaching of the text is equivalent to the injunction, "give up your stereotypes and prejudices."

Meynet makes sense of the same data in a slightly different way by combining the focus on the figure of the Samaritan as foreigner with Aletti's, Fitzmyer's, and my interpretation which reads the text as a call to faith/seeing. Then the teaching of the text is that the only one who has faith is a Samaritan, a non-Jew, a despised heretic; and more generally, that true faith is found among people such as the healed leper who was a Samaritan and not among the Jews.[30]

Still another interpretation was given to me by Philippine students of Union Theological Seminary (Dasmariñas, Philippines) who made sense of the same data by underscoring that the teaching of the text is that being a Samaritan, a foreigner, is a condition for having faith/seeing, because in such a case one is readily aware of the good things one receives from others. This is so because receiving these good things is a matter of survival for people such as the Samaritan, by contrast with people who can rely on powerful institutions—be they economic, political, or religious institutions. Thus the call to faith/seeing is also a call to become like a Samaritan, to be as free from the institution (represented by the priests, Luke 17:14) as the Samaritan was, in turning away from it so as to express his gratitude to his benefactor.

---

29. "His [the one leper's] behavior would be regarded as appropriate by most Christian readers." Tannehill, *The Narrative Unity of Luke–Acts,* 118–19.

30. "Le seul qui proclame ainsi sa foi, qui va jusqu'au bout du chemin en revenant vers Jésus et vers Dieu est un samaritain; il n'est pas juif, il est hérétique, encore plus méprisé que les étrangers. Une fois de plus, c'est le pire de tous, lépreux guéri mais pas encore reconnu comme tel, samaritain honni, dont la foi est plus grande que celle des juifs." Meynet, *L'Évangile selon Saint Luc,* 171. This is also the teaching which could (and possibly, would necessarily) follow from identifying the nature of the text as the outcome of a reshaping of the story resulting from "the switch to a mission to the Gentiles and inner dissociation from the Temple" as Theissen says, *The Miracle Stories,* 187.

Value Judgment. Why was I not affected by this powerful figurative dimension of the text? Why didn't I choose any of these three teachings? One possible reason is that this figurative interpretation easily becomes a teaching that I loathe, namely an anti-Jewish or even anti-Semitic teaching, as becomes clear in Meynet's commentary. Yet I do not have this problem with the two other conceptualizations of the teaching of this dimension of the text. I did not adopt Tannehill's interpretation for the same reasons that I did not adopt Bultmann's: such injunctions do not address the actual problem with which I and others (from my point of view) are confronted, and therefore are valueless for me.

But why didn't I adopt the Philippine students' interpretation as my *pro me* interpretation? It is not because I find it difficult to understand; indeed, it readily makes sense to me. In other contexts, I have chosen similar interpretations of other texts.[31] It is not therefore a matter of limitations regarding epistemological categories available in North American and European cultures. Furthermore, it is not because I find this interpretation loathsome or even simply useless; on the contrary, I find it quite valuable, now that I reflect on it. Yet in the context of reflections on what I owe to Robin Scroggs, while I was ready to acknowledge that I failed to express my gratitude to him in a timely manner, I did not feel the need to explore further the reasons for this failure. Is it not sufficient to have the scriptural text (Luke 17:11–19) as a prototype to help me recognize my failure to be grateful in a timely manner, in the same way that the prompting of friends and colleagues of Robin Scroggs was sufficient to help me become aware of what I owe to him? Possibly. But the Philippine students' interpretation challenges the appropriateness of the value judgment implied in my *pro me* interpretation. For these students, their reading is quite valuable, because they see themselves in the role of the despised Samaritan. Colonialism has made out of them foreigners in their own country; they are people who are readily aware of the truly good things they receive from others since they cannot truly rely on any institution, tainted as they are by colonialism. Thus such an affirmation of the Samaritan as a prototype of faithfulness is a valuable affirmation of their faithfulness. For me, the situation is different, since this teaching would become a call to become a "Samaritan"—a call to forsake my reliance on institutions. Did I subconsciously turn away from this inter-

---

31. See my interpretation of the parable of the Good Samaritan in my *Structural Exegesis for New Testament Critics*, 99–118. At any rate, I knew the Philippine students' interpretation before developing my *pro me* interpretation.

pretation, then, because I found it too costly? Is this really what is best for me?

WHITHER CRITICAL NEW TESTAMENT STUDIES? BRINGING TO CRITICAL UNDERSTANDING EXISTING INTERPRETATIONS AS A DISCOVERY PROCESS

The bringing to critical understanding of my *pro me* interpretation through its comparison with the preceding interpretations has the effect of clarifying the choices I have made among equally legitimate and plausible options, but also, in the last case, of questioning the value of my choice. Whither critical New Testament studies? Such results are, I propose, those that our critical studies should pursue. This is an on-going process that involves self-consciously seeking to bring to critical understanding our *pro me/pro nobis* interpretations, by analyzing them along with other existing interpretations to which we want to compare our own. In this way we become more and more aware of the charac-teristics of our own interpretation—a fascinating discovery process.

Negatively, this proposal means that we should not conceive of the goal of our critical exegetical task as the production of new interpreta-tions. Does this mean that critical New Testament studies would lose its creative edge? It would if the existing interpretations that we are to bring to critical understanding were exclusively *scholarly* interpreta-tions. But as the last example already suggests, we can and should include in our critical studies all the interpretations we encounter, espe-cially including those of our students and the faith interpretations of believers in various cultural contexts. *Reading with* these interpreters, one is constantly surprised by new insights and perspectives, and soon one has to wonder: Why would I seek to produce still another inter-pretation? Have I already exhausted the rich mine of interpretations that people bring to me as a gift for which I should be thankful (Luke 17:15–16)?

Another interpretation of Luke 17:11–19 that the Philippine stu-dents shared with me at Dasmariñas brought this point home for me.

To my puzzlement, they exclaimed that after all this text was simply about *utang na loob*. They soon explained to me that they referred to "the sense of indebtedness" that is a central feature of their cultures in the Philippines because it is the cement that holds together their society at all its levels. They explained: we have *utang na loob* toward our parents, our neighbors in the village, the authorities in it, because they have done and are doing so many things for us, from the time of our childhood. This means that we have the duty to express our gratitude toward them, by respecting them, offering them gifts, doing things for them, and taking care of them in time of need. Thus, *utang na loob* weaves a web of social relations that hold communities together and ensure that the needy are taken care of. One of the teachings of Luke 17:11–19 for Philippine people is, therefore, that this biblical text reaffirms a central feature of the original Philippine cultures as conforming to God's will and the gospel.

But *utang na loob* also is a problem and a source of many evil practices. Because of the strong sense of indebtedness, people feel they must do whatever a person to whom they are indebted asks them to do. There is no need to describe here all the abuses that are committed in the name of *utang na loob*, such as the chief of a village who demands exorbitant gifts from the villagers, or the colonialist authorities (be they political, economic, cultural, or religious) who exploit Philippine people after giving them a sense of indebtedness. Against this background the students at Dasmariñas quickly noted that Luke 17:11–19 offered a powerful teaching regarding the way in which these abuses can be avoided in the Christian communities and by Christians in the daily life. It is a matter of following the model offered by Jesus in this text.

Indeed, Jesus accepts the healed leper's expression of gratitude and praises him for it (Luke 17:17–18). But he does not stop here. At this point Jesus could have asked anything from the healed leper, who owed him his health (and indeed a place in society). He could have said to him: "Follow me," as he said to Levi (Luke 5:27). Like Levi, the healed leper would have had no choice but to leave everything and follow him and indeed, out of his sense of indebtedness to Jesus, to become Jesus' slave rather than a disciple. Yet Jesus does not tell the healed leper, "Follow me," but rather "Get up and go on your way" (17:19a). He frees the healed leper from his indebtedness. Furthermore, he adds, "your faith has made you well" (17:19b), which amounts to saying: "You are not as indebted to me as you may think. Yes, I was instrumental in your healing, and you were right in expressing your gratitude, but it is really your faith that made you well." In sum, Jesus further frees the healed leper of his sense of obligation toward him.

The value of this reading in the Philippine context is clear. But, one might wonder, does this amount to projecting upon the text something that is foreign to it? *Reading with* these Philippine students entails presupposing until proven otherwise that their reading is legitimate and plausible. Thus, one would need at this point to proceed to a detailed research project seeking to verify the legitimacy and plausibility of this interpretation. It is easy to recognize that taking Jesus as a model of discipleship is a perfectly legitimate way of reading Luke 17:11–19 along with many other passages of this Gospel. Here Jesus offers a model of the way in which we should deal with people who are indebted to us. But is it plausible (an appropriate epistemology judgment) to interpret this text in terms of the epistemological categories provided by the Philippine concept of *utang na loob*? Will not these categories be foreign to the text and betray it? The counter question could be: Which interpretation does not involve anachronistic epistemological categories? Yet a direct answer could be that the concept of *utang na loob* might not be as foreign to Luke and the New Testament as it first seems. An anthropological study of New Testament and of Hellenistic texts would be necessary to provide an answer. It is enough to say here that this concept seems to be directly expressed in the preceding verses, where we read "So you also, when you have done all that you were ordered to do, say, 'We are worthless slaves; we have done only what we ought to have done!'" (Δοῦλοι ἀχρεῖοί ἐσμεν, ὅ ὠφείλομεν ποιῆσαι πεποιήκαμεν, 17:10). The sense of duty (of "what we ought to do") is also a sense of indebtedness (the first meaning of the verb).

Whither critical New Testament studies? Geographically, to the Philippines and to all the cultural contexts of the world, including here at home (wherever home might be). This is where the future of critical New Testament studies is, in unexpected interpretations brought to us by all readers. Indeed, we should express our gratitude to them, by taking seriously their interpretations, and by *reading with* them.

18

Religious and Theological Studies as Religious Criticism

A Future for Biblical Studies

Vincent L. Wimbush

I

In this essay I do not propose to discuss in general "the crisis" facing religious studies, theological education, or biblical studies. I agree that all three arenas are—and have been for as long as I have been involved with them—in crisis. However, the term "crisis" means different things to different critics, institutions, and constituencies and has inspired different and conflicting proposals.[1] I propose instead to focus primarily upon *academic doctoral* programs in theological and religious studies, the former housed primarily in theological seminaries, the latter in humanities programs in universities. There are three major reasons for such a focus in this essay.

This essay is a revision of a paper that was commissioned by Auburn Theological Seminary's Center for the Study of Theological Education in connection with the conversations that were a part of the Center's Consultation on Doctoral Programs in Theological Studies. Although I would not claim that he would be in agreement with all that is argued in the essay, because of our six-year close personal and working relationship supervising the doctoral programs in New Testament and Christian Origins at Union Theological Seminary and in the Religion Department at Columbia University, and because of the conversations, debates, experiments, and proposals inspired by the relationship, it is fitting that this essay be included in this collection in honor of my friend and colleague Robin Scroggs.

1. See *Shifting Boundaries: Contextual Approaches to the Structure of Theological Education*, ed. Barbara G. Wheeler and Edward Farley (Louisville: Westminster/John Knox Press, 1991), for the latest collection of essays on theological education. Happily, it is a collection that is more than hand-wringing. There are several different provocative statements and proposals. Mark K. Taylor's essay, in particular, anticipated some of my arguments below, although he focused solely on professional theological education. As for religious studies, a number of books have appeared in recent years that attempt to address the crises and propose some solutions. See the very thoughtful review essay of some recent provocative books by Catherine Bell, "Modernism and Postmodernism in the Study of Religion," *Religious Studies Review* 22, no. 3 (July 1996) 179–90.

First, because of my now almost fifteen-year-long involvement in both religious studies (as a part of humanities studies division in a graduate school and university) and theology curricula (as part of two graduate theological schools' offerings), I am constantly forced to evaluate the challenges facing academic doctoral programs in these spheres. As a forty-something, midcareer scholar who has had to attempt to meet the demands of both professional theological schools and departments of religious studies, I can offer some perspective on the presuppositions, the character, and the challenges of both programs.

Second, from my work within the field of biblical studies, an area of specialization that within the last decade has undergone little self-critical discussion, I can offer some different, if not precisely field-representative, views. I say "different" because—given my ethnic background, but more important, given my self-chosen stance within the guild—it can hardly be said of me that I represent the typical biblical scholar or that my scholarship in its total effect represents "consensus" biblical scholarship in North America. It is important that certain heretofore not widely heard voices join the debate about the challenges facing academic programs in theological and religious studies. Little reform can be accomplished in theology and religious studies without a hearing of those voices that represent the probable future of the guild.

Third, my involvement in both professional and academic doctoral programs during the last several years leads me to argue that an important factor in the current crisis facing theological education has to do with those programs that are the primary suppliers of faculty personnel in both professional schools of theology and in college and university religious studies programs. Surely, these programs are highly influential in the setting of program standards, as well as in determining the professional and personal orientations of faculty.

Given the character and agenda of doctoral study in theology and religious studies for *our times*, how can theological education or religious studies be other than in or near crisis? If doctoral studies in theology and religious studies are without a clear focus, without consensus in terms of structure, requirements, and even nomenclature, how can professional degree programs, now sensitive to the need to be both academically respectable and attuned to the needs of religious professionals, be otherwise? And, given the appointment to teaching posts of scholars who have been socialized in such worlds, how can religious studies programs and theological schools realize any shared purposes or coherences of structure? Doctoral programs in the different fields in religious and theological studies have at least during the last fifteen years been almost pathetically silent about the structure and politics of disciplines and fields. How, then, can we avoid facing the challenge of a rethinking of such programs for our times and the times to come?

For these reasons, this essay will focus on academic doctoral programs in religious and theological studies, with biblical studies as the primary exemplum. Ultimately, it seems to me, a different ideological orientation and *structural reconfiguration* of such programs is required. I am not capable of offering so much in this paper, but I hope to offer pointers in the right direction. Before these pointers can be offered, however, an assessment of the current situations and challenges facing the culture in general and academic doctoral programs in theological and religious studies in particular, will be set forth. This is imperative because part of the problem has to do with the lack of awareness in current dominant programs of their own culture-specific presuppositions, assumptions, and orientations. I have reached the point at which it is impossible for me to begin thinking about any part of religious and theological studies—including biblical studies, that notorious metacultural field in religious and theological studies whose methods and argumentation are still assumed and claimed by many to be universally translatable!—without beginning *at home*. Thus, in full recognition of the criticism I am likely to incur from colleagues, I am prepared to argue for the domestication, in this case, the Americanization, of biblical studies. I see this process as a way of revolutionizing the current dominant paradigm in theological studies where the Bible serves either as a (theological-) ideological foundation (in almost all theological schools and in many religion-controlled colleges and universities), or as "scientific" source (in many self-styled "secular" schools and religious studies programs). The result is that the Bible, sometimes by intention, other times quite ironically and unwittingly, becomes a mirror and protector of the status quo religious and sociopolitical establishment. It either is rendered as a distant, ancient text, irrelevant to current concerns, or becomes the "canon" for those whose views are in vogue and in power.

II

Any serious rethinking today of educational programs and scholarly agenda must take inventory of our cultural situation in North America near the end of the twentieth century. Our situation, in what Fredric Jameson refers to as a late capitalist, postmodern society, would, in fact, seem to demand rethinking of all the givens around us. How could it be otherwise, given the enormous changes and modifications that have become standard in our world of transnational corporations and CNN, the rapid-fire global dissemination of everything from the fluctuations of the stock market to pop music and fashion trends?[2]

The smaller world that is created by transnationals and CNN is not more negotiable; it does not result in less, but more, conflict and modification. More of us now know about the privileges and stations of the rest. More of us now know more about the unnatural advantages accruing to the rest. More of us now know more about the lifestyles of the elites of the world and their consequences for the rest. More of us now come to know more quickly about the cruelties some of us inflict upon the rest. And some of us now know for the first time about real alternatives—to the known ideologies and structures and traditions, whether social, political, economic, or religious.

The situation is not a happy one for all. It is not simply the modern worldview that is at issue; it is the postmodern world's breakup of those things associated with modernity that is unsettling. The rapidity of change, the ever-shifting boundaries, the constantly changing parameters for everything from architecture and music to literary theory and history, the multiplicity of conflicts, and the breakdown of totalizations—these represent the new realities to be faced. For some, a type of "fundamentalism" is paradoxically both a product of, and a response to, the situation as described.

> In the . . . atmosphere of an uncontested postmodernism, more effortlessly secular than any modernism could have wished . . . religious traditionalisms [i.e., "mainline churches"] seem to have melted away without a trace . . . while the wildest and most unexpected forms of what is now called "fundamentalism" flourish, virtually at random and seemingly obedient to other climacterics and ecological laws.[3]

The paradox may be better understood, if not resolved, by addressing the question of "how the new [fundamentalist] religions compensate their irreplaceable absence in the depthlessness of the new social order."[4] This suggests that religion must be seen both as a reflection of culture and as culture-defining. The changes that are characteristic of the world we experience today make it impossible for religion not to be affected and to affect. Contemporary religion cannot be understood

---

2. Fredric Jameson, *Postmodernism: Or, The Cultural Logic of Late Capitalism* (Durham: Duke University Press, 1991) ix.

3. Ibid., 387–88.

4. Ibid., 388.

without attention to its relationship to culture and, therefore, to its own past.[5]

The situation of late capitalism in the United States near century's end requires that serious attention be given to religion. In *The American Religion: The Emergence of the Post-Christian Nation* Harold Bloom argues rightly that the United States is "religion-soaked," a "religiously-mad culture, furiously searching for the spirit."[6] There is even, he argues, such a phenomenon as the "American Religion" that is transdenominational, post-Christian, and "gnostic."[7] Although I am fascinated by Bloom's isolation of this phenomenon, I am much more interested in what is required in response:

> A nation obsessed with religion rather desperately needs a religious criticism, whether or not it is prepared to receive any commentary whatsoever on so problematical and personal a question as the individual's relation to group persuasions.[8]

Religious criticism parallels that which Bloom knows much about— literary criticism. The latter should seek, according to Bloom, to find "an irreducibly aesthetic element in one's experience." So with religious criticism,

> there must be a[n] . . . irreducible element when we study religion; our experience is prior to analysis, whether we call what we experience "the divine" or "the transcendental" or simply "the spiritual." Yet the work of literary criticism is done upon texts, or the relations between texts, or the relations between texts and authors. . . . I do not think that texts can give us the essence of the American Religion.[9]

The role of the religious critic, therefore, is not the same as that of the historian of religion, the sociologist of religion, the psychologist of religion, or even the theologian. It is more comprehensive, more difficult and challenging. The point is conveyed through another comparison with literary criticism:

> Religious criticism, like literary criticism, is a mode of interpretation, but unlike the critic of imaginative literature, the critic of religion, as I conceive her, is not primarily an interpreter of texts. A critic's function is to compare and judge perceptions and sensations not only represented by imaginative literature or by religion, but themselves the product of poetry

---

5. Ibid., 387.
6. Bloom, *The American Religion: The Emergence of the Post-Christian Nation* (New York: Simon & Schuster, 1992) 22.
7. Ibid., 28.
8. Ibid., 22.
9. Ibid., 28.

or of belief. While a literary critic must protect literature against belief, whether societal or transcendental, a religious critic cannot protect belief, whether from society or from rival modes such as psychoanalysis philosophy, science, and art. The function of criticism is to purge us not of selfhood (upon which the American Religion centers and relies) but of self-righteousness.[10]

Bloom provokes serious reconsideration not only of American culture and the force of religion within it, but also of the study of religion in general in America. If his arguments are taken seriously, how is it now possible for the study of religion in America to continue with the same set of disciplines? What would be required in order to carry out the academic study of religion on the doctoral level as *religious criticism?* The first thing required is an analysis of the current situation facing academic programs in the study of religion.

III

The academic or "critical" study of religion in North America, whether housed in graduate divisions in theological seminaries and university divinity schools, or in college and university departments of religious studies, has achieved something of a pyrrhic victory. Having won its hard-fought and legitimate independence from ecclesiastical controls and general religious dogmatisms, and having gained acceptance by arts and sciences faculties in colleges and universities, the study of religion all too often now seems able to interest only a few. Why should a phenomenon so intimately tied to the making and development and explosion of cultures and societies on the whole seem to be so uninteresting, so useless (it would seem) to so many? The generally recognized anti-intellectualism that is a hallmark of United States culture notwithstanding, why are so few in this most religious of cultures so little informed or affected by scholarship in religion?

Efforts to establish the study of religion as a program partner with the humanities have not resulted in the type of breakthroughs that were anticipated. Whether in the context of the seminary/divinity school or the department of religious studies, it is still generally the case that most doctoral programs are primarily (not exclusively) organized around classic texts, great events, and great personalities (and their texts). Although much needed and impressive scholarship has resulted from such a focus, its agenda has tended to reduce the study of religion

---

10. Ibid., 38.

to antiquarian, esoteric interests. Even social scientific studies, with their promise of conceptual breakthroughs, have tended, more often than anyone could have predicted, to see as the object of their study the classic texts, historical figures, and events. To be sure, some attention is given to the other elements, but such attention, when associated with scholars whose home is in departments of religious studies and in seminaries and divinity schools, does not affect the basic curricular presuppositions of their respective faculties.

One of the perduring problems for doctoral programs in religious and theological studies, then, is the failure to problematize their existence in the period after independence (from ecclesiastical control) and after initiation (into the mysteries of university humanities and other faculties). There is now no doubt that both the traditional and the newer areas of specialization within doctoral programs in religious studies make great contributions to our knowledge in many different areas. But these specializations do not create a comprehensive statement about religion as historical or contemporary cultural phenomenon. For example, the study of early Christianity has added much to our knowledge of early Roman social movements. But why should not the study of such a phenomenon now be carried out in a history department? What difference does membership on a theological or religious studies faculty make? What difference *should* it make?

I certainly would not want to argue that the member of a theological or religious studies faculty who is a student of early Christianity should be less the historian than the student of early Christianity who is a member of the history department! I would fight to ensure the continuation of a disciplinary division of labor within religious studies and theological faculties. No, the difference between the historian of early Christianity within the history department and the New Testament scholar/historian of early Christianity on the theological or religious studies faculty should include an effort on the part of the latter to account for early Christianity as an expression of the religious life. This accounting should not seek to make early Christianity identical to contemporary expressions of religion, but it should render it understandable as an expression of the universal religious experience.

What this means is that the scholar of religion, no matter what his or her discipline is, should be expected to contribute to the general discourse regarding the phenomenon of religion *qua* religion, religion as mediation of ultimate reality. Without this focus programs in theology and religious studies have no basis for existence. Every scholar of religion should be expected to discuss *religion in itself*—whence it comes, what it is, how it functions. Without this discussion no amount of in-depth research should be justified as part of a faculty of religious studies or theology. Moreover, no *doctoral* program in a theology or religious studies department at whatever level can justify its existence without a curriculum that is centered on what it means to be religious. Otherwise, why should not our more narrowly focused agenda be carried out on another faculty? If we as religious and theological studies faculty do not concern ourselves with religion itself, what do we contribute as scholars on religion and theology faculties that others on other faculties—history, literature, sociology, philosophy, anthropology, and so forth—cannot contribute?

IV

This leads to a proposal: Theological and religious studies doctoral programs should be put on an axis other than the current field divisions; they should be reoriented as *religious criticism,* around the quest to understand the essence of religion itself within *contemporary* culture (as the basis for inquiry into the *past*). The quest to understand religion as part of culture is, of course, not new. The works of individual scholars and schools of thought among and beyond scholars of religion on this topic abound. What would be new, however, is an effort to orient *entire programs, entire departments and faculties*—with all of their guild representation and field divisions—around such a concept. Further, the quest itself would be understood no longer as the need simply to understand how religion *x* functioned within a particular society at a particular point in time, or the original meaning(s) of a particular text. This is already in vogue today, with biblical studies dominating the scene. What I propose instead is that each field, each discipline, each course, agenda, and project in religious and theological studies be oriented around a common quest to understand *how* religion functions, *what* religion is—both as cultural product and as constitutive of culture.

This reorientation would require a different point of departure. No longer can classic texts *qua* classic texts hold first place in the curriculum. Their continuing primacy in curricula and in research projects can lead only to a continuation of the situation in which there is more often than not a lack of program coherence, and little substantive cooperation across fixed disciplinary and field boundaries. But this is just another way of saying that a more radical starting point is needed.

As mentioned above, an engagement of the religious in *contemporary* culture can provide a most useful beginning. Curricular offerings and research would then be focused upon religion in all of its varied manifestations, with the need to consider the impact of its *longue durée*. Programs would, in following this reorientation, be inspired and encouraged to seek deeper understanding and critical analysis of indigenous cultural expressions—although not in the same manner for every project or every course.

The academic study of religion understood *as religious criticism* that is understood as a type of *cultural criticism* is timely and is certainly supported by currents and movements within other sectors of the academy. The unsettled social, economic, and political situations in the world have inspired creative scholarly arrangements and shifts, especially in literary criticism, anthropology, cultural criticism, and history. These shifts fly under different banners, the New Historicism being one of the most exciting and colorful of them. It represents a bold frontal attack upon humanistic claims to objectivity, and it is disdainful of rigid disciplinary boundaries.

> New Historicism has given scholars new opportunities to cross boundaries separating history, anthropology, art, politics, literature, and economics. It has struck down the doctrine of noninterference that forbade humanists to intrude on questions of politics, power, indeed on all matters that deeply affect people's practical lives. . . . It encourages us to admire the sheer intricacy and unavoidability of exchanges between culture and power.[11]

The self-styled New Historicists in fact represent no one discipline or guild. They represent no single front. They are an aggressive, academically giddy bunch, prone to taking on their guilds and traditions. They refuse to be shut up or boxed in by departments, guilds, schools, or old curricular paradigms. Along with many others, they see themselves as part of the "postmodern, postparadigm age," with great capacities for toleration of difference, of disciplinary messiness, of political extremes. They are consequently prone to

> muddy the formal walkways that criticism has up to now generally followed. They refuse to apportion the discussion of character, language, and theme to literary scholars, of primitive customs to anthropologists, of demographic patterns to social historians. . . . [They] threaten all defenders of linear chronology and progressive history. . . . Those who would jealously enclose their private gardens against communal interference may well lock arms against a criticism that mingles disparate periods and upsets the calculus of Left and Right politics.[12]

---

11. H. Aram Veeser, ed., *The New Historicism* (New York and London: Routledge, 1989) ix, x.

12. Ibid., xv.

New Historicists and their types shun totalizing visions and grand schemas and theories. The focus is rather on attempts to describe more adequately textured social realities.[13] Yet the "crisis of representation," the pervasive doubt that we have found an adequate means of describing social realities, is very strong and must be faced. No academic program or enterprise can ignore it. Skepticism about all truth statements causes general academic claims to give way to an epistemology accepting of contradiction, paradox, and irony, and the embracing of the "jeweler's eye view of the world," i.e., "closely observed social and cultural processes."[14] Thus, in an era of "postconditions"— "postmodern, postcolonial, posttraditional"—careful ethnographic and cultural critical studies of many types are needed as "cultures" are constantly "rediscovered."[15]

V

The academic study of religion *as religious criticism* cannot possibly avoid responding to the cultural and academic situations and challenges described above. In other words, it is not possible to think of the study of religion as the study of cultural change without a reconsideration of disciplinary and field divisions. To assume that the latter can be carried out under the current reigning paradigms, while allowing a few individual faculty "firebrands" to transgress, is naive. Cultural criticism can hardly be done honestly and with power unless scholarly inquiry is to some degree critically focused on the scholar's own world. This focus on self-critique must be clear and explicit; it should be built into scholarly inquiry itself.

The academic study of religion would then, with religious criticism as its agenda, be put on an entirely different axis—away from the current pattern of discrete studies of texts and historical periods, of great personalities and their ideas, of doctrines and rituals and their histories, and so forth, with little or no critique of the presuppositions of our contemporary cultural situation that inspire such studies in the first place. It would move toward scholarly creative play, with the greater possibility for clearer understanding of the essentials of religion, insofar as the religions of the scholar's own world are understood and critiqued.

---

13. George E. Marcus and Michael M. J. Fischer, *Anthropology as Critique: An Experimental Moment in the Human Sciences* (Chicago: University of Chicago Press, 1986) 8–9.

14. Ibid., 15–16.

15. Ibid., 24.

This suggestion would mean that the study of religion would need to be oriented around the quest to understand religious impulses both as part of culture making in America and as part of a critique of contemporary domestic culture. It would not render the study of the religions and religious impulses of other times and cultures irrelevant; it would, on the contrary, have such studies function differently. Arguing the merits of "cultural critique" for the function and orientation of anthropology, G. E. Marcus and M. M. J. Fischer make the point about the importance of continuing scholarly interest in "the other"—other times and other cultures—for the sake of effecting "defamiliarization":

> Disruption of common sense, doing the unexpected, placing familiar subjects in unfamiliar, or even shocking, contexts . . . [using] the substantive facts about another culture as a probe into the specific facts about a subject of criticism at home.[16]

But such criticism cannot be accomplished without a rethinking and reconfiguring of the scholarly divison of labor. I agree with P. Joseph Cahill[17] that the four primary disciplinary divisions of labor constitutive of religious and theological studies—the literary, the historical, the comparative, and the theological—require the mediation of

> a relation of the interpreter to the subject matter . . . that is suitable to the manner in which religious texts or religious history present the subject matter. So the interpreters must first grasp their own existence as historical. . . . In a generic and abstract sense these are the boundaries of religious subject matter. If the interpreter has no relationship to the various possibilities for making human existence accessible to human beings . . . he or she is incapable of exercising a criticism of the subject matter, regardless of proficiency in the exegesis of the subject matter. In this instance much of the work will turn out to be . . . "busy work"; the blind man speaks of color.[18]

Other operations "consecutive to, consequent on, and auxiliary to" the primary operations, according to Cahill, include the psychological, sociological, anthropological, and philosophical.[19] Religious criticism must always presuppose engagement or empathy on the part of the critic, a genuine openness to the religious impulse and its varied expressions. And it should, of course, always presuppose the serious

---

16. Ibid., 137–38.
17. Cahill, *Mended Speech: The Crisis of Religious Studies and Theology* (New York: Crossroad, 1982), see p. 6 for first summary-listing of operations, and Part 2 for full explication.
18. Ibid., 41–42.
19. Ibid., 6.

engagement of one or more of the primary "mental operations" of the study of religion. The difference between the primary operations and the consequent and auxiliary operations is that the latter

> do not demand on the part of the interpreter a fully articulated prior relationship to the subject matter of religion. The distinction of operations . . . is grounded in the epigenetically differentiated consciousness of the interpreting subject. This epigenetically differentiated consciousness is itself based on the intentionalities and meanings that people have historically given to ultimate transcendence.[20]

VI

If religious criticism is to be carried out as the mediation between the interpreter's consciousness, religious texts and communities, and the larger culture in which religious communities are formed, then it is important to have some understanding of how it is that the four primary operations may be engaged for the task. Because Cahill's taxonomy has been adopted, I shall continue to use his language and follow his lead—to a point. I need at the outset to stress that no program in religious and theological studies envisioned as religious criticism need abandon all of the traditional disciplines; what is critical is that the disciplines be subsumed under the presuppositions and agenda of religious criticism. This means that the different operations may actually be collapsed in the creative play and shifts and modifications that are expected as part of *Sachexegese* (*exegesis* of the subject matter), as opposed to *Sachkritik* (*criticism* of the subject matter).[21]

The Literary Operation. It would be impossible in the West to study religion without studying texts. In the beginning was the word, first oral, then written—thus, the text. The literary operation seeks first to establish the text, then to understand it in its formal parts and as a whole, and finally to explain critically and persuasively its "religious force."

> The literary operation is that activity which understands a text by any operation proportionate to the object. This operation, however, is contrasted to any type of interpretation that would base itself in charism, authority, spiritual power, inheritance, institution, or the so-called conversion. . . . The intention of the operation is understanding of the body of religious literature in question. For this understanding there is required an exact textual knowledge, a sensibility for the historical and social set-

---

20. Ibid., 10.
21. Ibid., 39–40.

ting and environment, an ear attuned to the life of language, and a driving concern that the intention of the author be preserved. A religious text
comes to life only when the interpreter "gives it voice."[22]

No matter how expert the engagement of the literary operation as
defined above, it must, as a part of religious criticism, ultimately contribute to a comprehensive understanding of the particular culture that
is being studied. Of course, this assumes some interaction with the
other primary operations. But it also assumes that such inquiry
involves not only the recovery of the religious impulses behind the
texts of a tradition, but also the "mediation" of religious impulses in
the text for the scholar's world. Such "mediation" will likely be
imperfect; the literary operation can only mediate the religious
impulses, religious visions, and political challenges as they are brought
into speech by others.

The Historical Operation. The second of the four primary operations has also the religious text as its primary object of study, although
a wide range of other types of sources—like art, music, and
archaeology—are also increasingly engaged. Historical criticism must
be intimately related to the literary operation. This operation is based
on the assumption that all phenomena must be placed within the framework of time and space, and that all religion so framed can be studied
as meaningful responses to that particular time and space. Historical
study, therefore, will entail both apprehension and reconstruction of
"objective, certain facts" of the past (*Historie*), and the establishment
of the past "as direct concern to me (*Geschichte*), as . . . possibilities
for understanding my own existence, the existence of the community,
or human existence in general."[23] So as regards religion in particular,
the historical operation can be understood as *both*

> the objective reconstruction of the religious past (*Historie*) and the sub-
> jective dimension of understanding the past in such a way that the full
> potentialities of the human race will be disclosed (*Geschichte*).[24]

The emphasis upon both *Historie* and *Geschichte* is important but
deceptive: it should not be assumed that there are *two* types of history,
or *two* different ways of doing historical work. The essential point
being made here is that there are (at least) two *aspects* of the doing of
historical work. A different terminology, supplied by Cahill, may help
make the point:

---

22. Ibid., 116–17.
23. Ibid., 132.
24. Ibid., 133.

All historical study in the history of religions will be both idealistic and pragmatic. When the study of history justifies itself simply on grounds of antiquarian interest or the satisfaction of curiosity or as something that somehow or another should fit into all education and be part of the cultured person, then surely the serious study of serious history will disappear and become a matter for dilettantes. . . . The simple fact is that the time, energy, and resources of the individual . . . are limited. While the entire past of the world may be broadly described as constituting history, an indiscriminate reconstruction of this past (all the events constituting *Historie*) is neither desirable, necessary, nor possible. What one seeks is enough understanding of a field that discloses the potentialities of [humankind], without predetermining beforehand what these potentialities are. Hence . . . the historical operation is idealistic in its aims and intentions, and pragmatic in its selection and execution.[25]

The historical operation requires on the part of the historian some empathy, envisioning, and the exercise of "historical imagination," in order to discern the religious element behind the sources. This will in turn lead to an acceptance of historical work as the quest not merely to recover the "facts," but also to discern meaning, including religious meaning, within a tradition or culture.

The Comparative Operation. The comparative operation is always in evidence to some extent in the two operations discussed above. Comparing and contrasting and pointing out important relationships are important aspects of literary and historical work. But because this operation encompasses the whole range of religious expressions, it necessarily assumes research competence in particular single traditions.[26]

The hermeneutical circle is most clearly evident in this operation: every comparativist, while establishing relationships, patterns, similarities, and dissimilarities among religions, must nonetheless do so on the basis of one particular religion, with all its peculiarities. The comparativist should acknowledge the reality of doing comparative work from *a* place. In this way honest and bold criticism of the many different expressions of religious traditions can ensue. Moreover, it will then be possible to sustain criticism of a particular religious tradition or impulse, since criticism cannot be sustained without comparisons.

Is every movement that terms itself Buddhist authentic Buddhism? If not, what is the criterion of judgment? How does one arrive at norms that may be said to indicate what is constitutive of Buddhism and not merely con-

---

25. Ibid.
26. Ibid., 139.

sequent to it? Who are the true followers of Muhammed—the Kharijites or the Umayyads? Or, is the religious distinction of the Murji'ites correct, namely, that God alone can judge who is an authentic Muslim and who is not? Can the scholar judge whether a monarchical episcopate, first hinted at in the Ignatian letters, is regulative for the church but not constitutive? Is it possible in any religion that the so-called tertiary symbolism of speculative theology occasionally distorts the intention of the primary and secondary (the story and myth) symbolism? [27]

The comparative operation, then, in drawing upon the work of the literary and the historical, and in examining the different significations, rituals, texts, and orientations of a range of different traditions, as well as the scholar's own tradition, has the potential to help establish essentially "what an authentic tradition is . . . what is constitutive for a religion."[28]

The Theological Operation. According to Cahill, in most religious studies programs constructive theology is the field about which there is the most skepticism. It has been considered the field most susceptible to ecclesiastical control and to parochial vision—the one of all the other fields in theological studies that has historically adjusted rather poorly and slowly to the conceptual world opened up by historical consciousness. It is the field that has least embraced the historical critical method. There is, therefore, something rather ironic about structuring and orienting religious studies and theological studies around religious criticism, as is proposed here. The theological operation should actually have a prominent, focal place in the religious and theological studies understood as religious criticism.

If theology can be conceived of as the critical study of "intentionalities directed to ultimate meaning and immediate transcendence," then its object must include the religious impulses and expressions of all human beings. Given this scope, it is obvious that the other operations and their results will need to be employed. But the most important point that needs to be made here is that the theological operation, insofar as it concerns itself *explicitly* with the mediation and translation of that which is central to religious experience—ultimacy and transcendence—is an essential part of the hermeneutical circle in religious criticism.

The dance behind the dancers, the structure behind the transient forms, the transcendent behind the representations of divinity: this is what the theological operation seeks to disclose. And its disclosures will be crea-

---

27. Ibid., 140–41.
28. Ibid., 140.

tive transformations. For behind particular heuristic visions and their cultural mediation, is the one heuristic vision. Behind the many theological representations is potentially one theology.[29]

The search for the "dance behind the dancers," the theology behind the different religious representations, is not intended to collapse all religious experiences into one. It is, instead, the encounter with what is the specifically religious vision within certain traditions, arts of expression, particular orientations and praxes, key texts, rituals, and institutions. That which is "religious" in history and literature and across different cultures can potentially and ultimately be made "one" only as part of theology's rigorous conceptualizations in and about the present experience. In the same manner in which theology by definition seeks the religious aspect of all faith representations, so it must encompass and unify all other primary operations of mind. It is, in other words, a necessary step in the study of religion as religious criticism because it alone forces those analyses that are explicitly about the religious. Thus, a program in religious studies or theological studies ultimately cannot justify itself over against any other program or department, all the aforementioned operations notwithstanding, unless the theological operation as is defined here is included. The latter not only unifies the other operations, it also pushes them toward consistent consideration of the "religious" in the interpreter's present as the springboard for more self-critical consideration of religious history and religious literature across cultures. Unless such consideration perdures, the purely academic study of religion at any level in any context can hardly be justified. How otherwise can we come to know that we are talking about the same things when we reference "religion"? How can we distinguish our discourse from that of the sociologist or the mathematician?

VII

The study of religion as religious criticism, and as a type of cultural criticism, must assume the redesign of its primary disciplines—especially history (including comparative studies) and literary criticism—and associated "secular" disciplines. These disciplines must be reoriented in such a way that they all—in collaboration with, if not actually led by, theology—contribute to the quest for the specifically "religious" element within the different expressions of contemporary

29. Ibid., 148.

culture. So the study of religion as religious criticism must never stop at interpreting a text or work of art or music; it must push beyond this level of engagement to help mediate the specifically religious visions, impulses, or orientations of our situations and times. Ultimately, the different operations of mind—primary and secondary—in the program that constitutes religious criticism must collectively contribute toward an understanding of the religious forces that inform our thinking and orientations. To do less is not only to threaten a future for the academic study of religion by undermining its role in the academy, it is also to render it uninteresting—a fate most difficult to overcome.

Biblical studies can profit enormously from a serious consideration of the agenda of religious criticism. The place to begin in such studies is with the decentering of the text, that is, a stepping away from the historical privilege accorded the Bible as text (religious or cultural canon) in our still Protestant-dominated culture. In place of the text should be a focus upon contemporary social formations. This focus, facilitated by the intellectual operations discussed above, can in turn put the study of the Bible on a different intellectual and academic plane and actually invest it with even greater significance than ever before: It would surely explode the reputation of biblical studies that it serves merely naive antiquarian or hypersubjective (religious-theological) interests.

The study of the Bible as religious criticism would entail first and primarily the study of contemporary "scripturalizing" efforts among human beings, i.e., how peoples understand sacred texts and what peoples do with the sacred texts. The juxtaposition of "the text and the times," as Robin Scroggs[30] has otherwise put it, is imperative. Interpretation of the "times" will certainly include in the West the engagement of the "text." But it is the "times" that are basic, the starting point; they are what in some respect or another are found to be compelling or quizzical or problematic or contradictory; the "times" are what make relevant, define, and delimit the "text" that comes to be "sacred." Biblical studies on this order, i.e., one that begins with the (problematizing of the contemporary) "times," ought to be imagined and experimented with for its—and our—future.

---

30. See Robin Scroggs, *The Text and the Times: New Testament Essays for Today* (Minneapolis: Fortress Press, 1993), especially "Introduction: Education of the Interpreter," 1–5.

19

On Transforming
New Testament Theology
(Re)Claiming Subjectivity

Virginia Wiles

Intellectual liberty may be defined for our purposes
as the right to say or write what you think in your own words,
and in your own way.
—Virginia Woolf, *Three Guineas*

In the final essay of his book, *The Text and the Times*, Robin Scroggs asks the question "Can the New Testament Be Relevant for the Twenty-first Century?" The closing pages of this essay reverberate with Scroggs's answer:

> How then can the New Testament be relevant for the twenty-first century? It can be relevant in its invitation to "come and see." . . . It can be relevant by inviting us to join in that reality it perceived and partially realized. . . . The New Testament thus helps us to *become*, no, to *be* different people.[1]

The invitation that Scroggs envisions is specifically an invitation to *transformation*, to "a significant change in the perception of reality that alters every dimension of our being."[2] Thus, the relevance of the New Testament lies precisely in the ways that it invites the readers and hearers of these texts—in what*ever* generation—to transformation of self. It boldly sets before its hearers a new world, "a world that it claims really exists."[3]

---

1. Scroggs, "Can the New Testament Be Relevant for the Twenty-first Century?" in *The Text and the Times: New Testament Essays for Today* (Minneapolis: Fortress Press, 1993) 283–84.
2. Ibid., 282
3. Ibid., 284.

Every scholar has his favorite words. Without question, one of the words that Scroggs has ever ready in his bag of vocabulary is this word, *transformation*. Scroggs also likes to ask unsettling questions. In this same volume of essays where he asks "Can the New Testament be relevant?" Scroggs also asks, "Can New Testament theology be saved?"[4] The theological pun here cannot be missed. It is even slightly humorous. But those who have had the privilege of conversing with Robin in recent years know that the question does not humor him. It is, for him, a crucial question, one that expresses the commitment of his own career, his own glimpses of transformation, his own hope for the future.

As a scholar at the cusp of her career, I hear this question from a different horizon than that from which it is asked. *Can New Testament theology be saved?* My mind meanders around this question daily. I take stock of myself—of my practice, of my context, my colleagues and my students. I have wandered down some blind alleys; but I have also nudged up against some "hunches" about how New Testament theology might be possible for us in the twenty-first century.

Such "hunches," of course, are not easily set forth in an argumentative essay, and such is the genre of article to which we are accustomed—both in our reading and for our writing. A different genre, an alternate rhetorical presentation, will be needed for this exploration that I have in mind.[5] Call it, if you will, an "exploratory essay."[6] I follow the lead of Michel de Montaigne:

> This is simply a trial (*essai*) of my natural faculties, and not of my acquired ones. . . . Let the [one] who is in search of knowledge fish for it where it lies; there is nothing that I lay less claim to. These are my fancies, in which I make no attempt to convey information about things, only about myself.[7]

---

4. Scroggs, "Can New Testament Theology Be Saved? The Threat of Contextualisms," in *Text and Times*, 212–33.

5. Thus, *caveat lector!* As one of the functions of *genre* is to establish expectations on the part of the reader, readers of this essay will need to approach their reading with an altered set of expectations. I do not, for instance, build a cumulative argument herein. I *essay* several self-understandings and definitions of our discipline, some of which I abandon along the way as I move on to other possibilities. And, as the many discursive footnotes illustrate, I wander frequently into yet other possibilities that I cannot here explore. The process of my *essaying* here will lead to a clearer statement of why I believe a different genre is necessary for this exploration; see below, p. 324.

6. The more traditional label for the genre I use is that of "personal essay." For a good introduction to the genre of personal essay, see the introduction by Phillip Lopate in *The Art of the Personal Essay: An Anthology from the Classical Era to the Present* (New York: Doubleday, Anchor Books, 1994) xxiii–liv, esp. the section entitled "The Personal Essay as a Mode of Thinking and Being," xlii–xlv. Also see Nancy Mairs, *Voice Lessons: On Becoming a (Woman) Writer* (Boston: Beacon Press, 1994).

7. Montaigne, *Essays*, trans. J. M. Cohen (New York: Penguin, 1958) 159.

I write here, ostensibly, about myself—of my own journeys into blind alleys, of my own struggles to understand what it is I do and think. This is what the world of New Testament studies has looked like in my eyes. But this *essai* is not, in reality, a *self*-presentation. Rather, I invite the reader to reflect with me, to come to alternate conclusions perhaps, but to *explore your own experience* in this world we share and imagine with me new ways of thinking about our common discipline.[8]

Can New Testament theology be saved? *Only if it is transformed.* Thus, my title to this essay is dual. On the one hand I intend by this title to honor Robin and to concur with his assertions regarding the transforming possibilities that the discipline of New Testament theology can provide.[9] On the other hand I want to explore how we might transform our understanding of that very discipline so that we may continue to practice it with intellectual integrity in this day and age. For it is my suspicion that *if New Testament theology is to continue to be transformative, then the very notion of what constitutes New Testament theology will need to be transformed.*

WHAT IS THEOLOGY?

It's a question I ask of anyone who will stand still long enough to listen. I ask it of laypeople. I ask it of my colleagues in the humanities and social sciences. I ask it of my eighteen- and nineteen-year-old students. I have never stopped anyone on the street to ask them this question—but I would like to. What *is* theology? The answers are as vague as they are certain: "the study of God," "talk about God," "church dogma." I have learned the hard way that the word makes most people nervous. What was once the "Queen of the Sciences" has become the closeted, illegitimate child of the humanities. Were "theology" a *literal* child, our social conscience would be aroused. We would demand liberation. But every generation has its abuses. And, within the confines of any particular culture, the abuses that it allows always appear to be justifiable abuses.

---

8. As Phillip Lopate says of the personal essayist, "The trick is to realize that one is not important, except insofar as one's example can serve to elucidate a more widespread human trait and make readers feel a little less lonely and freakish" (xxxii). Several people read and responded to initial drafts of this essay. I especially thank John McClure, Mary Ellen Burd, Nadine Pence Frantz, and of course Alexandra Brown, for their insightful critiques of my meanderings herein.

9. The course of my thinking on these matters, as represented in this essay, has been significantly influenced by an interaction with Robin's thought and work. In addition to the two articles cited above, I also draw on his (unpublished) Schmiechen Lectures entitled "'Blowin' in the Wind': Recent Trends in Pauline Interpretation and Their Implications for Church Proclamation," Eden Theological Seminary, October 1989; Lecture 1, "The Sundering of Exegesis and Theology"; Lecture 2, "Theological Possibilities"; Lecture 3, "Reunification: Bringing the Two Together."

I use this venue to come out of the closet: I am a New Testament theologian. Let me be explicit. I am a member of a "community of faith" only in name, by tradition at best and not in present lived experience. "God"—in the sense of a personalized and beneficent being who inhabits some transcendent realm—makes no more sense to me intellectually than it does to my colleagues who call themselves agnostics or atheists. Thus, the reality for me—if I am honest—is that, like so many of our guild, I live and work apart from the Church and am rather a daily, active partner with the avowed secular colleagues where I teach. Here are my friendships; here is my community; here, among these secularists, is where I feel most comfortable and "at home." I no longer feel bound by the canons of any particular Christian tradition. Rather I have adopted the canons of rational public discourse.[10] And I want for my words to make sense in this (secular, academic) world in which I live. I don't teach "religion." I don't teach "spirituality." But, as a theologian, I *do* talk about "God." How can I make sense of myself?

During my first week on campus at the college where I currently teach I was startled by the number of times I had this conversation:

> *Introducing myself:* I'm Virginia Wiles . . . in the Religion Department.
>
> *Response:* Oh! Do you believe what you teach?

Say what? I learned, eventually, to parry question for question. "Oh, you teach English? Do you *believe* English?" What were they to say? "No, I don't believe in Milton." "I teach biology, but no, I don't believe in osmosis." So, yes, I talk about "God." Furthermore, I often *believe* what I say as I talk about "God." I believe this talk about "God" is important, even life-giving. I believe that thinking about "God" is a worthy discipline, a worthy profession. It is, in fact, my passion. And this from someone who could in most meaningful respects be described as a secular humanist. I am an oxymoron.

An oxymoron, but not, I trust, a moron. Words are our stock in trade. We write, we speak, we read, we assess *words*. Some words give us more trouble than other words. "God" is one of these problematic words. "Belief" is another. Do you believe God? Do you

---

10. I am far from unaware of the feminist critique of the adoption of such "rational public discourse." My comments on that problem will have to wait for another time. For the moment, however, my epigraph for this essay intends to point to my own struggle with this difficulty that I have speaking as a "woman in a man's world." If this difficulty is foreign to you, I recommend a reading of the work of Luce Irigaray.

believe in God? Do you believe that there is a God? These questions rouse anxieties. We relegate them to that misty sidebar of personal opinion and private reflection. These things, we confidently assert, have no place in rational public discourse.[11] They do not belong to secular academics, to rational inquiry. There is no testing, no assessing of *these* matters. Leave them to the church, to the synagogue, to the demagogues of popular spirituality.

My willingness to call myself a New Testament theologian arises, in part, from my refusal to exile such words as "God" and "belief" from the exercise of critical reflection or from rigorous rational discourse. "God" is not an irrational term. Perhaps we fear the many irrational ways this term is used. As people trained in rational reflection, however, we should be able to critique irrational uses of this term without being compelled to dispense with the term itself.[12] No, I suspect that the real irrationality lies in our anxiety about using the term "God." If that is the case, then it is this anxiety that we must confront if we are ever again to do New Testament theology with integrity in this post-Christian age. So let us begin here: How do New Testament scholars—of all stripes and methodologies—speak of "God"?

GOD-TALK IN THE GUILD

It is not, of course, only the New Testament theologians among us who talk of God. The texts that serve as the very basis of our discipline are saturated with this term. None of us who study these texts can avoid the term "God." In a simplistic way we might say that the difference between New Testament theologians and other New Testament scholars is that the theologians "believe in" this "God." They believe (so we assume) that the term "God" denotes—in some referential way—something/someone who is Real, who exists. The texts, for these theologians, point to something that is not only past, but is also present. The hermeneutical leap from then to now is shorter for these folks. *That* God is now.

---

11. I intend these assertions as caricature of how much of the academy treats religious discourse within the public sphere. It should be noted, however, that this assumption—that religious language or belief should have no place within secular, public discourse—is being challenged on several fronts today. See, for example, Stephen Carter, *The Culture of Disbelief*, and George Marsden, *The Soul of the American University*. Also, see Habermas, Derrida, Kristeva, and Lyotard, all of whom wrestle with the place of religion and religious discourse in a postmodern world.

12. I must confess that I have been known, in the past, to resort to placing a ban on the word in a class. Have you, like I, noticed that when people open their mouths to enunciate the word "God" it is as though their very breath expels all their rational capability? The emerging rationality of my young students is frequently hijacked into piousness when they breathe this word "God."

Belief is the problem. "God," as a term, seems to most of us to be inextricably bound up with this question of belief—the question of faith. The anxiety, so often hidden (or denied) behind our well-honed critical methodologies, is the assumed threat of that childhood question: Do I believe in God? In honor of Robin I could propose a Freudian analysis of this repressed anxiety.[13] Such an analysis would no doubt do us good. My offering, however, will be simpler. I suggest that we begin by temporarily disentangling these terms—"God" and "faith." How do we speak of God when we are able to leave aside that threatening question of belief?

For we *are* able to do this. Many new methodologies have arisen in the discipline of New Testament studies in recent decades.[14] These methodologies do not exempt us from using the term "God" in our discourse. They do, however, allow us to escape slanderous accusations of irrational piousity from our colleagues in other humanities and social science disciplines.[15] As social historians and sociologists we freely speak of "God" as a central term in the symbolic universe of the communities that gave rise to these texts. Witness Wayne Meeks as he talks about the "reference individuals" in the world of Pauline morality:

> It hardly requires documentation that Christ and God are the primary imagined reference individuals, either explicitly or implicitly, in all Paul's letters. As in 1 Thessalonians, we see in the other letters a fairly narrowly drawn narrative of Christ as not only reference individual but also model. Also, as in the early letter, we find a much broader conception of God that is, however, often focused by relating specific actions: raising Christ from the dead, making and keeping promises, calling his people, and acting as judge. . . . The narrative structure . . . offers a picture of God as active agent by which, in varied and subtle ways, the behavior and attitudes of the Christian groups are to be measured.[16]

---

13. For an example of Scroggs's use of a Freudian model of interpretation, see his article, "The Heuristic Value of a Psychoanalytic Model in the Interpretation of Pauline Theology," in *Text and Times*, 125–50.

14. See Scroggs's article "Can New Testament Theology Be Saved?" for a thoughtful treatment of the implications of these emergent methodologies for New Testament theology.

15. Traditional historical criticism, of course, also used "God" in its discourse. However, a historical critic of yesteryear was prevented from (relieved of?) taking this term very seriously. The critical analysis of historical cause and effect necessarily excludes God as an actor on this historical plane. The historical critic sought to answer the question of what "really happened," and no serious critic would have ascribed either cause or effect to God. The difference in these new methodologies, I am suggesting, is that they have (if unwittingly) allowed us to speak of "God" with intellectual integrity.

16. Meeks, "The Circle of Reference in Pauline Morality," in *Greeks, Romans, and Christians: Essays in Honor of Abraham J. Malherbe*, ed. D. Balch, E. Ferguson, and W. Meeks (Minneapolis: Fortress Press, 1990) 314.

Here Meeks speaks of "God." He discusses the logic of Paul's use of this term/symbol. He engages implicitly in theo-logic. But Meeks is not theologian. He speaks not of the present Church's theo-logic, nor of his own. His is a historical and descriptive task. That was then. Now, here, is irrelevant in this theo-logic. Hence, he is not theologian. He is critical social historian.

As literary critics of the New Testament texts, we encounter the character of God. Not as do systematic theologians: "God is just, holy, beneficent, omniscient," and so on. Rather we encounter God *as a character* within a narrative. God here is on equal terms with the human, animal, or other celestial characters. God plays a role in the developing plot. We need not ascribe to God any more reality than we do to any other narrative presence. God, Hamlet, Mrs. Dalloway, Jane Eyre. All characters within their plots. Their "reality" is embedded within the narrative. We "believe in" them only to the extent that we temporarily enter into the world of this particular story or novel.

The recent "biography of God" by Jack Miles serves as a strong and extended example of the ability of the literary critic to speak intelligently and critically of God:

> The Book of Genesis says that God turned Lot's wife into a pillar of salt, an event that obviously has no status as history but one that for the purposes of this work must be counted as a moment in the life of God and as evidence, however minor, about his developing character. We may allow the historians to tell us what really happened. We may allow the theologians to tell us whether the real God would ever do a thing like that. For literary purposes, however, which are the only purposes of this book, the fact that the protagonist of the book does indeed perform this action on its pages is enough to bring it into the reckoning.[17]

Thus, Miles attempts to follow the literary theo-logic of this character as God grows into his own unique complexity. He writes a "theography"[18] that neither requires nor prohibits religious belief in a "real God" who might (or might not) reside outside of this narrative. With "belief" left to the side, Miles does not count himself among the theologians. He is literary critic—as secular as any other literary critic who analyzes the protagonist of a narrative.

As rhetorical analysts of these particular historical texts, we cannot escape the term "God" in the developing argument of the particular text under study. *Whether or not* this God actually exists (or, more properly, *existed*) need not concern us. What matters is what the

---

17. Miles, *God: A Biography* (New York: Alfred A. Knopf, 1995) 13.
18. Ibid., 12.

speaker and hearers believed. *Our* belief is, again, irrelevant. Thus, we can (presumably) analyze the use of the term "God" in Paul's epistles much as we would analyze the use of the term "Zeus" in the discourses of Epictetus. Here again, we necessarily engage in theo-logic, for "God" is frequently a crucial term in the argument. We assess the cogency and persuasive impact of that theo-logic for the long-ago hearers of that text. But historical and cultural distance exempts us from assessing the cogency of that theo-logic for our own lives. We are not to be persuaded. We escape the question of our own belief.

I confess to some confusion here: We carefully follow the theo-logic of "God" as a social symbol, of "God" as a character in a narra-tive, of "God" as a term within a rhetorical argument. But we insist that we are not "theo-logians." Why not? What (fear?) compels us to shun that word? Why *not* call myself theologian if I am attending to the theo-logic of a text?

Biblical theology is a particular type of historical theology. It is at most a prelude to dogmatic or systematic theology. It behooves us to go back to the origin of the modern discipline of biblical theology. Johann Philipp Gabler, 1787:

> There is truly a biblical theology, of historical origin, conveying what the holy writers felt about divine matters; on the other hand there is a dog-matic theology of didactic orgin, teaching what each theologian philosophises rationally about divine things. . . . .[19]

Oh yes, we would say things so much differently today. "Holy writers" thinking about "divine matters." Worn old language that would surely not find a place in today's academy. But is our effort to articulate the theo-logic of a historical (biblical) text—whether as social symbol, character development, or rhetorical term—really so far from this description of Gabler's? Does biblical theology stop being biblical theology when it has thrown off its role as the handmaiden of dogmatic theology? In other words, can there be a genuinely historical biblical theology without dogmatic belief?

---

19. Gabler, "Discourse on the Proper Distinction between Biblical and Dogmatic Theol-ogy, and the Right Determination of the Aims of Each," Inaugural Address, Altdorf. See the dis-cussion of Gabler (and bibliographic data) in William Baird, *History of New Testament Research. Volume One: From Deism to Tübingen* (Minneapolis: Augsburg Fortress, 1992) 184–87. Gabler distinquishes between two types of biblical theology: one that is a historical description of what the biblical authors wrote and is derived from exegesis, and one (pure biblical theology) that pre-sents the universally valid principles expressed in the whole of the biblical record and depends upon exposition. Here I play off of the first type—biblical theology as a historical description and exegesis.

THE ANXIETY OF BELIEF

Can there be biblical theology without belief? It is a question that has become crucial for me in my current context. For, if biblical theology does require belief, then how can I with integrity teach biblical—*New Testament*—theology to Jews and Muslims, to Buddhists and secularists, as well as to my Christian students? If New Testament theology belongs to the Church, as some say, then what am I to do in my secular context?

But if I follow Gabler's definition to its logical conclusion then, yes, I can affirm that there can be a New Testament theology without belief. That is, if New Testament theology is genuinely a historical enterprise. If, for instance, the task of Pauline theology consists in describing Paul's God-talk, then there is no inherent reason or demand for me as Pauline theologian to believe, agree with, or adopt Paul's God-talk as my own. It is a historical, descriptive task. As objectively as I can: here's what Paul thought about God/Christ/Law/Sin/Righteousness. If this is not teaching Pauline theology, then what is it?[20]

In his article on contemporary biblical theology in the 1962 edition of *The Interpreter's Dictionary of the Bible*, Krister Stendahl articulated the basic distinction between discerning "what the text *meant*" and "what the text *means*."[21] The discipline of biblical theology, Stendahl asserts, is concerned specifically with "what it meant." It is the question of "what it means"—i.e., the normative question—that introduces the element of belief, of faith. Indeed, according to Stendahl, the contribution of biblical theologians lies precisely in our

---

20. Perhaps a distinction should be made between *teaching* Pauline theology (or platonism or Freudian thought) and *being* a Pauline theologian or platonist. If I *am* a Freudian, then I do adopt (i.e., believe in) Freud's intellectual categories as being adequate (and even superior) categories for explaining the phenomena under study. I continue to use these categories as useful constructs for my own creative thinking. Such adoption is not necessary if I am only teaching someone else's thought, however. Nevertheless, in our teaching of the thought of others—*while we are teaching*—it is, I would argue, necessary for us to "step into" the thought of the person we are presenting in such a way as to make the structure of their thought plausible to our students. But then there are those troubling words of William Blake: "Truth can never be told so as to be understood, and not be believed" (from the "Proverbs of Hell" section of "The Marriage of Heaven and Hell").

21. "Biblical Theology, Contemporary," *IDB* 1:418–32. Stendahl articulated with useful phrases a distinction that had long been recognized at least since Gabler. See the reprint of Stendahl's article in his *Meanings: The Bible as Document and Guide* (Philadelphia: Fortress, 1984), under the title of "Biblical Theology: A Program." Here, Stendahl distinguishes three steps to the task of biblical theology: (1) a descriptive, historical task; (2) developing an interpretative strategy for relating the historical theology to today's society; and (3) translating the historical theology into a theology for today. See John K. Riches's discussion in *A Century of New Testament Study* (Valley Forge, PA: Trinity Press International, 1993) 203–4.

refusal to violate the descriptive limits of our task by importing normative judgments or speaking towards belief.[22]

Thus, if I adopt this Gabler/Stendahl[23] distinction between biblical theology (as a historical and descriptive practice) and dogmatic or systematic theology (as an ongoing explication of the inspired faith of the Church), then I would have to say that inasmuch as we seek to explain the theo-logic of a biblical text—"what this theo-logic meant"—then we are doing biblical theology. It simply seems dishonest of us not to acknowledge this, at least at a fundamental linguistic level: anyone who analyzes the theo-logic of a New Testament text is engaging in the discipline of New Testament theology. Personal belief is moot in this objective, historical enterprise.

But somehow I suspect that many of my disciplinary colleagues would prefer not to be numbered among the biblical theologians. Many in our midst who self-consciously seek to provide objective, historical descriptions of the rhetoric, social worlds, or literature of the New Testament texts would adamantly refuse (or so I imagine) to wear the label of "biblical theologian."[24] That term "theology"—despite Gabler's and Stendahl's careful distinctions—still connotes for most people some relationship to faith, it implies some obligation to the church. In this regard, Robin Scroggs's definition of New Testament theology seems a more *accurate* description of how the discipline of New Testament theology is actually perceived and practiced:

> In the first place, [New Testament theology] is the description in coherent and structured form of the faith claims of the authors as revealed in their texts. In the second, it is the use of such descriptions to inform the faith affirmations of subsequent generations of believers.[25]

New Testament theology, according to this definition, is not just a description of the God-talk of these New Testament texts—whether

---

22. Stendahl, "Method in the Study of Biblical Theology," in *The Bible in Modern Scholarship* (Nashville: Abingdon, 1965) 207–9.

23. I use these two, Gabler and Stendahl, as "bookends" of the Enlightenment-informed era and its construal of the task of biblical theology.

24. In my doctoral program the field of biblical studies was divided into five sub-areas: the history of Israel, the literature of the Hebrew Scriptures, the history of the New Testament era, the literature of the New Testament, and biblical theology. Although never stated officially, it was understood by those in the program that the area of biblical theology was the catch-all category for those in other disciplines (theology, history, psychology, etc.) who wanted to take an exam in biblical studies. "Serious" biblical scholars were politely directed towards taking exams in the "hard-core" stuff like history and literature. This bias works both ways, of course, for I have also heard those who consider themselves to be biblical theologians cast aspersions upon sociologists or historians who are "theologically tone deaf."

25. Scroggs, "Can New Testament Theology Be Saved?" 213. For my own suggested description of New Testament theology see below, p. 331.

through sociological, literary, or rhetorical analysis. It is, according to Scroggs, specifically interested in "faith claims." Moreover, since "subsequent generations of believers" (including, of course, our own generation) continue to use these documents as the basis for their faith affirmations, New Testament theologians must also engage themselves in wrestling with the *truth claims* that these documents purport to make.[26] As descriptive historians we (presumably) need make no effort to evaluate these truth claims; as biblical theologians such evaluative work becomes a necessity. We cannot separate biblical theology from belief. We cannot escape commitment of self.

In the age of modernity such a confusion of history and faith, of the historian with the theologian, caused discomfort. The detached and objective world of scientific inquiry provided a safe refuge from the anxieties of belief.[27] We had neatly divided the world into the realm of science (reason) and the realm of belief (revelation). Even our professional identities evidenced such division: the Society of Biblical Literature (revelation) versus the American Academy of Religion (reason); Departments of Religious Studies (reason) versus Departments of Theology (revelation). We were "faithful" scholars who understood that our primary duty was to the churches who continued to live by these ancient documents (revelation), or we were "secular" scholars who owed allegiance to the objective, rational inquiry of the academy (reason).[28] Biblical theologians bore this split more onerously than most other scholars. They, by necessity, had to be multiple personalities. Committed to the objective, historical task of discerning "what the text meant," they also considered themselves bound to the task of explicating "what the text means" for today, of assessing (and implicitly proclaiming) the faith claims made in these documents.

It is the language of this split that has made me appear oxymoronic when I confess to being a *secular* New Testament theologian. In the language of modernity, such a moniker would perhaps be oxymoronic, for *secular* implied objectivity and *theologian* implied a faith commitment. This was the language of my mentors, trained in a

---

26. Scroggs, "Can New Testament Theology Be Saved?" 225, 231.

27. Stendahl acknowledges this phenomenon, though he gives it a more positive interpretation than what I am giving it. He says, " . . . we can achieve a common discourse among different kinds of believers and non-believers as long as we . . . distinguish the question 'what it meant' from the question 'what it means'" ("Method in the Study," 202). That is, as long as we leave belief out of the equation we can talk. But then we are talking, *not* as "different kinds of believers and non-believers," but as similar kinds of "descriptive historians."

28. Increasingly we are recognizing the inadequacy (absurdity?) of these divisions. If they once indicated some genuine distinctions between us, such distinctions have been altered somewhere along the way. But see the recent article by Charlotte Allen, "Is Nothing Sacred? Casting Out the Gods from Religious Studies," *Lingua Franca* (November 1996) 30–36.

now-rejected neoorthodoxy.[29] But I was born of a different generation. I was weaned not on neoorthodoxy but on that Berger–Luckmann volume that is ubiquitous in our bibliographies of the past thirty years, *The Social Construction of Reality*.[30]

I first read this volume during the fall of my freshman year in college. Looking back on the twenty-odd years that I have spent in academia since my initial reading of that book, I suspect that this single volume did more to define the context of my critical inquiry than anything else I have read. Although my graduate studies in New Testament were always couched in the language of modernity, I now recognize that I was unconsciously translating this language of "reason vs. revelation" into something more amenable to the insights of the sociology of knowledge. All of our lives and our knowledge, so Berger and Luckmann had taught me, rest upon faith claims. There is neither in nature nor in revelation the possibility of singular and absolute Truth. Or rather, I learned to say that, even if there *is* such a truth, we/all are so culturally and historically bound that all claims of accessing, knowing, articulating "objective truth"—as *either* historians *or* theologians— are deceptive and deceived. In *all* of our knowings we are bound to our own cultural belief, exiled from objective certainty. Like those members of the early Christian (or Epicurean or Mithraic) communities, *we are ourselves creatures of socially constructed faiths.*

Finally and late I have come to see that the bifurcated language of modernity—that language that divides reason from revelation, objectivity from faith, history or sociology from theology, secularity from ecclesial commitment—cannot account for my world. As pale as the descriptive label is, we *do* live *post*modern.[31] Current academic assumptions regarding the thorough "contextualization" of all knowledge led Scroggs to state his fear that "New Testament theology *as it has traditionally been conceived* is . . . seriously called into question.[32] I agree. The Enlightenment definitions of New Testament theology will not survive the postmodern world. But where Robin states this as fear, I see it as a sign of new possibility.[33] No, there can be no biblical

---

29. See Scroggs's account of the effects of the death of neoorthodoxy on New Testament interpretation in "Can the New Testament Be Relevant?" 277–80. What I am calling the "bifurcation" of modernity, Scroggs refers to as "dualism." He asserts that, "we live at the end of the twentieth century in a world that is in effect, if not explicitly, 'monistic'" (ibid., 278).

30. Peter Berger and Thomas Luckmann, *The Social Construction of Reality* (New York: Doubleday, 1966).

31. With my sincerest apologies to Robin for my use of this monstrosity of a label.

32. Scroggs, "Can New Testament Theology Be Saved?" 216–17, emphasis added.

33. Scroggs stated his fears regarding how this tendency toward radical contextualization will/does affect how we understand the discipline of biblical theology. My own sense, however, is that it is more the *historian* in us than the theologian that should be unsettled by such radical contextuality. Comments on that difficulty will have to wait for another essay on "Can we get

theology without belief. But then, from the perspective of the sociology of knowledge, *there can be no academic inquiry without belief.*

The question that my new colleagues asked me—"Do you believe what you teach?"—led me to acknowledge that I brought with me a different understanding of "belief." In contrast to them, I begin with the assumption that every single professor in the college where I teach *believes* what he or she teaches. We place trust not only in the methodologies that we have adopted and in the results of the application of those methodologies, but also, and more important perhaps, in the intrinsic value of what we are doing. Something, somewhere, sometime led us to *believe* that researching and teaching physics or political science or Latin American history or Bible or feminist philosophy has legitimacy and value. *Every academic discipline*—whether in the sciences, the humanities, the social sciences, or the arts—rests upon commitments to some fundamental beliefs, beliefs that are at best plausible, but never finally provable. Does this language of commitment, of trust in the legitimacy of what we do, lead you to suspect a youthful idealism on my part? But no, I myself have had long dry stretches already in this profession, arid deserts where I have doubted the value of my discipline—either in the classroom or in my study. But of course, doubt is the cohort of belief. And the fact that many of us anxiously (or flippantly) doubt both the legitimacy and the value of our work, even much of the time, indicates that we are at least subconsciously aware that it is precisely some sort of *belief* that undergirds our professional activity. Do I believe what I teach, what I write? I hope so . . . I try to . . . Sometimes . . .

Yes, this "believing" life is a life of anxiety. I cannot *know*, not for certain, not with the arrogant confidence that I am "right." But this lack of certainty is not peculiar to me because I talk about God. No, this lack of certainty is the context for all of us.[34] We tread less

---

there from here?" At this point it is sufficient to note that while the discomfiting hermeneutical question *was* "Can we get from the 'then' to the 'now', from 'what it meant' to 'what it means'?", the discomfort *today* arises from the question of whether we can get to the 'then' at all. The insights of deconstructionism would leave us with only "what it means," and assert that it is folly for us to think we could ever discover "what it meant." Contrast Scroggs's article, "The New Testament and Ethics: How Do We Get from There to Here?" (in *Text and Times*, 192–211) with the section entitled "The Failure of Analogy" in his essay, "Can the New Testament Be Relevant?" 275–77.

34. Herein lies my primary critique of the "modern" construal of the problem. "Faith," in that construal, belonged properly to Theology and was *verboten* in any truly scientific or academic analysis. See, for example, Riches's statement to the effect that every modern biblical theologian (save von Balthasar) has wanted *"to free the student of the New Testament from any particular faith requirement,* so that he may address himself freely to his colleagues in other disciplines and even faiths" (229, emphasis added). I suggest that the situation is quite the reverse! We should not be "freeing" ourselves or our students from "faith requirements," but should rather boldly insist that our students and our "colleagues in other disciplines" own up to their own implicit "faith requirements." That is, *faith* (in terms of the sociology of knowledge) refers *not*

arrogantly (or so we should do) on this postmodern soil. Our ability to speak across disciplines, across "faiths," across cultural boundaries derives not from some common ground of scientific certitude that we share but from our common anxiety, the anxiety of belief.

In the age of modernity we sought to escape the anxiety of belief and searched for haven in the presumed objective truth of science. Our discipline was formed within this haven, and thus the "claiming of our anxiety" chafes not only psychologically but generically as well.[35] This chafing has led me to look beyond the walls of our discipline to the work of novelists, poets, and above all essayists, for I find there a type of intellectual exploration that celebrates openness and affirms the value of intellectual anxiety.[36] The critical discourse of the essayist is more akin to a pas de deux than to a chess match. And I find myself wanting to engage in this ballet and to think afresh about how New Testament theology might be conceived in my world. The modern world bequeathed me gifts of critical rigor. For these I am grateful. But surely ballet is as rigorous as a chess match. How, then, can I reconceive my discipline and discourse in this postmodern world where we must acknowledge *the inescapability of faith,* while not disdaining the critical gifts that I have received from the modern world?

STARTING ELSEWHERE

I can no longer rest easy in those oppositions of history versus faith, of objectivity versus belief. The theorists do not help me much. This great antinomy infects our theoretical language, and I am unwilling to start a reimagining of my discipline that invokes the terms of that now-old debate. And so I start elsewhere.

---

just to "religious belief" or moral commitment; it refers to the necessary acknowledgment that even our *categories of thought* (i.e., our epistemology) rely upon a cultural framework—a framework that may be unconcious, but is surely not "absolute" or objectively provable. As many of us can attest, entry into any professional discipline requires the adoption of some "faith claims." Every discipline has its insiders, outsiders, and heretics.

35. The genre of articles written for publication in our professional journals relies implicitly on notions of presenting an "air-tight argument." Given that our discipline was born in the age of modernity, such rhetorical expectations are not surprising. But it is difficult if not impossible to write in that genre from a stance that embraces intellectual anxiety.

36. As Theodor Adorno says, "the essay shies away from the violence of dogma." Or, as William Zeiger describes Montaigne's essays, "The practice of experimenting, or trying something out, is expressed in the now uncommon sense of the verb *to prove*—the sense of 'testing' rather than of 'demonstrating validity.' Montaigne 'proved' his ideas in that he tried them out in his essays. He spun out their implications, sampled their suggestions. He did not argue or try to persuade. He had no investment in winning over his audience to his opinion; accordingly, he had no fear of being refuted. On the contrary, he expected that some of the ideas he expressed would change, as they did in later essays. Refutation represented not a personal defeat but an advance toward truth as valuable as confirmation." Both Adorno and Zeiger cited in Lopate, xliii, xlv.

This "elsewhere" is an unconventional place. I can give it a conventional name—the name of "experience"—but that name does not erase its historic unconventionality. This "elsewhere" is not an objective place, for it cannot be so. It is particular (and scandalous in that). It offers no universality in itself. This "elsewhere" is the painfully limited space of my own life and experience. My initial embarrassment at my scanty and scandalous resources for theology is lessened some when I read these words of Doris Lessing:

> At last I understood that the way over, or through this dilemma, the unease at writing about "petty personal problems" was to recognise that nothing is personal, in the sense that it is uniquely one's own. Writing about oneself, one is writing about others, since your problems, pains, pleasures, emotions—and your extraordinary and remarkable ideas—can't be yours alone. The way to deal with the problem of "subjectivity," that shocking business of being preoccupied with the tiny individual who is at the same time caught up in such an explosion of terrible and marvellous possibilities, is to see him as a microcosm and in this way to break through the personal, the subjective, making the personal general, as indeed life always does, transforming a private experience—or so you think of it when still a child, "*I* am falling in love," "*I* am feeling this or that emotion, or thinking that or the other thought"—into something much larger: growing up is after all only the understanding that one's unique and incredible experience is what everyone shares.[37]

It is my suspicion that more of us live here than will dare admit it. It is *au courant* to emphasize the magnitude of our cultural and historical boundedness; that we are estranged from and *cannot know* what others elsewhere and in other times thought or believed; that historical continuity and the transcendental self are falsifications of what is finally a series of unbreachable chasms. Yet most of us deny these things daily in the actual practice of our profession. We dare to give lectures on the ancient Greeks or medieval Spaniards. We risk attempting to present the thought of Maimonides or of Seneca. We cast these distant realities into our own culturally and historically bounded language . . . as though such translation were possible. We presume to know—at least in part. More, we presume to communicate to others who are equally bound, distant even in some ways from ourselves. We reenact ancient wars and loves, family struggles and friendships, as though we understand such things today, as though we experience such ancient realities here, within our own gaspingly distant time and space. We

---

37. D. Lessing, *The Golden Notebook*, "Introduction" to the 1971 edition, p. xiii in Bantam Book edition, 1981.

trust (our actions reveal this faith) that such things can be passed on—to another time, another space, still further in the distance.

Our practice gives me more courage than our au courant theories. I suspect that our problem is not that we are unable *to do* New Testament theology in this present world, but rather that we are unable *to describe what we do* in the theoretical language that is available to us at present. Toward the end of Scroggs's essay on "Can New Testament Theology Be Saved?" he narrates a brief but enlightening encounter he once had with a student:

> A student once told me (I was not certain whether it was compliment or complaint) that she never was sure where Paul stopped and Scroggs started. Whether compliment or complaint I have come to see that ambiguity as necessary to the doing of New Testament theology.[38]

And in the margins of my book I wrote, *"I think this may be the key to defining NT Theology."* I strongly suspect that Robin's "unique" experience is, as Doris Lessing says, "what everyone shares." What every Pauline theologian shares, at any rate. At least I know that I could have said exactly what this student said to any really good professor I ever had. I know that in my own teaching of Paul, in my own thinking *with* Paul, I myself can never *quite* tell where Paul stops and Virginia starts.

But this is dirty laundry. It displays our own embarrassing lack of objectivity. It confuses subjectivity (my horizon) with objectivity (the horizon of Paul, of the text). Scroggs calls this an "ambiguity." Indeed. Perhaps we should go further and simply call it a downright confusion.

What are the safeguards when we deliberately engage in this kind of confusion? How do we know we have not slid headlong into a mass/mess of narcissistic subjectivity? I must refer you to the hermeneuticians for clarification of these inherent methodological difficulties. I'd rather stay down here with the dirty laundry . . . because it is mine, . . . because I suspect it is yours as well. I will speak then, not of the theoriticians, but of my own experience of teaching New Testament theology and of speaking in God-talk.

---

38. Scroggs, "Can New Testament Theology Be Saved?" 232.

MAKING SENSE OF GOD-TALK
"Putting Body and Soul Together Again"

> *We tell the story the way we do precisely because*
> *it makes sense that way in our day and time.*
> —Robin Scroggs

New Testament theology as a discipline is specifically concerned with making sense of the faith claims articulated within the texts of the New Testament. In Scroggs's language, it is the "description in coherent and structured form" of those faith claims. We are concerned with understanding the sense of these claims, and that means assessing their coherency, their consistency, their interrelationships, and yes, even their adequacy. We assume that the God-talk of Paul, for instance, has *at some level* a logical coherence, that it is not just a bunch of statements made willy-nilly in some mystical jabberwocky, devoid of any intellectual consistency. That is, we assume the *intellectual integrity* of these authors/texts.[39]

Furthermore, as New Testament theologians we relate to the authors/communities of these texts primarily as *conversation partners,* rather than as *cultural artifacts.* In the tribute to Robin's scholarship at the beginning of this present volume, Graydon Snyder related the story of Ernst Käsemann's consternation over Scroggs's proposal of a sociological analysis of the New Testament texts. Käsemann feared that Americans would abandon theology for sociology. And indeed, Käsemann's fear would seem to be appropriate, for much current study of the New Testament texts does treat the authors/communities of these texts primarily as cultural artifacts, as instantiations of particular social worlds. In a world where biblical theology reigned, Robin had called for "putting *body* and soul together"—that is, for attending not just to the "soul" of the text but to the "bodies" of the communities who gave birth to these texts. We have, it seems to me, now explored in creative ways the "embodiment" of these texts/communities, and it is time

---

39. Perhaps Scroggs's fear of how radical "contextualization" might undo all possibility of New Testament theology is related to this assumption. Some interpretations do come mighty close to *reducing* a historical text to its social/psychological/cultural/economic context, as though such contexts explain the whole of an author's thought. (This sounds like the old dictation theory of inspiration, except here it is social context that dictates, whereas before it was God who dictated. I prefer to allow a bit more human agency than that!) There are times, that is, when we let our new theoretical insights get the best of our common sense. Who among us would be willing to say that *our* thought, our publications, our speech is completely explained by analyzing our psychological history or our social context? Should we not grant our historical predecessors the same possibility for creative thinking that transcends their context as we would hope later generations would grant us? Or is creative intellectual thought not possible?

again to return to the task of "putting body and *soul* together"—but this time from the opposite direction, from within a world where sociological analysis rules. Can we move beyond observing (and objectifying?) the *bodies* of these communities to some place where we could again hear their *souls?* Can we put body and soul *together?*

In short, how can we—how *do* we—have conversations with these ancient texts, with those long-ago humans (both body and soul) who expressed themselves herein? The hermeneutical model of interpretation as "conversation" still has much to commend itself, particularly because in conversation there is a necessary intertwining of subject and object, of subjectivity and objectivity.[40] The more I know about the life-experience of my conversation partner, the more intelligent my participation in the conversation can be. We all know the frustration of having a conversation partner (I use the term lightly!) who interprets everything we say from within his own world, in relation only to her own experience. Not much true conversation happens there! Rather, we are simply co-opted as a voice within the other's ideology. In such ways have we co-opted the New Testament texts for our own "theologies." But true conversation demands an intuitive and empathic listening to the other, an other who speaks out of concrete life experiences that are usually quite different from our own. I try to listen to you as objectively as I can, that is, without imputing to your statements my *own* meaning, a meaning derived from my own subjective experience. But my objectivity does not (or *should* not) reduce you to *object.* Rather, my objectivity enables me to hear you as speaking *subject.* Sociological analysis is essential if we are to listen responsibly to the subjectivity of the authors/communities of these texts. We study their "bodies" in order to hear their "souls."

But conversation also prevails upon us to speak. It requires us—as subjects in our own right—to engage the other. It is not enough for us to understand the other, to observe "where you're coming from."[41]

---

40. See Hans-Georg Gadamer's notion of the "game" of conversation, where the "players" give way to the "subject matter": "The attraction of a game . . . consists precisely in the fact that the game tends to master the players. . . . The real subject of the game . . . is not the player, but instead the game itself." Gadamer, *Truth and Method*, trans. G. B. Garrett and J. Cumming (New York: Continuum, 1975) 95–96. I would prefer to retain the integrity of the "players" along with the "play" of the game. (I prefer a metaphor of dance for it preserves the dancers as both "subjects" and "objects" of movement and emphasizes collaboration among the acting subjects rather than competition between players, as in a game.) In terms of "conversation" I would use the term "intersubjectivity" to denote the interplay of (at least) two speaking *subjects* in relation to the *subject* matter.

41. See M. M. Bakhtin's discussion of the importance of response: "Understanding and response are dialectically merged and mutually condition each other; one is impossible without the other." Bakhtin, "Discourse in the Novel," in *The Dialogic Imagination*, ed. M. Holquist, trans. C. Emerson and M. Holquist (Austin, TX: University of Texas Press, 1981) 282.

No, as Robin has said, the other makes a claim on us.[42] At least this is true if we take the other *seriously*. If it is frustrating to try to converse with someone who will not listen, it is no less frustrating to "converse" with someone who refuses to respond. In my own conversation I do not want simply to be "understood." I have seen too frequently how the other's "understanding" becomes yet one more way for him to objectify, to control. No, I want *response* from another speaking subject—agreement, disagreement, modification, amplification. The kinds of response are manifold. If we take the other (as speaking subject) seriously, then we will respond with our own subjective voice. To be *observed* but not responded to . . . To *observe* and not respond . . . This is no conversation. It is a kind of death. The body remains but the soul is gone. The text as cultural artifact is a dead text.

As New Testament theologians we take seriously our obligation both to hear the subjects who speak in these texts *and to respond* as thinking subjects ourselves to the voices in these texts. But I would assert that the seriousness of our task does not derive from a prior religious faith.[43] Rather, as responsible intellects we seek to take all our conversation partners seriously—as both body and soul. Students of Plato or Whitman or Rousseau or Simone de Beauvoir should seek no less than to hear and to respond to the texts they study. They seek intellectual coherence, as do we. They seek to listen empathically and contextually, as do we. They seek to respond to these speaking subjects with intellectual and experiential integrity, as do we. The texts our colleagues in other disciplines read are imagined to be alive: profitable for study, demanding our attention, calling for our response. These texts, no less than our own, convey the "faith claims" of their authors, "faith claims" informed by and formed within the particular sociological contexts in which the authors lived. What defines the particularity of our discipline is not, then, the seriousness with which we seek to respond to these ancient faith claims. Rather, it is simply that we engage in conversation with faith claims that speak of God, faith claims that employ God-talk.[44]

---

42. See Scroggs, "Can the New Testament Be Saved?" 228–30.

43. It can, of course, be an expression of such a faith. My point, however, is that it need not be.

44. In my judgment, Scroggs's rejection of the "Pagan Classic" treatment of the New Testament was misplaced. (See "Can New Testament Theology Be Saved?" 227–28.) The New Testament is not "theological" simply because it makes a *truth claim*. Many (maybe even most) texts make such a claim. Read almost any philosopher! It is (part of) the philosopher's job to read and assess the truth claims made by others. What makes these New Testament texts (and our job) "theological" is that these texts make truth claims that employ God-talk.

Then how are we, as theologians, to interpret this God-talk? What *does* it mean for us to speak of God? New methodologies in our discipline have shown us that we can intelligently speak of "God" as a social symbol, as a character, as a term in rhetorical argumentation. We do not, that is, need to revert to a premodern belief in a dualistic universe, where (so we have assumed) talk of God was primarily referential speech.[45] Nor do we need to concede to that modern worldview wherein academics, in order to be *true* academics, refused to allow any reference to God in a "scientific" discourse.[46] We live, rather, in a world where we recognize that all speech is *interpretive* speech: Language seeks to interpret embodied experience.[47] Nadine Pence Frantz has coined what I find to be a useful aphorism for describing how we engage in God-talk: *"Theology is to life as interpretation is to a text."*[48] That is, God-talk is an interpretation of embodied lives. It is a human language that seeks to make sense of the complexity of human lives. The use of God-talk indicates that the speaker experiences life in ways that transcend (mere) psychological, sociological, economic, biological, or political descriptions. There is something more. Life cannot be reduced to these scientific analyses—so the speaker of God-talk insists. There is more to our human experience than the sciences or social sciences can explain.[49] The term "God" does not (necessarily) refer to some being who inhabits a transcendent realm; rather the term "God" (and the language field of theology)

---

45. That is, we do not need to "mimic" the subjective voice of the text. We can—and should—respond (as subjects) from within our own "world" to the "world" of the text. True conversation sustains the (ongoing) *difference* between the conversants in the conversation and does not need to reduce the dialogic interaction to a monologic "truth."

46. In this respect Charlotte Allen's caricature of the "young radicals" (Cameron et al.) in her article, "Is Nothing Sacred?" is interesting. These "radicals" are actually articulating what is—from a postmodern perspective—a very conservative position, i.e., they argue that scientific analysis enables objectivity. Two hundred years ago, Cameron et al. would have been radicals. In today's academy, however, such confidence in "scientific objectivity" reflects, in my judgment, a certain naivete.

47. See Scroggs's excellent introduction to this notion in his *Christology in Paul and John*, Proclamation Commentaries (Philadelphia: Fortress Press, 1988) 1–8.

48. See Frantz's article, "The (Inter)Textuality of Our Lives: An Anabaptist Feminist Hermeneutic," *Conrad Grebel Review* 14 (Spring 1996) 131–44. Drawing on the work of Ricoeur and Kristeva, Frantz argues that "there is a mutually interactive process between the text and the interpretation of the text. In the same way, there is a mutually interactive process between our lives and the doing of theology. Both processes render meaning out of performative moments which are made up of texts and sub-texts, multiple in their vitality and voice. In both, the process seeks to articulate the presence and activity of God and to express the *jouissance* (the delight) of revelation, meaning and speaking truly" (132). See also the insightful article by Monika K. Hellwig, "Theology as a Fine Art," in *Interpreting Tradition: The Art of Theological Reflection*, ed. Jane Kopas, The Annual Publication of the College Theology Society, 1983, vol. 29 (Chico, CA: Scholars Press, 1984) 3–10.

49. Thus, we have the disciplines of the humanities and the arts as well as the sciences and the social sciences!

provides us with a useful construct in our efforts to speak intelligibly about observable dynamics in human experience.[50]

I am a New Testament theologian. With this statement I began this personal *essaying* of our discipline. I have learned some things in this *essai*. I have learned, for instance, that my own understanding of our discipline requires that I pursue a particular kind of question. That is, *What sense can we make of these ancient faith claims that speak of God?*[51] How can we engage these texts—both body and soul—in responsible conversation today?

I do not despair of the possibility of taking up this conversation. I have, in fact, been engaged in this conversation for years—as have many of you. On this matter, my essaying here has given me some confidence: I *am* a New Testament theologian, even in a liberal arts context, even as I converse with colleagues and students who claim no religious faith. This task in which I engage is a legitimate academic pursuit within the humanities; I need not hide behind either church or science. I am not, after all, an oxymoron.

But how, then, do I describe what I do when I do "New Testament theology" in my current context? I have rejected above the traditional descriptions of our discipline, those that rely on the bifurcation of reason and revelation, sociology versus theology. And, as did Robin in his paper on sociological method, I reject a disembodied reading of these texts. How can I, how *do* I, read the text body *and* soul? I do not yet know a theoretical language that coheres with my experience of reading the texts this way. Rather, all I can offer is a description of my own experience. This is how I put body and soul together in my own conversation with the text—

I have a life. Sometimes it doesn't seem like much of a life, but it's all I've got. I struggle with paying bills, buying cars, single-parenting two teenage daughters, worrying about the "tenure-thing." I

---

50. We use such constructs frequently in academic discourse. The Freudian terms "id" or "super-ego," for example, are "constructs." That is, we cannot locate such a construct in place or time; we cannot scientifically observe such constructs in a literal fashion. Rather, they are intellectual categories that help us make intelligible—even if only in heuristic ways—some elements of human experience that would otherwise be difficult to describe with precision.

51. One reader of an earlier draft of this essay expatiated on my desire to "make sense" in this way: "To 'make sense' implies rationality of a practical sort. But 'sense' also refers to much more than the mind. The *senses* are invoked and intensified by the statement of desire—'I want to make sense.' To me, the quiet passion of 'I want for my words to make sense' rubs up against and begins to irritate a slightly more 'rational' statement such as 'I want to explain.'" Mary Ellen Burd, letter to author, 18 September 1996. I would add to this that *"making sense of a text"* implies an acknowledgment of the interpreter's personal involvement in the act of interpretation; the near-synonymous phrase, *"understanding a text,"* implies more passivity, and perhaps presumes more "objectivity."

revel in love and friendship and humor and (sometimes) work. Things in my life rarely go as planned: Teenagers throw unscheduled fits, cars crash (repeatedly in my case), bill collectors call, and tenure . . . well, ask me next year. Life occasionally delights: love in unexpected places, friends who surprise me with a party, laughter in deliciously inappropriate places and times, pen and paper that helps me sort out my sometimes muddled mind. I notice that other people around me have lives, too. (I never promised brilliance here, just a simple effort to understand.) They struggle, revel, are unable to plan, know delight. Me being me, I wonder incessantly what these lives mean.

I read the New Testament. It says some strange things. Cultural oddities: *Now concerning food offered to idols.* Philosophical profundities: *Those who lose their lives shall find them.* Theological curiosities: *God justifies the ungodly. The wages of sin is death. No one is justified by works of the law.* Me being me, I wonder incessantly (and much to the distraction of most of my friends) what these words mean.

I have a life—and I struggle to know what it means. I read the New Testament—and I struggle to understand what it means. And I use Mortimer Adler's rule of understanding:[52] Can I put it in my own words? Can I give an example?

This explains, I think, my frustration with reading much of what passes as New Testament theology. They (these authors who frustrate me) explain, for example, Paul's text by using Paul's own language (God, Sin, Righteousness) and by using Paul's own illustrations (cross, ethical dilemmas, Paul's *peristasis* catalogues). *But what does it mean?* Or so my mind shouts when I read. Can you, dear author, put these things in your *own* words? Can you give this reader some illustration of your *own*? What *sense* can I make of all these foreign (or too-familiar) words? Show me that you understand. Bring me, your reader, into your conversation with Paul.

I interrupt my tirade to note that there are, fortunately, some authors who pass the Adler test. The scholar whom we honor with this volume is paramount among them in our generation. Reread *Paul for a New Day.* Turn again to his volume *Christology in Paul and John,* his essays in *The Text and the Times.* Time and again, Scroggs struggles to make sense of the New Testament text—*not* by falling back on some disembodied dogmatic belief, never that—but by putting things in Robin's own words, by painting an illustration drawn from the particu-

---

52. See Mortimer J. Adler and Charles van Doran, *How to Read a Book: The Classic Guide to Intelligent Reading*, rev. and updated ed. (New York: Simon & Schuster, 1972) 124–28.

larities of his/our own embodied lives. We get some sense of how a noetic transformation enables new ethical perception as Robin describes his own efforts (both failed and successful) to listen to a student who drops by his office.[53] We hear the implicit desire to live a life "beyond the performance principle," a life in that new creation of "erotic exuberance" as he describes for us his conversation with Paul, Brown, and Marcuse.[54] We recognize that "scary crisis which jolts us out of our familiar, if dreary reality," and claim, with Robin, that "new world of light and joy,"[55] because we hear his own voice of trauma, his own cry of joy as he encounters the embodied experience of the authors of these texts.

So, too, do I find myself drawing on my own experience and that of my students, using our own engagement with the world as illustrative fodder that can help us engage these texts from foreign worlds. I describe to my students the curse of the law as I live it in relation to my teenage daughters. I explore the hunger for righteous approbation and the anxiety such hunger arouses as I analyze with them my own desires to attain tenure. Paul's notion of Sin becomes explicit as my students and I probe the dynamics of addiction. We recognize Grace as we talk together—and with Paul—about the surprise of love in our own lives.

Does such "illustrative work" simply display a narcissistic subjectivity—my "dirty laundry"—in my reading of the apostle Paul? No, I think this is what we do when we teach New Testament theology. We draw illustrations for/with our hearers in order to help them/us understand the underlying dynamics, the real-life *logic* of the text before us. The test of a good illustration is, of course, whether our examples become windows through which our hearers can begin to construct their own examples. I have not led my hearers into understanding (either Paul's text or my illustration) unless and until they begin to put it in their own words, translating it into their own examples and illustrations.[56]

Teaching demands such illustration that begets further illustration. And I suspect that every good teacher engages in this kind of enter-

---

53. Scroggs, *Paul for a New Day* (Philadelphia: Fortress Press, 1977) 69–70.
54. See "The Heuristic Value of a Psychoanalytic Model," in *The Text and the Times*, 144, 146.
55. Scroggs, *Christology in Paul and John*, 113.
56. Repeating myself ad nauseum (for our ghettoized discipline I think such repetition is necessary), I would insist that this same kind of thinking/learning occurs in other "secular" disciplines. Again, a student (or professor, for that matter) does not adequately understand Plato (or Freud or Marx or whomever you please) unless they can (a) say it in their own words and (b) give an illustration/example of their own.

prise. We live with that kind of dirty laundry behind the closed door of the classroom. We (often) have time to wash our clothes before we put ourselves into print, before we present our refined (disembodied?) insights to our colleagues at professional meetings.[57]

But I will say more. I will dare to suggest that the soil in our garment (that garment which is our discipline) is too deep to wash out. The soil of our subjectivity becomes a constitutive part of the fibers of our work. For these illustrations that we use, I would argue, are not simply *pedagogical* devices. They are the way in which *theological thinking* occurs. The "illustration" provides a structure through which we respond intellectually to the text; through our efforts to construct an approximate "illustration" we become speaking subjects in our conversation with this text. That is, on this side of the "sociological revolution" (if I may coin a term for a historical moment), we recognize that all thought is *embodied* thought. Just as we now would never claim to understand Paul's thought—his soul—apart from understanding his social context—his "embodiment"—so we now can no longer rest in a mode of intellectual response that is disembodied, that whitewashes our own subjectivity. We have "embodied the text" through sociological analysis. And now we are ready to meet the text intellectually with our own embodiment. Here, in this embodied conversation, is where we put body and soul together.[58]

Thus do such real-life illustrations become trial-and-error experiments that help us test our intellectual understanding of the text before us. Rather than the historian's "analogies" they are instead what philosophers call "thought experiments"—imaginings that assist us in assessing the coherency, adequacy, and consistency of the faith claims made in this text. Our "illustrations" function to help us make sense of some of the real-life logical dynamics inherent in Paul's text. But in turn—or rather simultaneously—Paul's text, that is his embodied experience expressed in his theological language, helps us think construc-

---

57. We would do well, in my judgment, to model ourselves instead after Montaigne: "Had it been my purpose to seek the world's favour, I should have put on finer clothes, and have presented myself in a studied attitude. But I want to appear in my simple, natural, and everyday dress, without strain or artifice; for it is myself that I portray." Taken from his introduction to the reader, *Essays*, 23. Scroggs's volume of collected essays, *The Text and the Times*, where he introduces each essay with a "preface" that sets the essay in a concrete historical and experiential context, models for us a way to begin to claim our "subjectivity." As he explains in his introduction to these essays, "I have prefaced each essay with a statement that attempts to describe why I wrote, and why I wrote it as I did" (3–4).

58. I am tempted to say that "where body meets body we encounter soul." That is, when the embodiment of the text (through sociological analysis) converses with the embodiment of the interpreter (through public ownership of my own concrete life experience), then we are able to respond to the text intellectually and honestly.

tively about our particular embodiment. We wrestle with the real-life logic and dynamics of this text by imagining its conceptuality into our own lives and universe; in doing so we cannot avoid thinking about our own lives as we imagine them through this other language, through these other distant lives. We think constructively about both things at the same time.

No, we can never tell where Paul stops and Scroggs starts. We do "put body and soul together." This is New Testament theology. It is what we do.

In the world of modernity, such things were scandalous. Burn the filthy rags at the (academy's) stake! But in this world which has followed upon the missteps of modernity—in this postmodern world—this pile of dirty laundry may be our glory. No longer do we need to feign an objective purity that whitewashes our subjective experience or obscures our culturally determined beliefs. True, we cannot claim certainty. True, we are left in the midst of our own limited time and space, messy as it is. But at least we can be here, both soul *and* body. And we can be here with the rich resources of the past, both body and soul, to help us understand, to help us live more intelligently in our now.

Do I believe in God? I cannot speak to that. But I can say that I have found that conversation with Paul's God-talk does help me and some of my students make sense of our own messy lives. I have found that by "thinking our lives into Paul's God-talk" I have encountered new ways of imagining what Paul might have meant. Do I know what Paul thought? Do I know his God? Do I have the faith of Paul? I cannot answer. But I can affirm that in the struggle to read—and make sense of—this text before me, a fragment from another time and place, my mind happens upon new ways of imagining this present time and place. By struggling to understand and respond to these distant faith claims I encounter new faith claims that I can make in the here and now, faith claims formed within this culturally constructed universe that we inhabit. I cannot say whether I or my students have been transformed by a "new world that *really* exists." But I can acknowledge that my scholarly engagement (body and soul) with the New Testament texts has sometimes surprised me into hearing an invitation to new thoughts, to a new perception of what our world, of what I myself, might (yet) be.

Curriculum Vitae
of Robin Scroggs

Robin Scroggs was born in Raleigh, North Carolina, on October 14, 1930. Prior to entering theological education, Scroggs earned two degrees in music (piano) from the University of North Carolina, an A.B. in 1951 and a B.Music in 1952. In 1952 he began his theological training at the Divinity School of Duke University, graduating with the B.D. in 1955. He is an ordained minister of the United Methodist Church. During the 1955–56 academic year, Scroggs studied rabbinics at Hebrew Union College in Cincinnati, Ohio. The following year he entered the Ph.D. program at Princeton University where he studied New Testament under W. D. Davies, writing a dissertation that was subsequently published as *The Last Adam* (1967, see bibliography). Princeton University granted him the Ph.D. in 1963.

Scroggs began teaching at Dartmouth College in Hanover, New Hampshire, in 1959. While at Dartmouth, he was awarded two grants for study: in 1964, as the Dartmouth Faculty Fellow he studied in Heidelberg and Tübingen, Germany; and in 1967, as the recipient of the Dartmouth Comparative Studies Grant (Ford Foundation) he studied Greek religions in Cambridge, England. Scroggs served as chair of the Department of Religion at Dartmouth from 1967 to 1969.

In 1969, Scroggs moved from Dartmouth to the Chicago Theological Seminary. In 1974 Scroggs returned to Tübingen for study. While in Chicago he also served as visiting lecturer at the Divinity School of the University of Chicago in 1975 and 1978. In addition to teaching New Testament, Scroggs carried a variety of responsibilities at the seminary. He served as organist for the seminary; he led a choral group that specialized in Renaissance music; and he served in the administrative capacities of acting dean (1975) and acting director of recruitment and admissions (1979–80).

Since 1986, Scroggs has held the position of the Edward Robinson Professor of New Testament at Union Theological Seminary of New York City, where he is also an adjunct in religion for the Graduate School of Arts and Sciences at Columbia University.

Scroggs has been an active participant in professional societies. From 1977 to 1982 he served as the chair for the Seminar on the Social Background of the New Testament for Studiorum Novi Testamenti Societas. He was president of the Chicago Society of Biblical Research during the academic year 1979 to 1980. From 1982–87 he served as the chair for the Pauline Epistles Section of the Society of Biblical Literature. He has also been a member of the Catholic Biblical Association. Throughout his time in Chicago, Scroggs was an active member of the New Testament group of the Chicago Cluster of Theological Schools which later became the Association of the Chicago Theological Schools.

Works by
Robin Scroggs

Compiled by Kevin L. Smith

1960

Review of *Le Peche Originel dans L'Ecriture*, by André M. Dubarle. *Journal of Biblical Literature* 79 (March 1960): 84–85.

"John Wesley as Biblical Scholar." *Journal of Bible and Religion* 28 (October 1960): 415–22.

1963

"Romans VI.7: ὁ γὰρ ἀποθανὼν δεδικαίωται ἀπὸ τῆς ἁμαρτίας." *New Testament Studies* 10 (October 1963): 104–8.

1965

"The Exaltation of the Spirit by Some Early Christians." *Journal of Biblical Literature* 84 (December 1965): 359–73.

1967

The Last Adam: A Study in Pauline Anthropology. Philadelphia: Fortress Press, 1967.

"The Humanistic Pursuit of Values." *Dartmouth Alumni Magazine* 59 (May 1967): 29–31.

"Paul: Sophos and Pneumatikos [1 Cor 2:6–16]." *New Testament Studies* 14 (October 1967): 33–55.

Review of *Christianity According to Paul*, by Michael Bouttier. *Journal of Biblical Literature* 86 (summer 1967): 348–49.

1968

"The Earliest Hellenistic Christianity." In *Religions in Antiquity: Essays in Memory of Erwin Ramsdell Goodenough*, edited by J. Neusner, 176–206. Leiden: Brill, 1968.

1969

Review of *The Pre-Existence of Christ in the New Testament*, by Fred B. Craddock. *Journal of the American Academy of Religion* 37 (summer 1969): 170–73.

1970

"Tradition, Freedom, and the Abyss." *Chicago Theological Seminary Register* 60, no. 4 (1970): 1–13. Reprinted in *The Text and the Times*, 5–19.

"Mark: Theologian of the Incarnation." In Markan Task Force, Society of Biblical Literature, 1970.

1971

"Reflections on the Question: Was There a Pre-Markan Passion Narrative?" In *SBL 107th Annual Meeting Seminar Papers*, edited by J. White et al., 503–86. 1971. Coauthored with W. Kelber and A. Kolenkow.

"The Significance of Paul: A Vision for the Future." *Chicago Theological Seminary: The President's Newsletter* (1971).

Review of *Jesus and Man's Hope*, edited by David G. Buttrick. *Encounter* 32 (fall 1971): 331–33.

1972

"A New Old Quest? A Review Essay." Review of *Matthew*, by William Foxwell Albright and C. S. Mann. *Journal of the American Academy of Religion* 40 (December 1972): 506–12.

"Paul and the Eschatological Woman." *Journal of the American Academy of Religion* 40 (September 1972): 283–303. Reprinted (with additions from "Paul and the Eschatological Woman: Revisited") in *The Text and the Times*, 69–95.

"Paul: Chauvinist or Liberationist?" *Christian Century* 89 (15 March 1972): 307–9.

Translator. *Glory and the Way of the Cross: The Gospel of Mark*, by Ludger Schenke. Franciscan Herald Press, 1972. (*Herrlichkeit und Kreuz: Wie kam es zum Marcus Evangelium?* Katholische Bibelwerk, 1969.)

Review of *The Myth of Christian Beginnings*, by Robert L. Wilken. *Christian Century* 89 (16 February 1972): 204.

"Eros and Agape in Paul." Paper presented at the International Congress of Learned Societies in the Field of Religion, 1972. Published in *The Text and the Times*, 151–66.

1973

"Baptism in Mark: Dying and Rising with Christ [Mk 14:51–52; 16:1–8]." *Journal of Biblical Literature* 92 (December 1973): 531–48. Coauthored with Kent Groff.

"Introductory Essay." In *Victory over Violence: Jesus and the Revolutionists*, by Martin Hengel, ix–xxiv. Philadelphia: Fortress Press, 1973.

1974

"Paul and the Eschatological Woman: Revisited." *Journal of the American Academy of Religion* 42 (summer 1974): 532–37.

"Paul and Women's Liberation." Audiocassette. *Thesis Theological Cassettes* 4 (January 1974).

1975

"The Earliest Christian Communities as Sectarian Movement." In *Christianity, Judaism, and Other Greco-Roman Cults: Studies for Morton Smith at Sixty*, edited by J. Neusner, 2:1–23. Leiden: Brill, 1975. Reprinted in *The Text and the Times*, 20–45.

1976

"The Bible as a Weapon in Evangelical-Liberal Warfare." In *The American Religious Experiment: Piety and Practicality*, edited by C. Manschreck and B. Zikmund, 60–71. Chicago: Exploration Press, 1976.

"Interdisciplinary Perspectives on the House Church." In *The House Church Evolving*, edited by A. Foster. Chicago: Exploration Press, 1976.

"Marriage in the New Testament." In *The Interpreter's Dictionary of the Bible: Supplementary Volume*, 576–77. Nashville: Abingdon Press, 1976.

"Women in the New Testament." In *The Interpreter's Dictionary of the Bible: Supplementary Volume*, 966–68. Nashville: Abingdon Press, 1976.

"Paul as Rhetorician: Two Homilies in Romans 1–11." In *Jews, Greeks, and Christians: Religious Cultures in Late Antiquity. Essays in Honor of William David Davies*, edited by Robert G. Hammerton-Kelly and Robin Scroggs, 271–98. Leiden: Brill, 1976.

Editor (with R. Hammerton-Kelly). *Jews, Greeks, and Christians: Religious Cultures in Late Antiquity. Essays in Honor of William David Davies*. Leiden: Brill, 1976.

Review of *Man as Male and Female: A Study in Sexual Relationships from a Theological Point of View*, by Paul K. Jewett. *Foundations* 19 (October–December 1976): 374–76.

Review of *Studies in Paul's Technique and Theology*, by Anthony T. Hanson. *Interpretation* 30 (July 1976): 329–30.

1977

Paul for a New Day. Philadelphia: Fortress Press, 1977.

"The Heuristic Value of a Psychoanalytic Model in the Interpretation of Pauline Theology." Paper presented for the Society for the Scientific Study of Religion, 1977.

"A Theological Apology for Using Sociological Methodology." Paper presented at Seminar Session of the SNTS, Tübingen, 1977.

1978

"Beyond Criticism to Encounter: The Bible in the Post-Critical Age." In *Sources of Vitality in American Church Life*, edited by R. Moore, 83–93. Chicago: Exploration Press, 1978. Also published in *Chicago Theological Seminary Register* 68 (1978): 1–11. Reprinted in *The Text and the Times*, 257–71.

"The Heuristic Value of a Psychoanalytic Model in the Interpretation of Pauline Theology." *Zygon* 13 (June 1978): 136–57. Reprinted in *The Text and the Times*, 125–50.

"The Next Step: A Common Humanity." *Theology Today* 34 (January 1978): 395–401. Reprinted in *The Text and the Times*, 96–108.

Review of *Community of the New Age: Studies in Mark's Gospel*, by Howard C. Kee. *Catholic Biblical Quarterly* 40 (October 1978): 636–39.

Review of *Quest of the Christ of Faith: Reflection on the Bultmann Era,"* by William Baird. *Christian Century* 95 (26 April 1978): 449.

1979

"How We Understand Scripture When It Speaks with Forked Tongue." Address for the Omer E. Robbins Lecture Series, University of Redlands, 1979. Published in *The Text and the Times*, 109–24.

"Paul and Pederasty." Paper presented at Pauline Ethics Seminar, SBL annual meeting, 1979.

1980

"The Sociological Interpretation of the New Testament: The Present State of Research." *New Testament Studies* 26 (January 1980): 164–79. Reprinted in *The Bible and Liberation: Political and Social Hermeneutics*, edited by Norman K. Gottwald, 337–56. (Maryknoll, NY: Orbis, 1983); and in *The Text and the Times*, 46–68.

Review of *Jesus, Politics, and Society: A Study of Luke's Gospel*, by Richard J. Cassidy. *Journal of the American Academy of Religion* 48 (March 1980): 114–15.

Review of *Paul and His Letters*, by Leander E. Keck. *Interpretation* 34 (January 1980): 79–82.

"The Political Dimensions of Anti-Judaism in the New Testament." Paper presented at the Seminar for Social Background of the New Testament at the SNTS annual meeting, 1980.

1981

Review of *Sons of God—'Seed of Abraham,'* by Brendan Byrne. *Journal of Biblical Literature* 100 (December 1981): 662–63.

Review of *Social Aspects of Early Christianity*, by Abraham J. Malherbe. *Journal of the American Academy of Religion* 49 (September 1981): 496–97.

1982

"New Being: Renewed Mind: New Perception. Paul's View of the Source of Ethical Insight." *Chicago Theological Seminary Register* 72 (winter 1982): 1–12. Reprinted in *The Text and the Times*, 167–83.

"The Personology of Grace: A Study of Pauline Anthropology." *Word and World* 2 (summer 1982): 217–24.

"Psychology as a Tool to Interpret the Text: Emerging Trends in Biblical Thought." Fifth in a series. *Christian Century* 99 (24 March 1982): 335–38.

Review of *An Introduction to the Parables of Jesus*, by Robert H. Stein. *Chicago Theological Seminary Register* 72 (fall 1982): 44–45.

Review of *Jesus' Parables and the War of Myths: Essays on Imagination in the Scriptures*, by Amos Wilder. *Christian Century* 99 (1 December 1982): 1235.

Review of *Paul the Apostle: The Triumph of God in Life and Thought*, by J. C. Beker. 1980. *Interpretation* 36, no. 1 (1982): 74–77.

1983

The New Testament and Homosexuality: Contextual Background for Contemporary Debate. Minneapolis: Fortress Press, 1983.

Review of *A Commentary on the Epistle of James*, by Sophie Laws. *Chicago Theological Seminary Register* 73 (fall 1983): 44.

Review of *A Materialist Reading of the Gospel of Mark*, by Fernando Belo. *Catholic Biblical Quarterly* 45 (July 1983): 473–74.

Review of *Christian Tolerance: Paul's Message to the Modern Church*, by Robert Jewett. *Chicago Theological Seminary Register* 73 (spring 1983): 24–25.

Review of *Galatians*, by Charles B. Cousar. *Interpretation* 37 (July 1983): 300–302.

Review of *Homosexuality and Ethics*, edited by Edward Batchelor. *Chicago Theological Seminary Register* 73 (spring 1983): 47.

Review of *Jesus and the Constraints of History*, by Anthony E. Harvey. *Chicago Theological Seminary Register* 73 (spring 1983): 25.

Review of *Jesus and the Gospel: Tradition, Scripture, and Canon*, by William R. Farmer. *Christian Century* 100 (2–9 February 1983): 128–29.

Review of *The Other Gospels: Non-Canonical Gospel Texts*, edited by Ron Cameron. *Chicago Theological Seminary Register* 73 (spring 1983): 25.

Review of *Paul and Power: The Structure of Authority in the Primitive Church as Reflected in the Pauline Epistles*, by B. Holmberg. 1980. *Journal of Religion* 63, no. 1 (1983): 78–79.

1984

"The New Testament and Ethics: How Do We Get from There to Here?" *Perspectives in Religious Studies* 11 (winter 1984): 77–93. Reprinted in *Perspectives on the New Testament: Essays in Honor of Frank Stagg*, edited by Charles H. Talbert (Macon, GA: Mercer University Press, 1985); and in *The Text and the Times,* 192-211.

Review of *Die Begegnung des Führer Christentums mit der Antiken Sklaverei,* by Franz Laub. *Catholic Biblical Quarterly* 46 (July 1984): 578-79.

Review of *In Fragments: The Aphorisms of Jesus,* by John Dominic Crossan. *Chicago Theological Seminary Register* 74 (fall 1984): 46.

Review of *Jesus and the Future: Unresolved Questions for Understanding and Faith,* by Richard H. Hiers. *Chicago Theological Seminary Register* 74 (winter 1984): 47-48.

Review of *The Kingship of Jesus: Composition and Theology in Mark 15,* by Frank J. Matera. *Catholic Biblical Quarterly* 46 (January 1984): 171-72.

Review of *The Legend and the Apostle: The Battle for Paul in Story and Canon,* by Dennis R. MacDonald. *Christian Century* 101 (1-8 August 1984): 752.

Review of *The Resurrection of Jesus Christ in New Testament Theology,* by John F. Jansen. *Chicago Theological Seminary Register* 74 (winter 1984): 48.

Review of *The Shape of Scriptural Authority,* by David L. Bartlett. *Christian Century* 101 (1-8 August 1984): 752.

Review of *The Use of the Bible in Christian Ethics,* by Thomas W. Ogletree. *Chicago Theological Seminary Register* 74 (fall 1984): 44-45.

1985

"Ernst Käsemann: The Divine Agent Provocateur." *Religious Studies Review* 11 (July 1985): 260-63.

"How to Burn without Burning Out: A Sermon." *Chicago Theological Seminary Register* 75 (fall 1985): 20-23.

Review of *Ante Pacem: Archaeological Evidence of Church Life before Constantine,* by Graydon F. Snyder. *Chicago Theological Seminary Register* 75 (fall 1985): 25-27.

Review of *Crisis and Catharsis: The Power of the Apocalypse,* by Adela Yarbro Collins. *Chicago Theological Seminary Register* 75 (winter 1985): 42.

Review of *Feminist Interpretation of the Bible,* edited by Letty M. Russell. *Chicago Theological Seminary Register* 75 (fall 1985): 27-30.

Review of *Images of Christ: An Introduction to Christology,* by Glenn F. Chesnut. *Chicago Theological Seminary Register* 75 (fall 1985): 33.

Review of *In Memory of Her: A Feminist Theological Reconstruction of Christian Origins,* by Elisabeth Schüssler Fiorenza. *Chicago Theological Seminary Register* 75 (fall 1985): 27-30.

Review of *Luke: A Challenge to Present Theology,* by Eduard Schweizer. *Chicago Theological Seminary Register* 75 (winter 1985): 44-45.

Review of *Meanings: The Bible as Document and Guide,* by Krister Stendahl. *Christian Century* 102 (23 January 1985): 83.

Review of *The Old Testament in the Gospel Passion Narratives,* by Douglas J. Moo. *Catholic Biblical Quarterly* 47 (April 1985): 359-61.

1986

"Church Music at the Chicago Theological Seminary." *Chicago Theological Seminary Register* 76 (spring 1986): 1–2.

"The Judaizing of the New Testament." *Chicago Theological Seminary Register* 76 (winter 1986): 36–45.

"A Paul for Unitarian Universalists." *Unitarian Universalist Christian* 41 (spring 1986): 26–31. Reprinted as "The Theocentrism of Paul," in *The Text and the Times*, 184–91.

"Sociology and the New Testament." *Listening: Journal of Religion and Culture* 21, no. 2 (1986): 138–47.

Review of *Gods and the One God*, by Robert M. Grant. *Chicago Theological Seminary Register* 76 (fall 1986): 60–61.

Review of *Jesus und die Führer Israels: Studien zu den Sogenannt Jerusalemer Streitgespröchen*, by Jean G. Mudiso Mba Mundla. *Catholic Biblical Quarterly* 48 (January 1986): 146–47.

Review of *The New Testament in Its Social Environment*, by John E. Stambaugh and David L. Balch. *Chicago Theological Seminary Register* 76 (fall 1986): 61–62.

Review of *The Sacred Bridge: The Interdependence of Liturgy and Music in Synagogue and Church during the First Millennium, Vol. 2*, by Eric Werner. *Chicago Theological Seminary Register* 76 (fall 1986): 59–60.

1987

Review of *Bultmann, Retrospect and Prospect: The Centenary Symposium at Wellesley*, edited by Edward C. Hobbs. *Catholic Biblical Quarterly* 49 (January 1987): 172–73.

"Governmental Structures and Interrelationships in First Century C.E. Corinth." Paper delivered at the Seminar for Social Background of the New Testament, SNTS annual meeting, Göttingen, 1987.

1988

Christology in Paul and John. Proclamation Series. Philadelphia: Fortress Press, 1988.

"Can New Testament Theology Be Saved? The Threats of Contextualisms" (UTS Inauguration Lecture). *Union Seminary Quarterly Review* 42, nos. 1–2 (1988): 17–31. Reprinted in *The Text and the Times*, 212–33.

Review of *Der Kreuzigungsbericht des Markusevangeliums Mk 15:20b–41: Eine Traditionsgeschichtliche und methodenkritische Untersuchung*, by Johannes Schreiber. *Catholic Biblical Quarterly* 50 (July 1988): 547–48.

Review of *From Darkness to Light: Aspects of Conversion in the New Testament*, by Beverly Roberts Gaventa. *Journal of Biblical Literature* 107 (June 1988): 322–24.

Review of *Johannine Christianity: Essays on Its Setting, Sources, and Theology*, by D. Moody Smith. *Journal of Religion* 68 (Jan 1988): 94–95.

Review of *Things Unutterable: Paul's Ascent to Paradise in Its Greco-Roman, Judaic, and Early Christian Contexts*, by James D. Tabor. *Union Seminary Quarterly Review* 42, no. 4 (1988): 69–70.

"'A Time For . . . the Kingdom of God'." Three Addresses to the National Meeting of the Congregational Christian Churches, 1988.

1989

"Eschatological Existence in Matthew and Paul: *Coincidentia Oppositorum.*" In *Apocalyptic and the New Testament: Essays in Honor of J. Louis Martyn,* edited by Joel Marcus and Marion L. Soards, 125–46. Journal for the Study of the New Testament—Supplement Series 24, 1989. Reprinted in *The Text and the Times,* 234–56.

Review of *Metaphorik und Personifikation der Sünde: Antike Sündenvorstellungen und Paulinische Hamartia,* by Günter Röhser. *Catholic Biblical Quarterly* 51 (October 1989): 755–56.

Review of *There Is No Male and Female,* by Dennis R. MacDonald. *Journal of Biblical Literature* 108 (spring 1989): 168–69.

"'Blowin' in the Wind': Recent Trends in Pauline Interpretation and Their Implications for Church Proclamation." Schmiechen Lectures (3 lectures). Eden Theological Seminary, October 1989.

1990

Review of *The Ethics of the New Testament,* by Wolfgang Schrage. *Interpretation* 44 (April 1990): 188–90.

Review of *What Are They Saying about Paul?* by Joseph Plevnik. *Virginia Seminary Journal* 42, no. 1 (March 1990): 54–55.

1991

"Salvation History: The Theological Structure of Paul's Thought: 1 Thessalonians, Philippians, and Galatians." In *Pauline Theology. Volume I: Thessalonians, Philippians, Galatians, Philemon,* edited by J. Bassler. Minneapolis: Fortress Press, 1991.

Review of *Hear Then the Parable: A Commentary on the Parables of Jesus,* by Bernard Brandon Scott. *Princeton Theological Bulletin* n.s. 12, no. 1 (1991): 99–100.

Review of *Opposition to Paul in Jewish Christianity,* by Gerd Lüdemann. *Interpretation* 45 (July 1991): 298–300.

"Is the New Testament Relevant for the Twenty-first Century?" Lecture, Hendrix College, 1991. Published in *The Text and the Times,* 272–85.

1992

"Authentic Human Life." In *The Living Pulpit.* Bronx, NY: Living Pulpit, 1992.

"Women and Men in the Early Church." In *We Belong Together: Churches in Solidarity with Women,* edited by Sarah Cunningham, 43–55. New York: Friendship Press, 1992.

Review of *Präexistenzaussagen im Neuen Testament,* by Jürgen Habermann. *Catholic Biblical Quarterly* 54 (July 1992): 564–66.

Review of *The Corinthian Women Prophets: A Reconstruction through Paul's Rhetoric,* by Antoinette Clark Wire. *Journal of Biblical Literature* 111 (fall 1992): 546–48.

Review of *The Lordship of Christ: Ernst Käsemann's Interpretation of Paul's Theology*, by David V. Way. *Critical Review of Books in Religion* (1992): 253–54.

1993

The Text and the Times: New Testament Essays for Today. Minneapolis: Fortress Press, 1993.

"Christ the Cosmocrator and the Experience of Believers." In *The Future of Christology: Essays in Honor of Leander E. Keck*, edited by A. Malherbe and W. Meeks, 160–75. Minneapolis: Fortress Press, 1993.

Review of *A Marginal Jew: Rethinking the Historical Jesus. Vol. 1: The Roots of the Problem and the Person*, by John P. Meier. *Interpretation* 47 (July 1993): 299–302.

Review of *The Conversation Continues: Studies in Paul and John in Honor of J. Louis Martyn*, edited by Robert T. Fortna and Beverly Gaventa. *Journal of the American Academy of Religion* 61 (winter 1993): 823–25.

Review of *The Historical Jesus: The Life of a Mediterranean Jewish Peasant*, by John Dominic Crossan. *Interpretation* 47 (July 1993): 299–302.

Review of *Paul, In Other Words: A Cultural Reading of His Letters*, by Jerome Neyrey. *Virginia Theological Seminary Journal* 45, no. 2 (August 1993): 49–51.

Review of *Theological Ethics of the New Testament*, by Eduard Lohse. *Catholic Biblical Quarterly* 55 (April 1993): 381–82.

"Jesus the Messiah: Early Christian Appropriation of Jewish Teachings." Lecture at Jewish Theological Seminary, Franz Rosenzweig Lehrhaus, 1993.

1994

Review of *History of New Testament Research, Vol. 1: From Deism to Tübingen*, by William Baird. *Catholic Biblical Quarterly* 56 (April 1994): 355–57.

Review of *The Death of the Messiah: From Gethsemane to the Grave: A Commentary on the Passion Narratives of the Four Gospels*, by Raymond E. Brown. *Union Seminary Quarterly Review* 48, nos. 1–2 (1994): 187–90.

Review of *The Lost Gospel: The Book of Q and Christian Origins*, by Burton Mack. *Union Seminary Quarterly Review* 48, nos. 3–4 (1994): 155–58.

Review of *The Women's Bible Commentary*, edited by Carol A. Newsom and Sharon H. Ringe. *Journal of Biblical Literature* 113 (summer 1994): 311–13.

1995

Holy Week: Proclamation 6, Series A. Minneapolis: Augsburg Fortress Press, 1995.

"The Bible as Foundational Document." *Interpretation* 49 (January 1995): 17–30.

Review of *Paul the Apostle to America*, by Robert Jewett. *Princeton Seminary Bulletin* 16 (1995): 366–67.

Review of *Searching the Scriptures. Vol. 2: A Feminist Commentary*, by E. Schüssler Fiorenza. *America* 173 (21 October 1995): 26.

1996

"Paul and the Eschatological Body." In *Theology and Ethics in Paul and His Interpreters: Essays in Honor of Victor Paul Furnish*, edited by Eugene Lovering and Jerry Sumney, 14–29. Nashville: Abingdon Press, 1996.

Review of *A Guest in the House of Israel: Postholocaust Church Theology*, by C. Williamson. *Interpretation* 50 (January 1996): 79–81.

Review of *A Radical Jew: Paul and the Politics of Identity*, by Daniel Boyarin. *Princeton Seminary Bulletin* 17, no. 1 (1996): 101–3.

Review of *Scripture and Homosexuality: Biblical Authority and the Church Today*, by Marion Soards. *Princeton Seminary Bulletin* 17, no. 3 (1996): 392–93.

Review of *Studying the Historical Jesus: Evaluations of the State of Current Research*, edited by B. Chilton and C. Evans. *Catholic Biblical Quarterly* 58 (April 96): 380–82.

Index of Biblical Passages

Index of Modern Authors